READING THE PAST

READING THE PAST

Ancient Writing from Cuneiform to the Alphabet

Introduced by J.T. Hooker

University of California Press/British Museum

Reading the Past Series
The six sections in this volume are also available as individual booklets. Other titles in the series include

Mathematics and Measurement   O. A. Dilke
Maya Glyphs   S. D. Houston
Runes   R. I. Page

Cover Pictures

Left: Votive offering for the cure of a leg. Roman period. BM GR 1867.5–8.117

Centre: Columns of painted hieroglyphs, part of a religious text. Fragment from the tomb of King Seti I, Valley of the Kings, Thebes. Nineteenth Dynasty, *c.*1300 BC. BM 5610

Right: A tablet of the Jemdet Nasr period. BM 116730

University of California Press
Berkeley and Los Angeles

Library of Congress Cataloging-in-Publication Data
Reading the past: ancient writing from cuneiform to the alphabet/introduced by J.T. Hooker.
    Includes bibliographical references and index.
    Contents: Cuneiform/by C.B.F. Walker—Egyptian hieroglyphs/by W.V.Davies—The early alphabet/by John F. Healey—Linear B and related scripts/by John Chadwick—Greek inscriptions/by B.F. Cook—Etruscan/by Larissa Bonfante.
    ISBN 0–520–07431–9 (cloth)
    1. Writing—History.   I. Hooker, J.T.
P211.R37   1990
411'.7—dc20   90–11316

Printed in Great Britain by The Bath Press, Avon.

Contents

Introduction

J. T. Hooker

The six books brought together in this volume explore in detail specific stages in the story of writing, with special emphasis on the decipherment of ancient scripts, which has added so greatly to our knowledge of past civilisations. The purpose of the introduction is to explore the subject of 'writing' and to provide a link between the six individual contributions which follow.

The human race has adopted four main methods of making records or communicating information: pictograms, word-signs, syllabic signs and the alphabet. As we shall see, two or more of these could function together within the same system. This list is not meant to imply a hierarchy, with the alphabet at the culminating point. So-called 'primitive' societies using pictographs may be just as complex in their modes of thought as users of other methods but it is a different order of complexity. Pictographs have been used chiefly by hunting or farming communities, the best-documented examples being those of the North American Indians. The other methods have evolved in more complex economies with more advanced technology – usually therefore in an urban environment. There is a further, crucial difference between the pictographic method and the rest. Pictographs have no linguistic reference of any kind; they depict an event, or convey a message, by means of a series of drawings. Such a medium can hardly be called writing.

But although pictographs may not in themselves amount to writing, it has been argued that they may have led to true writing through a process of selection and organisation. Another view, equally strongly held, is that the next stage, word-signs, arose as a new independent invention and was not developed from pictographs. It would be unwise to maintain either dogmatically but we do know that at least in Egypt a royal victory was recorded by means of pictographs to which word-signs are appended. The Narmer Palette (*c*.3000 BC) is the most splendid of such monuments (p. 111) and included both a late stage of pictography and an incipient use of word-signs.

The origin of the word-signs bears upon another contentious question: was a system of word-signs perfected only once, in Sumer, and subsequently borrowed by the Egyptians and the Chinese; or did the idea arise independently in different regions? For reasons given by C. B. F. Walker, pp. 19–21, it appears possible that the earliest writing did not emerge in Sumer at all, but in regions to the east or north-west. Sumer could still, in theory, have been the centre from which writing spread to China and Egypt. That, however, is unlikely since it would imply that the Egyptians and Chinese, with their aptitude for the higher arts of civilisation, were incapable of devising a simple series of signs in which a round disc stood for 'sun', an animal's head for 'sheep', and countless others. The truly remarkable feature of early writing is not the creation of a system of word-signs ('logograms'), nor even their more sophisticated use to express abstractions, whereby a disc could signify the verbs 'shine' or 'be hot' as well as the noun 'sun', and so on. Far more striking is the next stage in Sumer, Egypt, and China. It became not merely desirable, but imperative, to incorporate elements of the spoken language: by this means, writing expressed grammatical relationships, which could never be indicated by logograms alone.

In China, as in Egypt, writing is early connected with royal ideology. The writing-system of the Shang Dynasty (c.1500–1027 BC) has no known antecedents. It is represented by short texts on bronze vessels and oracle-bones, the latter conveying questions put by kings to their ancestors. The literature of the Zhou Dynasty (1027 BC–256 AD), including the works of Confucius, is known principally from later copies; there are, however, inscriptions on metal and stone and on strips of wood or bamboo. The entire system was overhauled and simplified in the third century BC. A further revolution was brought about by the invention of a brush made of hair, later by the introduction of paper. The 'regular script', written with brush on paper, in which each sign occupied the same area, formed the basis of printing (eighth century AD). The script was regarded as an art-form in its own right, closely allied to painting. Its use down to the present day is an assurance of cultural continuity; but it also provides a practical means of communication among speakers of widely different Chinese dialects.

The cultural ascendancy of China in her Imperial period had a great impact on neighbouring peoples. In Korea, Chinese writing became dominant by the end of the fourth century AD. After some attempts to use a simplified version of the Chinese system for the writing of Korean, King Sejong promulgated a new alphabet of 28 characters, the shape of each being systematically related to its pronunciation (1446 AD). Japan followed another path. There, too, a problem arose with the adaptation of Chinese script to write a different language. The solution was to choose a number of Chinese signs, the sound value of which was approximately that of syllables in Japanese. This 'syllabic', or *kana*, system was developed in the ninth century AD, but, from the outset, *kana* writing was confined to the grammatical elements of Japanese, while the basic vehicles of meaning, the nouns and verbs, were represented by Chinese signs *(kanji)*. This mixed *kana-kanji* script still persists; no cure for its unwieldiness has yet become widely accepted.

The scripts of China, Sumer, and Egypt differ so greatly in outward appearance that they might seem to have little in common. But in fact, despite many variations in detail, they all developed in much the same way, with respect to their internal structure. So did a number of other Bronze Age systems, such as the Linear B of Crete and Greece (15th–13th centuries BC) and 'Hieroglyphic Hittite' (Asia Minor and Syria, 15th–8th centuries BC).

When scribes first used a logogram to represent not a word but a syllable of their own language, they made the most important advance in the history of writing. Working for the most part on the 'rebus-principle' explained by W. V. Davies, p. 103, they raised two theoretical possibilites: the representation of each syllable by one sign and the exclusive use of syllabic signs. These possibilities were rarely realised, owing partly to the nature of the languages being written, partly to conservatism (or even obscurantism) on the part of the scribes.

In Chinese, for instance, every word is monosyllabic, thus creating an ideal climate for the development of a syllabic script. But, on the other hand, many words are 'homophones', i.e. their pronunciation is the same, except that they have different 'tones'. A fully syllabic script is not satisfactory for the writing of such a language, and some means had to be found of distinguishing the various homophones. The Chinese method involved the use of a 'determinative', that is, a logogram (or part of a logogram) with its original significance as a word-sign and indicating the broad area of meaning to which the word belongs. The structure of the Chinese signs in 'regular script' was such that a determinative could easily be attached to a syllabic sign: the two parts thereafter forming an indivisible whole.

The Chinese system, combining logograms with syllabic + determinative signs, is paralleled in Sumer and Egypt, although there the scribes did not physically incorporate the determinatives into the syllabic signs; in both regions, the scripts comprised a mixture of logograms, syllabograms, and determinatives: these are distinguished by function, not by their outward form. The syllables, however, came to be represented somewhat differently in Egypt and in Sumer. In the Sumerian script it was essential to indicate the vocalic component of a syllable, whereas in Egypt the syllable was often reduced to its consonantal 'skeleton', with the vowel(s) left to be understood by the reader. These consonantal signs, discussed by Davies on pp. 103–4, do not form a true alphabet: they still represent syllables, even though the vowels are usually not marked. The Akkadian language, like Egyptian, is built up from a number of consonantal roots, and in consequence the Akkadian scribes had to make many modifications in the usage of Sumerian Cuneiform in order to write their own language (Walker, pp. 28–9).

Further changes still were needed to adapt Sumero-Akkadian Cuneiform to Hittite and other languages. Even when used as a vehicle for Hittite (an Indo-European language), the Cuneiform system retained Sumerian logograms and determinatives and many Akkadian elements spelt syllabically, the latter often mingled with Hittite forms.

Hittite Cuneiform is known only from the clay tablets at Boghazköy, and not later than the end of the Empire (c.1200 BC). Another script, 'Hieroglyphic Hittite', had a more widespread use and a longer life. It looks far more naturalistic than Cuneiform; but its signs, just like those of Cuneiform, can be classed as logograms, determinatives, and syllabograms. Many words are spelt by means of a logogram followed by a phonetic 'complement', which indicates the grammatical ending. But sometimes the logogram is accompanied by syllabic signs spelling out the whole word. We thus have a species of 'double writing', not entirely unknown in Sumerian Cuneiform: a word is fully expressed in two different forms, the logographic and the syllabic. Such 'double writing' is common in the Linear B system of the Minoans and Mycenaeans. In Linear B, a word written syllabically is followed by a logogram conveying the same meaning; but a logogram may also function as a kind of determinative (details in J. Chadwick, pp. 156–7; he prefers the term 'ideogram' to 'logogram').

We turn now from the logographic-syllabic principle to the alphabetic, i.e. the systematic representation of the individual sounds of a language.

Two adaptations of Cuneiform may be mentioned first. In the second millennium BC, some thirty signs were arbitrarily selected from the Cuneiform repertory and used for the writing of the Semitic language of Ugarit on the Syrian coast. Much later (6th–4th centuries BC) a completely different selection was made for a completely different language, Old Persian. The Persian script, often called an alphabet, is really a mixture of alphabetic and syllabic elements, with one or two logograms. Neither the Ugaritic nor the Persian script had any descendants.

In the early history and diffusion of the alphabet strictly so called, the Phoenicians are crucially important. Living on the coast of modern Lebanon and Syria, they were renowned traders and colonisers. Their language, like Hebrew, is a variety of 'North-west' Semitic (Akkadian belonging to the eastern branch). Short texts in Phoenician script are known from about 1000 BC, or even earlier. By this time, the script already displays a definitive order of twenty-two consonantal signs. It is a matter of dispute (not easy to resolve) whether this system is a genuine alphabet or a syllabary, with each sign representing 'consonant + vowel' (vowel-quality being determined by the context). The origin of the script is likewise disputed. The suggestion that the Protosinaitic script formed a link between Egyptian and Phoenician is discussed by Davies, pp. 129–132. Even if the Protosinaitic script did play a part, a place in the development of the Phoenician system should also be found for some of the other, poorly-attested scripts known from Palestine in the second millennium BC.

In the course of their seafaring, the Phoenicians made contact with other peoples living on the borders of the Mediterranean. Among these were the Greeks, who in the ninth century BC began their own great expansion. Now

Greek writing (attested, though very sparsely, as early as *c*.750 BC) closely resembles the Phoenician script, the salient difference being that the Greeks used signs for vowels, either by altering the sound-value of certain Phoenician signs or by introducing new signs. These facts are often explained on the assumption of a single act of borrowing by Greeks at a specific place (perhaps Al Mina in Syria) and at a specific time (perhaps early eighth century BC) (cf. Cook, pp. 265–6). However, another view is that there were several Greek alphabets, not one, and that these differ in ways difficult of explanation if they were derived from a single model. Different parts of the Greek world may therefore have made their borrowing at different times. Nor need the borrowing have taken place in the Semitic-speaking area. The discovery of a Phoenician inscription in Crete (*c*.900 BC) raises the possibility that at least some Greeks learnt Phoenician writing in their own homeland and began to make an experimental alphabet in the ninth century.

These and related problems are considered in J. F. Healey's contribution on the Early Alphabet, p. 196. A final solution is not yet possible, although the passing years bring more and more information about the emergence of the Greek alphabet, as one may see by comparing the original publication of L. H. Jeffery's *Local Scripts of Archaic Greece* (1961) with its revision (1990).

The statement that the Greeks had 'become literate' by the late eighth century BC, while strictly true, needs considerable modification if it is not to mislead. The truth is, rather, that some people in some cities could read and write: no doubt a higher percentage in democracies than in other regimes, and higher in commercial centres than in rural backwaters. The vast range of subject-matter found on public and private monuments is illustrated in B. F. Cook's section on Greek Inscriptions. Greek culture did not enter its fully literate phase until the fifth century BC: the *History* of Herodotus (*c*.430) shows oral habits of thought and expression giving way to written modes.

The Greeks gave to their Roman conquerors so much of their thought, literature, and art that it is customary to speak of a 'Greco-Roman' period, at least in the cultural domain. But the gift of writing had already been transmitted by a more circuitous route. The Greek expansion of the Archaic age, already referred to, affected parts of Italy, where several derivatives of the western Greek alphabet are known. Among these is Etruscan, in north-west Italy, surveyed by Larissa Bonfante in the last section of this book. In order to write their own language (which is unlike either Greek or Latin), the Etruscans were using an alphabet early in the seventh century BC, adapted from the Greek model just as the Greek had been adapted from the Phoenician. The Etruscan language was written in its own script until the beginning of the Roman Empire (27 BC); but long before that it had been eclipsed in importance by Latin, the speech of Latium in central Italy. According to a common view, the Latin alphabet was, in its turn, a direct adaptation from the Etruscan; but other Italic alphabets, themselves also based on Greek, may have helped the process.

The principal stages in the evolution of the Latin alphabet before the Imperial period were these. C, the curved form of Greek *gamma*, at first represented *g* (the sound of *gamma*) and *k*; during the third century BC the variant G was introduced for *g*, C being reserved for *k*. C and CN were, however, retained as abbreviations of the *praenomina* Gaius and Gnaeus respectively. In the order of the alphabet, G replaced Z, which had been dropped as redundant to the needs of Latin. The Greek aspirates *phi*, *theta*, and *khi* were spelt P (or B), T, and C respectively; H was added in the second century BC, as in the modern spelling. As a result of these developments, the Latin alphabet in the time of Cicero (106–43 BC) consisted of twenty-one letters:

A B C D E F G H I K L M N O P Q R S T V X

Y and Z were later added at the end, to spell Greek *upsilon* and *zeta*. Further reforms in the first century AD had no lasting effect.

The so-called *monumental* script, brought to perfection at the beginning of the Empire, flourished in the first two centuries of the Christian era. The square-shaped, regular letters, deep cutting, and careful preparation by outlining and ruling, produced a means of writing on stone which was not subsequently rivalled for clarity and dignity. Lesser public inscriptions tended to take a more flowing shape, reflecting the brush-drawn letters of an earlier age. Co-existing with these styles were the *cursive* (a kind of handwriting on materials other than stone) and the *uncial*, a rounded version of the monumental: in the uncial script, the letter V took on the shape of U *c*.200 AD.

A great diversity of material from the Roman period is still available for study but, of course, Roman writing holds interest for us not only for its own sake but because of its descendants, notably the minuscule (lower-case) letters which came into use in western Europe in the seventh century AD. The predominance of this system in large parts of the modern world is self-evident, but it does not prevail everywhere, partly because it is inadequate for the representation of certain languages (Arabic, Chinese, Japanese), partly because other languages (Greek, Russian) already have adequate alphabets of their own. On the other hand, the ever-increasing use of English as an international language seems bound to encourage the further spread of the Roman-based alphabet.

In the case of Latin and Greek, known alphabets spell known languages; the Etruscan alphabet is known, but the underlying language is only now being elucidated; there is also the situation, all too common with earlier systems long out of use, in which both script and language were completely obscure. Three examples of the last type are represented in this book: Cuneiform, Egyptian Hieroglyphs, and Linear B.

These scripts presented different problems, and consequently different methods had to be devised in their decipherment; but one or two remarks may be made which apply to all of them. In the first place, an essential condition for any decipherment is that there should be an understanding of the scope and nature of the inscriptions in question. Again, it is only rarely that a single person is responsible for the entire course of a decipherment from start to finish. More often, a decipherment is built upon an accumulation of knowledge of various kinds, historical, linguistic, and archaeological. Lacking such a stock of facts, mere 'flair' is of little avail – or, rather, it leads only to unverifiable hypotheses. But it is also true that, without the flair of such men as Rawlinson, Ventris, and Champollion, no amount of erudition would suffice to solve the outstanding problems.

As noted above, it is a property of the Linear B script that the subject-matter is usually indicated by logograms. These impose a check, of some rigour, upon any decipherment. In his approach to the script, Ventris followed two paths, more or less simultaneously. On the one hand he established a pattern of grammatical inflections by analysing the contents of inscriptions of similar type. On the other, he worked out the phonetic equivalents for the signs by constructing a 'grid', showing which signs shared the same vowel and which shared the same consonant. The convergence of these two methods (neither, in itself, original with Ventris) led to a successful decipherment: by applying the phonetic values of his 'grid' to the grammatical endings, Ventris showed that the basic language of the Linear B texts was an early form of Greek.

In an important respect, the Linear B inscriptions are less misleading than Hieroglyphic or Cuneiform. The writer of a Linear B text commonly demarcated the phonetic from the logographic components: hence the prospective decipherer is in no danger of confusing the two. But *all* Hieroglyphic signs have a naturalistic appearance, whatever their function within the system may be; conversely, all Cuneiform signs are built up from the characteristic 'wedges' and so fail to reveal whether they are playing a phonetic, a logographic, or a determinative role.

Champollion's decipherment of Hieroglyphic proceeded from his grasp of a fundamental concept: that, despite the naturalistic appearance of the Hieroglyphs, the phonetic character of many of them held good not only in the 'cartouches' containing royal names and titles but in much of the rest of the system. In *how* much it was Champollion's task, and his achievement, to determine. Moreover, despite the monumentality of the Hieroglyphs and their virtually unchanging aspect over long ages, script and language did evolve, and in time the scribes acquired new habits, sometimes representing a concept phonetically, sometimes by means of logograms, sometimes by blending the two. All these peculiarities Champollion came to appreciate in their essentials. He used, but did not rely exclusively upon, the 'triscript' on the Rosetta Stone, which gave the same text first in Hieroglyphs, then in Egyptian Demotic, finally in Greek. The Stone formed one of his sources of comparison, which embraced a larger amount of material than had been exploited by his predecessors.

Entry into the Cuneiform scripts was effected by way of the Persian 'alphabet', mentioned earlier. The problems presented by this alphabet were not solved within a short time, or by a single person. The establishment of a plausible context enabled Grotefend to take the first step. This he did by analysing some short inscriptions which, he argued, were likely to contain royal names and genealogies. Since the names and affiliations of the Achaemenid kings of Persia were already known, Grotefend could make some progress towards reconstructing the sound-values of the alphabet. But not until the Persian language was better understood, and integrated into the Indo-European family, were Lassen and finally Rawlinson able to allocate a value to each character. Rawlinson achieved virtually a complete decipherment, on the basis of which he translated much of the extant texts. And this decipherment offered the possibility of understanding the older Cuneiform scripts as well, because some of the Persian inscriptions were accompanied by the same text written in Babylonian Cuneiform. The parallel texts were sufficiently close for Rawlinson and others to gain an insight into the reading of Babylonian. Their realisation that a syllabary of some complexity was in question, also that many logographic elements were present beside the syllabic, was equal in importance, and in brilliance, to Champollion's insight into the structure of the Egyptian Hieroglyphs.

We may be sure that new scripts, and perhaps new languages, will be discovered in the future, presenting fresh opportunities to the decipherer and the linguist. Their work (we hope) will interest not merely scholars but everyone concerned with the intellectual and social history of mankind.

1 Neo-Babylonian stone monument commemorating Adad-eṭir and his son Marduk-balassu-iqbi. BM 90834.

Cuneiform

C. B. F. Walker

Contents

Author's Note

Archaeologists and historians alike have tended to be quite inconsistent in their use of place names, ancient or modern. So, to avoid confusion, I have kept to the ancient names where known, giving the modern names in brackets where common usage has made them well known. Since much of the subject matter is common to the civilisations of Sumer, Babylon and Assyria I frequently use the term Mesopotamia to cover all three.

Assyrian and Babylonian are both dialects of the Akkadian language, and I use all three terms. Transliterations of Akkadian are printed in italic script, while Sumerian is printed in Roman upper or lower case, and translations are printed in quotes.

1

Origin and Development

Pictographs

Writing was invented in order to record business activities in the early Near East. With the growth of centralised economies the officials of palaces and temples needed to be able to keep track of the amounts of grain and numbers of sheep and cattle which were entering or leaving their stores and farms. It was impossible to rely on a man's memory for every detail, and a new method was needed to keep reliable records.

When man first began to write he wrote not with pen and ink on paper but by scratching signs on to damp clay with a pointed stick or reed. The raw materials were readily available in the river valleys of the Near East and cost little effort to prepare. Clay can be easily worked into a suitably flat shape for writing on while moist, and if left to dry in the sun after being inscribed will soon be hard enough to stand up to considerable wear and tear.

On the very earliest texts pictures (sometimes called pictographs) were drawn on damp clay using a pointed tool. But quite soon the scribes found it was quicker to produce a stylised representation of an object by making a few marks in the clay rather than attempt an artistic impression by naturalistic drawing in straight or curving lines. These stylised representations then had to be standardised so that everyone could recognise them. Since the scribes were no longer trying to be great artists the drawing instrument did not have to be finely pointed but could be blunt or flat. The end of the wooden or reed stylus, which struck the clay first, made a wider mark than the shaft, and so came into being the typical wedge-shaped impression after which this writing system became known – cuneiform (from the Latin word *cuneus* meaning wedge). Many early tablets show a mixture of signs drawn and written in cuneiform.

Until quite recently the theory presented in most books on Mesopotamian archaeology was that writing was invented in southern Iraq *c.* 3000 BC, or slightly earlier, perhaps by a Sumerian living in Uruk. Whether or not he was Sumerian is uncertain since the very earliest texts of all are purely pictographic (picture writing) and without phonetic indications to show which language is being written. The suggestion that he lived in Uruk was based on the facts that the earliest evidence for writing was found there and that by 3000 BC the city had already enjoyed a long history.

Today the picture looks rather different. Evidence for early stages of writing in the form of tablets inscribed with numbers only, sometimes also bearing seal impressions, has been found not only at Uruk but also at Nineveh in Iraq, at Susa, Choga Mish and Godin Tepe in western Iran, and at Tell Brak and Habuba Kabira in north Syria; most of these can be dated to the later fourth millennium BC. Next, two tablets from Tell Brak, found in 1984, depict a goat and a sheep, each accompanied by the number 10. They are quite as primitive as anything from Uruk; if anything they may even be earlier, since they show the whole of the animals, whereas pictures on the earliest tablets from Uruk show only the heads of animals. In the east the pictographic texts found at Susa, known as

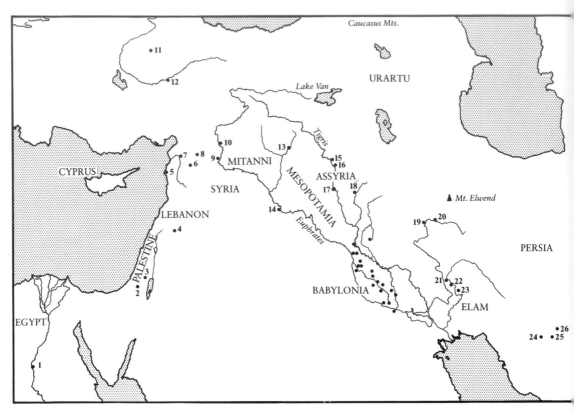

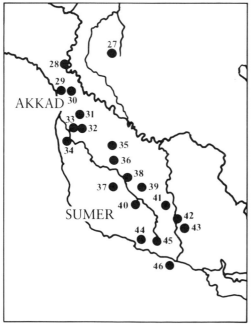

Above The Middle East.
Left Babylonia.

1 El-Amarna	24 Tall-i-Malyan
2 Lachish	25 Persepolis
3 Jerusalem	26 Pasargadae
4 Damascus	27 Eshnunna
5 Ugarit	28 Baghdad
6 Ebla	29 Sippar
7 Alalakh	30 Tell ed-Der
8 Aleppo	31 Jemdet Nasr
9 Habuba Kabira	32 Kish
10 Til Barsip	33 Babylon
11 Hattusas	34 Borsippa
12 Kanesh	35 Abu Salabikh
13 Brak	36 Nippur
14 Mari	37 Isin
15 Nineveh	38 Puzrish-Dagan
16 Kalhu	39 Adab
17 Ashur	40 Shuruppak
18 Nuzi	41 Umma
19 Behistun	42 Girsu
20 Godin Tepe	43 Lagash
21 Susa	44 Uruk
22 Dur-Untash	45 Larsa
23 Choga Mish	46 Ur

2 Pictographic tablets from Tell Brak.

proto-Elamite, appear in an archaeological level which shows marked differences from the previous level, suggesting the arrival of a new cultural group, and since these proto-Elamite texts have now been found as far east as Seistan on the border of Afghanistan, it may be that the script was invented on the Iranian plateau. Study of the early Uruk texts themselves has also suggested that they are dependent on an earlier tradition of pictography which has not yet been found or identified. Thus it is beginning to look as if we should think in terms of the invention of writing as being a gradual process, accomplished over a wide area, rather than the product of a single Sumerian genius.

In practice any meaningful discussion has to start with the tablets found at Uruk in the early archaeological level known as Uruk IV and a slightly later group found in Uruk III. Contemporary with the Uruk III tablets are tablets from Jemdet Nasr to the north and the proto-Elamite tablets from Susa. Historically the Uruk IV–III levels date to *c.* 3300 – 2900 BC. There are both similarities and differences between the tablets from Uruk and Jemdet Nasr and those from Susa, but while the Uruk and Jemdet Nasr tablets are regarded as the beginning of writing in Sumerian, the Susa tablets are seen as the first examples of the still little-understood Elamite language.

31

3

3 A proto-Elamite tablet.
Musée du Louvre, Paris.

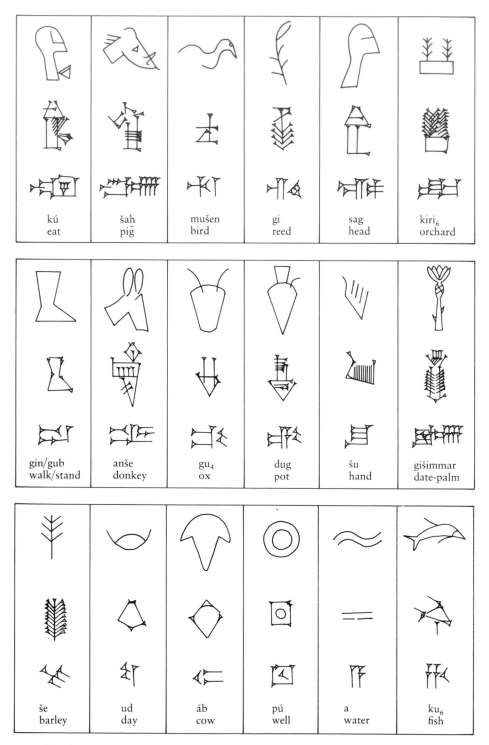

4 Table of cuneiform signs showing for each sign the pictographic form (c. 3000 BC), an early cuneiform representation (c. 2400 BC), and the Late Assyrian form (c. 650 BC), now turned through 90 degrees, with the Sumerian phonetic equivalent and meaning.

The inscriptions on these early tablets consist of brief economic records or lists of signs for the instruction of trainee scribes. The signs are mostly pictographic: that is to say the sign for an ox looks like an ox's head, the sign for barley looks like an ear of barley, and the sign for a day is a picture of the sun coming up over the horizon. The pictures quickly take on a cuneiform appearance and are regularly accompanied by numbers, which is enough to suggest that the texts were economic (receipts, delivery notes or inventories). An intensive study of all these early texts by a team from the University of Berlin from a mathematical point of view is slowly producing a better understanding of the meaning of the texts and the nature of the underlying economic system, although we are still a long way from being able to read the texts rather than interpret them.

Eighty-five per cent of the tablets from the early levels at Uruk are economic and are concerned with the income and outgoings of the city's temples in terms of food, live-stock and textiles. Remarkably, it has been possible to identify a large number of place names known from the later history of Sumer, mostly within the vicinity of Uruk, but including Kish and Eshnunna to the north, Aratta (somewhere in the mountains of Iran), and Dilmun (modern Bahrein). Fifteen per cent of the texts are lexical lists, including the names of various commodities, animals and officials. These lists were presumably compiled to establish and teach a definitive system of writing recognisable to every scribe. Significantly, exactly the same lists can be found from six hundred years later, showing the strength of the tradition. This continuity has been a great help in identifying many of the early signs which would otherwise have been quite unintelligible. Popular books on cuneiform have tended to give the impression that identifying the early signs is easy; in fact things are not so simple. Pictures of an ox or an ear of barley are identifiable, but there are many signs which we cannot yet explain as pictures even when by working back from the later lexical lists we are able to establish their meaning.

As soon as we are able to read the texts intelligibly, we are confronted by another difficulty. The early texts are not written in neat lines with every sign in the appropriate order – that came later – but with all the signs for each sense unit (or sentence) grouped together in a box (see front cover). The correct order in which to read the signs is thus a matter of interpretation.

Syllabic writing

The texts from Uruk and Jemdet Nasr, although slowly changing from a pictorial to a more linear or cuneiform script, are still largely logographic, that is to say that they use one sign or sign-group for each term or concept without adding grammatical elements. Even the nature of a transaction is not always clear; are the sheep being brought into or out of the temple? We do not know. In any case how could they tell us? Drawing an ox's head to represent an ox is straightforward. But how do you say that the ox is live or dead? How do you record that it has come or gone? And how do you record the name of the person who brought or took it? To communicate these things effectively you need to do more than draw pictures. You have to be able to express ideas. You have to be able to record a spoken language. The alphabet was not invented until 1,500 years later, so the first scribes used syllables instead.

This syllabic stage of the script's development is known from a group of texts from Ur corresponding to the archaeological levels Early Dynastic I–II (*c.* 2800 BC). In these

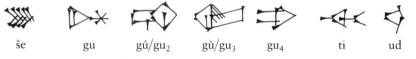

5 An archaic tablet from Ur,
c. 2900–2600 BC;
deliveries of barley and
meal to a temple.
BM 128897.

6 (*Opposite*) A tablet of the Fara
type (*c.* 2600 BC); a record of
numbers of workmen.
BM 21014.

texts we find the first identifiable use of purely phonetic elements and grammar, and as soon as we are able to identify the use of syllables in the cuneiform script we encounter the Sumerian language. The Sumerians may have been responsible for introducing writing at Uruk, but it cannot be proved. Because the script does not perfectly suit all the sounds which linguistic experts find in Sumerian, it has been suggested that the cuneiform script was devised by another people. In any case their origins are uncertain, and they have in the past been thought of as invaders from the eastern mountains. On the other hand the relative cultural continuity in the late Uruk period has suggested to others that the Sumerians were there all along.

še	gu	gú/gu₂	gù/gu₃	gu₄	ti	ud

In Sumerian the word for barley is še (pronounced 'she' as in shepherd), so the sign for barley also became the sign for the syllable še. The Sumerian for ox is gu; but the word for thread is also gu, so already you have two possible ways of writing the sound gu. There are, in fact, some fourteen ways of writing gu, so for convenience we (but not the ancient Sumerians) mark thread as gu and ox as gu₄. The word for arrow is ti, but so is the word for life, so to write 'life' you need only write the sign for arrow. The word for mouth is ka (represented as a head with the teeth clearly marked), but the sign ka is also used for the idea of shouting, which is again gu (gu₃ or gù); so the sign KA already has two values, ka and gu₃ (and in fact it can also be used for zú 'tooth', du₁₁ 'speak', and inim 'word'). Combining a syllable formed of consonant + vowel (like gu) with one formed from vowel + consonant (like ud 'day') allows you to make a closed syllable, gu-ud. In this way you can make up any combination of vowels and consonants, so long as you do not want to put more than two consonants together (no Sumerian cartoonist could write 'Psst!'). The principle of using several signs to represent the same sound (gu) is called homophony, and giving one sign several values (like KA) is called polyphony. Both principles are fundamental features of cuneiform writing throughout its 3,000 year history.

The early stages of Sumerian writing represented by tablets from Uruk, Jemdet Nasr

and Ur contain no historical material and generally fall outside the scope of historical discussion, being dated solely by archaeological considerations. The only history available for this period is in the form of a later tradition listing kings who lived before the Flood. With the next group of material we enter recorded history in what is known as the Early Dynastic period (II – III). Enmebaragesi, king of Kish (c. 2600 BC), is the first man known to be commemorated by his own inscription (to be seen in the Iraq Museum, Baghdad). Roughly contemporary with him are the tablets from Shuruppak (Fara), known in Sumerian literature as the home of the Sumerian Flood-hero Ziusudra. The tablets from Fara and the slightly later archives from Abu Salabikh and Ebla (in Syria) show the gradual development of the Sumerian script both in the form of the signs and in the flexibility of its use.

6
32

From these three cities come the first major groups of literary texts, including what one might call the first autographs in history, tablets on which the scribes have recorded their own names. The tablets from Abu Salabikh and Ebla show that literature and the study of cuneiform vocabulary were already highly developed. Slightly later again come the administrative archives from Girsu (Tello) and with these we also have a wealth of historical inscriptions to complete the setting. The Early Dynastic III period ends with the accession of Sargon of Akkad (2334–2279 BC), and the beginning of a strong Akkadian influence in politics and language. The Akkadian language is discussed below, but we should consider now one fundamental change in the writing system which seems to have taken place late in the Early Dynastic period – the change in the direction of writing.

39

The direction of the script

The pictographs on the earliest tablets are clearly meant to be read as naturalistic pictures. But when one traces their development through time it becomes apparent that at some point they have been turned through ninety degrees so that they are lying on their backs. The same applies to the overall direction of the script. The Uruk and Jemdet Nasr texts are mostly written on slightly elongated tablets, wider than they are high. The signs are disposed randomly within squares or rectangles. The rectangles are arranged in rows to be read from right to left, and when one row is filled a new row is started beneath it. When the front of the tablet is full up, the tablet is turned left to right and the back of the tablet is inscribed in the same manner but starting from the bottom up. In contrast by 2000 BC tablets are mostly higher than they are wide, and are inscribed with the signs written in order from left to right in long lines. In many cases there is only a single column of script on each face of the tablet, although on some Sumerian texts of the Ur III period (2112–2004 BC) there can be up to eleven columns on each side.

It had been thought that the change in direction of the script took place as early as the Jemdet Nasr period. It was also suggested that the change arose because scribes writing from right to left found they were smudging their handiwork; practical experience in writing cuneiform on clay shows, however, that with good quality clay very little smudging takes place and a conscious effort is needed to erase signs. More importantly, there are historical arguments against an early change in the direction of writing. Until 16 the middle of the second millennium most stone monuments and all inscribed cylinder seals preserve the archaic direction of script. So in reading the inscription on the great law code of Hammurapi one has to hold one's head down on the right shoulder. The direction of the script is obviously intended to preserve an ancient tradition, but it could hardly have become traditional if the direction of writing had changed already in the Jemdet Nasr period before any monumental inscriptions had been written.

The late Adam Falkenstein argued for a change at the end of the Early Dynastic period since some of the tablets from Girsu dated to that period have drawings of animals which can only be viewed the right way up if the script is read as in early times. This seems to be a forceful argument, although there is at least one stone monument from the late Early Dynastic (BM 117936 in the British Museum) which shows three standing figures and an inscription (still only partly legible) which must be read in the later direction (horizontally). There is another small point which seems to have been over-looked up to now. The earliest tablets inscribed in a single column date to the time of 7 Lugalzagesi, king of Uruk, the contemporary and predecessor of Sargon. This too suggests that the change had taken place shortly before. What induced it and how it was imposed remain obscure. One consequence was a reduction in the variety of wedges used to form signs. When read from the direction later customary, many signs used on Early Dynastic tablets have wedges pointing vertically upwards. From Old Akkadian times on, these wedges are almost entirely eliminated, so that the heads of wedges appear only at the top or the left side of a sign.

šu   da   ru   níg

7 A tablet of the time of Lugalzagesi, king of Uruk (2340–2316 BC). BM 114362.

It may be that the change seemed less significant to the ancient scribes than it does to us. Writing on a small tablet with the tablet held in one hand and the stylus held in the other is a two-handed operation, turning the tablet to impress wedges in different directions. Thus the scribes would have become used to seeing their writing from more than one angle. At all events the scribes of the Ur III and Old Babylonian periods must have been well accustomed to reading public monuments inscribed in the older direction. Today scholars are so familiar with the later direction of the script that most early tablets are published and exhibited the wrong way round.

Sumerian and Akkadian

So far the cuneiform script has been discussed only with reference to Sumerian. From the mid-third millennium onwards it was also used to write the Akkadian language in southern Mesopotamia and the Eblaite language at Ebla in Syria (see Chapter 4). So it may be helpful at this point to make some brief remarks on the nature of the Sumerian and Akkadian languages and the way in which the cuneiform script was used to record them.

The Sumerian language first became known from bilingual texts written in Sumerian and Akkadian and found in the seventh-century BC royal libraries at Nineveh. For some time many scholars refused even to believe that it was a language at all and suggested that it was a scribal trick or a form of cryptography. The discovery of vast archives inscribed unilingually in Sumerian put paid to that idea. The early doubters may, however, be forgiven since Sumerian is quite unlike the well-known Indo-European and Semitic language groups.

Linguists describe the language as agglutinative; each fundamental idea, nominal or verbal, is expressed by a single unchanging syllable (or polysyllable) which may be modified by a series of prefixes or postfixes, somewhat as in modern Turkish. Thus 'son' is dumu, 'sons' dumu-meš, 'his sons' dumu-meš-a-ni, 'for his sons' dumu-meš-a-ni-ir (for explanation of š see p. 22). The verb 'build' is dù, 'he built' ì-dù or mu-dù, 'he did not build' nu-mu-dù. So 'For Ningirsu his god Gudea built his temple' is Ningirsu dingir-ra-ni-ir Gudea é-a-ni mu-dù. So far so good, but the scribes were hardly consistent in their implementation of the system. In fact in the early periods many of the verbal prefixes and postfixes were not written at all; the sign dù expressed the idea 'build' and the rest had to be supplied by the reader. In some respects the Sumerian script never quite escapes from the fact that it was originally designed for the purpose of practical book-keeping rather than to express abstract ideas. When we reach the Old Babylonian period (2004–1595 BC), the time when most of the available literary texts were copied, we find that many duplicates of these texts use different groups of prefixes or postfixes. That does not make it easy to write a grammar of Sumerian.

The Sumerian language uses only four vowels: a, e, i, u; two half vowels: w and y; and the following consonants: b, d, g, k, l, m, n, p, r, s, t, z, ḫ, ĝ, š. The ḫ corresponds to a hard h, ĝ is a nasalised g, and š corresponds to English sh.

In addition to writing out a text phonetically the Sumerian scribes gave themselves extra clues for their own decipherment by adding certain specific signs to mark different categories of objects. So wooden objects might have the prefix giš, stone objects na$_4$, copper objects urudu, cities uru; birds have the postfix mušen, fish ku$_6$, cities ki (some cities are even uru-X-ki).

If all of this seems complicated, matters get worse when one tries to use the Sumerian system for the Akkadian language, for which it was not designed and to which it is not well suited.

Akkadian is one of the Semitic languages, together with Arabic, Hebrew, Aramaic, etc. It has three dialects: Old Akkadian, Babylonian and Assyrian; so by definition anything written in Babylonian or Assyrian can equally be said to be written in Akkadian. Each of these dialects tends to use a slightly variant form of the cuneiform script, although all handbooks to cuneiform take them as one. As in the other Semitic languages, Akkadian words basically have a root of three consonants, e.g. prs, which is then modified internally by the doubling of consonants or insertion of vowels, and externally by the addition of prefixes or postfixes, e.g. *iprus*, *purus*, *iparrasūni*. Thus in principle no single cuneiform sign could carry the meaning of an Akkadian word, and the practical solution was to write words out phonetically. To a large extent this happened, but additionally Akkadian-speaking scribes used Sumerian signs to express Akkadian terms, e.g. Sumerian udu-meš for Akkadian *immerū*, 'sheep', or mixed the two, e.g. Sumerian gal = 'great', but gal-*u* = Akkadian *rabû*, 'great'. (For clarity Assyriologists write Sumerian in normal script or capitals and Akkadian in italics.)

The Akkadian language as attested in the cuneiform texts uses the same four vowels as Sumerian: a, e, i, and u, having probably lost the vowel o under the influence of Sumerian. In addition to the semivowels w and y it uses the following consonants: b, d, g, k, l, m, n, p, q, r, s, t, z, ḫ, ṣ, ś, š, ṭ and the glottal stop ʾ. The Sumerian ĝ is not used in Akkadian but becomes g. The Semitic languages have three h-sounds, h, ḫ and ḥ; Arabic has all three, Hebrew uses only h and ḫ; Akkadian, under the influence of Sumerian, uses only ḫ. Akkadian originally had three sibilants s, ś, and š, but after the Old Akkadian period ś drops out of use. The three emphatic sounds ṣ, ṭ and q, the glottal stop ʾ, and the letter p which are used in Akkadian, do not occur in Sumerian. Thus the Sumerian script was never ideally suited to writing Akkadian. A new sign was invented for ʾ, but otherwise several different conventions were used at different times and in different areas to get over the problems. The distinctions between b and p, between d, t, and ṭ, and between g, k and q are never consistently marked in the script. It is curious that no single agreed solution was ever enforced, such was the strength of the old tradition.

In taking over and adapting the Sumerian syllabary the Akkadian-speaking scribes added to it still further values, increasing the aspects of homophony and polyphony. Thus the Sumerian sign á 'hand' corresponds to Akkadian *idu* 'hand'; hence the sign comes to be used for the syllable *id*, and also for *it*, *iṭ*, *ed*, *et* and *eṭ*. The total number of distinct cuneiform signs in use from the late third millennium onwards is about six hundred, and the number of possible values is far higher. The possible variations did not create as many problems as one might suppose, however, since at any given period and for any given class of text a rather more limited repertoire of signs was used, making life easier both for the scribe and the modern reader. Also in most cases the correct reading of a sign is made clear by the context and by the preceding and following signs.

Although Sumerian had dropped out of common use as a spoken language by the eighteenth century BC and was superseded by Akkadian, it continued to be used by the scribes both as a regular form of shorthand (as in writing udu for *immeru*), in composing many monumental inscriptions (for the sake of tradition), and in copying and recopying Sumerian word-lists and literary texts. By the first millennium for their own convenience the scribes frequently copied Sumerian literature with each Sumerian line followed by its Akkadian translation. The very latest of all cuneiform texts, astronomical texts of the first century AD, are almost entirely written in Sumerian logograms.

The historical divisions

The development of cuneiform during the early Sumerian period has been briefly sketched above. Its further progress is now briefly outlined in order to make the historical terminology intelligible. The accession of Sargon I in 2334 BC marked the beginning of the dynasty of Akkad; the basic language of texts written at this time was Akkadian, specifically the Old Akkadian dialect. With the decline of that dynasty around 2200 BC Akkad was eclipsed and Sumerian became the regular language of administration again, although throughout the next thousand years later kings frequently called themselves kings of Sumer and Akkad. Under the Third Dynasty of Ur (or Ur III) a massive growth of royal bureaucracy occurred which has left us a larger amount of administrative texts than all the other periods of Mesopotamian history put together. Almost every collection of tablets includes Ur III texts.

After the fall of Ur in 2004 BC the dominant dynasties were those of Isin, Larsa and Babylon, in that order. By 1900 BC with the ascendancy of Larsa, Sumerian had again ceased to be the prevalent language and finally gave way permanently to Akkadian. Although the dynasty of Babylon only took control of Sumer and Akkad in 1763 BC in the reign of Hammurapi, the time from 2004 to 1595 BC is commonly known as the Old Babylonian period, and all Akkadian texts of this time are described as Old Babylonian. Texts from the time of the succeeding Kassite Dynasty and the Second Dynasty of Isin are described as Middle Babylonian; this is also the date of the international correspondence found at El-Amarna in Egypt, mostly written in Babylonian, and the archives of Ugarit in Syria. In many respects tablets of the Middle Babylonian period retain a strong similarity in form and script to the earlier ones. The Babylonian texts written in the first millennium BC are quite distinct, but their nomenclature has caused problems. Some scholars describe tablets from 1000 BC to the beginning of the Chaldean (or Neo-Babylonian) Dynasty as Neo-Babylonian, and describe all later tablets as Late Babylonian. Others draw the dividing line after the defeat of the Chaldean Dynasty by Cyrus in 539 BC. There is also a separate literary dialect known as Standard Babylonian which is used in both Babylonia and Assyria.

From the time of Alexander the Great onwards the use of the cuneiform script is increasingly restricted, being superseded by Aramaic; a few legal and literary texts were still written in cuneiform as late as 40 BC, and the last astronomical text is datable to   8

75 AD. The latest texts have a very cursive script and can be extremely difficult to read.

Some of the earliest texts from Assyria are written in Old Babylonian, but a very distinctive group of tablets found at Kanesh (Kultepe) in eastern Turkey proved to be the commercial records of a trading colony from Ashur of the nineteenth century BC. They employ a quite distinctive script and dialect and are identified as Old Assyrian. From the area of Assyria come the fifteenth-century tablets found at Nuzi, but since they show the town to have been controlled by the Hurrian kingdom of Mitanni they are not regarded as Assyrian but are simply described as Nuzi texts. Middle Assyrian texts, mostly from Ashur, begin with the first expansion of Assyria outside its homeland in the thirteenth century BC. The great majority of Assyrian texts, however, belong to the Neo-Assyrian period (1000–609 BC), and come from the royal archives at Nineveh and Kalhu. There is one great advantage in dealing with these texts – they employ a very standardised script. It was fortunate for Assyriologists that these were the first large archives to become available.

The historical development of the cuneiform script which occupies scholars so much today also fascinated the ancient scribes. The collections from Babylon contain many late copies of early historical inscriptions or legal texts made in the seventh or sixth century BC by scribes who had found the originals in temples, private collections or even

Chronological table

Dates (BC)	Sumer/Babylon	Assyria	Elsewhere
3300–2900	Uruk IV–III and Jemdet Nasr periods Brak tablets		Proto-Elamite Susa archives
2900–2600	Early Dynastic I–II period Archaic Ur tablets		
2600–2334	Early Dynastic II–III Enmebaragesi of Kish, c. 2600 Fara tablets Abu Salabikh tablets Ebla archives Girsu (Enannatum I c. 2400) Lugalzagesi of Uruk (2340–2316)		
2334–2154	Dynasty of Akkad Old Akkadian Sargon of Akkad (2334–2279) Naram-Sin (2254–2218) Gudea of Lagash (2141–2122)		Puzur-Inshushinak of Elam
2112–2004	Ur III Dynasty Umma, Puzrish-Dagan and Girsu archives Ur-Nammu (2112–2095) Shulgi (2094–2047)		
2004–1595	Old Babylonian period Archives from Larsa, Nippur, Eshnunna, Sippar, Tell ed-Der, Ur, Kish Sin-kashid of Uruk (c. 1790)	Old Assyrian archives from Kanesh (19th century)	
1894–1595	First Dynasty of Babylon Hammurapi (1792–1750) Samsuiluna (1749–1712)		Mari archives Zimri-Lim (1775–1759)
c. 1550–1155	Kassite Dynasty (Middle Babylonian)		Hittite archives at Boghazkoy (17th–13th century)

8 An astronomical almanac for the year 61/62 AD. BM 40084.

tes (BC)	Sumer/Babylon	Assyria	Elsewhere
		Nuzi archives (15th century)	Mitanni kingdom (c. 1550–1260) Alalakh archives (15th century) (El-Amarna archives (c. 1400)
		Middle Assyrian archives at Ashur (13th century)	Ugarit archives (14th century) Middle Elamite Humban-numena I (c. 1275)
60	Elamite invasion of Babylonia		
57–1026	Second Dynasty of Isin		
1000–625	Neo/Babylonian	Neo-Assyrian archives from Ashur, Kalhu, and Nineveh Ashurnasirpal II (883–859) Shalmaneser III (858–824) Sargon II (721–705) Sennacherib (704–681) Esarhaddon (680–669) Ashurbanipal (668–627)	Urartian inscriptions
5–539	Chaldean Dynasty Archives from Babylon Nebuchadnezzar II (604–562) Nabonidus (555–539)		
9–331			Archaemenid Dynasty of Persia Old Persian inscriptions Late Elamite tablets Cyrus (559–530) Darius I (521–486) Xerxes (485–465) Artazerxes III (358–338)
6–323	Alexander the Great		
1	Seleucid Era began Antiochus I Soter (281–260)		
AD	The latest Babylonian tablet		

on rubbish dumps and who had faithfully copied the curious styles of early writing. Among the Neo-Assyrian tablets from Kalhu there is a small group of tablets on which the scribes have drawn archaic signs such as might have been typical of the mid-third millennium BC and annotated them with their modern equivalent, i.e. their Neo-Assyrian equivalent. A century later we find that the archaeologist king Nabonidus, who boasted of finding inscriptions of Hammurapi at Larsa and of excavating for inscriptions of Sargon I and Naram-Sin at Akkad, had some of his own royal bricks and cylinders stamped or inscribed in a script which attempts to imitate the Old Babylonian style.

Numbers

Numbers are found written on cuneiform texts of all types, from the very earliest, before 3000 BC, down to the very latest datable text in AD 75. Over that long time-span the system of writing numbers shows its own development alongside the development of the rest of the cuneiform script.

At all periods the numerical system used by the Sumerians, Babylonians, and those who borrowed from them, is a combination of the decimal system (counting in tens) and a sexagesimal system (counting in sixties). In the earliest periods there are separate symbols for each numerical power:

| 1 | 10 | 60 | 600 (60×10) | 3,600 (60^2) | 36,000 ($60^2 \times 10$) |

These numbers were written by pressing the larger or smaller ends of a reed stylus into the clay either vertically (to make a circle) or at a slant. When the script becomes truly cuneiform these numbers have a more angular form:

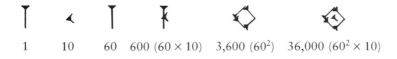

| 1 | 10 | 60 | 600 (60×10) | 3,600 (60^2) | 36,000 ($60^2 \times 10$) |

In the later Babylonian system (2000 BC to AD 75) for many purposes, especially pure mathematics, numbers were written with a simplified place-value notation whereby the place of a number in a sequence determines its value. There are only vertical and slanting wedges:

| 1 | 2 | 3 | 4 | 5 | 10 | 20 | 30 | 40 | 50 | 60 | 600 | 60^2 | $60^2 \times 10$ |

The same symbols were also used for writing fractions. So 1 can be $1/60$ or $1/60^2$, and so on. Everything depends on the order in which the numbers appear (higher values on the left, lower on the right) and on the context. So:

$$60 + 10 + 5 = 75$$
$$\text{or } 60^2 + 10 + 5 = 3615$$
$$\text{or even } 1 + (15/60) = 1.25$$

$$(2 \times 60) + 40 + 5 = 165$$
$$\text{or } (2 \times 60^2) + (40 \times 60) + 5 = 9605$$
$$\text{or } 2 + 45/60 = 2.75$$

A small group of signs were also used for simple fractions:

$\frac{1}{2}$ $\frac{1}{3}$ $\frac{2}{3}$ $\frac{5}{6}$

The result could be confusing even for the Babylonians. So, in practice, while the system described was regularly used for pure mathematics and astronomy, in many everyday economic operations numbers and fractions were written out in words (as we may write 100 or one hundred).

Sometimes numbers were also used as a sort of cryptography. Thus the names of some of the major deities could be, and frequently were, written as numbers:

Adad   Shamash   Sin   Ea   Enlil

There is a famous case of numerical manipulation in Assyrian history. Sennacherib had sacked Babylon in 689 BC. His son Esarhaddon on succeeding to the throne in 680 BC in a dramatic shift of policy decided to embark on its restoration, and justified it by announcing that whereas the god Marduk had decreed that the city should remain desolate for seventy years he had now relented and turned the number upside down. So seventy became eleven:

70   11

The use of sexagesimal numbers for astronomy by the Babylonians in the last centuries BC gave them a great advantage over contemporary Greek astronomers who had no convenient mathematical notation. As a result many Babylonian astronomical calculations were used by the ancient Greek and medieval Arab astronomers long after knowledge of cuneiform writing was lost. Our present system of counting sixty seconds in a minute, sixty minutes in an hour, and three hundred and sixty degrees in a circle is a survival of Babylonian mathematics.

2
Tablets and Monuments

Tablets and stylus

The overwhelming majority of cuneiform texts were written on clay. Monumental and dedicatory inscriptions can be found on stone, ivory, metal, and glass, and examples have been found of folding ivory writing boards which had a carefully preserved surface of beeswax; but the clay tablet was always the standard writing surface.

Clay was always widely available in Mesopotamia, but would have needed some preparation to ensure that it was of the right quality, at least for writing fine library tablets. Unfortunately the clay from southernmost Iraq has a high percentage of salt which means that some tablets from that area tend to disintegrate in unfavourable atmospheric conditions; but that would not have been a problem for the ancient scribes.

Learning how to make a tablet of the right size and shape with a good, smooth surface for writing on must have been one of the first tasks for trainee scribes. A few experiments show that it is not so easy. The Mesopotamian scribes turned out fine examples at all periods, not just of small single-column tablets but massive eleven-column tablets from the Ur III period measuring over 30 cm square. How they handled them is itself a mystery. One is reminded of the vase painters from Classical Greece who saw fit to record the names of the potters who made the vases; the Mesopotamian scribes might well have done the same, except that so far as we know they made their own tablets. The size of some of these Ur III tablets is probably also the explanation for one regular feature of tablets from that period onwards. The front of the tablet is regularly flat, while the back is convex. Making a tablet perfectly flat on both sides would have been unnecessary; but if the tablet was prepared with at least one side flat then the flat side could be inscribed first, and the tablet could then be lain on its flat face for the reverse to be inscribed without pressure distorting the signs on the front. This characteristic of tablets has often allowed modern scholars to determine which is the front and which the back of some broken fragment of a text.

Most tablets were simply left to dry out after being inscribed. Good quality clay when well dried can be extremely durable, and if not deliberately mishandled will last as long as needed for practical administrative purposes. If necessary it can be moistened again to alter the text. Some tablets, however, being intended for permanent record, whether for legal purposes or as part of a library, were baked. Additionally many of the tablets in museum collections today have been accidentally burnt, since they come from libraries or archives which were destroyed and burnt in antiquity when some foreign conqueror seized a city and sacked it. We owe most of the major collections of tablets to this kind of historical disaster. In the normal course of events unbaked tablets would probably have been re-used eventually as raw material for making new tablets. Where tablets have been baked their colour depends on the temperature to which they have been fired – mostly dark grey or black for tablets destroyed by fire, whitish for tablets baked to an excessive temperature, and a dark orange-brown for tablets baked in modern times under laboratory conditions for their better preservation.

9

Most tablets are square or rectangular, but not all. Some school texts of the Ur III and Old Babylonian periods, and some land-survey texts of Ur III date, are circular or bun-shaped. A few tablets prepared for magical purposes are shaped with a wide perforated lug at one end so that they can be specially mounted or threaded through and strung round someone's neck; and others designed for the same purpose are little more than inscribed clay beads. There are also a wide variety of cones, cylinders and prisms, to be discussed later.

These tablets were written with a stylus which was almost always cut from a reed. Its standard Babylonian name is simply *qan ṭuppi*, 'tablet-reed'. Styli in metal or bone were occasionally used, but not by the everyday scribe. Reed of great strength is common in the marshlands of the Near East and its exploitation was itself a large industry. The scribe needed only to take a short piece of reed and trim it to produce a rounded end, a

9 A tablet of the Ur III period; a register of fields. BM 110116.

sharp point, or a flat or sloping end. The manner in which he cut the reed would then affect the style of his writing. From this it is clear that in the third millennium many numbers were written with a round-ended stylus, while the rest of the text was written with a stylus flat at the end. Tablets from the late Old Babylonian period (seventeenth century BC) have a very distinctive slanting script which comes from a stylus with a diagonally cut end, while the Assyrian library texts were written with a flat stylus.

The stylus was not only used to inscribe the text on the tablet. It was also used to mark the lines and columns. From the very earliest periods a cuneiform text was broken up, mostly by natural grammatical or sense units, either into rectangular boxes, or, at least from the Old Akkadian period onwards, into lines separated by rulings. At first the signs were just written in the space between these rulings, but in the Ur III period the practice of using a top line as a guide from which to hang the signs seems to be quite regular; it is still common in the Old Babylonian period, especially for letters and literary texts. Occasionally examples can be found in the Kassite period, but for the most part, rulings in the Kassite and Neo-Babylonian periods separate the lines of text without the signs being hung from them. Some Neo-Babylonian school texts follow the earlier practice, but on literary texts the rulings may run through either the centre or the head of wedges. In general, however, Neo-Babylonian administrative and legal texts are not ruled. The Late Elamite scribes regularly used the side, not the point, of the stylus to make wider rulings, and this appears to be an innovation. The ruling would be made simply by impressing the point of the stylus into the clay and then laying it flat. On a small number of tablets from the royal libraries at Nineveh one can see that the stylus had been replaced by a piece of thread laid across the surface and pressed down.

The rulings made by the stylus marked not only horizontal lines but vertical divisions, or columns of text. Typically a multi-columned tablet would be inscribed first on the left-hand column of the front, or obverse, of the tablet, then on the right-hand column; then the tablet would be turned vertically over its lower edge, and inscribed first on the right column of the reverse and finally on the left column. This curious order harks right back to the days of the earliest pictographic texts. There are some exceptions but they are rare. In general, if a multi-columned tablet does not obey these rules, or if the tablet turns right to left (as the page of a book) then it suggests a forgery.

Very occasionally the stylus is used for some other marks; for instance, a few tablets have ornamental rulings around the outer edge. Some account tablets of the Old Babylonian period listing dozens of individuals have a small check-mark against every tenth person; and a few literary tablets from the Nineveh libraries have a mark against every tenth line, perhaps to give the scribe an easy check on whether he had left a line out. From the Middle Babylonian and Middle Assyrian periods onwards many literary tablets have 'firing holes', which are made by pressing the stylus (or some similar object) right through (or almost through) the tablet from front to back or side to side. It used to be suggested that the purpose of these holes was to help the tablet dry out and stop it from bursting if it was to be baked for better preservation. But consideration of the size of some large Ur III tablets, which could be successfully baked in antiquity without the use of firing holes, suggests that the idea is incorrect. In any case, whatever the reason for their first appearance, they quickly became a matter of tradition. One frequently finds on tablets from the Nineveh libraries that if one copy of a literary text has firing holes other copies of the same text not only have firing holes but have them in the same positions and often disposed in a purely ornamental arrangement. Firing holes are also of interest because close examination of them can show the precise shape of the scribe's stylus.

Occasionally the stylus was used for writing something other than cuneiform. Some tablets of the first millennium BC from Babylonia and Assyria have comments at the end or on the edges in Aramaic; with the gradual decline in use of cuneiform and the rise of Aramaic even in the court of the Assyrian king, remarks in Aramaic would have served as a quick guide to Aramaic-reading filing-clerks. In fact, from a somewhat later period there are also tablets inscribed wholly in Aramaic, and even a small group of tablets from Babylon with Babylonian texts written in the Greek alphabet. Tablets also

10 (*Left*) Neo-Babylonian copy (*c.* 600 BC) of an inscription of Hammurapi (*c.* 1750 BC); the colophon says that the copy was made by the scribe Rimut-Gula from the original text found in the temple Enamtila. BM 46543.

11 (*Right*) A literary tablet with 'firing holes' and a colophon stating that it was written for the royal library of king Ashurbanipal (668–627 BC) at Nineveh. DT 1.

occasionally have inscriptions added in ink or paint, in Egyptian (on a letter from El-Amarna), in Aramaic, or in Assyrian cuneiform.

Other marks were made on tablets by a variety of instruments for different purposes. Many tablets bear the impressions of the seals of witnesses or scribes (discussed below). Others, especially in the first millennium BC, have the impressions of the witness's thumb-nail on the edge, and in such cases the text often says, 'So-and-so has impressed his thumb-nail instead of his seal'. In the Old Babylonian period the same function was performed by impressing the hem of one's garment (*sissiktu*) on the edge of a tablet, though few cases of this have actually been found. Some fabric impressions on tablets may only be the marks of wrapping. Finally, when a tablet had outlived its purpose it could be cancelled by scoring across it with a stylus or some other sharp instrument.

Envelopes

Some tablets, once written, were placed in envelopes of clay, whether for transport, in the case of letters, or for security, in the case of disputed transactions. This practice started in the Ur III period, and was largely restricted to administrative texts. In order to prevent fraud once the record of livestock or materials entering or leaving the royal stores had been written, the tablet was wrapped in a clay envelope; the entire transaction was then re-recorded on the envelope and the responsible supervisor sealed it. In the

12 (*Left*) A Middle Babylonian legal tablet from Alalah, in its envelope. BM 131449.
13 (*Right*) An Old Babylonian letter and its sealed envelope. BM 82199.

event of a dispute about the quantities involved the envelope could be opened and the record checked. This elaborate precaution prevented anyone from attempting to moisten the clay of the original document and rewrite the numbers. In a few cases envelopes have been opened in modern times and found to contain not a duplicate record of the transaction on the envelope but the original letter authorising the transaction.

In the Old Babylonian period the practice extended to the use of envelopes for legal records, especially sales and disputes over inheritance. These became very elaborate documents, and were sealed by many witnesses in addition to the parties involved. At different periods the seals might either be rolled across the whole width of the envelope or over a space specially left blank, or the text was written on the right-hand side of the envelope and the seals were rolled down the left side or on the left edge. In a curious   12
extension of this practice a group of large legal tablets were prepared and sealed to look as if they were envelopes although they were not.

Envelopes for letters in the Old Babylonian and Old Assyrian period are typically   13
inscribed only with the name of the addressee, 'To my brother, Awil-Adad', or 'To Damqiya and Zikir-Shamash'. The sender normally seals the envelope with his personal seal. Very occasionally he also seals the inner tablet itself for security, and this is specially remarked on in the letter. A few envelopes from the Old Assyrian colony at Kanesh contain both the letter tablet and a small extra piece of clay on which the scribe, who had prepared too small a tablet for the letter, had to continue the message. The fact that literacy was restricted to the professional scribes is emphasised by the opening lines of all these letters, which follow a standard formula: 'Tell Mr A, Mr B sends the following message.' Having been written to dictation by one professional scribe, the letter would be read out to the recipient by another professional scribe.

Although envelopes later than the Old Babylonian period are uncommon, the practice of sending letters in them certainly continued, and examples survive from Neo-Assyrian times. One such, addressed to 'The second officer, my Lord' by Ashur-reṣua and sealed by him asks, 'Why does my lord refuse to reply to my letter?' To judge by the fact that the present letter still has its envelope, perhaps his lord was simply not opening his mail.

Seals
The practice of sealing tablets and envelopes has already been referred to. In fact seals,   14
either in the form of stamps or cylinders (which would be rolled across the clay), appear   15
long before the invention of writing. The very earliest tablets, which have mathematical   38
notation only, also bear seal impressions. The seals were carved from stone, bone or shell, and the different designs on them served to identify their owners. By the late Early Dynastic period some owners also had their names, or a dedication to a deity, inscribed on their seals. They were at first designed to mark property. When tying up a sack or tying down the cloth cover on a jar the careful Sumerian would squeeze a lump of clay around the knot and seal it; no one could then open the sack or jar without disturbing the seal-impression. Such sealings are known from prehistoric times down to the Old Babylonian period and then again in Neo-Assyrian times. The practice extended to using the seal to record who had authorised or witnessed a transaction, and so many tablets came to be sealed. This usage continued down to the Greek period in Babylonia when we find commercial contracts sealed by small stamp-seals bearing some of the signs of the zodiac as well as thousands of sealings from papyri which have long since decayed.

14 (*Left*) An Old Babylonian cylinder-seal. BM 132153.
15 (*Right*) A Kassite cylinder-seal. BM 89128.

Sometimes when the seal bears a personal name, especially a royal name, it can be useful as a means of dating the tablet on which its impression appears; but more often it is the dated and sealed tablets which allow us to study the artistic development of the seals.

As in any other activity anomalies occurred in the use of seals. So in the Old Babylonian period there briefly appear clay seals (known as *burgul* seals) which were one-off creations made for a particular occasion, perhaps because the witness had no personal seal. In Neo-Assyrian records we find that many tablets and clay sealings bear the royal seal of Assyria, depicting the king killing a lion; this would not have been the king's personal seal but a royal household seal. On one tablet of this time from Babylon a scribe making a copy of a royal grant confirming a man's right to temple income has carefully carved a copy of the royal seal in high relief on his tablet, since the royal seal was not available to seal the copy.

Monuments

Kings may have been illiterate, with the exception of Shulgi and Ashurbanipal, but they were well aware of the propaganda value of creating a permanent record of their exploits. They were also concerned to remind the watching gods of how they had cared for their shrines and supported their cults. So besides the everyday receipts and the literary creations we have a separate class of commemorative and dedicatory texts, inscribed at first mostly on stone. Some of the earliest are nothing more than large pebbles, selected simply because stone was more durable than clay, and rarer too in the delta areas of the Tigris and Euphrates.

The earliest such inscription, found on a sherd from an alabaster vase, says only, 'Mebaragesi, king of Kish'. He is to be identified with Enmebaragesi, the father of Akka (the legendary rival of Gilgamesh); the inscription probably dates to *c*. 2600 BC. The vase was prepared for dedication in a temple, and such vases in all varieties of stone continue to be inscribed by the Sumerian and Babylonian kings down to Neo-Babylonian times. More distinctive are the royal statues, mostly rather small but occasionally approaching 16 life-size, as in the case of a famous series of statues of Gudea, ruler of Lagash, *c*. 2130 BC, found at Girsu. The statues are frequently inscribed on the dress or down the back, and until Middle Babylonian times the tradition is preserved of inscribing them in the archaic direction. Over the years almost anything dedicated to a temple could be inscribed with the name of its royal patron, even the agate eyes of the statues of the gods; but some categories of objects became standard vehicles for commemorative inscriptions.

16 Statue of Gudea, ruler of Lagash (2141–2122 BC). Courtesy of Metropolitan Museum of Art, New York, Harrison Brisbane Dick Fund, 1959, 59.2.

17 A cone inscription of Ur-Bau, ruler of Lagash (2155–2142 BC). BM 91061.

17   The first category was the clay nail or cone. Decorating the walls of temples with a pattern of small clay nails, sometimes coloured, was a feature of Early Dynastic times, well attested at Uruk. At a later date Sumerian and Old Babylonian legal texts show that it was common for the purchaser of a house to hammer a nail into its wall in the presence of witnesses as a mark of his new ownership. Either the decorative or the legal tradition may lie behind the practice of kings from the time of Enannatum I of Lagash (*c.* 2400 BC) to Samsuiluna of Babylon (1749–1712 BC) to place inscribed nails, from 5 cm to 25 cm in length, in the walls of temples or chapels, sometimes by the hundred. The inscriptions often give no more than a brief statement, 'Ur-Nammu, king of Ur, who built the temple of Nanna'; but by the Old Babylonian period they have become lengthy recitals of historical and cultic events. In a few cases the inscription records the building of the king's own palace: 'Sin-kashid, the mighty man, king of Uruk, king of Amnanum, has built his royal palace.'

33   The second category was the brick inscription. Almost every building in Mesopotamia was built in brick rather than stone, mostly sun-dried mud brick, but with baked bricks used for the facades of temples and, in particularly prosperous times, even for private houses. From the time of Naram-Sin of Akkad (2254–2218 BC) the kings had their names inscribed or stamped onto at least some of the bricks used to build major public buildings. In view of the number of bricks involved, the scribes' time and effort were saved by preparing a stamp, in clay or wood, on which the inscription was carved in reverse so that it could be conveniently stamped onto hundreds or thousands of bricks in a short space of time. Almost every collection of Near Eastern antiquities has at least one

37   stamped brick of Nebuchadnezzar II (604–562 BC) from the great temple-tower (*ziqqurratu*) at Babylon. The kings of Assyria and Elam were less concerned with such economy of effort and most bricks from these kingdoms are laboriously inscribed along the edges; but this may also reflect their view of the purpose of the inscriptions. When one stamped the surface of a large square brick the inscription would become invisible as soon as it was built into a structure, and only the gods could read it; but if the brick were inscribed along the edge his fellow men too would remember the king's pious works. The inscriptions commemorate royal palaces as well as temples, and in some cases they even commemorate a particular part of a building, such as a well or the pedestal of a statue. A few late bricks have short Aramaic inscriptions, and there are one or two inscriptions in Greek and even in an early form of Arabic.

18   The third category of commemorative inscription was the cylinder or prism. In the

18 (*Left*) A prism inscription
describing the military campaigns
of Sennacherib, king of Assyria
(704–681 BC). H. 15 in (38 cm).
BM 91032.

19 (*Below*) Detail from fig. 18; the
account of Sennacherib's seige
of Jerusalem.

Old Babylonian period a number of prisms were inscribed with lexical lists or literary compositions, but apart from the great cylinders of Gudea (61 cm high, 32 cm diameter) this form was not used for royal inscriptions until Middle Assyrian times. From then on we have some fine examples of six-, eight-, or ten-sided hollow prisms inscribed with lengthy and detailed accounts of the king's military campaigns. (There are particularly fine examples from the reigns of the last great Assyrian kings, Sennacherib, Esarhaddon and Ashurbanipal.) The old idea of recording piety to the gods has been supplemented by the desire to create a permanent historical record, a record which might be updated many times during a king's reign. For most of the Neo-Assyrian kings our knowledge of the political course of their reigns is very largely dependent on an analysis of these prism inscriptions. In spite of the care with which they were prepared, these too were destined to be buried in the foundations of the walls of palaces or temples, much as today we place pennies and copies of newspapers in the foundations of new buildings. In Babylonia the favourite form of such inscriptions was the cylinder, but the cylinders of Nebuchadnezzar II and Nabonidus from Babylon have far less political information and concentrate on details of their temple building and even their own archaeological investigations. The cylinder form survives even in the time of Antiochus I Soter in 281–260 BC.

Most impressive of all were the great inscribed stelae and obelisks of the Assyrian kings, designed to stand out in the open for all to see in the squares and courtyards of the capital cities, depicting the king and describing his conquests. The only early monument comparable to these is the law code of Hammurapi of Babylon, 2.25 m high and inscribed with about 4,000 lines of Babylonian cuneiform. It so impressed the Elamite invaders of Babylonia in 1160 BC that they carried it off to Susa.

On a smaller scale, towns or wealthy private citizens recorded grants of land from the king or exemptions from taxation by preparing stone monuments, on which were carved copies of the original royal decree (written and sealed on a clay tablet) and the symbols of the gods who were invoked as witnesses. These monuments are known as boundary-stones, both from their outward appearance and from the Babylonian term used to describe them (*kudurru*), but almost all of those for which the find-spot is recorded have been found in temples.

1

3

Scribes and Libraries

Scribal training

Literacy was not widespread in Mesopotamia. The scribes, like any craftsmen, had to undergo training, and having completed their training and become entitled to call themselves dubsar, 'scribe', they were members of a privileged élite who might look with contempt on their fellow citizens. Writing 'Ibni-Marduk dubsar' was the equivalent of writing George Smith, B.A. The scribal profession was under the patronage of the Sumerian goddess Nisaba. Occasionally a scribe would end a long literary text with the comment ᵈnisaba zami, 'Oh Nisaba, praise'. In later times her place was taken by the god Nabu of Borsippa. Whereas other gods were symbolised by animals or stars, his symbol was the stylus.

Our picture of life in Babylonian schools is based on a group of Sumerian literary compositions of the Old Babylonian period. A few of them became part of the standard literary tradition and were still being copied for the library of Ashurbanipal. Schooling began at an early age in the é-dubba, the 'tablet-house'. The headmaster was called ummia (or *ummânu* in Akkadian). He might be assisted by an adda é-dubba, 'father of the tablet-house', and an ugula, 'clerk'. Much of the initial instruction and discipline seems to have been in the hands of a student's 'big brother', an elder student who is pictured as fluctuating between being a friend and a bully. Each of these had to be flattered or bribed with gifts from time to time to avoid a beating.

The French excavations at Mari revealed in the palace of king Zimri-Lim a room with rows of clay benches. This has often been taken as a model of what a Babylonian school would have looked like. Unfortunately no school tablets were found in it so its use cannot be proved. It seems just as likely that students were taught outside in the courtyard, which was the centre of life in any Old Babylonian house. Almost all the private houses of this period excavated at Ur and Isin have a few school texts of one kind or another, suggesting that in wealthy families all the boys were sent to school. At Nippur one part of the town was so full of literary tablets that it has become known to archaeologists as Tablet Hill; it may have been a special scribal quarter.

The first thing the schoolboy had to learn was how to make a tablet and handle a stylus. First steps in writing were made on any piece of clay, learning to impress a simple cuneiform wedge, known in Sumerian as a ge, Babylonian *miḫiṣtu*. The schoolboy practised the horizontal, vertical and sloping wedges over and over again. Then he started on the basic sign-list; but this had to be learnt not only as a series of individual signs but also with the different syllables that they could represent. Thus the sign A stood for á, ya, duru, e and a. He had to learn that A was the basic name of the sign. (He could not write A in capitals, but we do so sometimes to remind ourselves which sign we are dealing with.) Then he would go on to learn what were the many Babylonian equivalents of all these different signs and their alternative values. For instance, one type of sign-list reads di-i DI *di-nu-um* (i.e. the sign DI if read as di is the Sumerian equivalent of *dīnum*, 'lawsuit'); si-li-im DI *ša-la-mu-um* (the sign DI if read as silim is the equivalent of *šalāmum*, 'to be at peace'). After learning the basic signs the pupil had to go on to all the thousands of different Sumerian words that were expressed by more than one sign. Here we can see the continuity of scribal tradition, as the signs being learnt by the very earliest scribes at Uruk were learnt in the same order hundreds of years later by scribes at Abu Salabikh and Uruk, and the Old Babylonian sign-lists were still found in Ashurbanipal's library.

Learning to string signs together to write words seems to have been practised by writing names. That at least is the interpretation of the many small tablets inscribed in a clumsy hand with three or four Sumerian names. Babylonian scribes with few exceptions are remarkably consistent in their application of the cuneiform script to the Sumerian and Akkadian languages. The consonant at the beginning of a syllable is hardly ever linked with a vowel from a preceding syllable; thus the word 'to', Akkadian *ana*, is consistently written *a-na*, not *an-a*. That is a simple enough example, but the principle extends throughout the phonetic representation of the language, and must have been taught in the schools.

20   At this point the schoolboy was ready to go on to the next stage, which is marked by writing on a different kind of tablet, the round, bun-shaped tablet. On these the teacher would typically write out three lines on one side of the tablet, such as the names of gods, a list of technical terms, a short fragment of literature or a proverb; the schoolboy had to study these carefully, and then turn the tablet over and try to reproduce what the teacher had written. It is usually quite easy to see which side was written by the teacher and which by the schoolboy.

Finally the pupil reached the stage of learning and writing Sumerian literature. Much of Sumerian literature as known in the Old Babylonian period is preserved for us only in school copies. It seems that the boys were copying from dictation, as again and again we find that different copies of a text write the words out slightly differently. That some-

20 An Old Babylonian school tablet inscribed on the front (*left*) by a teacher and on the back (*right*) by a pupil; the text is a Sumerian proverb. BM 104096.

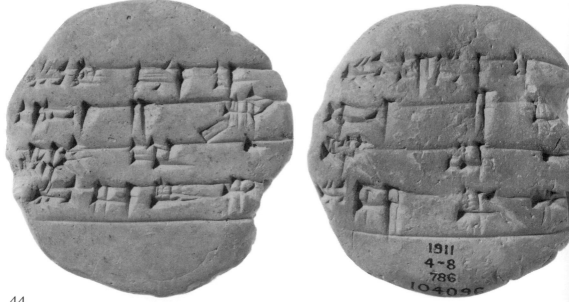

times makes it difficult for us to reconstruct the original form of the text. The literature curriculum was very large and mostly traditional, but even in the Old Babylonian period new compositions were being added, mostly hymns to the gods on behalf of the king.

A separate part of the curriculum was devoted to mathematics, taught by the dubsar nišid, 'scribe of accounting', the dubsar zaga, 'scribe of measurement', and the dubsar ašaga, 'scribe of the field' (i.e. surveyor). In a dialogue between schoolboys the senior boy asks the junior, 'Do you know multiplication, reciprocals, coefficients, balancing of accounts, administrative accounting, how to make all kinds of pay allotments, divide property and delimit shares of fields?' That summarises for us their mathematical curriculum. Museums have dozens if not hundreds of copies of mathematical tables: multiplication tables, tables of reciprocals (for division), of squares and cubes, of square roots and cube roots, and of coefficients. They are the Babylonian equivalent of '60 seconds = 1 minute, 60 minutes = 1 hour, 24 hours = 1 day; 12 inches = 1 foot, 3 feet = 1 yard, 1760 yards = 1 mile', etc., but extended to a wide variety of other purposes such as house-building and tuning musical instruments. There are also compilations of mathematical problems and their solutions designed to teach the students how to apply their knowledge to more or less practical situations, as well as problems in geometry and elementary algebra. The compilations have one curious feature: the numerical answer to all questions on the tablet is the same. If the answer to the first question is six, then so is the answer to the second and third question. This has the advantage that if the student arrives at the answer six then both he and the teacher know that he has correctly understood the necessary procedure. The technical terminology of mathematics is largely Sumerian even though the problem texts are written in Babylonian.

One gets the impression that apart from mathematics the Babylonian scribal education concentrated on Sumerian. One may compare this to the nineteenth-century English public-school tradition that a knowledge of the Greek and Latin languages and literatures and of mathematics were all the education that a man needed. In practice, however, the picture is incomplete. We have copies of Akkadian literary texts, and there is evidence for the more practical side of the curriculum. Just as the modern typist is taught the standard layout for a business letter or a contract, so the Babylonian scribes follow regular patterns in writing such texts, and one can often identify the nature of a tablet from a very small fragment on this basis. A small group of practice letters has a special terminology that marks them out as school letters, and there are similar model contracts. The lexical series, *ana ittīšu*, composed in the early Old Babylonian period but surviving only in a few copies from the Late Assyrian libraries, is a collection of Sumerian legal phrases with Babylonian translations, presumably also compiled for use in schools.

The picture given so far relates to the early second millennium BC, since that is the period for which we have the best evidence. As is so often the case, the surviving texts are quite unevenly distributed over time. A small group of copies of Sumerian literary texts of the Kassite period from Nippur shows that the old traditions still survived at that time. The next group of school texts while retaining the spirit of the old tradition have a quite different format. These are texts from Babylonia, and the majority probably come from Babylon itself, dating to the seventh or sixth century BC. They have extracts from more than one composition. Typically they quote two or three consecutive lines from a

21 Assyrian scribes recording booty on one of the campaigns of Tiglath-Pileser III (744–727 BC). BM 118882.

Sumerian text, giving a translation into Akkadian after each line, then quote from another part of the same text or from quite a different composition in the same manner, Sumerian with Akkadian translation, and end with an extract from a lexical text or the great list of gods known as 'An = *Anum*'. The fundamental change from the early tradition is the provision of translations of the Sumerian texts. The change is mirrored in the contemporary libraries, in which Sumerian texts written for permanent record also have interlinear translations.

21   Of the same late date are the few surviving pictures of scribes, all from the area of Assyria. The wall paintings at Til Barsip (eighth or seventh century BC) show pairs of scribes, one writing on a tablet with a stylus, and the other writing on a leather scroll with a pen, each holding his writing instrument differently. The papyrus was probably used for writing in Aramaic. Similar pairs of scribes can be seen on the reliefs from the palaces of Tiglath-Pileser, Sennacherib and Ashurbanipal at Kalhu and Nineveh (seventh century BC).

Colophons

11   Our knowledge of the scribes is mostly derived from the colophons of tablets. The word colophon (taken from Greek and meaning 'summit') describes the inscription formerly placed at the end of a book, containing the title, the printer's name, date and place of printing, etc. Nowadays books have title pages instead of colophons, but the term is regularly used by Assyriologists to describe the information which scribes wrote at the

end of tablets. There are three normal constituents to a colophon on a cuneiform tablet, the name of the scribe, the date, and the name of the town in which the tablet was written. Not all tablets have colophons, and some leave out one or another of these elements, but where they do include them all they generally follow this pattern.

Scribes wrote their names on tablets as early as the Fara period (c. 2600 BC). Most of the names have no great significance, but a few are of particular interest. Enheduanna, the daughter of Sargon I, and high priestess of the moongod Nanna at Ur, is one of the few female scribes known from Mesopotamia, and the earliest named author in history; her composition, named after its first line, nin-me-šár-ra, 'Lady of all aspects of life', is a celebration of the goddess Inanna. The next royal scribe is Ashurbanipal, king of Assyria, over 1,600 years later. Although on the whole the literary texts do not record their authorship, a catalogue preserved at Nineveh gives us a list of the authors of some of the best-known compositions such as Sin-liqi-unninni, editor of the Gilgamesh series, and Lu-Nanna, author of the Etana epic. A few texts are attributed to the god Ea or the mythical sage Adapa. Later scribes give not only their own names and the names of their fathers but also the names of an earlier ancestor, the founder of the family or scribal dynasty, and many of these ancestors are identical with the scribes named in the list of authors.

The scribes often describe themeselves simply as dubsar, but sometimes give them-selves other titles such as dubsar tur, 'junior scribe' (for instance Nur-Aya who copied out the Old Babylonian 'Flood story' of Atra-hasis), or mašmaššu, 'exorcist'. In a special class was the 'scribe of Enuma Anu Enlil', meaning the scribe of the astrological series entitled 'When the gods Anu and Enlil' – in effect a professional astrologer.

In a few cases even though no scribe's name is recorded we can see that a tablet was written by more than one scribe. A group of circular field-survey tablets of the Ur III period give the dimensions of various fields and the amount of barley that each field was expected to yield at harvest time. On a few tablets the space for the barley yield has been left blank. At first it was suggested that the tablets might only be school texts, but close examination revealed a different explanation. Wherever the barley yield was recorded it had been written in by a different hand, less deeply impressed than the rest of the text, probably when the clay had started to dry out. Apparently the surveyors were only responsible for recording the dimensions of the fields; the yield was worked out separ-ately by the accountants or tax inspectors.

The date on a tablet is the date of writing; in a very few cases we can see that a tablet was written on one day and its envelope on the next day. The dates normally take the sequence month, day, year. The year can be indicated in several ways. In Sumer and in Babylonia of the Old Babylonian period the year was named after an event of some importance occurring either in that year or in the preceding year. The scribes had to keep long lists of such names in order to remember the sequence of documents. The Old Assyrian archives and those from Mari are dated by the name of the limmu, a public official appointed for the year. Again lists of these officials had to be kept. In Kassite times the system of regnal years began, 'The first year of Kurigalzu', and so on, and this system remained standard in Babylonia until the fourth century BC. The Assyrians stuck to the limmu system. Finally in 305 BC a new system was introduced in which all years were numbered in succession from the first year of the Seleucid Dynasty, deemed to be 311 BC.

The place names given in the colophons are particularly useful for the reconstruction of archives which have been distributed through the antiquities trade. But occasionally they can have a different significance. Tablets excavated in one town can have another town's name in the colophon, showing how tablets were carried around the country for business purposes. Or an archaeologist scribe copying an earlier text may describe how he found it 'on the rubbish-tip at Nippur'.

Libraries

The archives in which tablets were stored and found have been referred to many times already. Excavations on almost any town or city site in southern Iraq will turn up at least a few tablets, and if one digs in a town of the Old Babylonian period it seems that one can find a few tablets in almost every house. Small private libraries existed at all periods; recent Belgian excavations at Tell ed-Der revealed a library of some 3,000 tablets in the house of a priest, datable to *c.* 1635 BC, and the agents of Ashurbanipal reported to him on the contents of several private libraries which they were sending to him from Babylonia. But it is the large state or temple archives that yield the most useful information about the nature of the contemporary economy and administration, and in most periods, with the exception of the Old Babylonian, it is the formal libraries from palace and temple that preserved the mass of literary texts.

The accidents of destruction and recovery have somewhat distorted our picture of the history and development of Mesopotamia. Some periods are extremely well known. The fall of the Ur III empire as a consequence of an Elamite raid in 2004 BC resulted in the accidental burial of huge archives in the ruins of Umma, Puzrish-Dagan and Girsu; only a fraction of the tablets from these sites have been published so far. Similarly the breaking of Babylon's domination of the south by the kings of the new Sealand Dynasty in the time of Samsuiluna (1726 BC) and the collapse of the First Dynasty of Babylon itself with the Hittite raid on Babylon in 1595 BC left large libraries for the archaeologist at Larsa and Sippar. Most famous of all is the library of Ashurbanipal at Nineveh, a priceless source for the reconstruction of Babylonian and Assyrian literature, which comes to us courtesy of the Babylonians and Medes who sacked Nineveh in 612 BC. On the other hand many historical developments are still quite obscure because for long periods we have no significant archives. We have the impression, for instance, that there was a low level of economic activity in Babylonia for a century or two after the end of the First Dynasty of Babylon and again after the end of the Kassite Dynasty; but does the absence of tablets really imply this, or does it only mean that the country was at peace and no one's library was being burnt down?

The great archives from Mari and Ebla have given us a good idea of the nature of a Mesopotamian library, because (for once) they were properly excavated by competent archaeologists who kept a record of what was found in each room and even how the tablets lay on the floor. At Ebla one can see how the library was scattered across the floor as the wooden shelves on which it was stored collapsed. The ancient librarians, like their modern successors, needed systems to record where to find their tablets. In the case of many large tablets from the Ur III period one can see brief notes written on one edge of the tablet, much like the title on the spine of a modern book, written so that the librarian looking along a shelf full of tablets could pick out the one he needed. Mostly this applies to economic texts, but marginal notes are found also, for instance, on tablets containing multiplication tables. Where a library could not afford the expense of wooden shelves tablets were normally stored in jars or baskets, which had an explanatory clay tag tied on. Such tags have been found for baskets of Sumerian literary texts, and matching up the titles recorded on the tags with the titles of known compositions shows us how much is still unknown. The idea of storing tablets in boxes is reflected in literature too: an Old Babylonian epic concerning Naram-Sin begins, 'Open the tablet-box and read the stele'. The scribe wishes to create the illusion that he is telling a story which has been preserved from distant days and lost in some forgotten corner or buried in a box in the foundations of a building.

One device occasionally used, especially in the Old Babylonian period, to ease the burden of storing and manipulating many large tablets was to compile summaries of several contracts on a single tablet. The same thing could apply to literary texts. A recent German excavation at Isin has produced a fragment of a finely inscribed tablet with five different poetic compositions, running to about 7,070 lines in total.

A simple system of keeping track of literary tablets was to add to the colophon a statement of the title of the series to which the tablet belonged and the number of the tablet within that series. So the famous *Epic of Gilgamesh* in its latest version consisted of twelve tablets; the story of the Flood was told on the eleventh tablet. The colophon reads, 'He who saw everything, eleventh tablet'. 'He who saw everything' is the first line of the epic and therefore its title. To ensure that the scribe found correctly the next tablet of the series its first line might also be added to the colophon of the preceding tablet.

The literary libraries largely consisted of standard texts copied and recopied from one generation to the next. Occasional new texts were added from time to time, but they were few by comparison with the great mass of traditional material. Much of this was not what we today would regard as literature, even if Assyriologists continue to call it such. The largest group of texts consists of omens, collections of observations made over hundreds of years concerned with the stars, the appearance of the liver of a sacrificial sheep, the movements of birds, etc. Other categories of texts were the lexical lists, incantations, prayers, and the well-known epic literature. The late Leo Oppenheim, in a summary of traditional Mesopotamian literature, calculated that the whole of the standard corpus as represented in a library like Ashurbanipal's could have run to as many as fifteen hundred different tablets of between eighty and two hundred lines each; for many texts Ashurbanipal had several copies.

Today the discovery of a new library of literary texts generates great excitement among Assyriologists, but such material is not really typical of the production of the Mesopotamian scribes. Most of them, after all their technical training, spent their lives writing lists of deliveries of sheep or issues of barley rations and occasionally taking a letter by dictation. The more successful scribes would end up as senior administrators in the state bureaucracy, but most of their colleagues would have been happy simply with their status as educated men and the knowledge that their training guaranteed them employment.

4

The Geographical Spread

The cuneiform script pioneered by the Sumerians and Babylonians came to be used for some fifteen different languages in its 3,000-year history. Most of these languages used the Sumero-Babylonian signs and syllabary, so the first stage of their decipherment was already done; but the fact that the Sumero-Babylonian system allows several signs to have the same value and each sign to have several values meant that each language in turn required an additional process of analysis and decipherment. A few peoples adopted the idea of writing in cuneiform, but created their own signs which therefore had to be quite separately deciphered (Old Persian, Ugaritic, and related alphabetic scripts). The decipherment of Old Persian and Babylonian is described in the next chapter.

Eblaite

After the pictographic tablets of Tell Brak there is a gap in the record in Syria of several hundred years before the cuneiform script is again found there. Recent Italian excavations at Ebla (Tell Mardikh, near Aleppo) from 1964 onwards have quite transformed the picture of Syria in the mid-third millennium. They revealed a major urban civilisation with widespread trade and commercial contacts and a scribal and literary tradition that had much in common with contemporary Sumer, especially as known from the tablets of Abu Salabikh. Some 10,000 tablets of the Late Early Dynastic period (c. 2500–2400 BC) have been found at Ebla mostly lying on the floor in orderly groups where the wooden shelves of the library had collapsed. Some are only small fragments, but many are huge tablets with 3,000 lines of writing or more.

   Much of what is written on these tablets is Sumerian and therefore gives us no clue to the nature of the local language. Thus we can read the Sumerian signs 3 udu-meš and know that they mean both to us and to the scribes of Ebla 'three sheep', but how the scribes of Ebla pronounced what they read is another matter. They had taken over from Sumer the use of clay as a writing medium and Sumerian cuneiform as their script, and for convenience they continued to use the Sumerian signs for most of the objects and transactions that their economic texts had to record. It has been estimated that eighty per cent of the words in the Ebla texts are Sumerian. Interspersed among these Sumerian signs the remaining twenty per cent reflect the local language, now called Eblaite. Broadly speaking most of the nouns, verbs and adjectives occurring in the economic texts are written in Sumerian, and most of the prepositions, pronouns, conjunctions and personal names are written syllabically in Eblaite. The fact that all the basic concepts of the texts are recorded in Sumerian makes it relatively easy to get an idea of their content, but since we have very few texts written entirely in phonetic Eblaite, and these mostly poetic, it is hard to get a good picture of the Eblaite language. It is certainly Semitic, but its exact relation to other Semitic languages such as Akkadian, Amorite and Hebrew is still a matter for academic dispute. The problem is not made any easier by the inadequacies of the Sumerian script for writing a Semitic language, discussed above.

Eighty per cent of the texts are administrative, concerning the textile industry, trade in metals, agriculture and personnel matters. A large group of lexical texts listing Sumerian words for animals, wooden objects, etc., form part of the Mesopotamian tradition of scribal education, and some are directly duplicated by texts found at Fara and Abu Salabikh. Some of them list both the Sumerian term and its Eblaite equivalent; but not all the Sumerian terms are translated, perhaps because they were simply too well known to the Ebla scribes. The few political and geographical texts were, when first found, thought to provide early references to the city of Ashur and to many of the place names of the Bible. But after the first excitement subsided further study has eliminated most of these speculative ideas. Only a few literary texts have been made available so far, Sumerian incantations, a Sumerian hymn to the Lord of Heaven and Earth, and some very problematic texts in Eblaite.

Elamite

The heartland of Elam corresponds very roughly with the area of the modern Iranian oilfields. Although Elamite was one of the three languages of the Persian empire, beside Old Persian and Babylonian, and was therefore inscribed on the various monuments which inspired the first decipherment of cuneiform scripts, including the great rock relief at Behistun, Elamite has long been the poor relation of the three. It is the more curious since, as described in Chapter 1, a native form of pictographic writing (known as Proto-Elamite) appears at Susa almost as early as the earliest texts from Uruk (3100–2700 BC). The nature of the texts suggests a society just as advanced as their Sumerian neighbours. The texts can be partially understood by comparison of the pictograms with parallels from Uruk and by means of mathematical analysis, but they cannot yet be read as a language even though, as at Uruk, the script develops from being purely pictographic to being syllabic.

At the time of the dynasty of Akkad the scribes of Susa had adopted the Sumerian script for commemorative inscriptions, but an Elamite invader, Puzur-Inshushinak, introduced a local variety of linear script based on the Proto-Elamite characters. Although we have a bilingual text inscribed in both Proto-Elamite and Old Akkadian the linear script is still only partly deciphered; it was in any case short lived, and for most of the next six centuries such documents from Elam as survive are written in Sumerian or Babylonian. Only four documents from this period are known to be written in cuneiform in Elamite. It is not until Middle Elamite times from the reign of Humban-numena I (about 1285–1266 BC) onwards that we have inscriptions in the Elamite language again. At this point they use a limited repertoire of signs borrowed from Babylonia to write phonetic Elamite with a few logograms. Most of the texts are on bricks or stone monuments from Susa or nearby Dur-Untash (Choga-Zanbil), but a group of economic texts have been found in American excavations at Tall-i-Malyan.

22 A Late Elamite letter, from Nineveh, c. 650 BC. Sm 2144.

Although the history of Elamite texts covers more than 2,500 years, the first large group of tablets which can be readily understood is the recently published economic archive of the Achaemenid Persian kings at Persepolis in the fifth century BC. In fact other evidence shows that the Persian court was already using Aramaic for much of its business.

The Elamite language is non-Semitic, and is not directly related to any of the other languages of the Near East. Its decipherment was naturally aided by the availability of the trilingual inscriptions of the Persian kings, but since the available inscriptions cover only a restricted range of subjects our knowledge of the language is still limited, and not more than a dozen scholars are involved in studying it.

Hittite

23   Until the present century the Hittites, who ruled much of present-day Turkey from the seventeenth to the thirteenth century BC, were known only from scattered references in the Old Testament and the histories of the kings of Egypt and Babylonia. They came to light again in 1906 when Dr Hugo Winckler began to excavate their capital city of Hattusas (Boghazköy). In the great palace of the Hittite kings he found a royal archive of 10,000 tablets. Many of these were easily readable in Babylonian, but the large majority were in the previously unknown Hittite language. Fortunately the Hittite scribes used the Babylonian script and a large number of Sumerian or Babylonian words to express Hittite terms – just as the Babylonians had taken over Sumerian terms. When writing historical, legal or ritual texts the scribes would freely alternate between their native Hittite term and its Sumerian or Babylonian equivalent. So a very convenient starting point was provided for deciphering Hittite.

The process of decipherment, begun by the Czech scholar B. Hrozny, was essentially completed by 1933 thanks to the combined efforts of F. Sommer, J. Friedrich, H. Ehelolf and A. Goetze. Hittite belongs to the Indo-European group of languages, although the use of the Sumero-Babylonian syllabary somewhat obscures this fact. Syllables consisting only of vowel + consonant, consonant + vowel, or consonant + vowel + consonant, are not suited to writing groups of more than two consonants, or two consonants at the beginning of a word such as commonly occur in Indo-European languages. It is now agreed that the true name of the language should be Nesite or Nesian (from the Hittite adverb *nešili*) but the name Hittite is now well established by tradition.

The tablets from Hattusas give a good picture of Hittite politics and society. They consist of historical records, international treaties and correspondence, a law code including a table of standard prices, title-deeds for private estates, many religious and magical rituals, and a few mythological stories which have parallels in Greek literature. Historical references to a neighbouring people, the Ahhiyawā, have been seen as early evidence of Homer's Achaeans.

In addition to Hittite two other closely related Indo-European languages were spoken in the Hittite kingdom, Palaic and Luwian. A small number of texts in these two languages have been found in the archives at Hattusas, together with short passages in the pre-Hittite language Hattian. All three languages are written in the Hittite cuneiform script.

Hurrian

This is the language of the Hurrian peoples who appear in the Near East at the end of the third millennium BC in the area of the upper Euphrates in north Syria and survive there

23 A bilingual tablet written in Hittite and Luvian; a ritual against plague. BM 108548.

until *c.* 1000 BC. About 1500 BC they set up the independent kingdom of Mitanni. The first known reference to this kingdom appeared in a letter from Amenophis III (1417–1379 BC) of Egypt to their king Tushratta. It was found in a large archive of international correspondence at El-Amarna in Egypt in 1887 and is still the most important single source of information about their language. A number of texts in Hurrian have been found in the Hittite archives from Hattusas (*c.* 1400 BC), where passages in Hurrian are introduced by the word *ḫurlili*, at Mari (*c.* 1750 BC) and at Ugarit (*c.* 1500 BC). The texts from Ugarit are written in a consonantal script and include a Sumero-Hurrian vocabulary, and there are fragments of a Hurrian translation of the Babylonian *Epic of Gilgamesh* from Hattusas. Hurrian names and terminology also appear in a wide variety of texts throughout the cuneiform milieu in the mid-second millennium BC. Hurrian is an ancestor of the Urartian language, but otherwise its relation to other languages is quite obscure; modern scholars have often named it Mitannian.

The Hurrians are of particular historical interest as the people who introduced the horse and chariot warfare to the Near East. A treatise on horse-training by Kikkuli of Mitanni found at Hattusas includes a number of technical terms in yet another language, which seem to have Sanskrit elements; it is not otherwise known and no satisfactory name has yet been found for it.

Urartian

The Urartians appear in history as the northern neighbours and rivals of the Assyrians from the thirteenth to the seventh centuries BC. They took over from them both the cuneiform syllabary and the Assyrian sign forms, but their own language was related to Hurrian. Since the Urartian homeland lay around Lake Van, A. H. Sayce, who published the first lengthy study of the language in 1882, called it Vannic. The chief deity in Urartu was the god Haldi, so others have called the language Haldian or Chaldian, but today the name Urartian is agreed on.

Such Urartian inscriptions as survive are mostly written on stone monuments and are the historical records of the kings of Urartu. Some texts are found inscribed on helmets, shields and metal vessels, naming their owners or donors, and there are about thirty clay tablets recording economic transactions. Already in 1826 E. Schulz copied forty-two cuneiform inscriptions in the area of Lake Van, but after he was murdered by a Kurdish chief in 1829 his copies were not published until 1840. Already by 1848 the Irish scholar Edward Hincks had taken the first steps towards the decipherment of Urartian, and this even before the decipherment of Babylonian and Assyrian had made much progress. The work of decipherment was continued by F. Lenormant and A. D. Mordtmann and was essentially completed with Sayce's publication (though, as with any newly deciphered language, vast progress has been made since his day). Since the Urartian kingdom extended over the Caucasus mountains much of the basic research into Urartian language and archaeology is being done by Soviet scholars.

Ugaritic

24 In 1929 French excavations at Ugarit (Ras Shamra) on the Syrian coast produced a quite unexpected new variety of cuneiform script datable to the fourteenth century BC. Unlike the Sumero-Babylonian form this one had only thirty signs (and a vertical word divider)

24 Part of the Ugaritic epic of Aqhat.
Musée du Louvre, Paris.

and was plainly alphabetic. Remarkably the script was deciphered within a year by the independent efforts of H. Bauer, E. Dhorme and C. Virolleaud. The language proved to be related to Hebrew, and the mythological texts found at Ugarit concerning the god Baal and his entourage have been a fruitful source of material for scholars seeking early parallels to the poetic texts of the Hebrew Bible. In practice economic documents in both Ugaritic and Babylonian were also found at Ugarit, but it is the mythological texts

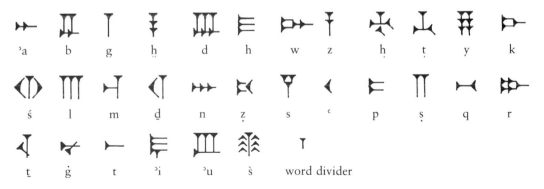

25 The Ugaritic alphabet.

which have stolen the limelight. There are over 1,000 tablets altogether written in Ugaritic, and the order of the alphabet is known from some tablets on which teachers or students wrote their ABC. It is almost identical with the traditional order of the Hebrew and Phoenician alphabets, and it is now apparent that it was the existence of contemporary linear alphabetic scripts that inspired the invention of the Ugaritic system. The full alphabet of thirty signs was only used in administrative texts. In the literary texts the scribes used a shorter alphabet, leaving out the last three signs.

It was probably the local use of the Ugaritic script that inspired a shorter cuneiform alphabet in Cyprus, Syria, Lebanon and Palestine. It is based on the Ugaritic script but has only twenty-two signs. Unfortunately very few such texts have been found so far, so we are unable to determine which of the local Semitic languages or dialects was being written in each case. The relevant texts have been conveniently assembled in a recent publication by É. Puech.

Old Persian

This cuneiform script was the first to be deciphered. In retrospect this is a remarkable fact since the normal requirement for the decipherment of a script is the availability of a large body of text to work on, and by comparison with Babylonian and Sumerian the amount and variety of Old Persian texts are very limited. However, at the time they were both more accessible and more legible than the other varieties of cuneiform. All of these points are in fact the result of the circumstances of the script's invention.

It has recently been suggested that the Old Persian script was invented on the instructions of the Achaemenid Persian king, Darius I (521–486 BC), in order to give him a distinctive script, comparable to those used by the kings of Babylon and Assyria, with which to inscribe his royal monuments. Even the cuneiform inscription on the stela of Cyrus (559–530 BC) is now thought to have been placed there on the orders of Darius I. The script is found on rock reliefs, the stonework of the Achaemenid buildings at Pasargadae and Persepolis, gold, silver and stone commemorative tablets, and a number of seals and calcite vases, but on very few clay tablets. For everyday purposes the Persian court and administration used either Elamite cuneiform or Aramaic, and the use of Old Persian was entirely abandoned after the time of Artaxerxes III (358–338 BC). Darius's inscription on the rock at Behistun, which was used by Rawlinson to complete Grotefend's decipherment of the script, remains the longest of all texts in Old Persian.

The script has thirty-six characters. Apart from three vowels (a, i, u) all are syllables consisting of a consonant and one of the three vowels. In addition a single slanting wedge is used as a word divider, and there are five separate ideograms for 'king', 'country', 'earth', 'god', and Ahuramazda (the name of the Persian deity), and numerical symbols. There are variant forms of the word divider and the ideograms for country and Ahuramazda. Some Old Persian texts are given in Chapter 5. In the accompanying table the conventions used by R. G. Kent have been followed: x represents Scottish ch as in loch, c represents English ch as in church, θ represents English th as in thin, ś represents a hard s, š represents English sh.

In addition to the languages discussed above a number of languages not normally written in cuneiform are represented by personal names or technical terms appearing in cuneiform texts. For instance in the Ur III and Old Babylonian period a large population of Amorites migrated into Mesopotamia and exercised considerable political influence. Almost all the kings of the Old Babylonian Dynasty bear Amorite names, and all that we know of this Semitic language is derived from the study of these names. The Kassite language is also known only from personal names and from two Babylonian tablets which are dictionaries for translating Kassite names. Similarly in the first millennium BC many Egyptian, Greek, Arab, Jewish and Iranian names appear in the Late Babylonian economic texts.

a	i	u	ka	ku	xa	ga	gu	ca	ja	ji	ta

tu	θa	ça	da	di	du	na	nu	pa	fa	ha	ma

mi	mu	ya	ra	ru	la	va	vi	sa	ša	za	ha

xšāyaθiya 'king'	dahyānš 'country'	būmiš 'earth'	baga 'god'	Auramazdā Ahuramazda

1	2	3	10	20	40	100

26 The Old Persian script.

5

Decipherment

The story of the decipherment of cuneiform starts in the eighteenth century with travellers visiting the ruins of Persepolis, the capital city of the Achaemenid Dynasty of Persia (559–331 BC). There they found and copied a number of short inscriptions from the doorways of the palaces, each of which was written out in three different forms of cuneiform script. In the eighteenth century the identity of the site was unknown, but study of the Greek histories eventually led people to believe that it was indeed Persepolis, and that its construction might have been the work of the Persian kings famous from the histories of Herodotus – Cyrus, Darius and Xerxes.

The time of the Achaemenid Dynasty saw the rise to prominence of the Zoroastrian religion and the worship of its supreme god Ahuramazda. The sacred literature of the Zoroastrians, the so-called Zend-Avesta, had fortunately become known to European scholars from the publication of its text by A. Duperron in 1771, and knowledge of the Avestan language and the related Pahlavi texts which were published about the same time was to give many clues to the decipherment of the Old Persian cuneiform script.

27
28

The first success in deciphering Old Persian was achieved by the German G. F. Grotefend. It had already been seen that the simplest version of each text used only a limited number of signs, and was therefore probably written in an alphabetic script. It had also been suggested that the single slanting wedges represented word dividers. Examination of the texts suggested that the script was written from left to right: for instance the sign group which we now transliterate as xa-ša-a-ya-θa-i-ya appears in fig. 28 at the ends of lines 1 and 3 complete, but also broken into two parts at the end of line 2 and the beginning of line 3. The texts illustrated here in figs 27 and 28 were both known to Grotefend. On the basis of the recently translated Pahlavi texts Grotefend guessed that this sign group (xa-ša-a-ya-θa-i-ya) would be the word for king, and that in lines 2–3 its repetition meant 'king of kings'. So the text of fig. 28 probably said, 'A, king . . ., king of kings'. The king's name at the beginning of fig. 28, line 1, appears again in line 3 of fig. 27, followed again by xa-ša-a-ya-θa-i-ya. So he presumed that in this inscription King B was describing himself as son of King A. Grotefend suspected that the texts might concern the kings Darius and his son Xerxes, so using forms for these two names which he derived from Greek, Hebrew and Avestan he suggested reading the signs as follows:

| d | a | r | h | e | u | sh | | kh | sh | h | e | r | sh | e |

Three signs, e, r and sh, seemed to be the same in the two names.

He then tackled the word for king (which we have transliterated as xa-ša-a-ya-θa-i-ya in the light of modern knowledge). The values already arrived at gave him:

kh   sh   e   h   ?   ?   h

In Duperron's edition of the Avesta he found the royal title khscheio. This he took as confirmation that the language of the cuneiform inscriptions was Avestan, and he assigned the values i and o to the two previously unidentified characters. Looking for the name of Darius's father, Hystaspes, in the first inscription he fitted it to the signs which we now transliterate as vi-i-ša-ta-a-sa-pa:

g   o   sh   t   a   s   p

The signs o, sh and a were in the right places and he now had the signs for g, t, s, and p.

This much he had already achieved by 1802. Comparing his results with the modern transcriptions one can see that the values of some signs were incorrect, and that he had not yet discovered that the script was not fully alphabetic, since in many cases the consonants have a specific vowel linked to them. Still it was a start, and a slow process of comparing various inscriptions with names known from historical sources gradually yielded approximate values for other signs.

The next big step forward was taken by the Englishman Henry Rawlinson, who began in 1835 the lengthy process of copying the huge inscriptions of Darius carved on the side of a mountain at Behistun in western Iran. Rawlinson had already managed to reach the same kind of results as Grotefend on the basis of the triple texts of two inscriptions found at Mount Elwend, but he saw the need for lengthy texts of varied content to give a better chance of thoroughly understanding the language being deciphered.

The texts carved for Darius at Behistun commemorated his victories in establishing his rule over the Persian Empire, and were accompanied by a relief depicting Darius and some of the kings whom he took captive. Like the shorter inscriptions already known, Darius's inscriptions were in three languages, now identifiable as Old Persian, Elamite and Babylonian. The task of copying the Old Persian text (414 lines in all) was completed little by little over some ten years, since the texts were inscribed on a steep cliff, needing all Rawlinson's skill and daring as a climber to reach them. It was well worth the effort, since the complete text and the many shorter captions contained the names of all the peoples of Darius's empire, and comparison with the Greek histories allowed Rawlinson correctly to identify many more cuneiform signs. Armed with these and his knowledge of Avestan and Sanskrit Rawlinson was able to go on to produce a complete translation of the whole text in 1846. Other scholars, notably Edward Hincks in Ireland, had made significant contributions to the progress of decipherment, but it was Rawlinson's work at Behistun which set the seal on the whole enterprise.

Continued on p. 62

27 Old Persian: carved above the figure of Xerxes in the doorways of his palace at Persepolis.

xa-ša-ya-a-ra-ša-a : xa-ša-a-ya-θa-i-ya : va-za-ra-
ka : xa-ša-a-ya-θa-i-ya : xa-ša-a-ya-θa-i-ya-a-
na-a-ma : da-a-ra-ya-va-ha-u-ša : xa-ša-a-ya-θa-
i-ya-ha-ya-a : pa-u-ça : ha-xa-a-ma-na-i-ša-i-ya

Xšayârša xšâyaθiya vazraka xšâyaθiya xšâyaθiyânâm Dârayavahauš xšâyaθiyahyâ puça Haxâmanišiya
Xerxes, the great king, the king of kings, the son of Darius the king, an Achaemenian.

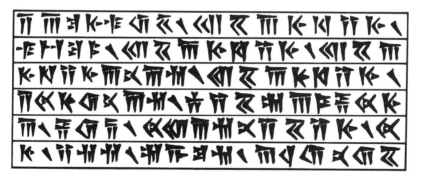

28 Old Persian: carved above the figure of Darius in the doorways of his palace at Persepolis.

da-a-ra-ya-va-u-ša : xa-ša-a-ya-θa-i-ya :
va-za-ra-ka : xa-ša-a-ya-θa-i-ya : xa-ša-a-
ya-θa-i-ya-a-na-a-ma : xa-ša-a-ya-θa-i-ya :
da-ha-ya-u-na-a-ma : vi-i-ša-ta-a-sa-pa-ha-ya-
a : pa-u-ça : ha-xa-a-ma-na-i-ša-i-ya : ha-
ya : i-ma-ma : ta-ca-ra-ma : a-ku-u-na-u-ša

Dârayavauš xšâyaθiya vazraka xšâyaθiya xšâyaθiyânâm xšâyaθiya dahyunâm Vištâs-pahyâ puça Haxâmanišiya hya imam tacaram akunauš
Darius, the great king, king of kings, king of countries, son of Hystaspes, an Achaemenian, who built this palace.

29 The Elamite version of fig. 28 ([1] represents the word divider; in line six a horizontal word divider is used. The sign sunki is a 'logogram' for the word 'king' and is not written out phonetically.)

[1]da-ri-ya-ma-u-iš [1]sunki ir-šá-
ir-ra [1]sunki [1]sunki-ip-in-na [1]sunki [1]
da-a-ú-iš-be-na [1]mi-iš-ba-za-na-
áš-be-na [1]mi-iš-da-áš-ba [1]ša-ak-
ri [1]ḫa-ak-ka₄-man-nu-ši-ya ak-ka
ḫi [1]da-iṣ-ṣa-ra-um ḫu-ut-taš-da

Darius, the great king,
king of kings, king
of all lands,
son of Hystaspes,
the Achaemenian,
who built this palace.

30 The Babylonian version of fig. 28. As explained on p. 63, in texts of the first millennium BC Sumerian words are transliterated in capitals.

[1]da-ri-ia-a-muš LUGAL GAL-ú
LUGAL LUGAL.MEŠ LUGAL KUR.KUR.MEŠ
ša nap-ḫa-ri li-šá-nu gab-bi
A [1]uš-ta-as-pa
[1]a-ḫa-ma-an-ni-iš-ši-iʾ
ša É a-ga-a i-pu-uš

Dariamuš šarru rabû šar šarrāni šar mātāti ša napḫari lišānu gabbi apal Uštaspa Ahamannišši ʾ ša bīta agâ īpuš
Darius, the great king, king of kings, king of the lands of all tongues entirely, son of Hystaspes, the Achaemenian, who built this palace.

Once the meaning of the Old Persian texts had been established the Elamite and Babylonian texts had to be tackled. The Behistun texts in these languages were copied by Rawlinson in 1844 and 1847, with even greater difficulty than he had faced when copying the Old Persian texts. The Elamite texts of the Achaemenid period use 123 different signs, so the texts were clearly written syllabically, not alphabetically. Again the values of the different signs were established by comparing the writing of names in the Elamite and Old Persian texts. This would not always have been easy – compare the various writings of Hystaspes in figs 28–30: Old Persian vi-i-ša-ta-a-sa-pa-ha-ya-a, El-amite ¹mi-iš-da-áš-ba, Babylonian ¹uš-ta-as-pa. Since the Elamite language was not related to any other known language there was not the help available which Avestan and Sanskrit had provided for Old Persian, but by 1855 Edwin Norris, to whom Rawlinson had given his notebooks, had arrived at the correct decipherment of most of the script. Rawlinson and Hincks meanwhile concentrated on the Babylonian texts, which were the more interesting since they could be related to the stray texts in Babylonian and Assyrian which had been found in Mesopotamia in the preceding decades and to the flood of texts which were now coming from Layard's excavations at Kalhu (Nimrud).

The Babylonian texts were altogether more difficult in some respects, since, as fig. 30 shows, they were not written entirely phonetically but used a number of 'logograms' (signs each standing for a word). Thus in fig. 30 LUGAL is the Sumerian sign for king, and is used in place of the Babylonian word šarru (in its various forms); KUR is Sumerian for Babylonian mātu, land, and in this case plurality is expressed by doubling the sign KUR and adding the Sumerian plural sign MEŠ. In the case of GAL-ú, the Sumerian GAL has a phonetic complement ú to indicate that the signs are to be read as rabû. None of this was at first apparent to the decipherers, who found themselves confronted by a far larger and more confusing set of signs than had been the case with Old Persian and Elamite (over 600 signs are in use in Babylonian and Assyrian in the first millennium BC). However, the decipherers, Rawlinson, Hincks and Jules Oppert, had an advantage in that it was supposed that the Babylonian language (which they assumed was hidden in this script) would be related to Hebrew and Aramaic and other languages of the Semitic group. The Semitic languages as then known were typically written out without regular indication of the vowels in a word. So when Rawlinson came across the different signs for ba, bi, bu, ab, ib, ub he would at first have regarded them all as different ways of writing b, and only later did he realise that the signs were significantly different and included the vowels which would contribute much to the understanding of Babylonian grammar.

In the case of the decipherment of Babylonian the tortuous path by which Rawlinson and his competitors arrived at their goal is only partly hinted at in his notebooks, now preserved in the British Library. It was a path which often reduced him to despair, and in old age he was himself quite unable to account for how he had achieved success. International argument has returned frequently to the question of how much of the credit for success is due to Rawlinson himself. There is no doubt that Hincks in particular made significant contributions for which he has been given little credit. But the fact remains that the first major landmark was Rawlinson's publication of the cuneiform text, transliteration and translation of the Babylonian inscription from Behistun in 1851. Even then the varied nature of Babylonian cuneiform, its contemporary equivalent in Assyria, and its predecessor in Sumer, was only partially apparent, and in some senses the decipherment of this branch of the cuneiform scripts continues to this day.

6

Sample Texts

Assyriologists habitually write out Sumerian in lower case Roman script and Akkadian in italics. But for texts of the first millennium words taken over from Sumerian are written in Roman capitals. There is no good reason for the difference; it is merely arbitrary.

š represents sh; ṣ and ṭ are emphatic consonants; ḫ is a hard h.
ā ē ī ū are long vowels.
Accents and subscript numbers are used to distinguish cuneiform signs which have the same sound, e.g. ša, šá, šà, ša₄.
[1,d] and [ki] are the cuneiform markers for personal names, divine names and towns. GIŠ and URU are markers for wooden objects and towns. Writing [ki] rather than KI, etc., is again only an Assyriological convention.

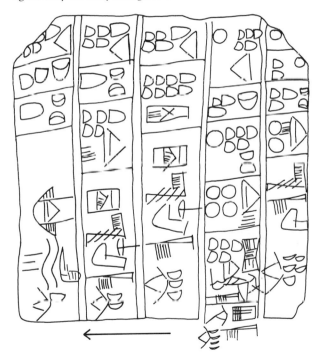

31 A tablet of the Jemdet Nasr period. BM 116730.
The tablet is shown oriented in the late direction. However confusing this may be, scholars persist in exhibiting and publishing the early texts as if they had been written

and read in the late manner. To see the tablet as an early Sumerian scribe would have read it, turn this page so that the arrow points upwards, not sideways. Turning the page back to its natural direction the horizontal lines of the tablet have become vertical columns. Compare fig. 7, in which the little squares have expanded into lines.

This text cannot yet be fully translated, but it illustrates the general character of the early texts. Each column concerns the issue of commodities as rations for a particular day. The day number is given at the bottom of the column, 'day 1', 'day 2', 'day 3', ('day 4' is out of sight on the bottom edge), 'day 5'. Five different commodities are being issued; we shall call them A, B, C, D and E.

| day | A | B | C | D | E |

On day 1 they issue 5 A, 1½ B, 1 C; on day 2, 5 A, 1 C, 5 D; on day 3, 5 A, 8 E; on day 4, 15 A, 3 B, 15 C, 40 D; on day 5, 10 A, 2 B, 3 C, 20 D. The various commodities are summarised on the reverse of the tablet. On day 4 there is also an issue of 5 items of another commodity identified by a lengthy group of signs. The remaining signs at the end of each column are not yet understood.

32 A tablet of the Fara period; Sumerian. BM 15833.
Like the previous tablet this one would probably have been read in antiquity from a different angle. It is a list of cattle being received from or distributed to various temple herds. The signs are still grouped in boxes; in a later text 'from Enlil' would be written ki ᵈen-líl

1 še gu₄	1 barley-fed ox	3 ^{d}en	3 from the god Enlil
6 ú gu₄	6 grass-fed oxen	ki lil	
^{d}šuruppak	the god Shuruppak	2 gu₄	2 oxen
3 še gu₄	3 barley-fed oxen	6 ú gu₄	6 grass-fed oxen
6 ú gu₄	6 grass-fed oxen	kin nir	Mr Kinnir
^{d}gi	the god Gibil	7 gu₄	7 oxen
bil		ki ^{d}en zu	from the god Suen

33 A brick inscription of Ur-Nammu, king of Ur (2112–2095 BC); Sumerian. BM 90015.
^{d}inanna nin-a-ni ur-^{d}nammu nita-kala-ga lugal-uri^{ki}-ma lugal-ki-en-gi-ki-uri-ke₄ é-a-ni
mu-na-dù
For Inanna his lady Ur-Nammu, the mighty man, king of Ur, king of Sumer and Akkad,
has built her temple.

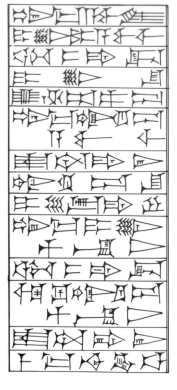

34 Part of the code of laws of Hammurapi, king of Babylon (1792–1750 BC); Babylonian.

1. *šum-ma a-wi-lum i-in* dumu *a-wi-lim úḫ-tap-pí-id i-in-šu ú-ḫa-ap-pa-du*
šumma awīlum īn mār awīlim uḫtappid īnšu uḫappadū
If a man destroys the eye of another man, they will destroy his eye.

2. *šum-ma* gìr-pad-du *a-wi-lim iš-te-bi-ir* gìr-pad-du-*šu i-še-eb-bi-ru*
šumma eṣmet awīlim ištebir eṣmetšu išebbirū
If he breaks the bone of another man, they will break his bone.

3. *šum-ma i-in* maš-en-kak *úḫ-tap-pí-id ù lu* gìr-pad-du maš-en-kak *iš-te-bi-ir* 1 ma-na
kù-babbar *i-ša-qal*
šumma īn muškēnim uḫtappid ū lū eṣmet muškēnim ištebir 1 mana kaspam išaqqal
If he destroys the eye of a subordinate or breaks the bone of a subordinate he shall pay
one mina of silver.

35 The inscription above a picture of Sennacherib, king of Assyria, at the seige of Lachish. Assyrian.

1. ¹ᵈsin-PAP.MEŠ-SU šar₄ ŠÚ šar₄ KUR aš-šur
   Sin-aḫḫē-erība šar kiššati šar māt aššur
   Sennacherib, king of the world, king of Assyria

2. ina GIŠ.GU.ZA ni-me-di ú-šib-ma
   ina kussī nēmedi ūšibma
   sat on a throne and

3. šal-la-at URU la-ki-su
   šallat Lakisu
   the booty of Lachish

4. ma-ḫa-ar-šu e-ti-iq
   maḫaršu ētiq
   passed before him.

36 Alternative writings of the names of some Assyrian kings.

Ashurnasirpal, Aššur-naṣir-apli – ¹AŠ-PAP-A, ¹aš-šur-PAP-A

Shalmaneser, Šulmānu-ašared – ¹ᵈšul-ma-nu-MAŠ

Sargon II, Šarru-kīn – ¹šárru-GIN, ¹LUGAL-GI.NA

Sennacherib, Sin-aḫḫē erība – ¹ᵈsin-PAP.MEŠ-eri₄-ba, ¹ᵈEN.ZU-ŠEŠ.MEŠ-SU

Esarhaddon, Aššur-aḫ-iddina – ¹AŠ-PAP-AŠ, ¹ᵈaš-šur-PAP-AŠ

Ashurbanipal, Aššur-bāni-apli – ¹aš-šur-DÙ-A, ¹ᵈAN.ŠÁR-DÙ-A

37 A brick inscription of Nebuchadnezzar II, king of Babylon (604–562 BC);
Babylonian.

1. ᵈnabu-ku-du-úr-ri-uṣur LUGAL KÁ.DINGIR.RAᵏⁱ
   Nabû-kudurri-uṣur šar Babili
   Nebuchadnezzar, king of Babylon,

2. za-ni-in é-sag-íl ù é-zi-da
   zānin Esgila u Ezida
   patron of Esagila and Ezida,

3. IBILA a-ša-re-du
   aplu ašarēdu
   eldest son

4. ša ᵈnabu-IBILA-URÙ LUGAL KÁ.DINGIR.RAᵏⁱ
   ša Nabû-apla-uṣur šar Babili
   of Nabopolassar, king of Babylon.

7

Fakes

Any form of document can became a subject for the collector, and cuneiform documents are no exception. Whether one seeks examples of calligraphy, literature, postal history, or merely curios, a cuneiform tablet can be an attractive item. Vast quantities of tablets were brought to Europe and North America between 1890 and the early 1930s and found their way into private collections and local museums. Along with the genuine tablets came many fakes, and both continue to circulate as collections are formed and dispersed. The difficulties of the cuneiform script mean that an experienced Assyriologist has little problem in recognising a fake except in the case of really well-made casts. However, few museums and even fewer dealers have any expertise in cuneiform, and most have to rely heavily on advice from a small number of scholars. Some comments on the subject of cuneiform fakes may therefore be interesting and helpful both to potential collectors and to museum visitors.

Whenever someone starts to collect, and especially when he is prepared to pay good money for objects, someone else sees an opportunity to make an easy profit by supplying the new market with forgeries. So the first cuneiform forgeries of modern times appear already in the 1820s, in the collections of C. J. Rich, British Resident in Baghdad. His manuscript collection contains a number of faked tablets and cylinder inscriptions of Nebuchadnezzar II moulded in the local clay from originals found at Babylon. No doubt these were the product of the local merchants of the nearby town of Hillah. Since the decipherment of cuneiform still lay in the future it would not have been too easy to detect the forgeries, but it is suggestive that none of them are illustrated in the beautiful drawings of Rich's cuneiform collection made by Carl Bellino.

Later in the nineteenth century casts of tablets appear in larger numbers, and with some of these one encounters a special problem, as they were made by two of the most professional people in their field, the Ready brothers. They were not in fact made as fakes at all, but as bona fide replicas, and as such have occasionally caused problems for later museum curators. The Ready brothers were employed to make official copies of many works of art for the British Museum, and had access to numerous very well preserved cuneiform tablets on which to try their skill; some of the resulting casts have even caused confusion within the Museum.

The first warning of a cast of a tablet is its weight; a plaster cast tends to be noticeably lighter than a clay tablet of similar size. The second indication is the mark around the edge of the cast where the two pieces of the cast, front and back, have been fitted together. Occasionally the truth also appears from the direction in which the tablet turns. When reading a book we turn the pages from right to left; but cuneiform tablets were turned bottom to top. Only a handful of genuine tablets break this rule. So if a tablet appears to turn right to left it is almost certainly a forgery.

A very simple warning is carried by a large number of fakes made in Turkey in the early years of this century – a slip of Turkish newspaper pasted on to one edge. It is remarkable how many tablets still circulate in the market today with this forger's trademark surviving so visibly.

Another danger sign is the nature of the inscribed object itself. The vast majority of inscriptions written in antiquity were written on clay. Inscribed seals are much less common, although very durable, but are quite often faked simply because they are so much prized by collectors. But inscribed statues surviving from antiquity, especially complete statues, are very rare. Despite that there is nowadays a flourishing trade in the Levant in crude statues made in some easily worked stone brazenly carrying on the front or back large cuneiform inscriptions which immediately proclaim them forgeries. On the whole forged inscriptions on metal vessels and weapons seem to be incised by a rather more competent group of craftsmen. With all objects other than clay tablets there is the added difficulty that many items were also made in antiquity by second-rate craftsmen. A wealthy Babylonian bureaucrat could well afford a perfectly cut cylinder seal from the best seal-cutter in town while a small-time merchant in north Syria might carry a seal of very indifferent workmanship cut by a man who had only a slight knowledge of cuneiform. Even experienced curators often find it hard to tell the difference between third-rate antiquities and fakes.

The easiest test of authenticity is to take a long hard look at the cuneiform inscription itself. As explained before, from the later third millennium onwards cuneiform signs are almost exclusively created from three different types of wedges, vertical wedges having the head at the top, horizontal wedges with the head at the left, and slanting wedges with the head either in a central position or at the upper left end. The forger frequently ignores this rule. So any inscription where individual wedges point upwards, to the left, or slant up to the right, should be treated with suspicion. Excessive repetition of a small group of signs is also a common hallmark of an unimaginative forger.

Ultimately the best defence against fakes is to acquire some visual familiarity with the genuine article, whether by frequent visits to those few museums that display cuneiform inscriptions, or by building up a library of photographs. One should bear in mind that although some tablets are masterpieces of calligraphy, the vast majority of inscriptions were written by ordinary scribes for purely practical or commercial use, and that these are the texts that one will most commonly find in local museums or private collections.

38 An Old Babylonian cylinder-seal. BM 103314.

Where to see Cuneiform Inscriptions

The following is a summary of the principal collections of cuneiform inscriptions. It includes some quite small collections which hold material from particular sites or have published catalogues. Many collections have been built up entirely from purchases on the antiquities market. Others are largely the result of sponsoring excavations; these are briefly summarised. The references to excavations will give some idea of the history of archaeological exploration, especially in Iraq. On many sites excavation has continued to the present day.

Belgium
Brussels, Musées Royaux d'Art et d'Histoire.

Canada
Toronto, Royal Ontario Museum.

Denmark
Copenhagen, The National Museum.

Eire
Dublin, The Chester Beatty Library and Gallery of Oriental Art.

France
Paris, Musée du Louvre – tablets from excavations at Girsu (1877–1933), Susa (1884–1978, Mari (1933–), Ugarit (1929–), etc.
Paris, Collège de France.
Paris, Ecole pratique des Hautes Etudes, IV^c Section.
Strasbourg, Bibliothèque Nationale et Universitaire.

Germany
Berlin, Staatliche Museen, Vorderasiatisches Museum – tablets from excavations at Babylon (1899–1917), Fara (1902–3), Ashur (1903–14) and Uruk (1928–39).
Jena, Friedrich-Schiller-Universität, Hilprecht Sammlung – tablets from the University of Philadelphia's excavations at Nippur.

Iraq
Baghdad, The Iraq Museum – tablets from all Iraqi excavations and many foreign excavations from 1920 onwards.

Italy
Aosta, Collegiata dei SS. Pietro e Orso.
Florence, Archaeological Museum.
Rome, Vatican Museum.

Netherlands
Leiden, University of Leiden, Böhl Collection.

Switzerland
Geneva, Musée d'Art et d'Histoire.

Syria
Aleppo National Museum – tablets from Ebla.
Damascus, The National Museum – tablets from Mari and Ugarit.

Turkey
Ankara, Museum of Anatolian Civilisations – Old Assyrian tablets from Kanesh and Hittite tablets from Hattusas.
Antakya, Hatay Museum – tablets from Alalah.
Istanbul, Archaeological Museums (Ancient Orient Museum) – tablets from various excavations in Mesopotamia conducted by foreign institutions during the time of the Ottoman Empire. Over 85,000 tablets in total.

UK
Birmingham, City Museums and Art Gallery.
Edinburgh, Royal Scottish Museum.
Liverpool, Merseyside County Museum.
London, British Museum – tablets from excavations at Kalhu (Nimrud) (1845–1963), Nineveh (1846–1932), Babylon and Sippar (1879–82), Tell ed-Der (1890–1), Ur (1922–34) and Alalah (1937–49), etc., and large collections acquired by purchase. Over 130,000 in total.
Manchester, The Manchester Museum.
Oxford, The Ashmolean Museum – tablets from excavations at Jemdet Nasr and Kish (1923–33).

USA
Ann Arbor, Kelsey Museum, University of Michigan.

Baltimore, The Walters Art Gallery.

Berkeley, University of California, Lowie Museum of Anthropology.

Berrien Springs, Mi., Andrews University, Horn Archaeological Museum.

Cambridge, Harvard University, The Semitic Museum – tablets from Nuzi (1927–31).

Chicago, Oriental Institute Museum–tablets from Nippur (1948–), Eshnunna, (1930–37), etc. Over 20,000 tablets in total.

New Haven, Yale University – over 30,000 tablets.

New York, Columbia University Libraries.

New York, Metropolitan Museum of Art.

Philadelphia, Free Library.

Philadelphia, University Museum of the University of Pennsylvania – tablets from Nippur (1889–1900), Ur (1922–34), etc. Over 30,000 tablets in total.

Urbana, University of Illinois, World Heritage Museum.

USSR

Leningrad, State Hermitage Museum.

Moscow, State Pushkin Museum of Fine Arts.

39 A pre-Sargonic tablet from Girsu; a census of sheep from the time of king Uruinimgina (2351–2342 BC). BM 96591.

Further Reading

B. André-Leicknam and C. Ziegler, *Naissance de l'écriture*. Paris, 1982 (catalogue of an exhibition, containing a wealth of illustrations)

C. Bermant and M. Weitzman, *Ebla: an archaeological enigma*. London, 1979 (contains an excellent chapter on the decipherment of cuneiform)

E. Chiera, *They wrote on clay*. Chicago, 1938; reprinted 1975

A. Curtis, *Ugarit (Ras Shamra)*. Cambridge, 1985

G. R. Driver, *Semitic writing from pictograph to alphabet* (The Schweich Lectures of the British Academy 1944). Third revised edition, London, 1976

R. G. Kent, *Old Persian: Grammar, Texts, Lexicon*. New Haven, 1950

O. R. Gurney, *The Hittites*. Penguin Books, Harmondsworth, UK, 1981

W. Hinz, *The Lost World of Elam*. London, 1972

S. N. Kramer, *The Sumerians*. Chicago, 1963

A. L. Oppenheim, *Ancient Mesopotamia*. Revised edition, Chicago, 1977

G. Pettinato, *The Archives of Ebla: An Empire Inscribed in Clay*. Garden City, New York, 1981

É Puech, 'Origine de l'alphabet', *Revue Biblique* 93/2, 161–213 (Paris, April 1986)

World Archaeology 17/3: Early writing systems (Henley-on-Thames, February 1986) [a summary of recent research into the origins of writing]

1 Limestone wall panel, decorated with figures and hieroglyphs, from the tomb of a man called Iry. Fifth Dynasty. H. 95 cm. BM 1168.

Egyptian
Hieroglyphs

W. V. Davies

Preface

The limitations of this section should be stated at the outset. It is simply too brief to do justice to a system of communication as complex and many-sided as the hieroglyphic writing of ancient Egypt. The account of the subject presented here has had to be very selective, covering, in an introductory manner, only those areas that I believe to be of the greatest importance and interest. For more detailed and scholarly treatments of the various aspects of the system, readers are recommended to consult the works listed in the Bibliography.

In preparing this work I have been kindly and ably assisted in various ways by a number of colleagues. Mr T. G. H. James made several valuable suggestions concerning its organization and content; Professor A. F. Shore and Miss Carol Andrews provided information on Coptic and demotic matters; Mrs Christine Barratt drew the line illustrations and the hieroglyphs in the text; Mr Peter Hayman prepared the bulk of the photographic material; Miss Felicity Jay typed the final copy. To all these I offer grateful thanks, as I do also to those institutions who have allowed me to use illustrations of objects in their collections.

Contents

1
The Language

Ancient Egyptian occupies a special position among the languages of the world. It is not only one of the very oldest recorded languages (probably only Sumerian is older) but it also has a documented history longer by far than that of any other. It was first written down towards the end of the fourth millennium BC and thereafter remained in continuous recorded use down to about the eleventh century AD, a period of over 4,000 years. Egyptian, or Coptic (as the last stage of the language is called), expired as a spoken tongue during the Middle Ages, when it was superseded by Arabic. It is now, strictly, a dead language, though it continues to 'live on', albeit in a fossilised form, in the liturgy of the Coptic church in Egypt. Although it can only be a minute fraction of what was actually produced, the body of written material to have survived in Egyptian is, nevertheless, enormous. It consists, in large part, of religious and funerary texts, but it also includes secular documents of many different types – administrative, business, legal, literary and scientific – as well as private and official biographical and historical inscriptions. This record is our most important single source of evidence on ancient Egyptian society.

Since the decipherment of the writing system in the third decade of the last century (see Chapter 5), the language has been among the most thoroughly researched areas of Egyptology. As a result, although a great deal of vocabulary and many points of grammar remain to be fully elucidated, our understanding of the basic structure of Egyptian and of the rules governing its operation can now be considered to be on a reasonably firm footing. It is not only Egyptologists who have taken an interest in the language. In recent years increasing attention has been paid to Egyptian by linguists concerned with the study of human language as a general phenomenon. In this area, Egyptian is of particular importance to comparative and historical linguists, its longevity offering a rare opportunity for the testing of theories concerning the nature and rate of language change and development.

Egyptian is one of a group of African and Near Eastern languages (many of them still living tongues) which have sufficient similarities in their grammar and vocabulary to suggest that they are derived from a common linguistic ancestor. This group is known to scholars as Afro-Asiatic (or Hamito-Semitic). The Afro-Asiatic family is deemed at present to consist of six co-ordinate branches, of which Ancient Egyptian forms one. The other five are: Semitic (sub-branches of which include such well-known languages as Akkadian, Hebrew and Arabic), Berber (found in north Africa to the west of Egypt), Chadic (found in the sub-Saharan regions to the east, south and west of Lake Chad), Cushitic (found in the Sudan, Ethiopia, Somalia and north-west Kenya) and Omotic (found in southern Ethiopia). Of these, only Egyptian and Semitic are favoured with substantial written traditions; in the case of the others, written sources are minimal or even non-existent and a great deal of basic recording and analysis still remains to be achieved. There is as yet no consensus as to the date when the various branches separated from the proto-language. Recent estimates, based largely on the degree of differentiation between early Egyptian and Akkadian (the oldest recorded form of Semitic), vary widely. One scholar has placed the likely date of separation at around 6000 BC, another at around 12000 BC.

There is no evidence that the ancient Egyptians took a serious interest in the analysis of their own language. If works of grammar, such as those written in antiquity for Greek

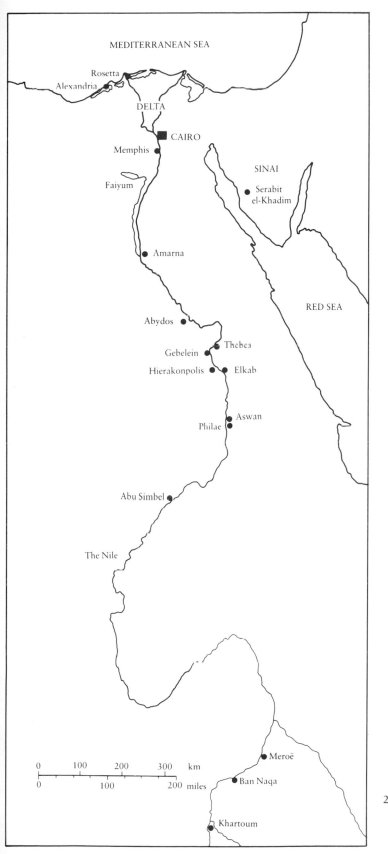

2 Egypt and the Sudan.

79

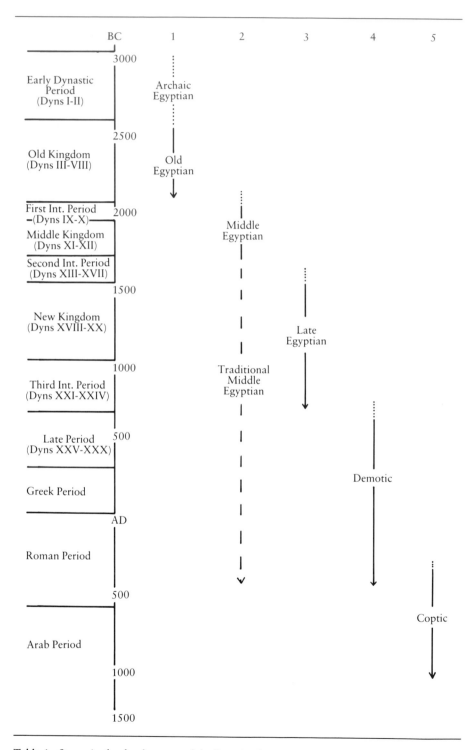

Table 1: Stages in the development of the Egyptian language.

and Latin, were composed for Egyptian, they have not survived. Our knowledge of Ancient Egyptian is entirely the product of modern scholarship. Egyptologists identify five, somewhat arbitrary, stages in the development of the language (see table opposite), each characterised by certain distinctive features of grammar and orthography, with the most fundamental point of division perceived as lying between the first two stages, on the one hand, and the last three, on the other. They have been arrived at by analysis and comparison of a large number of dated texts, covering the whole period of the recorded use of the language. Scholars, engaged in such work, have had always to keep in mind that the evidence at every stage consists of the language as *written*, and that written language rarely corresponds exactly to the spoken variety. Written language is more conservative: it frequently includes spellings that are partly or even wholly historical as well as words and grammatical constructions that have long ceased to be used in actual speech. Such redundancy is well evidenced in the case of Egyptian. In the following outline of the five stages it should be noted that the language of the very earliest inscriptions (from the late Predynastic and Early Dynastic Periods (*c.* 3100–2650 BC)), sometimes called 'Archaic Egyptian', is not included as a stage. This is because the inscriptions in question are too brief and limited in content to allow any meaningful analysis of the underlying language.

Old Egyptian
The language of the inscriptions of the Old Kingdom (*c.* 2650–2135 BC), the period in which the first continuous texts appear.

Middle Egyptian
The idiom, in particular, of the First Intermediate Period and the Middle Kingdom (*c.* 2135–1785 BC); regarded as the 'classical' stage of the language, used in literary, religious and monumental inscriptions through to the Graeco-Roman Period. Very close to Old Egyptian in structure.

Late Egyptian
The everyday language of the New Kingdom and Third Intermediate Period (*c.* 1550–700 BC), as witnessed particularly in secular documents of the Ramesside Period (*c.* 1300–1080 BC); also found to some extent in literary and monumental inscriptions. Very different from Old and Middle Egyptian, especially in its verbal structure.

Demotic
Vernacular successor of Late Egyptian, written in the script known as Demotic (see below, Chapter 2), attested from the beginning of the Late Period down to late Roman times (*c.* 700 BC—fifth century AD).

Coptic
The final stage of the language, as written in the Coptic script (see below, Chapter 2), from the third century AD onwards. The only stage of the language of which the vocalic structure is known and in which distinct dialects are recognisable. The two major dialects are: Sahidic, the standard literary dialect until the tenth century AD, its place of origin uncertain, possibly Thebes or Memphis; and Bohairic, originally the dialect of the west Delta, which supplanted Sahidic as the official dialect in the eleventh century.

2
The Scripts

By the Late Period of Egyptian history three distinct scripts were in use for writing the Egyptian language. They are known as hieroglyphic, hieratic and demotic respectively. They are superficially different from each other in appearance but actually represent the same writing system, hieratic and demotic being merely cursive derivatives of hieroglyphic. All three were eclipsed during the Roman Period by a fourth script, called Coptic, which was based on the Greek alphabet and operated on quite different principles. The present chapter will be devoted mainly to an account of some of the more important external features and conventions of the scripts; the principles underlying the native system will be dealt with in the next chapter.

Hieroglyphic

This was the earliest form of Egyptian script, and it was also the longest-lived. The first hieroglyphs appear in the late Predynastic Period, in the form of short label-texts on stone and pottery objects from various sites, probably to be dated within the range 3100–3000 BC, while the last datable examples are to be found in a temple inscription on the island of Philae carved in AD 394, nearly three and a half thousand years later. Originally the script was employed to write different kinds of texts, in a variety of media, but as its cursive version, hieratic, developed, hieroglyphic was increasingly confined to religious and monumental contexts, where it was rendered most typically in carved relief in stone. It was for this reason that the ancient Greeks called the individual elements of the script *ta hiera grammata*, 'the sacred letters', or *ta hieroglyphica*, 'the sacred carved (letters)', from which our terms 'hieroglyph' and 'hieroglyphic' are derived.

The signs of the hieroglyphic script are largely pictorial or 'iconic' in character. A few are of indeterminate form and origin, but most are recognisable pictures of natural or man-made objects, which, when carefully executed, may exhibit fine detail and colouring, although they are conventionalised in form and their colour is not always realistic. There is little doubt that the best examples of the script have 'an intrinsic beauty of line and colour' that fully justifies the claim, often made, that 'Egyptian hieroglyphic writing is the most beautiful ever designed'. Its pictorial character should not, however, mislead one into thinking that the script is a kind of primitive 'picture-writing'. It is a full writing system, capable of communicating the same kinds of complex linguistic information as our own alphabet, though it does so by different means. Typologically the script is a 'mixed' system, which means that its constituents do not all perform the same function; some of the signs convey meaning, others convey sound (see Chapter 3).

The system was never limited to a fixed number of hieroglyphs. It contained a relatively stable core of standard signs throughout its history, but, in addition, new signs were invented as required, while others fell into disuse. Developments in material culture were influential in this process. Innovations in Egyptian weaponry at the beginning of the New Kingdom, for example, saw the introduction of hieroglyphs for the horse and chariot, ⟨glyph⟩, ⟨glyph⟩, and for a new type of sword, ⟨glyph⟩. By the same process, other hieroglyphs became obsolete and were either changed in form or entirely replaced; the sign for the royal *khepresh*-crown was ⟨glyph⟩ in the Thirteenth Dynasty and ⟨glyph⟩ in the

Eighteenth Dynasty; the sign for the common razor was ⬭ in the Old Kingdom, ⬭ in the Middle Kingdom, and finally ⬭ in the New Kingdom. In these cases developments in fashion and technology produced corresponding changes in the script, each sign in turn depicting the current form of the actual object. There was no consistency in the process, however. Many hieroglyphs, even those in culture-sensitive categories, retained a more or less regular form; others changed temporarily and then reverted. The common hieroglyph depicting scribal equipment, for example, was written ⬭ in the Old Kingdom, 'up-dated' to ⬭ in the First Intermediate Period, and then changed back to the Old Kingdom form, which remained standard thereafter.

Taken over the whole period of the script's use, the total number of known hieroglyphs is huge; over 6,000 have so far been documented. The figure is misleading, however. The vast majority of these signs are found only on the temple walls of the Graeco-Roman Period, when, perhaps for special religious and esoteric reasons, the number of hieroglyphs was deliberately increased. In earlier periods the repertoire in standard use at any one time was always fewer than 1,000 (for example, about 700 are attested for the period covered by Middle Egyptian proper), and of these only a relatively small proportion occurs with real frequency.

3 *Left* Temple inscription carved in AD 394. These are the latest firmly dated hieroglyphs yet attested. They label a representation of a god, whom they name as 'Merul, son of Horus'. Temple of Philae.
4 *Right* Inscription in a tomb of the early New Kingdom including some of the very earliest examples of hieroglyphs representing the chariot and the horse. Elkab.

A hieroglyphic inscription is arranged either in columns or in horizontal lines, the former being the more ancient arrangement. The sequence of signs is continuous. There are no punctuation marks or spaces to indicate the divisions between words. Orientation is usually rightward, with the individual signs and the inscription of which they form a part read from right to left, and with upper taking precedence over lower. It has been suggested by one authority that this preference for rightward orientation is derived from the fact that human beings are generally right-handed; quite simply, in producing a text, 'the scribe began on the side where the hand that did the writing happened to be situated'. Leftward orientation does also occur but as a rule only in certain contexts; it was employed, for example, in inscriptions that accompany figures facing left, or to provide balance or symmetry in a larger composition. Examples of horizontal and columnar inscriptions orientated in both directions are given below. The direction of writing is indicated as well as the order in which the signs are to be read. It will be seen

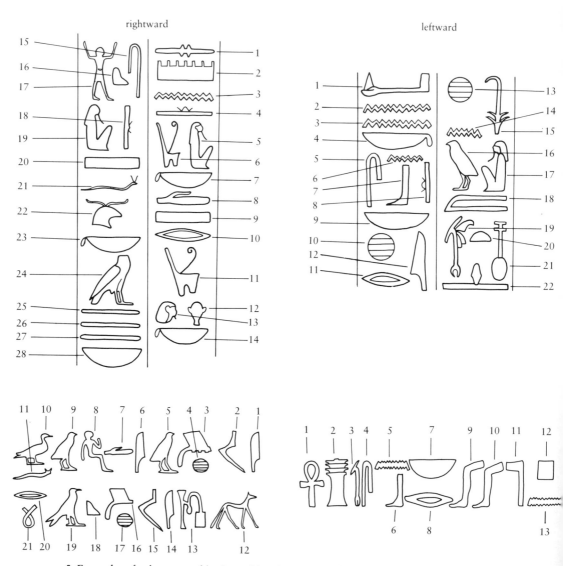

5 Examples of columnar and horizontal inscriptions, in rightward and leftward orientation. The numbers indicate the order in which the signs are to be read.

that a clue to the direction of reading is given by those signs, especially human or animal, that have a recognisable front and rear. Such signs in normal writing always face the beginning of the inscription.

Aesthetic or calligraphic considerations played a large part in the internal organisation of an inscription. Hieroglyphs were not written in linear sequence, one after another, like the letters of an alphabetic script, but were grouped into imaginary squares or rectangles so as to ensure the most harmonious arrangement and to minimise the possibility of unsightly gaps. Such requirements affected the relative size and proportions of individual signs and determined whether a word was written in full or in an abbreviated form. It is not uncommon to find hieroglyphs switched in their order for reasons of better spacing. Indeed 'graphic transposition', as it is called, is virtually the rule for some sign combinations, particularly those in which a bird hieroglyph is written next to a small squat sign or a tall thin one. Many such transpositions were initially designed to make the most effective use of space in columnar inscriptions, but became so standard that they were often retained in horizontal texts as well.

Sign order was similarly affected by considerations of prestige. Words for entities of high status (such as 'king', 'god', and the names of specific gods) were usually given precedence in writing over words which, in speech, they followed. Typical examples

6

6 Examples of graphic transposition. The transposed signs are marked with a cross.

occur in the lines of an inscription on a tomb panel belonging to a man called Iry (written

1, 7 ⎘). The first three signs of the inscription form the beginning of a common funerary formula which translates as 'An offering which Anubis gives'. In the order of signs the jackal hieroglyph occupies initial position in the group, whereas the word it represents, 'Anubis', actually comes third in the order of Egyptian speech. The jackal takes precedence because Anubis is a god. Similarly in the group ⎘ , which is a title meaning 'priest of the king', the hieroglyphs for 'king', ⎘ , are written before the hieroglyph for 'priest', ⎘ , in reversal again of the actual word order. Graphic reversals of this kind are referred to as 'honorific transposition'.

The hieroglyphic script was always more than just a writing system. The Egyptians referred to it as ⎘ , 'writing of the divine words', or simply as ⎘ , 'divine words'. The individual hieroglyph was termed ⎘ , 'sign', 'image', 'form', the same word as was sometimes used to denote a representation in Egyptian art. This terminology reflects two points of fundamental importance about the script: it was closely related to representational art and, like the art, it was endowed with religious or magico-religious significance.

36 The interrelationship between art and writing, which can be seen already on some of the earliest inscribed monuments, is evident in a number of ways. Most obviously the hieroglyphs are themselves miniature pictures. In fact, in all essentials, they are small-scale versions of the larger 'actors' in an artistic scene. It is important to remember that Egyptian art was not a free form. It had a distinct purpose: to 'make to live' for eternity the things it depicted. In keeping with its purpose it was governed by strict rules as to content and manner of representation. A basic convention was that a figure should be depicted as objectively as possible, with no account taken of the effects of visual distortion. A figure was reproduced, two-dimensionally, in what was deemed to be its most 'characteristic' aspect; in the case of a complex figure, it might be necessary to embody more than one aspect in a single representation. The hieroglyphs follow this convention. Three instances, again from the inscriptions of Iry, may be taken to illustrate the point.

7 The sign below the jackal is a single hieroglyph with two parts. The lower rectangular part is a reed mat; the conical object centred above it is a loaf of bread. It is actually a picture of a loaf standing on a mat. The two are depicted, however, from different 'characteristic' view points. The loaf is shown in profile, the mat as if seen from above.

8 The same combination of views is apparent in the hieroglyph depicting items of scribal equipment. Side views are given of the narrow brush-holder and the round pigment bag, but a top view is shown of the rectangular palette with its characteristic paint-holes.

9 Even more illustrative is a third hieroglyph, representing an old man leaning on a stick. It is a very skilful carving, showing fine naturalistic detail, but it is not an organic whole. Close inspection will show that the figure is a composite, with the major parts of the body shown from different points of view. The head, the front breast, the arms and the legs are in profile view; the eye, the shoulders, and the rear breast in frontal; and the navel in three quarters. It is a picture of the body that combines in a single figure as many as possible of its essential aspects. The same diagrammatic approach informs the figures of Iry and his retinue on the same monument. It is the standard manner of representing the human body in Egyptian two-dimensional art.

The relationship between the figures and the hieroglyphs in the scene is not only a matter of internal structure. Each of the human figures has a separate inscription of its own, which identifies it by name and sometimes by title as well. The largest of the figures is identified as 'Priest of the king, Iry'. The smaller figure immediately in front of Iry is described as the 'scribe, Kai-nefer', the one behind as 'Iry-nedjes'. The three others

7 Panel of Iry. Detail of horizontal inscriptions at the top.

8 Panel of Iry. Detail of hieroglyph representing scribal equipment. H. 6.6 cm.

9 Panel of Iry. Detail of hieroglyph representing an old man. H. 9.2 cm.

10 Limestone statuette of Min-nefret; view showing inscription on the right side. Fourth Dynasty. H. 47 cm. BM 65430.

11 *Left* Limestone stela of Wennekhu and his son Penpakhenty, the names in each case followed by a 'name determinative' (). Nineteenth Dynasty. H. 35.3 cm. BM 1248.

12 *Above* Granite squatting figure of Sennefer. Such statues, because of their peculiar 'block' form, came to be regarded as suitable vehicles for long texts. Eighteenth Dynasty. H. 83.8 cm. BM 48.

shown facing the tomb owner are, from top to bottom, 'Nen-kai', 'Nefer-seshem-nesut' and 'Itjeh' respectively. In each case the writing follows in general the direction of the figure to which it belongs – rightward in the case of Iry, Iry-nedjes and Kai-nefer, leftward in that of the others. This correlation leads to a further point of identity. When a name occurs in an Egyptian inscription it is normally followed by a hieroglyph in the form of a male or female figure, called by Egyptologists a 'name determinative'. Its function is quite simply to clarify whether the name is that of a man or woman. In this case every one of the names lacks a small-scale determinative. The reason for this is that the larger figures, because of their proximity to the names, themselves act as determinatives. In other words, they function as large-scale hieroglyphs.

This kind of interdependence is not confined to two dimensions. The statue of the lady Min-nefret shows the same principle at work in three dimensions. The statue is inscribed with hieroglyphs on the right and left sides of the seat. On each side the hieroglyphs are orientated in accordance with the figure. On the natural right side, they face rightwards; on the natural left, leftwards. The inscription ends with the lady's title and name, ⟨hieroglyphs⟩, 'the confidante of the king, Min-nefret'. Again there is no determinative, in this case because the statue serves as the determinative; it is actually here a three-dimensional hieroglyph.

The panel of Iry and the statue of Min-nefret both date to the Old Kingdom. This is the period when the relationship between art and writing is most consistently in evidence. The relationship remained in existence throughout the whole of Egyptian history but, after the Old Kingdom, a partial 'disengagement' gradually took place. Certain rules, such as those concerning orientation, continued to be observed, but there was an increasing tendency for the inscription on a monument to be treated as an entity in its own right. The virtual unity of name and figure was still sometimes respected on monuments as late as the New Kingdom, but more often than not it was disregarded and name determinatives were appended even when a figure of the name's owner was depicted nearby. At the same time texts began to 'take over' the statues on which they were inscribed. Whereas in the Old Kingdom inscriptions were appropriately situated, on the seat or the pedestal of a statue, from the Middle Kingdom onwards they intrude, inorganically, on to the dress of the owner and eventually on to the body itself. The impression is, in the case of certain statues, that the figure has been viewed as primarily a vehicle for the text that it bears.

As an integral part of a system of recreative art the hieroglyphs were naturally believed to have the power to bring to life what they depicted or stated. A funerary formula invoking benefits from a god was enough in itself, if written in hieroglyphs, to ensure the reception of those benefits by the deceased owner, as long as the owner was named, as in the case of Iry. The name of a person, inscribed in hieroglyphs, was believed to embody that person's unique identity. If the representation of a person lacked a name, it lacked also the means to ensure his continued existence in the after-life. To destroy the name(s) of a person was to deprive him of his identity and render him non-existent. On several occasions in Egyptian history the cartouches (name rings) of a dead ruler were systematically mutilated or removed from monuments on the orders of a vengeful successor. Even the gods were not immune from such attack. When King Akhenaten sought, in the late Eighteenth Dynasty, to institute a new religion of the sun disk and abolish the old regime, he ordered, among other things, that the name of the existing chief of the gods, Amun, be removed from the monuments of the land, with effects that can still be seen on many surviving pieces. By similar means the monument of one person was often appropriated for the use of another. The essential act in such 'usurpation' was the change of name. The name of the original owner was removed; the name of the new

13 Detail of a basalt statue of a man holding
a shrine. The hieroglyphic inscriptions
include the cartouches of King Amasis
deliberately effaced. Twenty-sixth
Dynasty. H. of shrine 27 cm. BM 134.

14 Red granite statue of King Amenophis II of the
Eighteenth Dynasty with inscriptions added by kings of
the Nineteenth Dynasty. H. 2.6 m. BM 61.

one added; the monument might otherwise be left untouched. A statue of a king in the   14
British Museum provides a good example. On grounds of style and iconography it can be
identified as a portrait of Amenophis II of the Eighteenth Dynasty (*c.* 1400–1350 BC).
The cartouches it bears, however, are those of Ramesses II and Merenptah of the Nineteenth Dynasty (*c.* 1290–1200 BC). The statue was usurped for these later kings simply
by adding their names; no attempt was made to change the appearance of the piece to
make it conform to the style of their time.

Belief in the magical efficacy of the 'divine words' found further expression in the
attempts that were occasionally made to limit the power of certain hieroglyphs, especially those depicting humans, birds and animals. These were deemed to have considerable
potential for harm when located in magically 'sensitive' areas, like the walls of a burial
chamber or the sides of a sarcophagus. The fear was that they might assume an independent hostile life of their own and consume the food offerings intended for the deceased or
even attack the dead body itself. Steps were therefore taken to neutralise the danger that
they posed. Sometimes such hieroglyphs were simply suppressed and replaced by
anodyne substitutes. On other occasions they were modified in some way to immobilise
them. The bodies of human figures and the heads of insects and snakes were omitted, the
bodies of birds truncated, the bodies of certain animals severed in two, and the tails of   15
snakes abbreviated. Particularly dangerous creatures, such as the evil serpent, called
Apophis, the great enemy of the sun-god Rēʿ, were sometimes shown as constrained or
'killed' by knives or spears.

15 Examples of inscriptions with mutilated
hieroglyphs.

Other hieroglyphs were regarded as having beneficial properties and were rendered in three dimensions to serve as amulets or charms. When worn on the body these amulets were believed to confer 'good luck' on their owners, whether living or dead. The amulet
16 in the form of the *sa*-sign, meaning 'protection', was one of several that offered protection against the powers of evil; the so-called *udjat*-eye of the god Horus was another.
17 The *ankh*- and the *djed*-signs offered the benefits of 'life' and 'endurance' respectively,
18, 19 while the hand, leg and face, and others like them, helped to restore the functions of the
19 bodily parts after death. The sign meaning 'horizon' shows the sun rising over a mountain. It allowed the deceased to witness and identify with the sun's daily rebirth and thereby be reborn himself.

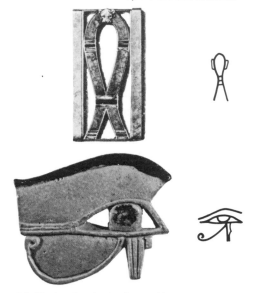

16–19 Amulets in the form of hieroglyphs.
16 *sa* (H. 3.9 cm, Cairo Museum, CG 52044, gold and semi-precious stones), *udjat* (H. 4.9 cm, BM 23092, faience).

17 *ankh* (H. 11 cm, BM 43211, wood), *djed* (H. 7.4 cm BM 50742, faience).

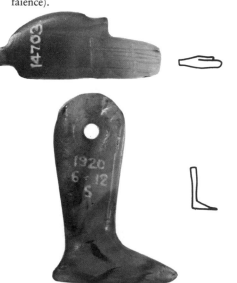

18 hand H. 0.7 cm, BM 14703, carnelian), leg (H. 1.9 cm, BM 54747, carnelian).

19 face (H. 1.7 cm, BM 57812, steatite), horizon (H. 2 BM 8300, glass).

Hieratic

Hieratic is an adaptation of the hieroglyphic script, the signs being simplified to facilitate quick reproduction of a kind required in non-monumental contexts. It was Egypt's administrative and business script throughout most of its history, and was also employed to record documents of a literary, scientific and religious nature. It is found on all sorts of media, but most typically on rolls or sheets of papyrus or on bits of pottery and stone called ostraca. Documents in hieratic were usually written in black ink, applied by means of a brush made out of a stem of rush. Red ink was occasionally employed to mark out a special section, like the beginning of a text or a numerical total, or to indicate punctuation points in literary compositions. There are also monumental examples where the script was incised in stone, but these are quite rare and of a relatively late date.

The earliest substantial body of texts in hieratic yet attested are estate records of the Fourth Dynasty, although sporadic examples of the script are known from much earlier. Its origin clearly goes back to the very beginning of writing in Egypt, since the first stages in its development are observable in the semi-cursive hieroglyphs that occur as labels on vessels of the late Predynastic Period. The 'day-to-day' script of Egypt for nearly two and a half millennia, hieratic was finally ousted from secular use by another cursive script, demotic, at the beginning of the Late Period (*c.* 600 BC). Thereafter its use was confined to religious documents, which is why it was called *hieratika*, 'priestly', by the Greeks. The latest known hieratic documents are religious papyri dated to the third century AD. Like hieroglyphic, hieratic could be written either in columns or in horizontal lines but, unlike hieroglyphic, its orientation was invariable. Hieratic proper always reads from right to left. This is one of the features that distinguishes it from 'cursive hieroglyph', a script that resembles early hieratic and was the preferred form, for example, for reproducing certain kinds of funerary text (such as the Coffin Texts and the 'Book of the Dead') from the Middle Kingdom down to the Third Intermediate Period.

20,21

37

22

20 *Right* Scribe's palette of ivory. It has two holes, one for black ink, one for red, and a slot for holding brushes. On the bottom are scribal jottings in hieratic. Eighteenth Dynasty. H. 30 cm. BM 5524.

21 *Below* Scene from a tomb painting showing a scribe conducting a census of geese. He stands reading from an unrolled papyrus with his palette tucked under his arm. Thebes. Eighteenth Dynasty. H. of scribe's figure 33.4 cm. BM 37978.

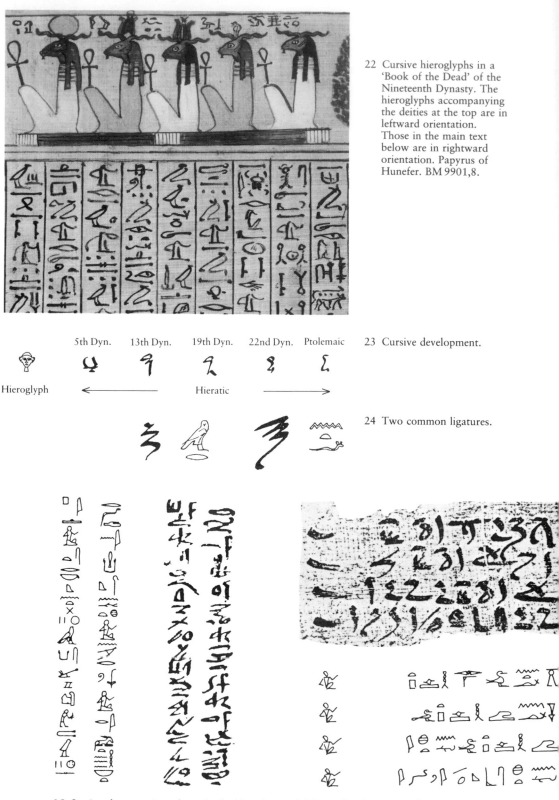

22 Cursive hieroglyphs in a 'Book of the Dead' of the Nineteenth Dynasty. The hieroglyphs accompanying the deities at the top are in leftward orientation. Those in the main text below are in rightward orientation. Papyrus of Hunefer. BM 9901,8.

	5th Dyn.	13th Dyn.	19th Dyn.	22nd Dyn.	Ptolemaic

23 Cursive development.

Hieroglyph ←—————— Hieratic ——————→

24 Two common ligatures.

25 Section from a private letter in the hieratic script, written in columns on papyrus. Eleventh Dynasty. New York, Metropolitan Museum of Art.

26 Part of an inventory of names written in the hieratic script, in horizontal lines. Twelfth Dynasty. Papyrus Reisner I. Boston, Museum of Fine Arts.

It is probably true to say that hieratic never completely lost touch with its monumental parent. It is always possible, with varying degrees of ease or difficulty, depending on the period and type of inscription, to transcribe a hieratic text sign by sign into its hieroglyphic equivalent. However, it followed its own course of evolution, the signs showing a definite tendency to become progressively more cursive, and it also developed 23 other conventions and features appropriate to a running hand. Certain groups of two or more signs came to be rendered by one stroke of the brush in what are called 'ligatures', 24 and complicated signs were often avoided or replaced by simple substitutes (for example, the bird 🦅 was abbreviated to ℗) – these in turn were sometimes borrowed by the hieroglyphic script, a reverse influence that is hardly surprising when it is considered that in all probability many hieroglyphic inscriptions were initially drafted in hieratic.

A crucial period in the history of hieratic was the Middle Kingdom. Up to the Eleventh Dynasty hieratic texts were usually written in columns. For some reason during the 25 Twelfth Dynasty there was a major change in practice. Scribes began to write in horizon- 26 tal lines, a mode that soon became universal. At the same time different styles of script began to appear, which developed along their own lines. By the New Kingdom they had become quite separate. One was a cursive 'business' hand used for writing mundane documents, the other an elegant 'book' hand employed for literary texts and in contexts 27 where a 'traditional' hand was thought more appropriate. Out of the business hand of the late New Kingdom there developed in turn, during the Third Intermediate Period, two regional variants, both even more cursive – the so-called 'abnormal' hieratic in 28 Upper Egypt and demotic in Lower Egypt. Abnormal hieratic was completely supplanted by demotic in the Twenty-sixth Dynasty, following the conquest of the south by kings of the north.

27 Line from a literary text. Nineteenth Dynasty. Papyrus d'Orbiney. BM 10183,3.

28 Papyrus with witness subscriptions in traditional hieratic (above) and abnormal hieratic (below). Twenty-sixth Dynasty. Papyrus Brooklyn 47.218.3. New York, The Brooklyn Museum.

Demotic

For the rest of Egyptian history demotic was the only native script in general use for day-to-day purposes. The name demotic, ancient Greek *demotika*, 'popular (script)', refers to its secular functions, as does its Egyptian name *sḫ šꜥt*, 'the writing of letters'.

29 Like hieratic, demotic was mostly confined to use on papyri and ostraca and it maintained the scribal tradition of writing in horizontal lines with rightward orientation. It is otherwise an almost independent form, barely recognisable as a descendant of hieratic, let alone hieroglyphic. It is a very cursive script, almost wholly lacking in iconicity and replete with ligatures, abbreviations and other orthographic peculiarities, making it difficult to read and virtually impossible to transcribe meaningfully into any kind of hieroglyphic 'original'.

The demotic record is dominated by legal, administrative and commercial material. However, it also includes, from the Ptolemaic Period on, literary compositions, as well as scientific and even religious texts, which were written in a more calligraphic hand, the

30 ink now increasingly applied with the reed pen introduced by the Greeks, which by the end of the period had virtually supplanted the traditional brush. Another development of the Ptolemaic Period was that the script began to be used monumentally, particularly on funerary and commemorative stelae. The best-known example is the so-called

39 Rosetta Stone (see Chapter 5), which contains a single text, a priestly decree, repeated in three scripts, hieroglyphic, demotic and Greek (the latter included as Greek was now the official language of Egypt). All three versions, including the demotic, are incised in the stone. Present evidence suggests that demotic outlived the two other native scripts by a century or so before finally falling into disuse in the fifth century AD. The latest demotic inscription is a graffito in the temple of Philae dated to AD 450.

29 *Right* Demotic ostracon: a receipt for the delivery of wine in year ten of the Emperor Antoninus Pius. AD 145. H. 8.7 cm. BM 21426.

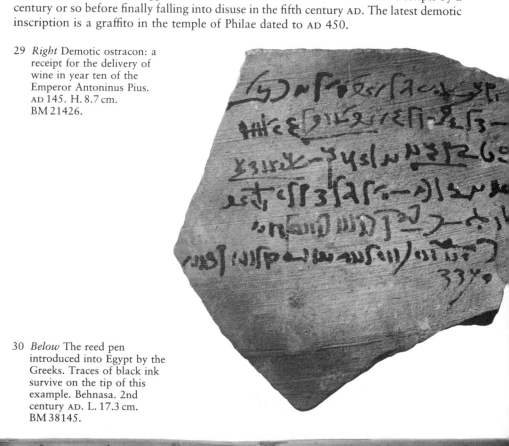

30 *Below* The reed pen introduced into Egypt by the Greeks. Traces of black ink survive on the tip of this example. Behnasa. 2nd century AD. L. 17.3 cm. BM 38145.

Coptic

As the old native scripts went into decline and finally disappeared during Egypt's Roman and Christian period, so a new script, Coptic, as used by the 'Copts', took their place to write the Egyptian language. The name 'Copt' is derived from the Arabic *gubti*, itself a corruption of the Greek *Aiguptios*. It means simply 'Egyptian'. It was the term used by the Arabs after their conquest of Egypt in the seventh century, to denote the native inhabitants of the country. Coptic represents a distinct departure from the other scripts. It consists of the twenty-four letters of the Greek alphabet, supplemented, in its standard, Sahidic, form, by six characters taken from demotic to denote Egyptian phonemes not known to Greek. It is thus a fully alphabetic script in which the vowels of the

31 Egyptian magical papyrus written in Greek and demotic letters. Behnasa. 2nd century AD. H. 29 cm. BM 10808.

language are represented, as well as the consonants. The letters borrowed from demotic and their phonemic values are as follows:

Demotic	Coptic	Value
ϣ	ϣ	sh
ϥ	ϥ	f
ϩ	ϩ	h
ⳡ	ⳝ	j
ϭ	ϭ	g
ϯ	ϯ	ti

The development of this standard form of the alphabet, which was well established by the fourth century AD, is closely associated with the spread of Christianity in Egypt. It has been suggested that the impetus for its development was provided by the need to furnish translations of the New Testament and other religious texts for the native population in a regularised and easily accessible form, a task for which the demotic script appears to have been considered both inadequate and inappropriate. The Coptic script was not, however, initially devised for Christian purposes. The earliest recognisable form of Coptic (datable to the end of the first century AD) was used to write native magical texts, where the motive for the use of the Greek letters probably lay, it is thought, in the desire to render as accurately as possible the correct pronunciation of the magical 'words of power'. In 'Old Coptic', as it is called, the Greek letters are supplemented by several more demotic characters than are retained in the later standardised form of the script.

The surviving literature in Coptic is extensive, with a huge quantity, coming mostly from the libraries of monasteries, being devoted to religious, mainly Biblical, subjects. Non-religious material, much of it again originating from monastic communities, includes private and official correspondence and administrative, business and legal documents, but very little of a purely 'literary' or scientific nature. Most of the surviving texts were written in ink, again with the reed pen, on papyrus or ostraca, though wooden tablets, parchment and, later, paper were also utilised, and the script was adapted without difficulty for monumental use. Many of the documents are in the form of the 'codex', the ancestor of the modern book, made up of individual leaves of papyrus or

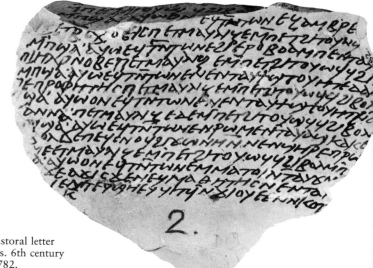

32 Coptic ostracon: a pastoral letter from a bishop. Thebes. 6th century AD. H. 13 cm. BM 32782.

33 Wooden lintel from a Coptic church with (left) invocation to 'The Lord Jesus Christ' for the blessed Jōkim and his wife. The damaged text on the right bears the date AD 914. L. 1.93 m. BM 54040.

parchment connected at the spine, which was introduced during the early centuries AD. Whatever the text or format the arrangement and direction of Coptic writing follow the common Greek mode. It is written or carved in horizontal lines reading from left to right. No gaps were left between words and punctuation was minimal (if present at all). A feature peculiar to Sahidic Coptic was the use of a superlinear stroke, unknown to Greek, which was regularly placed above certain consonants or groups of consonants to indicate a syllable.

Literacy

Although it is clear from the quantity and range of the extant record that writing played an immensely important part in ancient Egyptian society, it is very unlikely that literacy can have been widespread among the population. The production of writing, and direct access to it, was almost certainly the preserve of an educated élite, consisting, at the highest level, of royalty and high officials of state and, below them, of people for whom the ability to read and write was a necessary part of their job. There is no doubt that the routine exercise of literacy was largely a function of the professional scribe, who was a central figure in every aspect of the country's administration – civil, military and religious.   21

Recent estimates, admitted to be no more than informed guesses, suggest that less than 1 per cent of the population would have been literate during most of the Pharaonic Period, rising to about 10 per cent in the Graeco-Roman Period, when Greek was the official language of Egypt. Within this generality, allowance must, of course, be made for considerable local variation deriving from special circumstances, such as existed, for example, in the village of Deir el-Medina, the home of the community of workmen who built and decorated the royal tombs at Thebes during the New Kingdom. Draughtsmanship and writing played such an important part in the daily work of these men that they were probably significantly more literate than the general populace. Among the latter, literacy, if it existed at all, is likely to have been restricted to the ability to write one's name and probably not much more. An illiterate person, requiring a document to be written or read, would simply have had recourse to a scribe.

Egyptian writings on the subject indicate that literacy was a very desirable acquisition, conferring status, securing a position and providing a means to advancement that might lead ultimately to the very highest office. A thorough training in scribal skills was held to be an essential prerequisite for any young man with professional or political aspirations. There appear to have been elementary schools at which the basic skills were taught; more advanced training was obtained actually in the job, the system being akin to that of 'apprentice' and 'master', the latter in many cases being a father or near-relative.

School texts of the New Kingdom, which form the bulk of our evidence on Egyptian educational methods, indicate that basic reading and writing were laboriously learned by copying out excerpts from well-known 'classics', at first in cursive hieroglyph and then in the hieratic script. Countless such excerpts survive, written in schoolboy hands

34 Limestone ostracon, the
largest of its kind, bearing a
copy in school-boy hieratic of
part of 'The Story of Sinuhe'.
Nineteenth Dynasty.
H. 88.5 cm. Ashmolean
Museum, Oxford.

of varying competence, on scraps of papyrus, wooden tablets or, most commonly, on limestone ostraca. One of the most famous is the Ramesside ostracon, the largest of its 34 kind, which bears a copy of a sizeable portion of a well-known literary text of the Middle Kingdom, 'The Story of Sinuhe'. Like most efforts of this type, it is a poor version of the text. It contains, in the words of the modern editor of the ostracon, 'every kind of mistake – misspellings, confused constructions, and senseless interpolations – which show that its writer did not know, and suggest that he and his instructors did not care, what the words that he was writing meant'. At a higher level pupils progressed to writing texts actually designed for the purpose of training scribes. Such documents are often cast in the form of letters written by one scribe to another and deliberately include strange words, foreign names, technical terms and difficult calculations – all designed to test the pupil thoroughly. A fine example on a papyrus in the British Museum is devoted 35 to one of the favourite themes of such literature: the advantages of the scribal life as compared to alternatives, in this case military conscription. It is executed in a good literary hand, probably that of an advanced student. The three groups written above the main text are thought to be corrections by the instructor of signs that he felt to be not quite properly formed. The passage begins, 'Apply yourself to writing zealously; do not stay your hand ...', and ends, 'Pleasant and wealth-abounding is your palette and your roll of papyrus'.

35 Advanced exercise in hieratic, including a passage extolling the scribal life. The instructor's corrections are written above. Nineteenth Dynasty. Papyrus Anastasi 5. H. of sheet, approx. 21 cm. BM 10244,4.

3
The Principles

The Egyptian writing system may be regarded as containing three major types of sign, each of which performs a different function. The first type is the 'logogram', which writes a complete word; the second is the 'phonogram', which represents a sound (a phoneme of the language); the third is the 'determinative', which helps to indicate a word's precise meaning. More broadly, since the logogram and the determinative are both concerned with 'sense' or 'meaning' rather than with 'sound', they can be classed together as 'semograms' (or more traditionally, and less adequately, as 'ideograms'). In the nature of the system there is a certain amount of overlap between the categories, and it is not always easy in practice to distinguish clearly between a semographic and a phonographic usage. Moreover, 'there are degrees and varieties within the groups of sense-signs and sound-signs'. The conventional three-fold division of the system presented here covers the essential ground and provides a useful working model, but it should be kept in mind that the categories are not absolutely hard and fast.

An important feature of the system, seen also in scripts of the Semitic branch, is that it records only the consonantal phonemes; the vowels are not specifically indicated. One of the chief characteristics of both the Egyptian and the Semitic languages is that they contain basic word-roots made up of consonants (usually three in number) that are generally invariable; within these roots such features as grammatical inflexion are often indicated by internal vowel variation. It is thought that the neglect of the vowels in writing is a direct reflection of their 'instability' in relation to the consonants.

By the time of Middle Egyptian there were twenty-four consonants in the language. A complete list is given below under 'uniconsonantal signs'. To render their phonemic values Egyptologists are accustomed to transliterate them, as far as is possible, into modern alphabetic characters, some with additional points or marks written above or below (so-called 'diacritics') to differentiate them.

Logograms
The simplest form of logogram is that in which a word is represented directly by a picture of the object that it actually denotes:

⊙ , depicting the sun, signifies 'sun' (r^c)

▭ , depicting the ground-plan of a house, signifies 'house' (pr)

☺ , depicting the human face, signifies 'face' ($ḥr$)

A more developed form works through a kind of extension or association of meaning:

⊙ , depicting the sun, signifies 'day' (r^c or hrw)

, depicting writing equipment, signifies 'scribe' or 'writing' ($sẖ$)

∧ , depicting a pair of legs, signifies 'come' (iw)

It is clear that a writing system based entirely on such logograms would be quite impractical. Firstly it would require many thousands of signs to cover the vocabulary of a language. Secondly it would find it very difficult to express, clearly and unambiguously, words for things that cannot easily be pictured. It is these considerations, scholars suggest, that, early on, led to the development of the second category of sign, the phonogram.

Phonograms

These were derived by a process of phonetic borrowing, whereby logograms were used to write other words, or parts of words, to which they were unrelated in meaning but with which they happened to share the same consonantal structure. For example:

the logogram ⬭, *r*, meaning 'mouth', was used as a phonogram with the phonemic value *r*, to write such words as ⬭, *r*, meaning 'towards' or to represent the phonemic element *r* in a word like ⬭, *rn*, 'name'.

the logogram ▭, *pr*, meaning 'house', was used as a phonogram with the value *pr*, in words such as ▭△, *pr*, 'go', or ▭⬭⊙, *prt*, 'winter'.

the logogram ☺, *ḥr*, meaning 'face', was used as a phonogram with the value *ḥr*, in such words as ☺, *ḥr*, 'upon', and ☺⬭▭, *ḥrt*, 'sky'.

The basic principle at work here is that of the *rebus*, whereby 'one thing is shown, but another meant'. By the same principle the English verb 'can' could be written with the picture ▯, representing a (tin) can, or the word 'belief' with the pictures 🐝 🍃, representing a bee and a leaf. Using this method the Egyptians were able to develop a large corpus of phonographic signs which was more than adequate to meet their linguistic needs. These phonograms fall naturally into three main categories.

1. Uniconsonantal signs, which represent a single consonant; the most important group. There are twenty-six of these including variants:

Sign	Translit.	Sound-value	Sign	Translit.	Sound-value
🦅	ꜣ	glottal stop	🪶	ḥ	emphatic h
❙	i̓	i	⊖	ḫ	ch as in Scottish loch
❙❙ \ ❙	y	y	⬭	ẖ	slightly softer than last
⌐▫	ꜥ	gutteral, the ayin of the Semitic languages	⎾⎿ }	s	s
🐦	w	w	▭	š	sh
◺	b	b	△	ḳ	q
▯	p	p	⬭	k	k
⌐	f	f	▨	g	hard g
🦉	m	m	◠	t	t
∿∿∿	n	n	⬭	ṯ	tj
⬭	r	r	⬭	d	d
⊓	h	h	⎨	ḏ	dj

103

Among these, 🐦 , 𝟙 , and 🐥 are weak consonants. They were readily assimilated in speech to a preceding vowel, especially at the end of a syllable, and consequently were often omitted in writing; the consonant ⌒ was similarly unstable. Egyptologists sometimes indicate the graphic omission of a consonant by enclosing its transliteration in brackets.

2. Biconsonantal signs, which represent pairs of successive consonants; the largest single group of phonograms, though fewer than a hundred in all. We have already encountered ☐ , *pr*, and 😊 , *ḥr*. Here are some others:

Sign	Translit.	Sign	Translit.	Sign	Translit.
	ȝw		*mn*		*sȝ*
	ȝb or *mr*		*mr*		*sw*
	ir		*mr* or *ȝb*		*sn*
	wȝ		*ms*		*šs*
	wp		*nb*		*kȝ*
	wr		*ns*		*ti*
	wḏ		*ḥm*		*ḏȝ*
	bȝ		*ḥn*		*ḏd*

3. Triconsonantal signs, which represent groups of three successive consonants. There are between forty and fifty of these, the following being among the most common:

Sign	Transliteration	Sign	Transliteration
	'iwn		*rwḏ*
	'nḫ		*ḥtp*
	'ḥ'		*ḫpr*
	wȝḥ		*ḫrw*
	nfr		*šm'*
	nṯr		*tyw*
	nḏm		*ḏ'm*

It should be noted that although the signs in the last two categories do occur as individual hieroglyphs, they are more often accompanied by uniconsonantal signs, which record part or even the whole of their phonemic value. This is referred to as 'phonetic complementing'. In general it is a single consonant, more usually the last of the group, that is complemented:

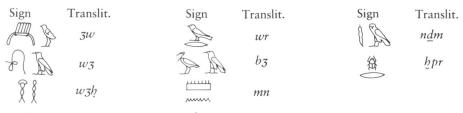

Sign	Translit.	Sign	Translit.	Sign	Translit.
	3w		wr		nḏm
	w3		b3		ḫpr
	w3ḥ		mn		

Fuller complementing is, however, by no means rare:

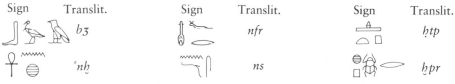

Sign	Translit.	Sign	Translit.	Sign	Translit.
	b3		nfr		ḥtp
	'nḫ		ns		ḫpr

The original function of such complements was to emphasise that the complemented sign was indeed a phonogram and not a logogram, but they were also exploited as calligraphic devices, to be deployed, for example, when there was a need to fill an unwanted space.

In theory, the system allowed a word of more than one consonant to be written in a number of different ways. In practice, however, a degree of economy was excercised, with the full range of possibilities being left unexploited and with spellings being relatively standardised. Thus, for example, the preposition ḥn', 'together with', is always written ⌇⌇⌇⌇ and never as ⌇⌇⌇⌇; the verb mn, 'to remain', always takes the form ⌇⌇⌇⌇ or the like, and is never written as ⌇⌇⌇⌇ ; the adjective nfr, 'good', though written variously as ⌇⌇, ⌇⌇⌇, or ⌇⌇⌇, never lacks the triconsonantal ⌇ ; and the biconsonantals ⌇⌇ and ⌇ , though they can both represent mr, are used each in a particular set of words (related by root) and are not interchangeable. Many words do have variant forms but their orthography has a sufficiently consistent 'core' to make them recognisable without undue difficulty. This process of word recognition is further aided by the third major category of sign, the determinative.

Determinatives

Determinatives, which like phonograms were derived from logograms, were placed at the end of words to assist in establishing their meaning, where otherwise there might be uncertainty. For example, a determinative in the form of a stroke was commonly appended to a logogram to emphasise that its function was logographic: ⌇ , 'sun', ⌇ , 'face', ⌇⌇ , 'house'. Similarly, to remove ambiguity, a sign or group of signs subject to more than one interpretation would be written with the determinative appropriate to the intended meaning. Thus the logogram ⌇⌇ , sḫ, would be written ⌇⌇⌇ , with the determinative depicting a man, when the word 'scribe' was meant, and ⌇⌇⌇ , with the determinative representing a book-roll, when the word 'write' or 'writing' was meant. We have already noted in Chapter 2 the use of determinatives (in the form of male and female figures) to disambiguate names. So also with other phonograms. For example, the group ⌇⌇⌇ , mn, could stand for a number of different words, among them 'remain' and 'weak'. To distinguish between them, the former was written ⬚, with the book-roll determinative (indicating an abstract notion), the latter ⬚, with the determinative of a small bird (indicating something small, bad or weak).

Some determinatives are specific in application, which means that they are closely tied to one word:

	ꜣsḫ	'to reap'	(determinative of a man reaping)
	ssmt	'horse'	(determinative of a horse)

Others identify a word as belonging to a certain class or category. These are called 'generic determinatives' or 'taxograms'. The following form a small selection:

	man, person		walk, run		metal
	woman		limb, flesh		town, village
	god, king		skin, mammal, leather		desert, foreign country
	force, effort		small, bad, weak		house, building
	eat, drink, speak		wood, tree		book, writing, abstract
	enemy, foreigner		sun, light, time		several, plural
	force, effort		stone		

Words could be written with one determinative or more:

	ikm	'shield'	('shield' determinative)
	wšb	'answer'	('speak' determinative)
	wgs	'cut open'	('knife' and 'force' determinatives)
	bhꜣw	'fugitives'	('legs', 'man' and 'plural' determinatives)

The determinatives of a word could also be changed or varied, so as to indicate a nuance of meaning. Take the word *ikm*. It is often followed by the specific determinative as above, but it was also written with the leather or metal determinatives (⬚, ⬚), when it was felt to be important to distinguish its material. The information conveyed by the determinative in either case is additional to that which is implicit in the word *ikm* itself. It is a special attribute of the Egyptian system that it could convey by pictorial means extra-linguistic information of this kind.

As well as performing a semantic function, determinatives were useful aids to reading. Since they mark the ends of words, they would have helped the reader to identify the 'word-images' or 'word-pictures' in a continuous text. Such 'images' once established were very slow to change, resulting in a stability for the system which certainly had its advantages but which was also one of the major reasons for the gradual divergence between the written and spoken forms of the language (a divergence already well advanced, it is believed, by the time of the Middle Kingdom). As the one failed to keep pace with the other, the script became increasingly 'historical', with a somewhat fossilised orthography no longer accurately reflecting contemporary pronunciations.

As any routine line of inscription will demonstrate, all the categories of sign mentioned above occur regularly, side by side, in Egyptian writing, sometimes together with other, less important, types, called 'orthograms' and 'calligrams', which convey neither meaning nor sound but may be present for special orthographic or aesthetic reasons:

wḏ ḥm.f ḥr wrryt.f nt ḏᶜm ỉb.f ꝫw

'His Majesty departed upon his chariot of electrum, his heart joyful'

In this line the signs (*w*), (*f*), (*r*), (*y*), (*n*), (*t*), and (*m*) are uniconsonantal, with (in both cases), ., and , acting as phonetic complements; (*wḏ*), (*ḥm*), (*ḥr*), (*wr*), and (*ꝫw*) are biconsonantal; (*ḏᶜm*) is triconsonantal; (*ỉb* = 'heart') is a logogram; the first is an orthogram; and , , , , and are determinatives.

Such apparent complexity has led the Egyptian system (and others like it) to be treated rather disparagingly by many commentators. Dismissing it as 'cumbrous' and 'illogical', they have found it difficult to understand 'the process of thought by which it was evolved, and even more difficult to imagine why it should have continued with so little development over so long a period'. The central complaint is that the Egyptians, evidently lacking in imagination, failed to take what is deemed to be the 'obvious step': simply to use their uniconsonantal signs in the manner of an alphabet, abandoning the other types of sign. Such criticism, which is based essentially on the assumed superiority of alphabetic scripts over all others, is quite misplaced. It not only overrates the efficiency of alphabetic systems, it also seriously undervalues the merits of others. The Egyptian system has the 'disadvantage' of containing a relatively large number of signs. In compensation, however, its mixed orthography creates visually distinctive word patterns that actually enhance legibility. Direct support for this view is provided by those few attempts at 'alphabetic' writing, which were carried out, perhaps experimentally under the influence of Greek, during Egypt's Late Period. The experiment, if such it was, was short-lived and it is not hard to see why. These 'alphabetic' texts, consisting of a succession of consonantal signs, written in unbroken sequence like Greek of the time, are very difficult to read, considerably more so than contemporary inscriptions written in the traditional orthography. The verdict of one percipient authority is that 'writing Egyptian with only an alphabet of consonants sacrificed legibility to simplicity, and thus did more harm than good ... Perhaps it is now time to stop chiding the Egyptians for not "taking the step which seems to us so obvious"'.

There is, of course, a further dimension to the matter. The reduction of the system in the way suggested would have meant the abandonment of what was evidently to the Egyptians an exceedingly important attribute of the script: namely, its capacity, because of its pictorial and unrestricted nature, to be exploited for purposes other than straightforward linguistic communication. Some of the ways in which the hieroglyphs functioned as part of a larger system of artistic representation were mentioned in the previous chapter, where certain non-scriptorial uses and significances were also noted, while earlier in this chapter attention was drawn to the script's ability to convey 'extra-linguistic' information. It is relevant to add here the way in which the script could be manipulated to produce so-called 'sportive' or 'cryptographic' writings, designed, it has been suggested, 'to clothe a religious text in mystery' or simply 'to intrigue the reader'. The extent to which such manipulation was possible is shown most strikingly by the systems of orthography employed in certain temple inscriptions of the Ptolemaic and Roman Periods. They are characterised, among other things, by an enormous increase in the number of signs and variants, in the values and meanings that the signs could bear, and in the possible combinations of signs and sign-groups, an elaboration achieved not by artificial means but simply by exploiting to the full the inherent properties of the hieroglyphic script. To a reader accustomed only to the classical orthography these texts are unintelligible, though it is now doubted that they were actually designed to be deliberately cryptographic. Whatever the reason for such elaboration, it is clear that it was not an original invention of the Ptolemaic Period. On the contrary, it was the final stage of a tradition that is strongly in evidence already in the New Kingdom and can be traced back sporadically as far as the Old Kingdom. Indeed some 'sportive' writings are to be found as regular components of the standard system from a relatively early date. A prime example is the common occurrence, from the Middle Kingdom on, of the hieroglyph ⌐, as an abbreviated writing of the title 𓅓𓄿 *imy-r*, 'overseer'. The basis of the usage, which is a 'kind of graphic pun', becomes clear, when it is understood that ⌐ represents a tongue and that the title *imy-r* means literally 'he who is in the mouth'.

Vocalisation

The general absence of vowel notation means that our modern transliterations represent only the consonantal skeletons of Egyptian words. Many of these are difficult to communicate verbally, being, as they stand, virtually unpronounceable. As an aid, therefore, to pronunciation (in discussion, lectures, teaching), Egyptologists insert a short 'e' between the consonants and render 3 and ꜥ as 'a'. Thus, for example:

s3	'sa'	*ḥnꜥ*	'hena'
wrs	'weres'	*ꜥḏꜥ*	'adja'
mn	'men'	*nfrt*	'nefret'
wbn	'weben'	*sḥtp*	'sehetep'

It must always be borne in mind, however, that the resulting vocalisations are artificial devices serving as a convenience and bear little or no relation to the ancient pronunciation of the words.

Our knowledge of the original pronunciation of Egyptian is very incomplete but not a total blank. The vocalic structure of a considerable number of words can be deduced from their form in Coptic, the last stage of Egyptian and the only stage in which the vowels are written. Although Coptic contains a large number of Greek and other foreign words, the bulk of its vocabulary is of Pharaonic ancestry, in many cases going back to the earliest stages of the language. A selection is given below of some common Egyptian words together with their Coptic descendants:

	mn (remain)	ⲘⲞⲨⲚ	(moun)
	mdw (speak)	ⲘⲞⲨⲦⲈ	(moute)
	pḏt (bow)	ⲠⲓⲦⲈ	(pite)
	nfr (good)	ⲚⲞⲨϤⲈ	(nūfe)
	r(m)ṯ (man)	ⲣⲱⲘⲈ	(rōme)

	r^c (sun)	рн	(rē)
	sf (yesterday)	сау	(saf)
	kmt (Egypt)	кнме	(kēme)

The Coptic forms cannot, of course, be accepted as accurate indications of the way in which the words were actually pronounced in earlier periods. Coptic is the end product of centuries, even millennia, of linguistic evolution, in the course of which the grammar of Egyptian, including its phonology, was subject to constant modification and change. One has only to consider that Coptic is separated from Old Egyptian by over 2,000 years – a span of time that is twice as long as that which covers the evolution of modern English from Anglo-Saxon – to realise the potential for change. Coptic is the single most important source of information on the Egyptian vocalic system but its evidence must be used with caution.

There are other, earlier sources of evidence on the subject. A number of ancient scripts (for example, Greek, Assyrian, Babylonian), which themselves indicate vowels, contain fully vocalised transcriptions of contemporary Egyptian words. Such evidence is invaluable, though unfortunately it is very limited in quantity and scope. The earliest and most important of these transcriptions occur in cuneiform documents contemporary with the New Kingdom in Egypt. They include the names of several Egyptian kings, among them such well known ones as 'Imn-ḥtp (Amenophis) and R'-mss (Ramesses), which are transcribed as Amanhatpi and Riamesesa respectively.

Such vocalisations coupled with careful inferences from the Coptic evidence have enabled scholars to make considerable headway in ascertaining the rules governing Egyptian syllabic structure and vowel quantity and even to get some idea of the quality of the vowels. The indications are that up to the Eighteenth Dynasty Egyptian had only three vowels, namely 'a', 'i' and 'u', all of which could be either long or short. The vowels 'e' and 'o' were relatively late developments.

It should be mentioned at this point that some scholars disagree with the conventional view, followed above, that the phonograms are essentially consonantal. They argue that these signs are really syllabic, standing, in the case of the 'uniconsonantal' signs, for consonant + any vowel. The question is too complex to consider in detail here. Suffice it to say that the 'syllabic' interpretation fits very well with current theories on script development, but is problematic in other respects and is generally rejected by Egyptologists. This theory should not, incidentally, be confused with the phenomenon referred to in Egyptological literature as 'syllabic orthography', also called 'group writing'. This is a method of writing characterised, among other things, by the use of biconsonantal signs, or pairs of uniconsonantal signs, instead of single uniconsonantal signs (for example, ⟨⟩, ʿ₃, for ʿ; ⟨⟩, ḥ₃, for ḥ). In such groups the second element is often a weak consonant indicating the presence of a vowel. Employed mostly to write words of foreign origin, this kind of orthography was particularly popular during the New Kingdom, when its wider usage may have been encouraged by the example of the contemporary cuneiform system, employed very generally throughout Western Asia, in which the vowels are recorded.

Origins

Although the principles underlying Egyptian writing are now fairly well understood, it is still unclear how the system came into being in the first place. Was it the end-product of a process of gradual development or was it the invention of a single person? Was it indigenous or was it introduced from abroad? It is impossible to give definitive answers to these questions. All that can be said in the present state of knowledge is that some alternatives seem more probable than others. Unfortunately, the Egyptians themselves give us no direct help on the subject of the origin of their script. Hieroglyphic writing was traditionally regarded by them as the invention of the gods, in particular of Thoth, the divine scribe, who is often referred to in texts as the 'lord of writing'. We are left to deduce what we can, therefore, from the evidence provided by the earliest examples of the script itself.

Writing makes its first appearance in Egypt at the very end of the Predynastic Period, in the reigns of the immediate predecessors of the kings of the First Dynasty. That it should do so at this time is not altogether surprising. It was a period of great cultural change and technological innovation, with a system of government increasingly concentrated around the royal court. It is reasonable to see writing, within this context, as itself a new technology, invented, or adopted, in response to the needs of the system; the ways in which it was used suggest that it served to further central control both ideologically and administratively.

To the ideological category belong those inscriptions that occur on a series of votive objects decorated with representations in low relief – the first examples of Egyptian 'monumental' art. The most famous of these objects is the palette of King Narmer, in which the king is represented engaged in acts symbolic of his status and authority. The administrative function is to be seen in those labels or dockets usually written in ink, or roughly incised, on the outsides of stone and pottery vessels. The inscriptions in both contexts are short and restricted. They consist almost wholly of titles and names (personal, mainly royal, names, place-names and the names of commodities). In the case of the vessels they identify the owner, the contents and sometimes the source. In the case of the ornamental objects, where the hieroglyphs form an integral part of a larger scene, they identify the representations with which they are associated – the unity between 'caption' and 'figure' in these latter, carefully carved cases, showing clearly how in style and form the hieroglyphs were direct offshoots of the new pictorial art of the period.

Few of these early inscriptions are completely unambiguous. It is not simply a matter of unfamiliar vocabulary. The signary itself had yet to stabilise into its standard dynastic form. It contains several hieroglyphs that do not survive into later usage and whose reading, therefore, can only be guessed at. What is clear, however, is that the basic 'mixed' structure of the writing system is already fully formed – it consists not only of logograms but of phonograms as well; moreover, all the different types of phonogram (uni- and multi-consonantal signs) are present. Thus, for example, among the signs that can be definitely identified on the pottery vessel, the Horus-bird, ⟨glyph⟩, denoting the king as 'the Horus' is a logogram, while ⟨glyph⟩, ⟨glyph⟩, and ⟨glyph⟩ are phonograms, the last two uniconsonantal (i and p), the first triconsonantal ($šm^c$). In the case of the palette, in addition to what is traditionally regarded as a *rebus* writing the king's name, Narmer (the two hieroglyphs, ⟨glyph⟩, and ⟨glyph⟩, one depicting a cat-fish, the other a chisel, supplying the phonetic values n^cr and mr respectively), there are, among others, the phonograms ⟨glyph⟩, w^c and ⟨glyph⟩, $š$, quite possibly writing a name $w^c š$ and ⟨glyph⟩, t, and ⟨glyph⟩, t, combined in what is probably an abbreviated writing of the title $t\underline{3}ty$, 'vizier'. In short, although it was to be some considerable time before its potential was fully exploited – long continuous texts, for example, are not known before the early Old Kingdom – the writing system, already at its inception or very shortly afterwards, had the capacity to express almost everything that was later to be required of it. Elsewhere in the Near East writing is first

36(a) *Left* Slate palette of King Narmer, obverse. The King is represented as the dominant figure smiting an enemy with a mace, in a pose that was to become part of standard royal iconography. His name, written above him with two hieroglyphs, one depicting a cat-fish, the other a chisel, is enclosed in a rectangular structure called the *serekh*. The other figures in the scene are also labelled. Hierakonpolis. Late Predynastic Period. H. 63 cm. Cairo Museum, JE 32169.

36(b) *Below left* Slate palette of King Narmer, reverse. The King is shown in the upper register engaged in a ritual procession. His name occurs twice, written with the same signs as on the obverse, once in a *serekh*, once without. Other identifiable hieroglyphs are present.

37 *Above* Pottery vessel with ink label in cursive hieroglyphs, now somewhat faded. The intelligible signs include a *serekh* enclosing a king's name possibly to be read as *Ka*, surmounted by a falcon denoting the royal title 'Horus'. To the right are three hieroglyphs, *šmꜥ*, *i* and *p*, which can be read as *ip-šmꜥ*, 'tax of Upper Egypt' or the like. Abydos. Late Predynastic Period. H. 27 cm. BM 35508.

111

attested in contexts of record-keeping and accounting, and the indications seem to be that it developed gradually out of a system of numerical notation. No such 'prehistory' is convincingly traceable for Egyptian writing. On present evidence, admittedly sparse and possibly very misleading, it appears to come into use almost 'ready-made', as it were.

It is generally thought unlikely that full writing could have been invented independently in more than one place in the ancient Near East. This belief coupled with the apparently sudden appearance of writing in a developed form in Egypt has led to the suggestion that the Egyptian system was borrowed from outside. The areas of Mesopotamia and Elam have been cited as the most likely sources, where in the last quarter or so of the fourth millennium BC a pictographic system, similar in appearance and structure to the hieroglyphic script, was used to write first the Sumerian language and then, a little later, the language known as Proto-Elamite. On present estimates the earliest Sumerian writing appears to ante-date the first hieroglyphs by a century or more. That there was contact between Egypt and these areas is beyond doubt. Mesopotamian and Elamite influences are discernible in a number of features of Egyptian culture during the late Predynastic Period, most clearly in the form of various artistic designs and motifs (the intertwined felines on the reverse of Narmer's palette are a case in point). The importation of writing into Egypt can, therefore, be viewed, it has been suggested, as part of a larger process of cultural transmission.

Reasonable as this hypothesis is, there can be no question of the Egyptian system being a direct borrowing of the Sumerian. One obvious objection is that there is little, if any, discernible overlap between the two sets of signs. The Egyptian signary, though pictographic in character like archaic Sumerian, is clearly derived from indigenous sources. Several of the hieroglyphs depict objects, such as certain kinds of tool and weapon, that are known from the archaeological record to have been in contemporary use in Egypt. Others have representational antecedents among the motifs and designs on painted pottery of the earlier Predynastic Period and among the 'mnemonic' symbols, thought to mark possession or ownership, that occur on pots and implements of the same date. More importantly, although both are mixed systems, their structures are not the same. In the first place, the balance of their 'mix' is different. In the earliest Sumerian logography is predominant. Phonography is present at first to a very limited extent, and takes several centuries to become fully developed. By comparison the earliest Egyptian, as noted above, is a system that already contains a substantial, if not complete, phonographic component, in this respect being considerably more advanced than the contemporary Sumerian. In the second place the basic phonetic unit of the system is different in each case. Sumerian is syllabic; its signs represent syllables of the language, each one consisting either of a vowel or of a consonant plus a vowel. Egyptian, on the other hand, is consonantal; its signs represent only the consonants of the language; the vowels, being 'unstable', are not specifically recorded. These differences are rooted in the structures of the languages that the two scripts represent. They are so fundamental as to be decisive against the theory that one system was simply borrowed from the other. The present consensus is, therefore, that if Egyptian writing is to be regarded as not wholly indigenous and Sumerian is to be seen as somehow influential in its invention, then the influence was imparted through a process of what has been called 'stimulus diffusion'; in other words, Sumerian provided the example or the idea of writing, together with some of its operating principles, not the system itself.

4
A Little Basic Grammar

Egyptian grammar is a large and complicated subject, important areas of which are still imperfectly understood. It cannot, without distortion, be reduced to a series of simple rules. This present chapter is intended merely to give a flavour – to a non-Egyptological readership – of how the language works. It is *highly selective* and is confined to Middle Egyptian, the 'classical' stage of the language and the one with which the study of Egyptian is usually begun. It includes also a brief account of other important topics; numerals, kings' names, dates and the offering formula.

Gender and number
There are two genders in Egyptian, masculine and feminine. Masculine nouns have no special ending; feminine nouns end in ◁, *t*.

	sn 'brother'		*snt* 'sister'
	b3k 'servant'		*b3kt* '(female) servant'
	pr 'house'		*nht* 'tree'

There are three numbers, singular, plural and dual. The plural endings are ⟨⟩, *w*, for masculine and ⟨⟩, *wt*, for feminine, though the ⟨⟩ is often omitted in writing. The determinative of plurality, written ١ ١ ١ or ١ is normally present at the end of plural words.

	snw 'brothers'		*snwt* 'sisters'
	b3kw 'servants'		*b3kwt* '(female) servants'
	prw 'houses'		*nhwt* 'trees'

The dual is used for pairs of things. The masculine ending is ⟨⟩, *wy*, the feminine is ◁\\, *ty*:

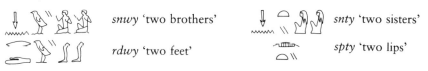

	snwy 'two brothers'		*snty* 'two sisters'
	rdwy 'two feet'		*spty* 'two lips'

Adjectives take their gender and number from the noun they describe and are placed after the noun:

	s nfr	'good man'
	st nfrt	'good woman'

113

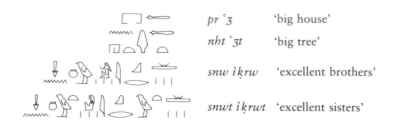

pr ʿз	'big house'
nḫt ʿзt	'big tree'
snw iḳrw	'excellent brothers'
snwt iḳrwt	'excellent sisters'

The article and co-ordination

There are no direct equivalents of the English definite and indefinite articles, 'the' and 'a'. Thus, for example, , *pr*, may be rendered 'house', 'a house' or 'the house' according to context. Similarly there is no special word for 'and', co-ordination being expressed more often than not by direct juxtapositioning:

sn snt 'brother and sister'

nṯrw nṯrwt 'gods and goddesses'

The cases

Egyptian is not an inflected language, like Latin or German. There are no case-endings to indicate the syntactic function of a noun. Whether a noun is the subject or the object of a verb is indicated by its position in a sentence, the normal word order being verb + noun-subject + noun-object:

(verb)   (subject)   (object)

sḏm s ḫrw, 'the man hears the voice'

The genitive is expressed in two ways, direct and indirect. In the direct genitive the second noun follows the first without a connecting link. It is thought that in this form the genitive expresses a particularly close relationship:

nbt pr 'mistress of the house'   *sз Rʿ* 'son of Re'

In the indirect genitive the second noun is preceded by the genitival adjective , *n(y)*, plural , *nw*, which agrees in number and gender with the first noun:

sbз n pr 'door of the house'

niwt nt nḥḥ 'city of eternity'

wrw nw зbḏw 'great ones of Abydos'

When the genitive is pronominal it is expressed by the so-called suffix pronoun, the forms and meanings of which are as follows:

i	'my'		or	*s*	'her', 'its'
k	'your' (masculine singular)			*n*	'our'
t	'your' (feminine singular)			*tn*	'your' (plural)
f	'his'			*sn*	'their'

These pronouns serve also as the subject of verbs and the object of prepositions (see below). Note that in transliteration it is customary to place a dot before a suffix.

The dative is rendered simply by means of the preposition ~~~~, *n*, 'to' or 'for', which always precedes its object, whether noun or pronoun:

~~~~ ▽ ⬠ *n nbt pr* 'for the mistress of the house' ~~~~ *n.s* 'for her'

Prepositions

The most common prepositions are:

𓄿	*m*	'in, from, with'		*ḫr*	'before, under'
~~	*n*	'to, for'		*ḥr*	'upon'
⬡	*r*	'to, towards'		*ẖr*	'under'

𓄿⬠ *m pr* 'in the house'   ~~~~ *n st* 'for the woman'

⬡⊗ *r niwt* 'towards the town'   *ḥr tꜣ* 'upon the land'

ẖr rdwy 'under the feet'   *ḫr nswt* 'before the King'

Such phrases are usually placed at the end or towards the end of a clause:

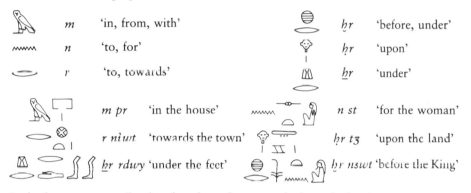

sḏm s ḫrw m pr
'the man hears the voice in the house'

Sentences

Sentence structure and, in particular, the nature and role of the verb, are the most problematic areas of Egyptian grammar. The traditional view is that there are two types of sentence in Egyptian, verbal and non-verbal. Although according to present theory this is not an accurate formulation, it may still serve for the practical purpose of translating Egyptian into English. It is important to note that, in Egyptian, distinctions of 'tense' and 'mood' and the difference between 'main' and 'subordinate' clauses are rarely indicated clearly in the writing and can often only be determined by reference to the context.

In the non-verbal sentence the link between subject and predicate is left unexpressed:

rꜥ m pt 'the sun (is, was) in the sky'

nb m pr 'the master (is, was) in the house'

In the verbal sentence the predicate is a verb, most typically one belonging to the so-called 'suffix-conjugation', the basic pattern of which is verb stem + suffix-pronoun.

115

Egyptologists refer to it as the *sḏm.f* (sedjemef) form, after the verb traditionally used as the model. The *sḏm.f* is not a simple unity. Owing to the lack of vowel notation, the word as written 'conceals' several different forms, each of which has its own meaning. The most frequently encountered is the 'indicative' *sḏm.f*, which expresses an event as an objective fact. Conventionally translated as a present tense, it is actually 'tenseless', and, depending on context, may have past and future, as well as present, reference. It conjugates as follows:

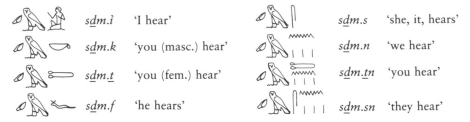

	sḏm.i	'I hear'			*sḏm.s*	'she, it, hears'
	sḏm.k	'you (masc.) hear'			*sḏm.n*	'we hear'
	sḏm.t	'you (fem.) hear'			*sḏm.tn*	'you hear'
	sḏm.f	'he hears'			*sḏm.sn*	'they hear'

The subject of the verb may also, of course, be a noun, which, like the pronoun, follows the verb, as in the sentence 'the man hears the voice' cited above.

The numerals

The numerals are denoted by seven special signs:

	wʿ	1		*ḏbʿ*	10,000
	mḏw	10		*ḥfnw*	100,000
	št	100		*ḥḥ*	1,000,000
	ḫȝ	1,000			

When written together to form a single number they are placed in descending order of magnitude. Multiples of each are indicated by simple repetition of the sign:

7 = ||||||| 369 =

24 = 142,235 =

The numeral is placed after the noun, which is generally in the singular:

s 7 'seven men' *niwt ḫȝ* 'a thousand towns'

The King's names

When a king ascended the throne he assumed five 'great names', the two principal among them being what Egyptologists call the *prenomen* and the *nomen*. These names are easily distinguished because they are enclosed within so-called 'cartouches' or royal rings: . The Egyptian name for the cartouche was , *šnw* (shenu), 'that which encircles'. It is thought that the cartouche symbolised the fact that the bearer of the name ruled over everything that the sun encircles. The *prenomen* is often preceded by the titles , *nṯr nfr*, 'good god', , *nb tȝwy*, 'lord of the two lands', and, most importantly, , *nswt-bity*, 'King of Upper and Lower Egypt', while the *nomen* is introduced by , *sȝ Rʿ*, 'son of Re'. Frequently the epithet , *di ʿnḫ*, 'given life', or ⟨glyph⟩, *di ʿnḫ ḏt*, 'given life eternally', follows the names. Here is a titulary featuring the names of Tuthmosis III of the Eighteenth Dynasty:

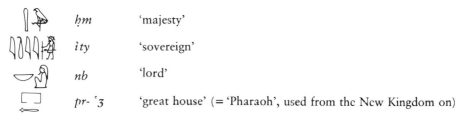

nṯr nfr nb tȝwy nswt-biȝty Mn-ḫpr-Rˤ sȝ Rˤ Ḏḥwty-ms di ʿnḫ ḏt

'The good god, lord of the two lands, king of Upper and Lower Egypt, Men-kheper-Re, son of Re, Tuthmosis, given life eternally'

The ordinary word for king, already encountered above, is *nswt*, ⟨glyph⟩, often abbreviated to ⟨glyph⟩. Here are some other common designations with their conventional translations:

glyph	transliteration	translation
⟨glyph⟩	*ḥm*	'majesty'
⟨glyph⟩	*ity*	'sovereign'
⟨glyph⟩	*nb*	'lord'
⟨glyph⟩	*pr-ˤȝ*	'great house' (= 'Pharaoh', used from the New Kingdom on)

Such designations are often followed by the 'wish formula', ⟨glyph⟩, *ʿnḫ(w) wḏȝ(w) snb(w)*, 'may he live, be prosperous, be healthy', usually abbreviated to ⟨glyph⟩.

Dates

Dating in Egypt was not continual but was based on the year of the reigning king. The year was subdivided into seasons, months and days. The full system consists of the following categories:

1. regnal year	⟨glyph⟩	*ḥȝt-sp*	
2. month (four in a season)	⟨glyph⟩	*tpy*	(the first month)
	⟨glyph⟩	*ȝbd*	(the remaining months)
3. season (three in a year)	⟨glyph⟩	*ȝḫt*	(inundation)
	⟨glyph⟩	*prt*	(winter)
	⟨glyph⟩	*šmw*	(summer)
4. day (thirty in a month)	⟨glyph⟩	*sw*	

Here are some typical dates:

⟨glyph⟩ *ḥȝt-sp 2 ȝbd 3 ȝḫt sw 1*
'year 2, month 3 of the inundation season, day 1' (of the reigning king)

⟨glyph⟩ *ḥȝt-sp 12 tpy prt sw 11*
'year 12, month 1 of winter, day 11' (of the reigning king)

Commonly, dates are abbreviated giving only the year of the king, as on a stela in the British Museum:

38 Hieroglyphic inscription from a stela mentioning year nineteen of King Nubkaure (Ammenemes II). Twelfth Dynasty. BM 583.

ḥ3t-sp 19 *ḫr ḥm n nṯr nfr nswt-bìty Nbw-k3w-r'*

'year 19 under the majesty of the good god, king of Upper and Lower Egypt, Nub-kau-re' (Ammenemes II of the Twelfth Dynasty)

The offering formula

A very large number of Egyptian texts, particularly those on funerary stelae, begin with the hieroglyphs [glyph], *ḥtp dì nswt*, probably to be translated as 'an offering which the king gives' or similar. It is referred to by Egyptologists as the 'offering formula' or the 'hetep-di-neswt-formula'. A common variant of the formula, [glyph], *ḥtp dì 'Inpw*, 'an offering which Anubis gives', has already been encountered on the panel of Iry. Its purpose was to procure for a named beneficiary a perpetual supply of the provisions deemed necessary for continued existence in the after-life. The underlying idea seems to have been that the king first provided for the gods, prominent among them [glyph], *Wsìr*, 'Osiris', and [glyph], *'Inpw*, 'Anubis', and that they in turn provided for the dead person or, more strictly, for the dead person's [glyph], *k3*, 'spirit'. In the full writing of the formula, the provisions invoked from the gods are collectively referred to as [glyph], *prt-ḫrw*, conventionally rendered as 'invocation offerings' and are then individually itemised. The standard provisions are: [glyph], *t*, 'bread', [glyph], *ḥnkt*, 'beer', [glyph], *k3w*, 'oxen', [glyph], *3pdw*, 'fowl', [glyph], *šs*, 'alabaster', and [glyph], *mnḫt*, 'clothing'. The following is a typical example:

ḥtp dì nswt Wsìr nb Ḏdw nb 3bḏw dì.f prt-ḫrw t ḥnkt k3w 3pdw šs mnḫt n k3 n nbt pr Mrrt

'an offering which the king gives (to) Osiris, lord of Busiris, lord of Abydos, that he may give invocation offerings (consisting of) bread, beer, oxen, fowl, alabaster and clothing, for the spirit of the mistress of the house, Mereret'

5
Decipherment

The spread of Christianity in Egypt, and the consequent development of the Coptic script, sounded the final death-knell for the ancient 'pagan' writing system. The evidence suggests that by the end of the fifth century AD knowledge of how to read and write the old scripts was extinct. A long dark age – destined to last thirteen centuries and more – descended upon the ancient records. The break in knowledge was complete. The hieroglyphs were fully surrendered to the larger myth of ancient Egypt – the land of strange customs and esoteric wisdom – fostered and handed down by classical writers. Although the Egyptians had been respected throughout classical antiquity as the inventors of writing, this respect does not seem to have been attended by any serious attempt to understand the basic principles of their writing system. The belief that the hieroglyphs, as opposed to the everyday 'popular' script, were not elements of an ordinary writing system but were somehow symbolic and imbued with secret meaning had already become well rooted by the time the historian Diodorus Siculus visited Egypt in the century before Christ. 'their writing does not express the intended concept by means of syllables joined to one another, but by means of the significance of the objects which have been copied, and by its figurative meaning which has been impressed upon the memory by practice.' During the early centuries AD, this 'figurative meaning' received further elaboration. For the influential philosopher Plotinus, writing in the third century, the hieroglyphs were nothing less than Platonic ideas in visual form, 'each picture ... a kind of understanding and wisdom', revealing to the initiated true knowledge as to the essence and substance of things.

Within, and out of, this tradition, there grew a genre of literature specially devoted to the explanation of hieroglyphs. The best preserved and most famous treatise on the subject is the *Hieroglyphika* of Horapollo, which was probably compiled in the fourth or fifth century AD. Here is one of its entries:

> 'What they mean by a vulture
> When they mean a mother, a sight, or boundaries, or foreknowledge ... they draw a vulture. A mother, since there is no male in this species of animal ... the vulture stands for sight since of all other animals the vulture has the keenest vision. ... It means boundaries, because when a war is about to break out, it limits the place in which the battle will occur, hovering over it for seven days. Foreknowledge, because of what has been said above and because it looks forward to the amount of corpses which the slaughter will provide it for food ...'

There is a germ of truth in this account, in as much as the Egyptian word for 'mother', , *mwt*, is written with the hieroglyph representing a vulture, but the 'explanations', conceived wholly in allegorical terms, are otherwise complete fantasy.

The importance of the *Hieroglyphika*, however, lies not in its content but in the influence that it exerted over the formation and direction of later opinion and research. When, following the Renaissance in Europe, there arose a new curiosity in things Egyptian, the Neoplatonic tradition, embodied in such 'authoritative' ancient sources as Horapollo, encouraged a line of research that was to prove a long blind alley for scholars attempting to elucidate the 'enigmatic' hieroglyphs. A good example of its influence is to be seen in the conclusions reached after years of extensive study by the German polymath Athanasius Kircher (1602–80). A linguist of great ability, Kircher's translations of hieroglyphic texts, based entirely on preconceived notions as to their symbolic functioning, are wholly wide of the mark, to the point of absurdity. One oft-quoted example may suffice. The name of the king Apries written in hieroglyphs was taken by Kircher to mean 'the benefits of the divine Osiris are to be procured by means of sacred ceremonies and of the chain of the Genii, in order that the benefits of the Nile may be obtained'. Despite his mistaken views of the meaning of the hieroglyphs, Kircher, nevertheless, occupies an honourable place in Egyptological history. He was the author of the first Coptic grammar and vocabulary, works that proved to be an enormous stimulus to the development of Coptic studies. Since knowledge of Coptic was to be a vital element in the eventual decipherment of the hieroglyphs, modern Egyptology owes a considerable debt to the pioneering efforts of Kircher in this field.

Though the myth of the secret hieroglyphs was to remain deeply entrenched, the century following Kircher's death saw a generally more cautious approach to their interpretation. While Kircher's translations were wholly rejected, few complete solutions were offered as alternatives. In 1785 the French orientalist C. J. de Guignes (1721–1800), tried to prove the unity of the Egyptian and Chinese scripts, under the false belief that China had been an Egyptian colony. More valuable, and to the point, was his elaboration of an idea first mooted in 1762 by another French scholar, J. J. Barthélemy (1716–95), that the rings or 'cartouches' to be observed frequently in Egyptian texts enclosed royal names. This was the first hint of a breakthrough, but in the state of knowledge then prevailing the means of making further progress were lacking. In due course, following the discovery of the Rosetta Stone, the means became available and the royal cartouche was to prove the very key that unlocked the secrets of the hieroglyphs.

39   The Rosetta Stone was discovered in July, 1799, near the town of Rashid, ancient Rosetta, which is situated in the Delta, on the western arm of the Nile near the sea. It was unearthed, quite fortuitously, by a gang of French soldiers who were part of Napoleon Bonaparte's invading army. Under the command of an officer named Pierre Bouchard, they were digging foundations for a fort and, according to one account, found the monument built into an ancient wall. The 'stone' – a substantial slab of black basalt, 118 cm high, 77 cm wide, 30 cm thick, and weighing 762 kg – is actually a commemorative stela, which was once set up in an Egyptian temple. It is broken and was probably about 50 cm or so higher when intact. Incised on one face, it bears an inscription dated to year 9 of the reign of Ptolemy V Epiphanes, corresponding to 27 March 196 BC, the main part of which is a copy of a decree issued by a general council of Egyptian priests recording the honours bestowed upon the king by the temples of Egypt. The point of crucial importance about the inscription is that it is reproduced in three different scripts: hieroglyphic at the top, demotic in the middle, and Greek at the bottom. None of the sections has escaped damage, the worst affected being the hieroglyphic. The bilingual nature of the text and the potential that this offered, since Greek was a known language, for the decipherment of the Egyptian versions, were immediately apparent to the French *savants* who first examined the stone after its transference to Cairo. To their enormous credit they lost no time in making ink impressions of the inscriptions and in distributing them among the scholars of Europe. After the defeat of Napoleon's army, the stone itself, which had been moved to Alexandria, was ceded to the British in 1801, together with other antiquities, under Article XVI of the Treaty of Alexandria. It was shipped back to Britain in February, 1802, and was deposited for some months at the Society of Antiquaries of London, where a translation of the Greek section was read out in April of that year by the Rev. Stephen Weston and where further reproductions were subsequently made. It was transferred to the British Museum towards the end of 1802, where it remains to the present day.

39 The Rosetta Stone bearing a single text written in three different scripts: hieroglyphic at the top, demotic in the middle, Greek at the bottom. 196 BC. H. 1.18 m. BM 24.

The distribution of the various copies of the stone inaugurated a period of intense study, with scholars competing anxiously and even jealously to be the first to achieve the prize of decipherment. The 'devil of hieroglyphics', as it has been called, was let loose in no uncertain terms. A stream of lectures and publications ensued and new theories and 'solutions' were espoused, most of them hopelessly erroneous and some of them as bizarre as the translations offered by Kircher a century and a half before. In fact the hieroglyphic portion of the stone was to remain intractable for many years more. It was the study of the demotic section, recognised as the 'popular' writing mentioned in ancient Greek sources, that yielded the first positive results.

Already by the end of 1802, before the stone had had time to settle in its new home at the British Museum, two important contributions to the subject had appeared, the first by the French scholar Sylvestre de Sacy (1758–1832), the second by the Swedish diplomat and orientalist, de Sacy's pupil, Johan Åkerblad (1763–1819). The former had decided to concentrate on the demotic section as it was virtually complete, missing only the beginnings of a few lines, whereas the hieroglyphic section was incomplete and was, in any case, a less-promising proposition since 'the hieroglyphic character, being representative of ideas, not sounds, does not belong to the domain of any particular language'. De Sacy's approach to the demotic was eminently sensible. He began with the Greek proper names and attempted to isolate their demotic versions. He believed that this would enable him to identify the values of the demotic letters, which could then be used as stepping stones to further correlations. In practice the process proved to be more difficult than he had anticipated. He met with partial success in isolating the demotic groups for the names of Ptolemy and Alexander, but he found it impossible to identify the values of the individual characters.

Åkerblad, following de Sacy's method, made more substantial progress. He was able to identify in the demotic all the proper names occurring in the Greek, among them, in addition to Ptolemy and Alexander, Arsinoe, Berenice and Aelos. From the sound values thus obtained, he built up a 'demotic alphabet' of twenty-nine letters, almost half of which were actually correct. He then demonstrated that the phonetic signs used to write the names were also used to spell ordinary words, thus providing the first definite indication of the general phonetic character of the demotic script. Among several individual words, apart from names, that he correctly identified are those for 'Greek', 'Egyptian', 'temple', 'love', 'him' and 'his', all of which he was able to correlate with their Coptic equivalents. These were impressive achievements, but, ironically, Åkerblad's very success in establishing the values of so many demotic characters now led him astray. He became convinced that the script was entirely phonetic or 'alphabetic', as he called it. This belief proved an insurmountable barrier to further progress on his part.

After these early successes with the demotic, virtually nothing of value was achieved for another twelve years. Then, at the beginning of 1814, fragments of a papyrus written with 'running Egyptian characters' were submitted for study to the Englishman Thomas Young (1773–1829), a scientist of international distinction and an accomplished linguist. The study of this material aroused his interest in the Rosetta inscriptions and in the summer of that year he began to subject them to the most careful scrutiny. He began, like de Sacy and Åkerblad before, with the demotic or 'epistolographic' as it was also known. Within a few weeks Young had been able to isolate in the demotic most of the graphic groups representing individual words and to relate them to their equivalents in the Greek, but he found it difficult to go further:

> 'You tell me that I shall astonish the world if I make out the inscription. I think it on the contrary astonishing that it should not have been made out already, and that I should find the task so difficult as it appears to be ... by far the greater part of the words I have ascertained with tolerable certainty, and some of the

most interesting without the shadow of a doubt; but I can read very few of them alphabetically, except the proper names which Åkerblad had read before ...'

An important observation was soon to follow, however:

'after having completed this analysis of the hieroglyphic inscription, I observed that the epistolographic characters of the Egyptian inscription, which expressed the words God, Immortal, Vulcan, Priests, Diadem, Thirty, and some others, had a striking resemblance to the corresponding hieroglyphs; and since none of these characters could be reconciled, without inconceivable violence, to the forms of any imaginable alphabet, I could scarcely doubt that they were imitations of the hieroglyphics, adopted as monograms or verbal characters, and mixed with the letters of the alphabet.'

These are the first intimations of two crucially important points: firstly that demotic was not a wholly separate script from hieroglyphic; secondly that the Egyptian system was a mix of different types of character.

In the year or so following, Young spread his researches beyond the Rosetta texts, drawing also on other material, an increasing amount of which was now becoming available. Particularly useful for him were the inscriptions newly published in the volumes of the *Description de l'Égypte* (the scholarly fruits of the Napoleonic expedition) and some unpublished papyri, 'funeral rolls', recently brought from Egypt and placed at his disposal. His eye for significant detail is revealed by his observation that the hieroglyphic group ⌒, which he commonly found attached to what were evidently personal names in the funerary papyri, was in fact a 'female termination', a sound conclusion that was to be of considerable value at a later stage of the decipherment. Even more significantly, by the judicious comparison of parallel texts occurring in the funerary documents, he was able to confirm the relationship of the various Egyptian scripts by tracing the 'degradation from the *sacred* character, through the *hieratic*, into the *epistolographic*, or common running hand of the country'. This conclusion led him on directly to what was to be his single most important contribution to the process of decipherment: the partial subversion of the great myth that the hieroglyphic script was entirely 'symbolic'. Turning back again to the Rosetta texts, he now quickly established the equivalence of many of the demotic and hieroglyphic signs. One of the outcomes of this process was the firm identification of the only personal name that occurs in the hieroglyphic section, that of King Ptolemy. Since the demotic expressed the name phonetically, it was logical to conclude, in Young's view, that the hieroglyphic equivalent did so also.

The name of Ptolemy occurs six times in the hieroglyphic section, three in a short cartouche and three in a longer one:

'Ptolemaios'   'Ptolemaios, may he live for ever beloved of Ptah'

Deducing that the shorter contained the name Ptolemy alone, while the longer contained the name plus title, Young conjectured the phonetic values of the name signs to be as follows:

Hieroglyph	Young Value	Correct Value
□	p	p
⌒	t	t
𓊪𓏏	'not essentially necessary'	o

Hieroglyph	Young Value	Correct Value
	lo or ole	l
	ma or simply m	m
	i	i or y
	osh or os	s

He followed this with a similar analysis of the name of the Ptolemaic queen, Berenice, which he had isolated, somewhat fortuitously, on a copy of an inscription from the temple of Karnak at Thebes:

Hieroglyph	Young Value	Correct Value
	bir	b
	e	r
	n	n
	i	i
	'superfluous'	k
	ke or ken	a
	'feminine termination'	female determinative

These two analyses, with the hieroglyphs treated as phonograms (and four or five of them quite correctly identified), represent an enormous step forward conceptually. The door was now open at last to a real understanding of the largely phonetic nature of the hieroglyphic script. Sadly, at the very threshold, Young's progress came to an abrupt halt. The old myth still exercised a potent influence. Young was convinced that the phonetic principle could only be of limited validity, that the 'hieroglyphic alphabet' was a 'mode of expressing sounds in some particular cases, and not as having been universally employed where sounds were required'. In other words, the hieroglyphs were mostly symbolic; only in special cases, such as in the rendering of foreign names, were they used to represent sounds. Drawing on an analogy from Chinese, he viewed the cartouche surrounding the royal name as a mark denoting that this special process was in operation:

> 'it is extremely interesting to trace some of the steps by which alphabetic writing seems to have arisen out of hieroglyphical; a process which may indeed be in some measure illustrated by the manner in which the modern Chinese express a foreign combination of sounds, the characters being rendered simply 'phonetic' by an appropriate mark, instead of retaining their natural signification; and this mark, in some modern printed books, approaching very near to the ring surrounding the hieroglyphic names.'

The results of Young's researches, of four years' duration in all, were published by him in 1819 in a splendid article entitled 'Egypt' for the *Supplement to the fourth edition of the Encyclopaedia Britannica*. In the years following he continued to work, with intermittent success, on the problems of the hieroglyphs, but he entirely failed to capitalise on his own initial breakthrough. The prize of final decipherment was to fall to another scholar, Young's contemporary and rival, the brilliant young Frenchman, Jean-François Champollion (1790–1832).

40

The latter's route to the decipherment was also via the name of Ptolemy, the identity of

40 *Right* Jean-François Champollion (1790–1832). Portrait by Coignet, 1831. Musée du Louvre, Paris.

41 *Below* A plate from Champollion's *Lettre à M. Dacier*, published in 1822. Listed are the various demotic and hieroglyphic signs which form the Egyptian 'phonetic alphabet' together with their Greek equivalents. At the bottom enclosed in a cartouche is Champollion's name written by him in demotic.

Pl. IV.

Tableau des Signes Phonétiques
des écritures hiéroglyphique et Démotique des anciens Égyptiens

125

which he appears to have determined by a similar process of deduction to that of Young. To what extent, if any, Champollion's initial discoveries were dependent on Young's work has long been a matter of dispute. Champollion's famous paper on the phonetic nature of the hieroglyphs, *Lettre à M. Dacier relative à l'alphabet des hiéroglyphes phonétiques*, appeared in 1822, three years after Young's article 'Egypt'. Whether or not Champollion learned anything from Young, it is beyond dispute that he rapidly overtook him. Young's results, though they pointed in the right direction, were limited and inconclusive. Champollion was the first to *prove*, by systematic analysis of the available evidence, that the hieroglyphic script operated on the phonetic principle, and to build on this effectively. Champollion realised that to make real progress it was necessary somehow to isolate a pair of already known names having several hieroglyphs in common. These would act as an independent check on each other and would provide a firm basis for further identifications. In early 1822, by a happy chance, a copy of another bilingual inscription containing just such a pair of names came into his hands.

In 1819 the English traveller, W. J. Bankes, had transported back from Egypt to his home in Kingston Lacy, Dorset, an obelisk and its base block, which had once stood in the temple of Philae near Aswan. On the base was a Greek inscription mentioning two royal names, Ptolemy and Cleopatra, while on the obelisk itself was a hieroglyphic text including two different cartouches. Bankes inferred from the Greek that the cartouches contained the names of Ptolemy and Cleopatra and noted that the hieroglyphs in one corresponded exactly to those in the cartouche on the Rosetta Stone identified as Ptolemy by Young. In 1821 Bankes had a lithograph made of both the Greek and hieroglyphic texts, copies of which, annotated by Bankes with the suggested identifications of the names, were widely distributed. For Champollion the receipt of one of these copies was, in the words of one commentator, 'the moment which ... turned bewildering investigation into brilliant and continuous decipherment'.

Omitting the epithets accompanying the name of Ptolemy and the signs representing the 'female termination' in the other, the cartouches on the Bankes' obelisk read so:

Ptolemaios   Cleopatra

Champollion identified the values of the individual signs as follows:

□	= p	⊿	= c
◠	= t	(sign)	= l
(sign)	= o	(sign)	= e
(sign)	= l	(sign)	= o
◡	= m	□	= p
(sign)	= e	(bird)	= a
(sign)	= s	◡	= t
		◠	= r
		(bird)	= a

There was an encouraging degree of correspondence between the signs which occurred in both names. Only the ◠ and ◡ did not correlate but for this Champollion had a ready explanation. He deduced correctly that the two signs were actually 'homophones' – separate signs that could represent the same value, here a *t*.

Champollion knew that if these identifications were correct it should be possible to apply the values gained from the names of Ptolemy and Cleopatra to other cartouches and to produce further recognisable names. This he now proceeded to do, beginning with the cartouche:

From the known values the following elements could be identified:

When the range of possible names was considered, it was not difficult to fill the gaps with k, n, and s to yield the name *alksentrs* = Greek Alexandros (Alexander), with ⌀, ᗰ, ⊶ identified as k, n and s respectively, the first and last understood as homophones for ⊿ and ∩. By the extension of this method there quickly followed further identifications, including the name of Queen Berenice (confirming and correcting Young's suggestions) and the names and titles of several Roman emperors:

B N K
| | |
R E A
Berenice

—K
—E
—S
—R
—S
Caesar

A— —W
T— —K
R— —T
—R
Autocrator

It seems that during at least the initial stages of the decipherment Champollion had believed, like Young, that the phonetic system operated only for the expression of foreign names and elements of the Graeco-Roman Period. It was to these that his *Lettre à M. Dacier*, published in late 1822, was largely devoted. At the end of the *Lettre*, however, he announced an entirely new and astonishing discovery: the phonetic system was of wider application and could be extended back into earlier times. The final breakthrough had been achieved.

It appears that in September 1822 Champollion had received copies of various reliefs and inscriptions from Egyptian temples. One of them, from the temple of Abu Simbel in Nubia, contained cartouches enclosing a name repeated in a variety of ways but in its simplest form as ⬭. The last two signs were familiar to him from the cartouches of the Graeco-Roman rulers as bearing the phonetic value s. But what of the first two signs? Champollion had an excellent knowledge of Coptic and here it came fully into play. The first hieroglyph appeared to represent the sun, for which the Coptic word was ⲣⲏ (rē). Supplying this value for the first hieroglyph produced the sequence

$Re + ? + s + s$. There immediately sprung to Champollion's mind the combination $Re + m + s + s$ yielding the well-known name Rameses or Ramesses, identified as a king of the Nineteenth Dynasty in the history (written in Greek) of the Ptolemaic historian, Manetho. By this analysis, the sign 𓏠 should logically be accorded the value m. More evidence was at hand. A second sheet of drawings included the cartouche 𓅱𓏠𓇳. Here again was the group 𓏠𓋴 already conjectured to be $m + s$, in this case preceded by a hieroglyph that Champollion recognised as the picture of an ibis, known to be the symbol of the god Thoth. Surely the name was none other than Thoth-mes, the Tuth-mosis of Manetho's Eighteenth Dynasty. For confirmation of the value of 𓏠 Champollion was able to turn to the Rosetta Stone, where the sign occurs, again in conjunction with 𓏤, as part of a group corresponding to the Greek *genethlia*, 'birth day', which at once suggested to Champollion the Coptic word for 'give birth', ⲙⲓⲥⲉ (mīse). It should be noted that Champollion was actually in error in interpreting 𓄟 as having the value m. It does, in fact, have the value ms, being a biconsonantal sign to which 𓋴 had been added as a phonetic complement. At this stage, understandably, Champollion was unaware of the possibility of multiconsonantal signs. Fortunately the error was not crucial.

Champollion published these and many other subsequent discoveries in his *Précis du système hiéroglyphique* (1824), a work in which he conclusively demonstrated that the phonetic principle, far from being of limited application, was, as he called it, the 'soul' of the entire writing system. For the first time the true relationship between the semo-grams and the phonograms, including the function of the determinative, was revealed. In addition a huge quantity of new data was presented and identified – royal, private and divine names, titles and epithets, as well as ordinary vocabulary. Furthermore there was grammatical analysis and translation of phrases and sentences. Inevitably there were mistakes, but the fundamental approach was absolutely sound. With the appearance of the *Précis*, the ancient myth of the hieroglyphs was finally laid to rest and the science of Egyptology was born.

6
Borrowings

No account of the hieroglyphic script would be complete without some consideration of its contribution to the writing of languages other than Egyptian. The other great writing system of the ancient Near East, cuneiform, was adapted through the course of three millennia to write a large variety of languages. By comparison the Egyptian contribution was small but was not completely insignificant. Some scholars believe that the example of Egyptian hieroglyphs may well have stimulated the development of Cretan and Hittite 'hieroglyphs' in the first half of the second millennium BC. More certainly, in the case of two other scripts – Protosinaitic and Meroïtic – there was the direct borrowing of Egyptian signs.

Protosinaitic

Protosinaitic is a script that was initially noted in various localities in the Sinai peninsula, hence its name. Serious attention was first drawn to it in 1906 by the British archaeologist, Flinders Petrie (1853–1942), following his expedition to Sinai where he explored the sites of the turquoise mines worked anciently by the Egyptians. The most important of these sites, Serabit el-Khadim, bore the remains of a temple dedicated to Hathor, the chief goddess of the Sinai mining area. It was here that Petrie made his most substantial discoveries, including a large number of inscriptions, many dedicated to Hathor, by the personnel of the expeditions. The vast majority were written in Egyptian, but some of the monuments bore texts in a script (there were eleven such texts in all) that contained 'a mixture of Egyptian hieroglyphs ... though not a word of regular Egyptian could be read'. One of these, a sphinx-statuette, is particularly interesting in that it bears texts written both in ordinary Egyptian script and in the Sinaitic script. The Egyptian is inscribed between the paws and on the right shoulder, where it reads 'beloved of Hathor, 42

42 Sandstone sphinx statuette with inscriptions in Egyptian hieroglyphs and in Protosinaitic. Second Intermediate Period. Serabit el-Khadim. L. 23.7 cm. BM 41748.

43 Sphinx statuette, detail. Part of the Protosinaitic inscription on the left side including the group identified as 'Balat'.

mistress of turquoise', the Sinaitic is written on both the right and left sides on the upper surfaces of the pedestal. Petrie was unable to offer any suggestions as to the reading of the script but he did make some perceptive observations. He noted, for example, that in view of the limited number of signs the new script was likely to be alphabetic and that in view of the context it probably represented the Semitic language of the Asiatic workers on the staff of the expeditions. Petrie dated the material to the middle of the Eighteenth Dynasty but in this he was probably wrong. The sculptural style of the sphinx and of some of the other pieces indicates an earlier date, in all likelihood the late Middle Kingdom or Second Intermediate Period.

Table 2   The Sinaitic script appears to consist of at least twenty-three separate signs, the forms of nearly half of which are clearly borrowed from Egyptian. Like the hieroglyphs the signs are arranged either in columns or in horizontal lines but they seem generally to read from left to right. There appears to have been no strict rule as to which direction the individual signs should face, though within a single text the direction is consistent. The first breakthrough in deciphering the system was made in 1916 by the English scholar, A. H. (later Sir Alan) Gardiner (1879–1963). He noticed that a number of the signs depicted objects or things, the Semitic names for which correspond to the names of letters in the later Phoenician/Canaanite alphabet. Gardiner was led to the conclusion that the linear forms of the latter were actually derived from the Sinaitic 'pictograms' and showed that the transition in form from one to the other was in many cases traceable without undue difficulty. Moreover in assigning to the Sinai pictograms the phonetic values of their alphabetic descendants he was able

43   to read the commonly occurring group ⟨⟩ as b'lt, 'Balat'. This makes very good sense in the context, since Balat is the name of a Semitic goddess closely identified with Hathor, whose name, in addition, occurs written in Egyptian hieroglyphs, on the sphinx that is one of the monuments bearing the group in question. Gardiner was unable to make further progress with the material at hand, but the fact that by a process of logical deduction, unforced by prejudice, the Sinai texts had been made to yield perhaps the one name most likely to occur in the area has been regarded as a powerful factor in favour of his interpretation of the script.

Since Gardiner's initial contribution, a great deal of scholarly work has been carried out on Protosinaitic. The stock of available texts has more than trebled and these now include inscriptions from places other than Sinai. Unfortunately the texts are invariably short and often crudely executed. Progress in further understanding has been slow, and has been limited on the whole to small gains in vocabulary. A complete decipherment of the script published in 1966 by the American scholar W. F. Albright (1891–1971) has

Protosinaitic	Egyptian		Protosinaitic	Egyptian	
		(ox)			(water)
		(house)			(snake)
		(throw-stick?)			(eye)
		(fish)		?	
	?			?	
		(man with upraised arms)		?	
		or (mace or oar)		?	
		(door)			(head)
		(twisted flax)			(lotus pool)
		(hand)		?	
		(palm)			(crossed planks)
		(crook?)			

Table 2: Protosinaitic signs and Egyptian prototypes (Protosinaitic forms after Albright).

not received general acceptance. Probably the most important development has been the realisation that the Sinaitic texts are not an isolated group. Inscriptions written in what appear to be basically the same script have been identified in various localities in Palestine. Some are roughly contemporary with the Sinaitic texts, others are later. The corpus as a whole, including the Sinai material, is now referred to by some scholars as Proto-Canaanite.

That the system represents an early stage in the history of the alphabet seems very feasible. Recent studies in the palaeography of the texts have tended to confirm its suggested relationship with the later Canaanite or Phoenician alphabet, though a link is not demonstrable in the case of every individual sign. The system is not strictly 'alphabetic' in the proper sense but is really an 'economical syllabary' in which each sign stands for a consonant + any vowel. In its creation the Egyptian writing system is thought to have been influential, supplying not only the actual sign-forms, or at least some of them, but also providing with its uniconsonantal signs a partial model for just such a restricted signary. If this view is correct (and it is not accepted by all scholars), it has an interesting implication. Since the Canaanite/Phoenician syllabary formed the basis of the Greek alphabet, and the Greek in turn of the Latin, it means, in the words of Gardiner, that 'the hieroglyphs live on, though in transmuted form, within our own alphabet'.

Table 3

Egyptian	Protosinaitic	Phoenician	Early Greek	Greek	Latin
				A	A
				B	B
				Γ	G
				E	E
				k	K
				M	M
				N	N
				O	O
				P	R
				T	T
				Σ	S

Table 3: From hieroglyphic sign to alphabetic letter.

Meroïtic

Meroïtic was the native language of a great African civilisation, known to the Egyptians as the 'Kingdom of Kush', which during the later periods of Egyptian history had its capital at Meroë (modern Begrawiya in the Sudan).

The language was first recorded in writing in the second century BC in an 'alphabetic' script consisting of twenty-three symbols, most of which were borrowed or at least derived from Egyptian writing. The system is quite different from Egyptian. Every sign has a phonetic value, and vowels as well as consonants are represented. There is also a special symbol for marking the division between words. The script has two forms, hieroglyphic and cursive. Hieroglyphic inscriptions are normally written in columns, cursive in horizontal lines reading from right to left. Unlike Egyptian the individual signs read in the direction which the figures face.

Although it looks alphabetic, Meroïtic is in fact a syllabic system. A 'consonantal' sign does not represent a single consonant but a consonant plus the vowel a, except when it is followed by one of the signs i, o and e. The special sign for the vowel a is used only at the beginning of words. There are separate signs for the combinations n + e, s + e, t + e, and t + o. In addition the sign for e has two uses: not only does it represent the vowel e, but it can also denote the lack of a vowel following a consonant.

The corpus of known Meroïtic inscriptions is much larger than that of Protosinaitic but is still relatively small. To date fewer than 1,000 individual texts have been properly

Table 4

Hieroglyphic	Cursive	Value	Hieroglyphic	Cursive	Value
		a			*l*
		e			*ḫ*
		i			*h*
		o			*š (s)*
		y			*se*
		w			*k*
		b			*q*
		p			*t*
		m			*te*
		n			*to*
		ne			*d*
		r			word divider

Table 4: Meroïtic syllabary (after Hintze).

133

documented, though this total is increasing steadily. They have been found throughout the length of the Sudanese and Nubian Nile valley from Philae in the north to Naqa near Khartoum in the south and occur in a wide range of contexts – on temple walls, shrines, altars, offering tables, stelae, statues, pottery vessels, ostraca, papyri, and in the form of rock-graffiti. Inscriptions in the hieroglyphic script are comparatively rare and are largely confined to royal and divine 'prestige' contexts. Cursive is much more common. It was the 'everyday' script and gradually supplanted its ornamental companion. The earliest dated text in Meroïtic is a hieroglyphic temple inscription of Queen Shanakdakhete (*c.* 180–170 BC). There is no evidence for its use, in either form, after the fifth century AD.

The fundamental work on Meroïtic was carried out by the British Egyptologist, Francis Llewellyn Griffith (1862–1934), in the first decade or so of this century. By a detailed comparison of parallel funerary formulae occurring on offering tables and stelae, Griffith was able to determine the size of the Meroïtic syllabary, to prove the correlation between the hieroglyphic and cursive scripts, and to show in which direction the signs were to be read. He then went on to establish the phonetic values of the signs. The key to this achievement was an inscription carved on the base of a sacred boat from the temple of Ban Naqa in the Sudan, now in the Berlin Museum. Included in this inscription are the cartouches of two rulers of Meroë, a king and a queen, Natakemeni and Amanitere, who were dedicators of the monument. The vital point is that the names are written in both Meroïtic and Egyptian hieroglyphs. Since the phonetic values of the Egyptian signs were known, it was possible for Griffith to deduce the values of the Meroïtic equivalents. The values of eight separate signs, over one third of the complete syllabary, were thus more or less correctly established from this one inscription. By cleverly isolating in other Meroïtic texts various well-known names such as those of the gods Osiris and Isis and place names like Philae, Griffith quickly established the values of the remaining signs. The system established by Griffith has since been refined and modified in points of detail, most notably by the German scholar Fritz Hintze, but it is agreed to have been essentially correct.

This success in transliterating the scripts has not, unfortunately, been followed by an equivalent progress in understanding the language which they write. Some words and phrases have been made out with reasonable certainty and some grammatical constructions tentatively identified, but the meaning of the vast majority of inscriptions remains obscure. The task of deciphering the language would be considerably aided if a link between Meroïtic and some other known language could be established. This has yet to be achieved. Meroïtic does not apparently belong to the Afro-Asiatic family and attempts to place it within one of the African groups of languages have hitherto proved inconclusive. It seems likely that really significant progress will have to await the discovery of a bilingual text, another 'Rosetta Stone', written in Meroïtic and some other known language, like Egyptian or Greek.

44 Stand from Ban Naga with inscriptions in Egyptian and Meroïtic hieroglyphs. 0-AD 20. H. 1.18 m. East Berlin, 7261.

Bibliography

Albright, William Foxwell, *The Proto-Sinaitic Inscriptions and their Decipherment*, Harvard/London, 1966

Andrews, Carol, *The Rosetta Stone*, London, 1981

Assmann, Aleida and Jan, and Christof Hardmeier (eds), *Schrift und Gedächtnis. Beiträge zur Archäologie der literarischen Kommunikation*, Munich, 1983

Baines, John, 'Literacy and Ancient Egyptian Society', *Man* 18,' 1983, pp. 572–99

Baines, John R., 'Schreiben' in Wolfgang Helck and Wolfhart Westendorf (eds), *Lexikon der Ägyptologie*, V, Wiesbaden, 1984, cols 693–8

Bynon, James and Theodora (eds), *Hamito-Semitica. Proceedings of a Colloquium held by the Historical Section of the Linguistics Association (Great Britain) at the School of Oriental and African Studies, University of London, on the 18th, 19th and 20th of March 1970*, The Hague, 1975

Callender, John B., *Middle Egyptian*, Malibu, 1975

Caminos, Ricardo, and Henry G. Fischer, *Ancient Egyptian Epigraphy and Palaeography*, New York, 1976

Černý, J., *Paper and books in ancient Egypt*, London, 1952

Davies, Nina M., *Picture Writing in Ancient Egypt*, Oxford, 1958

Faulkner, Raymond O., *A Concise Dictionary of Middle Egyptian*, Oxford, 1962

Fischer, Henry George, *L'écriture et l'art de l'Égypte ancienne. Quatre leçons sur la paléographie et l'épigraphie pharaoniques*, Paris, 1986

Fischer, Henry George, *Egyptian Studies*, II. *The Orientation of Hieroglyphs*, Part 1 *Reversals*, New York, 1977

Fischer, Henry G., 'Hieroglyphen' in Wolfgang Helck and Wolfhart Westendorf (eds), *Lexikon der Ägyptologie*, II, Wiesbaden, 1977, cols 1189–99

Galeries nationales du Grand Palais, *Naissance de l'écriture. Cuneiformes et hiéroglyphes*, exh. cat., Paris, 1982

Gardiner, Alan H., 'The Egyptian Origin of the Semitic Alphabet', *The Journal of Egyptian Archaeology* 3, 1916, pp. 1–16

Gardiner, Sir Alan, *Egyptian Grammar. Being an Introduction to the Study of Hieroglyphs*, 3rd edn (rev.), Oxford, 1957

Gaur, Albertine, *A History of Writing*, London, 1984

Gelb, I. J., *A Study of Writing. A discussion of the general principles governing the use and evolution of writing*, rev. edn, Chicago, 1963

Griffith, F. L., *Meroitic Inscriptions*, Parts I and II, London, 1911 and 1912

Harris, J. R. (ed.), *The Legacy of Egypt*, 2nd edn, Oxford, 1971

Harris, Roy, *The Origin of Writing*, London, 1986

Hawkins, J. D., 'The origin and dissemination of writing in western Asia' in P. R. S. Moorey (ed.), *The Origins of Civilization*, Oxford, 1979, pp. 128–66

Henderson, Leslie, *Orthography and Word Recognition in Reading*, London, 1982

Hintze, Fritz, 'The Meroitic Period' in *Africa in Antiquity The Arts of Ancient Nubia and the Sudan* I. *The Essays*, Brooklyn Museum exh. cat., Brooklyn, 1978, pp. 89–105

Hodge, Carleton T. (ed.), *Afroasiatic. A Survey*, The Hague, 1971

Iversen, Erik, *The Myth of Egypt and its Hieroglyphs in European Tradition*, Copenhagen, 1961

Lewis, Naphtali, *Papyrus in Classical Antiquity*, Oxford, 1974

Lichtheim, M., *Ancient Egyptian Literature*, 3 vols, California, 1973–80

Meltzer, E. S., 'Remarks on ancient Egyptian writing with emphasis on its mnemonic aspects' in Paul A. Kolers, Merald E. Wrolstad and Herman Bouma (eds), *Processing of Visible Language* 2, New York/London, 1980

Millard, A. R., 'The Infancy of the Alphabet', *World Archaeology*, 17, no. 3, 1986, pp. 390–8

Pope, Maurice, *The Story of Decipherment from Egyptian hieroglyphic to Linear B*, London, 1975

Quaegebeur, J., 'De la préhistoire de l'écriture Copte', *Orientalia Lovaniensia Periodica* 13, Leuven, 1982, pp. 125–36

Ray, John D., 'The Emergence of Writing in Egypt', *World Archaeology* 17, no. 3, 1986, pp. 307–16

Sampson, Geoffrey, *Writing Systems. A linguistic introduction*, London, 1985

Schäfer, Heinrich, *Principles of Egyptian Art*, ed., with an epilogue, by Emma Brunner-Traut; trans. and ed., with an introduction, by John Baines, Oxford, 1974

Shinnie, P. L., *Meroe: a civilization of the Sudan*, London, 1967

Schenkel, Wolfgang, 'Schrift' in Wolfgang Helck and Wolfhart Westendorf (eds), *Lexikon der Ägyptologie*, V, Wiesbaden, 1984, cols 713–35

Schenkel, Wolfgang, 'The structure of hieroglyphic script', *Royal Anthropological Institute News*, 15, 1976, pp. 4–7

Williams, R. J., 'Scribal training in ancient Egypt', *Journal of the American Oriental Society* 92, 1972, pp. 214–21

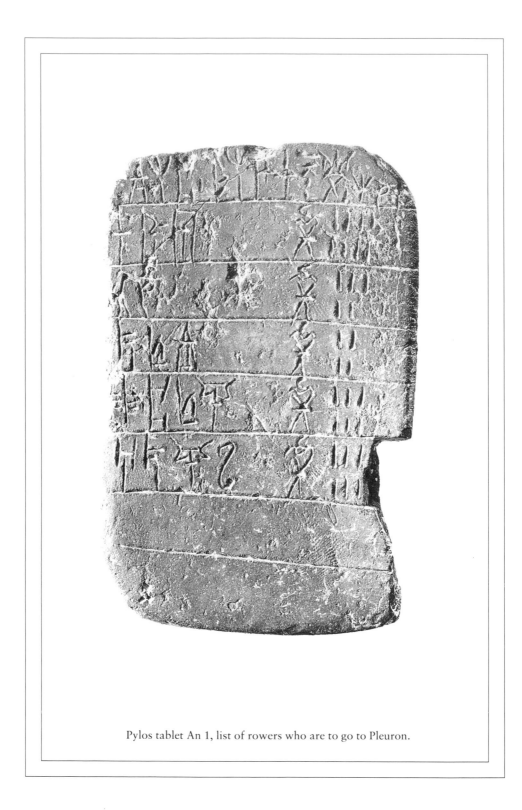

Pylos tablet An 1, list of rowers who are to go to Pleuron.

Linear B
and related scripts

John Chadwick

Acknowledgments

I should like to thank my friend and colleague, Dr J. T. Killen for reading and criticising the text of this section. The views expressed are entirely my own responsibility.

I am indebted for photographs to the Department of Classics of the University of Cincinnati, USA (figs. 2, 5, 17, 23). I should like also to thank the École française d'Archéologie of Athens for fig. 37, and the Cabinet des Médailles, Bibliothèque Nationale of Paris for fig. 35.

The line drawings have been based with their permission on the originals by E. L. Bennett, Jr, J-P. Olivier, L. Godart, E. Masson and O. Masson. I am grateful to all of these for their interest and help. Fig. 22 is reproduced from A. J. Evans, *Scripta Minoa* I, p. 156, Clarendon Press, Oxford, 1909, by permission of the publisher.

Contents

1
The Discovery
of Linear B

The revelation of the Bronze Age in the Aegean area began with the epoch-making discoveries of Heinrich Schliemann at Troy and Mycenae towards the end of the nineteenth century. At that date the science of archaeology had hardly come into existence, and we ought not to blame Schliemann for the irreparable damage that he did to the sites he attacked. At Troy he dug a great cutting through the middle of the hill to expose the earliest layers. But at least he demonstrated that there had been civilisations in the Aegean long before the historical Greeks came on the scene, even though we now know that what he originally identified as Priam's Troy was in fact a thousand years too early for the Trojan War of Greek tradition.

Now that the chronology has been well established, we can confidently assert that the greatest pre-classical civilisation flourished in what is called, after the first of its sites to be excavated, the Mycenaean period. This can be dated roughly between the sixteenth and twelfth centuries BC. It is generally believed that the epics of Homer describe the Aegean world towards the end of that period; but the more facts we learn about it, the more it is evident that Homer's knowledge was incomplete and imperfect. We have moved a long way from Schliemann's faith in the literal truth of Homer.

An English student of archaeology, Arthur Evans (later Sir Arthur), was so impressed by the level of culture these Mycenaeans had achieved on the mainland of Greece, that he formed the opinion that such a civilisation could not have functioned without a knowledge of writing. Yet neither at Troy nor at Mycenae had Schliemann's excavations yielded a single inscription. Whether Evans' opinion was justified may be disputed, but his hunch proved to be right, and it was he who succeeded in finding the proof, though it led to such important new discoveries that he later lost interest in the problem that had started his search.

He noted that dealers in antiquities in Athens sometimes had engraved stones for sale, which had clearly been intended for use as seals. They were unlike any later seals, and were covered with small pictures of objects arranged in such a way that they might be a system of writing. It may be hard in such cases to be sure whether the signs are really writing, or merely a pictorial representation of a name. Heraldic shields, for instance, often have devices which suggest the owner's name. But Evans thought the system on these seal-stones was more like a script, and his researches led him to the conclusion that they had come from the great island of Crete.

At this date Crete was still occupied by the Turks, and successive Greek revolts throughout the nineteenth century were unsuccessful until 1899, when the Turks finally withdrew. Evans had already travelled widely through the island, and had decided where to dig. The site he chose was Knossos, a few miles inland from the principal town of the island, now known as Iraklion. Greek traditions told of a King Minos who had in prehistoric times ruled a sea-empire in the Aegean from Knossos. It seemed therefore a promising site to investigate, and local diggers had already recovered interesting finds from it. When the Turks left, Evans was able to purchase it, and he began digging there in 1900.

1   Knossos tablet Co 907, listing sheep, goats, pigs and cattle

It became clear at once that he had found a major Bronze Age site, and he was rewarded by the discovery of large numbers of inscribed clay tablets. The writing was much more highly-developed than on the seal-stones, and there could be no doubt that this was a true script. But the characters were unlike any script then known, and although Evans started with high hopes of deciphering it, his work came fairly soon to an end, for it was overshadowed by more exciting finds.

Evans had hoped to find a Mycenaean site on Crete to rival Mycenae on the mainland. Sure enough, the huge complex of buildings he unearthed at Knossos must have been a major palace, and it had flourished during the Mycenaean period. But it differed in type from the site at Mycenae, and what was quite unexpected was that it went back much further in time. The king of Knossos was living in some degree of luxury long before the walls of Mycenae were built. In fact, it is now accepted that a high level of civilisation developed in Crete as much as two hundred years before the mainland began to imitate it. It was no longer possible to call this Mycenaean, and Evans coined the new term 'Minoan' to describe the Bronze Age culture of Crete.

Many archaeologists followed Evans to Crete, and important new palaces were excavated at Phaistos in the south and Mallia further to the east along the north coast. Both of these sites and several others, notably Haghia Triada only a few miles from Phaistos, produced small quantities of clay tablets, but these were rather different from the Knossos ones. Evans thought at first this might be due to a special royal script at Knossos, but later it was seen that the differences correlated with the date. The earliest inscriptions were those on the seal-stones, rarely found on clay; Evans named this script 'hieroglyphic' because of a supposed resemblance to the early Egyptian script known by that name, but there is no reason to think that they are related. A little later the pictures of objects become more stylised and thus less recognisable, especially when written on clay. Evans named this script Linear A, because the signs were simple outlines. Few examples of this were found at Knossos, for there the bulk of the inscriptions were in a later version of this script, which he called Linear B. This was restricted to the latest phase of the Palace, which we can now date as from about 1450–1375 BC.

The clay tablets had not been baked when they were made, but only dried in the sun, so that they survived only if they happened to be in a building which had been burnt. Thus tablets were only found in destruction layers, and must date to the very end of the period of the building's use. Unfortunately, at Knossos there has been since Evans' time a long argument over the date of the final destruction, and although most scholars accept a date somewhere around 1375 BC, it has been seriously proposed that a date in the thirteenth century would be possible. There is nothing in the documents to settle the argument, but on the whole a fourteenth century date still seems more likely.

Evans studied his Linear B tablets and drew some obvious conclusions. But although he prepared an edition of all the hieroglyphic material then known, his preparations for an edition of the Linear B tablets were still incomplete when the outbreak of the Balkan Wars, and then the First World War, diverted his attention to other matters. After the war he produced his vast work on the palace at Knossos, which he confidently named the Palace of Minos. This contained a section on the tablets, and a number of them were illustrated, but the vast bulk of the documents still remained unpublished and hence inaccessible to scholars. It was not until 1952, eleven years after Evans' death, that an old friend and colleague, Sir John Myres, finally published the volume that Evans had planned and largely compiled around 1911–12.

It was unfortunate in many ways that it had been so long delayed. Earlier publication would have made a great deal of information available, so that serious work on the decipherment could have 'started much earlier; even those who succeeded in seeing material in Iraklion Museum were inhibited by the rule that no one may anticipate in print the finder's first publication of his finds. When it became possible for scholars to work on the originals, it was quickly discovered that the edition had been imperfect and incomplete. Three separate collections of fragments of tablets recovered in Evans' excavations have since come to light in

Iraklion Museum, but none of these appear in the 1952 publication. Their study at once revealed that no serious effort had been made to join the fragments, and so to reconstruct complete, or more nearly complete, tablets. This task has fallen to a devoted band of scholars of several different nationalities, who have worked together as a team to reconstitute the tablets and publish a complete and trustworthy text.

But as early as 1939 a major new discovery had totally changed the situation as regards Linear B. In that year a joint American–Greek expedition under Carl W. Blegen of the University of Cincinnati had begun to excavate a site in the south–west of the Greek mainland. It lies a little to the north of the modern town of Pylos, just inland from the Bay of Navarino, one of the finest natural harbours in the Mediterranean. It proved to be a Mycenaean palace destroyed by fire at the end of the thirteenth century BC. By a stroke of luck the first trench laid out by the excavators ran across what we now know as the Archive Room, since it contained hundreds of clay tablets, hardened by the fire which destroyed it. As soon as the first pieces were lifted from the ground, they could be identified as written in the same Linear B script already well known from Knossos.

This news did not perhaps create the sensation it should have done. The world had more serious matters on its mind in 1939–40 than Bronze Age writing. For the

2   Pylos tablet Tn 996, showing numbers of bath-tubs and other vessels, some of bronze, some gold

first time Linear B was seen to be not restricted to Knossos, or even to Crete, but to be in use on the mainland, for such an archive is hardly likely to have been transported from where it was written. Yet if it were simply, as Evans asserted, a modified version of Linear A, a purely Cretan script, did this mean that the Cretan language too was used on the Greek mainland? Was this the proof Evans had sought to show that all southern Greece had once been under Minoan control?

The difficulty was that most scholars at this time believed that the Mycenaeans known to archaeology were the Achaeans described by Homer as masters of Greece at the time of the Trojan War. Of course poets, like novelists, are liable to make their characters speak their own language; but the fact that most of Homer's characters have names which are significant in Greek implied that Greek was already spoken in Greece in the Mycenaean age, if Homer's stories were not pure fiction. So what was the king of Mycenaean Pylos, Nestor, if we can trust Homer, doing keeping his accounts in a foreign language?

An easy answer to this question is provided by the parallel of the Middle Ages, when kings all over Europe kept their records in Latin, whatever language they spoke themselves. However, further discoveries from other sites on the mainland have now totally altered the picture. Linear B is now seen to be the script of the Mycenaean palaces on the mainland, and it is its intrusion into Crete which is the feature which demands explanation. The solution to the problem came in 1952–3, with the demonstration that the language of the Linear B tablets was Greek. Evans would have been profoundly shocked to learn that his Minoan palace in the last phase of its existence had used the Greek language. This story will form the subject of the next chapter, but we need first to complete the account of discovery.

Even before Linear B tablets had been found on the mainland, it was known that large pottery jars with painted inscriptions in this script had been found on the mainland. The largest collection is from Thebes, to the north-west of Athens, but other contemporary sites have provided specimens. These jars were often used for the transport of olive oil and wine, and it was suggested that these were containers for Cretan produce. This suggestion has now been confirmed in a remarkable way. It was noticed that some of the words on the jars were also found on the Knossos Linear B tablets, where they appeared to be place names; and it would be natural for the exporter to record his name and address on his product. But much more recently an analysis of the clay used to make these jars has revealed that they almost certainly come from Crete.

Small numbers of clay tablets have been found at Mycenae itself, the first significant find being made by the British archaeologist A. J. B. Wace in 1952. He dug some large houses outside the Citadel Walls, and found in them collections of Linear B tablets. This does not prove that Linear B was in widespread use throughout the population, for such houses must have been occupied by members of the royal establishment. Some more, rather badly damaged tablets, have come from a house within the walls, but there is no trace of the main palace archive. Since the palace is at the top of the hill, its site has long been exposed to the weather, and its archives are likely to have perished. But it is a sobering thought that if Schliemann had known what to look for, he might have been the first to find Linear B tablets. As they come out of the ground, it is only too easy to dismiss fragments of tablets as pieces of coarse pottery, which the early excavators threw away without a thought.

At Tiryns, only a few miles away from Mycenae, stood a huge castle with massive walls. It may have been intended to guard the port, but the sea has now retreated from the site. It would be incredible if this were, as Homer implies, the seat of an independent kingdom. It must have been in some sense under the control of the king of Mycenae, who may have been an overlord having the allegiance of several lesser rulers. From 1971 onwards excavations in the lower town outside the castle walls have revealed a number of fragmentary Linear B tablets. It looks as if these have come down from their original position higher up, and all we can say at the moment is that somewhere on this site there must have been a major archive, but only fragments of it have been recovered.

The situation at Thebes is rather different. The problem here is that the same site has been continuously occupied for at least four thousand years, and it is now a thriving provincial town. This has been built over successive layers of occupation, Turkish, Frankish, Byzantine, Roman, Hellenistic, Classical, Archaic, Mycenaean and even earlier. It is rarely possible here to find a place to excavate, and only when it is necessary to put up a new building are the archaeologists able to investigate what lies beneath the ground. Rescue digs of this kind have so far yielded two small collections of Linear B tablets, and a group of clay sealings, small lumps of clay stamped with a seal and then in some cases inscribed with a few words in Linear B. This evidence makes it almost certain that somewhere below the centre of the modern town lies an archive of tablets. Thebes was clearly the site of a palace which controlled a large kingdom in this part of Greece, and its records would be very important, if we could only find them. But for the moment we can say very little about this kingdom.

The finds show that writing was not in widespread use in Mycenaean Greece. No tablets have been found at minor sites, and all those where they have been found are either palaces or so close to palaces that they can be regarded as dependencies. There is no trace of any private use of writing. This contrasts with the history of the Greek alphabet, which as early as the eighth century BC was used by private citizens to write light-hearted verses on a cup; and during the next two centuries began to be used for laws inscribed on stone in places where all could read them. Nothing of the kind has ever been found in Linear B. Writing seems to have been exclusively a bureaucratic tool, a necessary method of keeping administrative accounts and documents, but never used for historical or even frivolous purposes. As we shall see, the contents of Linear B tablets are almost without exception lists of people, animals, agricultural produce and manufactured objects. But first we must see how it became possible to read a script which had been forgotten for more than three thousand years.

2

The Decipherment

The first step in trying to decipher an unknown script is the analysis of the texts. We need to know what sort of a script it is, and what can be deduced about the contents of the inscriptions. All scripts can be classified as one of three types: *a*) phonetic, *b*) ideographic, *c*) mixed. Phonetic scripts represent by their signs the sounds of the language. They do not of course give a detailed picture of those sounds; for one thing, it would be confusing if every speaker wrote exactly as he spoke, for then the same utterance would be recorded in many different ways. There is therefore a conventional element in scripts which eliminates most of the individual differences between speakers. Secondly, to represent even roughly the range of sounds employed would demand a much larger alphabet that the twenty-six letters we use in English; many languages employ diacritical marks on letters to indicate special values, but even so all phonetic scripts are only a notation adequate to permit someone who knows the language to reconstruct the word for himself. The segments into which the stream of speech is analysed for notation may vary in size. Alphabetic scripts aim at the ideal of one sign for each sound, though English, for example, often departs from this ideal. Other languages in the past have used syllabic scripts, where each sign represents a pronounceable syllable. These may vary from the simple type where each sign denotes a consonant followed by a vowel, to more complex types where there are signs for vowels followed by consonants, and for groups of consonant, vowel and consonant, and so on.

Ideographic scripts have basically one sign for each word, and this sign usually represents the meaning of the word, not primarily its phonetic form. They can therefore be easily transferred from one language to another. So the Japanese borrowed the Chinese ideographic script, and wrote the same signs for the same meanings, but gave them quite different sounds. The problem with ideographic scripts is that they need enormous numbers of signs, which have to be very complex in order to be different, and are therefore hard to learn and to write. However, the advantage for the decipherer is that they are easily recognisable by the large number of different signs and their complexity. Ideograms usually begin as pictures of objects, and they may despite development still remain recognisable, but they may also evolve to unrecognisable patterns, the meaning of which is simply conventional. A familiar set of ideograms, the numerals *1, 2, 3, 4, 5,* can be read in English as *one, two, three, four, five,* but the same signs may be used in other languages with quite different phonetic values, although their meaning remains the same.

Mixed systems are not uncommon, that is, ones where some signs are ideographic and some phonetic. When we read *1st* as *first,* and *3rd* as *third,* we are using ideograms with a phonetic complement. This serves to prevent us giving the wrong sound to the ideogram, and in some languages allows us to indicate inflected forms. Examples of mixed scripts are Hittite (a cuneiform script) in antiquity, and in modern times, Japanese.

This explanation is essential in order to understand how Linear B was deciphered. It was immediately obvious that there was a simple numeral system; virtually all tablets record numerals, and there are examples of addition to verify the system. There are signs for units (short upright bars), tens (horizontal bars), hundreds (circles) and thousands (circles with rays). Each sign can be repeated up to nine times. Thus the number 1357 would be written:

With this clue it is then possible to identify certain signs which occur only in isolation before numerals. Many of these are obvious pictures, or 'pictograms' as they are called:

𐀂	MAN	𐀁	WOMAN	𐂇	HORSE	𐃇	CHARIOT
𐂐	WHEEL	𐂌	JAR	𐂟	BATH	𐂝	CUP

But many others bear only a distant relationship to the pictures that must underlie them, and at this stage these are therefore still unidentified. Even so it is clear that some of these were animals:

There is also a special set of signs which occur before numerals and sometimes following an ideogram. The analysis of a Knossos tablet will illustrate this.

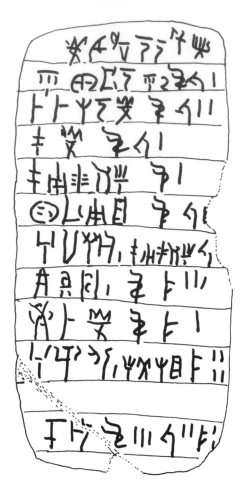

3   Knossos tablet Fp1

Now if we call ⸙ *A* and the signs ⸲ and ⸳ *x* and *y* respectively, we can tabulate the entries thus:

A	x	y
0	1	–
0	2	–
0	1	–
1	–	–
0	1?	–
0	1?	–
0	0	3
0	0	1
0	0	4
3	2	2

The last line is a much higher figure than any of the preceding ones, and this would be explained if it were a total. But since this is a sum like our old-fashioned pounds, shillings and pence, we need to know the relationship between the three columns to check this, because it will be necessary to carry over the appropriate figure from one column to that to the left of it. If we add up the figures in the right-hand column, they come to 8; but the total in the last line is only 2. It follows therefore that $x = 6y$ or $3y$, either of which would give the remainder 2, if divided into 8. But since one entry has the figure $4y$, if $x = 3y$, this would have been written $1x\ 1y$. Therefore $x = 6y$, and 1 must be added to the middle column.

The figures in the middle column add up to 6, to which must be added the 1 carried over from the y column. But two of the figures are shown as 1?, because either or both of these could be read as 2. However, when the total of x is reduced to A units, there is again a remainder of 2, as shown by the total. Since only $1A$ is recorded in the left-hand column, 2 must be carried over from the x column to make the total $3A$. It follows that the total of x units, before being reduced to the higher unit A, must be an even number, if when divided by twice the value of x it leaves a remainder of 2. Therefore only one of the doubtful figures must be restored as 2, and the other is 1. Thus the real total for the x column will be 8, and therefore $A = 3x = 18y$. By such means we can establish that the word � � (and elsewhere � �) is used to introduce a total, and must have an appropriate meaning.

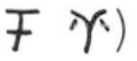

Inspection of other tablets shows that x and y are fractions of other ideograms too, and thus we can can deduce that they are units of a system of measurement, like hundredweights, quarters, pounds and ounces, or bushels, gallons, quarts and pints. Thus the numerals lead directly to the identification of three series of metric signs: one, since its highest unit is a pictogram of a pair of scales, is clearly weights; the other two share the two lowest units, so they presumably represent volume, one for dry and the other for liquid measure.

By such deductions it is easy to see that the tablets are for the most part lists of men and women, livestock, agricultural produce and manufactured objects. Without any knowledge of the language, we can still give a useful account of the subject matter of the records. As we shall see later, this is also the situation as regards the earlier, Linear A, script.

The real problem concerns the remaining signs, which constitute the bulk of the text. The first question to ask is: how many are there? This is not so easy to answer as might be thought. The scribes did not write a 'copy-book' hand, but showed a great deal of individual variation. One sign appears as:

These are fairly obviously variants of one sign. But another, rather similar sign, appears as:

⊡   ⊙   ⊜

Is the number of strokes inside the circle significant, or are they all simply variants? Is it the same as the previous sign? The answers to these questions depend partly on judgment, but a hunch can often be confirmed if two forms behave alike and replace each other in the same sign group. Simple as this sounds, it does of course depend upon having a large body of material to work on. Statistical methods cannot be used when there are very few examples of a particular sign. For fifty years after the first discovery of Linear B, very few people had access to enough material to make this kind of work practicable. Evans produced some lists of signs based upon the Knossos tablets; but it was impossible to check his work, and when the fuller evidence was published in 1952, the job had already been done for the Pylos tablets by an American, Emmett L. Bennett. His signary still stands today, with minor modifications, as the definitive list of signs. But there are still a very few signs whose status is unclear. For instance, Bennett quite properly listed as separate signs 𝄢 and 𝄡, although this would be the only case in the script in which the distinction between two signs depended on one being the mirror image of the other. Subsequently it has become clear that these were really variants of one sign, since new material has shown that one replaced the other in the same sign-group. Bennett in his table listed 87 signs, and even with corrections it is safe to say the total number in use was no more than 90.

Once the signary was established, it became possible to count the signs and list their frequencies. It is highly convenient for the decipherer that the Mycenaean scribes divided their signs into groups by using a short upright bar placed just above the line, thus:

𝉣𝉤 𝉥𝉦𝉧𝉨. ⊕𝉩𝉪𝉫 𝉬𝉭 𝉮𝉯𝉰. 𝉱𝉲𝉳

The groups so divided off range from two to eight signs. Contrast this with the habit of Greek alphabetic inscriptions, which usually string the words together in a continuous sequence.

The direction of the writing is obvious, since most lines begin at the left-hand edge of the tablet and unfilled spaces are left at the right-hand edge. This left-to-right direction is uniform throughout Linear B. Tablets with several lines of writing usually have them separated by transverse lines running the full width of the tablet. It is tempting to call them rules, but they are in fact drawn by hand, before the text was written. Elongated tablets often have the first word of the text in large signs, and after this there is a division into two lines. In places a word, or even a complete line of writing, is added over the text; this is either an annotation, or may be a continuation of the main text for which there was not enough room.

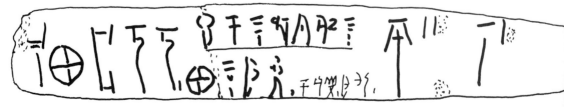

4 Pylos tablet Eo 269, showing division into two lines

The tablets are generally speaking small enough to be held in one hand, while being written on by the other; they sometimes have the marks of fingers on the reverse. The largest tablet so far known is about six inches across, ten-and-a-half inches high, and about an inch thick, but the majority are very much smaller.

Thus it is possible to produce frequency lists of signs, showing not only their overall frequency, but also in initial, medial and final positions. It will often appear that a sign has a particular liking for one position in sign-groups. At this stage it is useful to compile an index of sign-groups, not merely to find repetitions of groups, but also to discover groups which begin alike but have different endings. Likewise a reverse index, that is to say, one in which the groups are arranged in the order of their signs working from the end of the word, is useful to find groups that have the same ending.

All of this work was performed for Linear B by the small number of people who had access to sufficient texts, but it did not at first lead to any significant advances. The most important step, seen with hindsight, was the discovery by the American scholar Alice Kober of a number of sign-groups at Knossos which occurred in three different forms, which she thought must represent some sort of inflexional endings.

The decipherment proper was the work of a British amateur named Michael Ventris. He had been fascinated by the mystery of Linear B since he was a schoolboy, and when he had qualified as an architect, he continued to devote much of his spare time to this hobby. In the autumn of 1951 the publication of the first batch of Pylos tablets, those found in 1939, gave him for the first time an adequate supply of material. He had already analysed the script and concluded that in view of the size of the signary it was likely to be a relatively simple syllabic system. He also understood the ideographic system, as outlined above.

If the language of the inscriptions had been known, it should not have proved too difficult to find values which would give appropriate words. However, as explained above, Linear B was seen as a Cretan script, which had unexpectedly appeared on the mainland of Greece in a Mycenaean palace. Evans had been in no doubt that his 'Minoan' Cretans were not Greek-speakers, and it could be held that the Pylos tablets supported his belief that the Minoans had for a time controlled southern Greece, as they certainly did the islands of the Aegean. Other scholars were less certain, for Homer gives what is acknowledged to be a picture of the Mycenaean age, however much the details are garbled. All his characters speak Greek, whether they are on the Greek or Trojan side; and many have names which are significant in Greek, and this too is true of the Trojans. But this could be simply a literary convention, and it is unsafe to deduce from Homer's poems that the Mycenaean inhabitants of Greece were Greek-speaking, though this certainly appeared for other reasons too to be probable. The upshot was that it was clearly impossible to predict the language of Linear B, and Greek would have been regarded as an outsider if this had been a betting matter.

There was however another valuable clue. At the easternmost fringe of the early Greek world lay the island of Cyprus, which was largely Greek-speaking in classical times, though early inscriptions in other languages showed that it had not always been wholly Greek. Down to about the third century BC the Greeks of Cyprus had not used the alphabet, but a peculiar script of their own. This had been deciphered in the 1870s, since it was assumed to be Greek, and few short inscriptions were known in which the same text was given both in the later Greek alphabet and in the native script. Fuller details will be given in chapter 6, but it was important that here was a simple syllabic script used for writing Greek. Even more interesting was the fact that a few of the simple signs were identical with or very similar to signs in Linear B. Evans had already noticed that a Knossos tablet listing horses contained the word 𐊾𐊾 and that 𐊾𐊾 in the Cypriot script would read *po-lo*. Now *pōlos* is the Greek word for 'foal'. Evans dismissed this as a coincidence, and in principle he was right to do so. For one thing the word is very short; a coincidence involving a longer word would be less easy to dismiss. To prove that Linear B was Greek would require a number of such coincidences, where the meaning of the word could already be deduced from the context. Evans was of course in any case irrevocably prejudiced against the Greek solution.

Ventris started by deliberately ignoring the Cypriot clue as the point of departure. Observing that the formula for 'total' varied between 𐊾𐊾 and 𐊾𐊾, he argued that in an inflected language this might correspond to a difference of gender, since one form appears with the ideogram for 'man', the other with the ideogram for 'woman'. If the gender difference was expressed by a change in the vowel of the termination, then 𐊾 and 𐊾 probably differed in their vowels, but had the same consonant. Detailed analysis of a number of such pairs of words enabled Ventris to build a 'grid', a table in which the signs sharing the same consonant were arranged in horizontal lines, and those sharing the same vowel in vertical columns. Once this stage had been reached for a fair number of signs, it was only necessary to obtain values for a few of the signs and it would become possible to read off the values of the rest.

At this point the Cypriot clue afforded some help, but the key discovery concerned the groups noticed by Alice Kober. Ventris, seeing that they did not occur on the Pylos tablets, deduced that they might be the names of Cretan towns, with their adjectival variants; and since the names familiar from classical Crete are not of Greek origin, it was not unreasonable to suppose that they came from the earlier language of Crete. He was quickly able to suggest that *ko-no-so* was a spelling for what in Greek is *Knōsos*, *a-mi-ni-so* was the name of its port, *Amnisos*, and a few other well-known names were identified. Up to this point the decipherment was still not linked to any language. But application of the values so obtained from the 'grid' to other words revealed that, for instance, the totalling formula would read *to-so* and *to-sa*, which bore a striking resemblance to the Greek word meaning 'so much' or 'so many', *tosos*, feminine *tosā*. A few other words also appeared which recalled Greek words of appropriate meaning.

Ventris therefore set out to test the hypothesis that the language was Greek, not expecting it to lead anywhere. But as he applied his values to more and more words,

Greek words kept on appearing, but their spelling was nearly always incomplete, and the written skeleton needed to be filled out before it became intelligible as a Greek word. Even so, the form of the word was sometimes unfamiliar, as might be expected in a form of Greek far older than our earliest text, the poems of Homer.

For example, there were tablets from Pylos listing numbers of women, clearly recognisable from the ideogram, together with numbers of two other items written in the syllabic script. It was a fair assumption that these were the words for 'children', or more precisely 'girls' and 'boys'. Homeric Greek has for these the words *kourai* and *kouroi*, but the Linear B spellings emerged as *ko-wa* and *ko-wo*.

5   Pylos tablet Aa 62, showing women and children

Only a knowledge of the etymology and early history of Greek could show that the original form of these words had been *korwai* and *korwoi*. The letter pronounced *w* had been lost from Homeric Greek, though it was still heard in a few dialects. But it was necessary to set up rules stating that *r* might be omitted before *w*, and that diphthongs might have their second element dropped, so that the ending might be read as -*ai* and -*oi*.

It was at this point that Ventris formed an alliance with John Chadwick, a lecturer in Classics at Cambridge University, whose special interest was the early history of the Greek language. Together they worked out the rules governing the spelling, which will be discussed more fully in the next chapter; they were able to show that in many cases the archaic form of the words they reconstructed was supported by what was already known about the language.

The increasing number of Greek words which appeared in promising contexts soon provided good evidence for the correctness of the decipherment. For instance, previous decipherments had sometimes yielded weird names, which their authors claimed as gods and goddesses; the Ventris decipherment applied to a Knossos tablet yielded no less than four divine names well known from Greek literature. But it was necessary to present these results in a scientific manner, so that any scholar with the skill and patience to apply the solution could see for himself the match between the interpreted forms and their contexts. Even where the context was itself obscure, the interpretation often produced a plausible sequence of Greek words.

All this was demonstrated in an article entitled 'Evidence for Greek dialect in the Mycenaean archives', written jointly by Ventris and Chadwick and published in *The Journal of Hellenic Studies* for 1953. The theory was so unexpected, and its testing demanded so much technical and archaeological knowledge, that its reception was at first mixed. But powerful support soon came from distinguished Greek scholars, and others began to contribute to the elucidation of the texts.

But the main reason why the decipherment carried conviction was an unforeseen event. In the summer of 1952, almost precisely at the critical period when Ventris was getting the first hint of Greek words, the American excavators of Pylos, whose work had been interrupted in 1939 by the outbreak of the Second World War, at last resumed digging. More Linear B tablets were quickly found, but as they came out of the ground they could not easily be read, and they were carefully stored for cleaning and consolidation during the ensuing winter. In the spring of 1953 the leader of the American team, Carl Blegen, returned to Greece to work on his finds. He had been supplied with an advance copy of the article reporting the decipherment, which was still being printed. Studying his new tablets Blegen quickly noticed a large one which bore pictures of three-legged cauldrons. He applied the values given to the accompanying signs, and was astonished to read *ti-ri-po-de*, almost exactly the Greek word *tripodes*, which of course means 'tripods' and is used of cauldrons of this type.

Even more remarkable was a series of vessels pictured on the same tablet with different numbers of loops at the top, clearly indicating the number of handles. Here the text revealed a word which read *qe-to-ro-we* accompanying the vessels with four handles, and one reading *ti-ri-o-we-e* or *ti-ri-jo-we* with those with three handles. Obviously the second word began again with *tri-*, the Greek form for the number 'three' in compounds; and those who knew about the history of the language could accept that *quetro-* was a possible form in very early Greek for 'four'. The classical form corresponding to this would be *tetra-*. There was even a pictogram of a vessel without handles; here the text read *a-no-we*, and Greek regularly has *an-* as a negative prefix. The second part of these words is related to the word for 'ear', which is also used in Greek to mean 'handle'.

As soon as the 'tripod' tablet became known, most scholars accepted the validity of the decipherment. The odds against a coincidence of this sort would be astronomical. In other tablets too, new examples were found of ideograms

6   Pylos tablet Ta 641, showing tripod-cauldrons

corresponding to the syllabic text. The Knossos tablet listing horses has already been mentioned; a new fragment joined to this gave the Greek words for 'horses' in one line and 'asses' in the other. Added to the word for 'foals' already suggested, but rejected, by Evans, this made three words on one tablet in close agreement with the evident subject.

This did not mean that all was now plain sailing. A number of the rarer signs remained to be solved, and there are still a few left in this class. Some signs appeared to have an optional function, and the limits within which they could be used had to be determined. The nature of the spelling rules had to be elucidated, and the new dialect revealed had to be studied. The vocabulary proved, not surprisingly, to differ from that current a thousand years later, and only gradually has it become possible to suggest meanings for some of the new words.

Some of the early difficulties turned out to be due to wrong readings of the originals, and a great deal of effort has gone into their study. As a result we have much better texts now than were available to the decipherers. In particular, the joining of fragments in the material from Knossos has revealed many new facts. It is pleasant to record that all this work has been performed by the co operation of scholars all over the world.

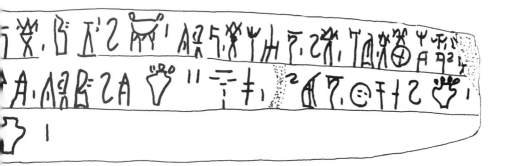

3
How the Linear B
Script was used

The Linear B script is now fairly well known and understood, though there are still many unsolved problems. It consists of three elements: syllabic signs, ideograms and numerals. The syllabic signs are used to spell out the phonetic shape of the word. The ideograms were not used as a means of writing a word, but merely as symbols to indicate what the numerals were counting. This means that ideograms are normally found only before numerals. In some cases the word describing the object being counted is first spelled out syllabically, and then the relevant ideogram is written before the numeral. The metric signs form a special class of ideograms, and these often occur after an ideogram specifying the commodity which is being measured.

As now known in the light of the decipherment, the Linear B syllabary consists of 87 signs. These may be divided into three classes, shown in the following tables.

The first of these (fig. 7) is the basic syllabary, which consists of signs for the five vowels, and signs for each of the twelve consonants combined with each of these vowels. Gaps in the table may indicate that there never existed a sign for that value, but one or two may be absent because they are still unidentified.

The forms shown are merely typical specimens, and there are a number of variant forms in use. Since we are dealing with handwriting, it is impossible to illustrate here all the varieties that may be encountered. There are some differences to be observed between the forms used at Knossos and on the mainland; but generally speaking the range of variation found at one site is as great as between different sites.

There is also a supplementary group of signs (fig. 8), which are in some sense optional. They are not strictly necessary, but may be employed to give a more accurate spelling and so reduce the risk of misinterpretation; or they may serve as abbreviations, allowing one sign to do the work of two. Their use will be explained further below. Some of the values are marked as uncertain; this is because we do not yet have enough examples in recognisable words for the value to be regarded as certainly determined. It is probable that the unidentified signs (fig. 9) belong mainly to this optional class.

The values shown must not be taken as a strict representation of the sounds; they are merely conventional notations, and interpretation is needed to reconstruct from them the spoken form. All scripts are in some sense merely an outline notation which the reader has to fill in for himself, and there are words in English which we need to recognise before we can read them correctly. But the Linear B spelling is far more incomplete, and the Mycenaean reader must have been left with a lot of guesswork in order to make intelligible words out of what he read on the tablet. This would be quite intolerable if the script were used as we understand writing; it would be very difficult to use it for letters or histories. But in fact, with one exception, it seems to have been used solely for writing lists and accounts; and these too were hardly intended to be read by anyone but the writer and his colleagues working in the same office. The one exception is the inscribed jars, which seem to record the name, and sometimes other details, of the producer of the contents. In these circumstances a much more abbreviated script may be acceptable. But for us, trying to read these texts more than three thousand years later, with no knowledge of the affairs of the office where they were written, the difficulties are immense, and it is no wonder if we have still many unsolved problems.

The following is a brief outline of how the syllabary is used to write words in this early dialect of Greek; but it is not possible here to go into much detail. All the vowels may be treated as either short or long; there is no separate notation, as in the later Greek alphabet, for long *e* and *o*. Initial *h-* is not usually written, but there is no reason to think that it was not pronounced. A vowel may be ignored when two, or even three, signs are written to represent a syllable containing a cluster of consonants, as *ti-ri-* for *tri-*. The letters *j* and *w* stand for the semivowels, the sounds we write in English as consonantal *y* and *w*. The *y* sound is generally absent from the later Greek language, though it may have been heard as a glide between the vowel *i* and an immediately following vowel. The signs *ja, je, jo, ju* are used in this way when another vowel follows an *i*. But they have a second use, to indicate that the preceding vowel is to be read as forming part of a diphthong in *-i*; so the ending *-o-jo* is to be read as answering to the Homeric *-oio*. The letter *w* stands for another sound which disappeared from later Greek, though early inscriptions of some dialects write it with a letter F, which survived by a remarkable series of changes to become the Roman letter we still know as *f*. The *w* sound was frequently to be found in the Mycenaean dialect of Greek. The letter *r* is a convention standing for either *r* or *l*.

The transcription *ka, ke, ki, ko, ku* is really a shorthand for any velar stop followed by these vowels. Greek has three velar stops, *k, kh* and *g* (written K, X and Γ in the later Greek alphabet), and the reader had to choose for himself which value to give the sign in any word. Likewise *pa, pe, pi*, etc. can stand for *p, ph* or *b*. But the series *ta, te, ti*, etc. stands only for *t-* or *th-*, and there is a separate series *da, de, di*, etc. for *d-*. The letter *q-* in transcription must be understood as *kw* (much like *qu-* in English *queen*), *khw* (the same with aspiration) and *gw* (as in *Gwen*). All of these sounds were lost before the classical period, when they were replaced according to

7   The basic Linear B syllabary

8   The optional signs of Linear B

9   The unidentified signs of Linear B

context by *t* or *p*, *th* or *ph*, and *d* or *b*. Almost all classical words containing *b* come from an earlier *gw*, and it was facts like this which made the decipherment convincing to those acquainted with the history of the language. Difficult as it is for us, the system was no doubt clear enough to Mycenaean scribes; after all, we have no difficulty in giving six different values to the spelling *-ough* in different words *(though, through, thought, borough, tough, cough)*.

Greek has only three consonants which can stand at the end of a word: *-n*, *-r* and *-s*. The use of final *-k* was restricted to certain special contexts, and probably did not occur in Mycenaean Greek. It was therefore possible to adopt the rule that final consonants should be omitted in writing. The same licence was extended to these sounds when they occurred in the middle of a word immediately followed by another consonant, and the same applied to the similar sounds *l* and *m* when they occurred in the same position. Double consonants are not indicated by the script, but they doubtless existed in speech. Other clusters of consonants have to be written by inserting extra vowels, which were not pronounced. The vowel *-i* as the second part of a diphthong *(ai, ei, oi, ui)* might be omitted, though it could optionally be inserted using the sign for *i*, or before another vowel by using the signs *ja, je, jo, ju*.

A few examples will show better how these rules work. These are isolated words, not a coherent text. The first line below gives the spelling as it occurs in the Linear B script. The second line gives the conventional transcription into syllables, separated by hyphens. The third line gives the phonetic form as we think it should be reconstructed from the syllables; letters in brackets have to be supplied by the reader. The fourth line gives an English translation of the word:

ka-ko	pa-ka-na	ti-ri-po	i-je-re-ja	qa-si-re-u
kha(l)ko(s)	pha(s)gana	tripo(s)	(h)iereia	gwasileu(s)
'bronze'	'swords'	'tripod'	'priestess'	'chief'

po-me	tu-ka-te	ko-wo	re-wo-to-ro-ko-wo
po(i)mē(n)	thugatē(r)	ko(r)wo(s)	lewotrokhowo(i)
'shepherd'	'daughter'	'boy'	'bath-pourers'

The use of the optional signs (fig. 8) needs to be explained. Some are straightforward, for instance *dwe*, *nwa* and *pte* are used in place of spellings with two signs: *de-we*, *nu-wa* and *pe-te*.

160

The sign a_2 is used in place of a to denote aspiration, that is, it is equivalent to ha. But it is optional, and ha is also written with the simple a. For example, a_2-te-ro is written for $hatero(n)$, 'other' (classical Greek $heteron$). But unlike later Greek this Mycenaean dialect used -h- between vowels in the middle of a word, and we have spellings like pa-we-a_2 (as well as pa-we-a) for $pharweha$ (classical $phar\bar{e}$), 'cloaks'. The sign a_3 is used only at the beginning of words and has the value ai-, as in a_3-ku-pi-ti-jo, a man's name, $Aiguptio(s)$, 'the Egyptian'. au is also restricted to the initial position; au-ro is for $aulo(i)$, 'pipes' (in this context, some part of a chariot).

The sign pu_2 normally has the value phu; pu-te-re is $phut\bar{e}re(s)$, 'planters'. The exact values of ra_2 and ro_2 are disputed, but they were probably in origin rya and ryo, though by the date of our documents they may have advanced to rra, (lla) and rro, (llo). ra_3 has the value rai (lai); e-ra_3-wo is $elaiwo(n)$ (classical $elaion$), 'olive-oil'.

The signs with the conventional values za, ze, zo pose a problem. The transcription was adopted because in many cases the corresponding classical words have the spelling Z, but at that date this letter had the value zd. There is good reason to think that in Mycenaean times these words were pronounced with the group reversed dz; so to-pe-za is $to(r)pedza$ (classical $trapezda$), 'table'. But in other words z- appears to stand for ts, a group that was eliminated from all classical forms of Greek.

This difficulty is a good example of the kind of problems which arise as the result of our ignorance of this dialect of archaic Greek. If we had alphabetic spellings of the same date, it would be much easier to reconstruct the Mycenaean form. We can only do this by comparing the Mycenaean spelling with the alphabetic form of the same word, which may be as much as a thousand years later, and will in many cases have altered a great deal in the interval. In some cases we also need to take into account what we know of the earlier history of the word from a comparison of cognate words in other early languages. To take a very complicated case, the syllabic spelling i-qo can be reconstructed as $(h)i(k)kwo(i)$, 'horses', partly on the evidence of classical $hippoi$, but also of Latin $equi$ and Sanskrit $a\acute{s}v\bar{a}h$. Although Linear B has answered some of our questions about Greek words, it has also left us with a lot of new ones.

It is quite certain that the Linear B script was borrowed from the earlier Linear A of Minoan Crete; this will be discussed in Chapter 5. Many of the signs are identical or very nearly so; but some are rather different in form, and there are some which appear in one script but not the other. Where and when the borrowing took place is unknown, but we have reason to think it may have been much earlier than the date of the Linear B tablets we have preserved. But this does not mean that even when the signs are the same, the values were necessarily also similar, though this is probably true in many cases. One reason for this is that in the course of time the pronunciation of words changes, and although sometimes a new spelling is introduced, there is a tendency to keep the old spelling but to give it the new value. Some of the appalling confusion of modern English spelling is due to this. In rather the same way, the Greeks may have modified the values of the signs that they took over from the Minoans; and we cannot be sure that they did not take the signs for which they had no use and give them totally unrelated values. Only a full decipherment of Linear A will resolve this question.

The difficulties in interpreting Linear B are not confined to those associated with the reconstruction of the phonetic forms. The 'Greek' of the Mycenaean period is quite certainly Greek, but it is far older than any other Greek known to us. The earliest alphabetic inscriptions belong to the eighth century BC, and our earliest literary source, the epic poems of Homer, were probably composed at the end of that same century. For some Mycenaean words we can only compare much later spellings. It is inevitable that between the end of the Mycenaean period, at the beginning of the twelfth century, and the time of Homer the language will have undergone drastic changes, not merely in pronunciation, but in the grammar and vocabulary.

We can classify the changes which languages undergo during the course of time into three types. We may find words which have changed their pronunciation. So in Greek the word for 'son' which was in Mycenaean *korwos* had become by the time of Homer *kouros; gwasileus*, 'chief', had become *basileus; newos*, 'new', had become *neos; lewotrokhowoi*, 'bath-pourers', had become *loutrokhooi; dleukos*, 'new wine', had become *gleukos*, and so on.

When we turn to grammar, we find changes have taken place in the inflexions. Mycenaean regularly has genitive endings in *-oio*, a poetic variant preserved by Homer, but replaced by *-ou* in standard Greek. It has a dative case in *-ei*, where later Greek uses *-i; di-we* is the dative of *Zeus, Diwei* for classical *Diï*. The verb has a third person singular ending in the middle (or passive) voice *-toi* instead of *-tai; eukhetoi* for *eukhetai*, 'vows'. Some of our unsolved problems may be due to difficulties of this kind.

We may also encounter lexical changes. Over such a long period words tend to change their meanings, and new words have then to be found to express the original concept. Classical Greek has two words for 'king', *basileus* and *anax*, but the second of these is only used in poetic language, so it was known to be archaic. Mycenaean has *wanax*, the same word as *anax*, as its ordinary word for 'king'; but the equivalent of *basileus* is used in a wider sense, more like the English 'chief'. The Mycenaean word for 'wheel' is *harmo*, but the same word in the form *harma* means 'chariot' in later Greek, a development rather like our use of *wheels* to mean a vehicle. The Mycenaean word for 'chariot' is *hikkwiā*, literally 'the horse-(vehicle)', a word which disappeared from later Greek. Undoubtedly many other words died out in the gap between Mycenaean and our later texts; one reason for this may be the progress of technology, for new processes often demand new words. Similarly changes in political institutions call for the introduction of a new vocabulary.

Thus the interpretation of a Mycenaean word is hardly possible without a detailed knowledge of the history of the Greek language; it is little use looking up a classical lexicon to find the meaning of Mycenaean forms. There are, not surprisingly, still a number of words whose meaning we do not know for sure, though in some cases we can deduce from the context the approximate meaning.

When we turn to the ideograms, we have problems of quite a different kind. Some of these, as shown earlier, are recognisable at first sight. Others have become clear by identifying the contexts in which they were used. For example, one which appears with the Greek word for 'cloth' (fig. 10) was probably in origin a picture of an upright loom with weights at the bottom to keep the warp under tension. This identification is further confirmed by its association with the sign for 'wool', and this in turn is associated with the sign for 'sheep' (fig. 11).

	CLOTH		WOOL
	WHEAT		BARLEY
	WINE		OLIVE OIL
	BRONZE		GOLD

10   Some Linear B ideograms for commodities

Things like grain and liquids cannot of course be drawn recognisably, so the signs were probably intended as pictures of the plants which produced them. The signs for 'wheat' and 'barley' had in Linear B become merely conventional, but we can trace their origin back to Linear A, and there we find forms which look much more like the plants. Similarly 'wine' pictures a vine growing on a trellis, and 'olive oil' was probably to begin with a picture of an olive tree.

The domestic animals too are merely conventional forms, as they appear in Linear B (fig. 11).

SHEEP	GOAT	PIG	OX
RAM	HE-GOAT	BOAR	BULL
EWE	SHE-GOAT	SOW	COW

11   Ideograms for domestic animals

The male sex is indicated by two cross-bars on the upright, the female sex by a divided upright; but the male forms are often used for the species as a whole, and may in some cases stand for castrated males. Any of these signs may be accompanied by syllabic signs used as abbreviations to denote special types, such as young, old, last year's and so on.

In some cases syllabic signs are used alone as ideograms. Some of these are straightforward abbreviations of Greek words; for instance, the word *o-pe-ro* meaning 'deficit', is often abbreviated to *o*. But others (fig. 12) are more interesting, since the syllabic value does not occur in the Greek name. These were probably taken over from Linear A, where the sound may have been that of the initial syllable of the name in the pre-Greek language of Crete. In fact, this is probably how the syllabary was invented, by using the pictogram of an object for the initial syllable of its name in that language.

⚹	*ni*	FIGS
⚹	*sa*	FLAX
⚹	*ra₃*	SAFFRON
⚹	*qi*	SHEEP
⚹	*mu*	OX

12   Syllabic signs also used as ideograms

The case of 'wool' (fig. 13), however, is more complicated. The skin of an animal may be roughly drawn, and then a syllabic sign inserted to suggest the Greek word; thus an ox-hide bears the sign for *wi* standing for *wrinos*, 'ox-hide'. But 'wool' belongs to the category of things which cannot be drawn recognisably. The solution chosen here goes back to Linear A; there two syllabic signs, *ma* and *ru*, were combined to form a ligature, presumably because this represented the name of 'wool' in that language.

LINEAR A   LINEAR B

13   The signs for 'wool' in Linear A and Linear B

Now it is probably no accident that Greek has a word *mallos* meaning 'flock of wool', which might well be borrowed from this pre-Greek language. But the ideogram of Linear B is no longer recognisable as a ligature, though it is very close to the syllabic sign *ma*.

But the principle of inventing an ideogram by stringing two or three syllabic signs together remained valid. We have several examples of this in Linear B, where the words are Greek and sometimes appear in syllabic spelling in the context (fig. 14).

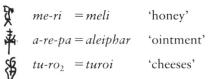

me-ri	= meli	'honey'
a-re-pa	= aleiphar	'ointment'
tu-ro₂	= turoi	'cheeses'

14 Syllabic signs of ligatures

The metric signs are a special type of ideogram. There are three series, for weight, dry measure and liquid measure. The Mycenaeans must have also had a system of linear measure, but no trace of this appears in our documents.

Heavy materials such as bronze or lead are measured by the largest units of the system of weights; the smallest are used for such things as saffron. The signs and their relationships are shown in fig. 14.

$$
\begin{array}{ll}
& \times 6 \\
= & \times 12 \\
= & \times 4 \\
= & \times 30 \\
=
\end{array}
$$

15 The Linear B system of weights

The highest unit is clearly a picture of a pair of scales, and probably stands for the talent, the major unit of weight throughout antiquity. Its value varied widely, and until a satisfactory series of weights is found on a Mycenaean site we cannot hope to obtain a precise value. But there is reason to think that it was very roughly around 30 kg. The talent was divided into sixty *minas*, so the second largest unit, which has a double sign, was almost certainly a double-*mina*. The other units do not seem to correspond to those in later use. If the value for the talent suggested is about right, the smallest unit will come out at around 3.5g.

The two systems of measurement of volume agree in their two lowest units. The next up is the same size in both systems, but has a different sign, which implies a different name. There is no sign for the highest unit in either system, but it is simply represented by the ideogram for the commodity directly followed by the numeral. Fig. 16 shows the two systems:

DRY MEASURE   LIQUID MEASURE

⌣ × 4   ⌣ × 4

= Þ × 6   = Þ × 6

= ⊤ × 10   = ⸉ × 3

= ⼤ (WHEAT)   = 𐄬 (WINE)

16   The volumetric systems of Linear B

The two lowest units stand in the same relationship as the classical *kotylē* and *khoinix*, but the higher ones are different. The determination of their values is much harder than in the case of the weights. No measuring vessels have been reliably identified from any Mycenaean site. The size of the smallest unit probably lies between 0·2 and 0·4 l., and there is some reason to prefer a value near the top of this range. This will give a major unit of up to 96 l. in dry measure, or 29 l. in liquid. The difference is probably due to the fact that a litre of wine weighs more than a litre of grain. The highest units may well represent the maximum load an average man could carry.

4
The Tablets as Historical Documents

The excavation of palaces in the Near East has revealed immense archives of tablets, far larger and more detailed than anything we have from Mycenaean Greece. But there have also been found among them annals, if not real histories, diplomatic correspondence, treaties, and even literary and religious texts. Linear B has produced nothing of the kind, and it may be doubted if the writing system was adequate to serve such purposes; it appears to have been devised solely as a means of keeping records, a way of extending the collective memory of the administrators.

Another major difference is that, unlike the Near Eastern tablets, Mycenaean tablets were never deliberately baked; they were accidentally baked in the fires that destroyed the buildings where they were kept, and in the absence of a fire no records survive. This means that at any one site we have only such tablets as were stored there at the time of the destruction. Moreover, there is a remarkable absence of dates on the tablets; only a small proportion have the name of a month, and years are only mentioned in such formulas as 'last year' or 'this year'. This implies that the tablets were rarely kept for more than a year; indeed, it seems likely that every winter the records of the past year were scrapped and a new collection begun. It is of course possible that on this occasion an abstract was transferred to some more expensive, but perishable, writing material; but if so, we have no trace of it.

It would seem at first sight almost impossible to glean any historical information from such records, and we must admit we know nothing about such matters as the names of kings or the lengths of their reigns. But within the limits imposed by the nature of the documents, it is possible to make some firm deductions and at least to advance hypotheses to explain the records. It is obvious that each tablet recorded a fact which was meaningful to the writer. Without his knowledge of the circumstances in which the tablet was written, we may find the record meaningless; but if we can conjecture the circumstances, we may be able to offer some explanation, or choose between different possible interpretations.

An example may help to explain this. Among the Pylos tablets is a large document (fig. 17) recording contributions of bronze from thirty-two officials all

17   Pylos tablet Jn 829,
listing contributions of bronze

over the kingdom. This bronze is described by a word which might mean 'of ships' or 'of temples'. The fact that some of the districts named are known to lie inland means that the official would be unlikely to have available 'ship bronze', whatever that might be. But temples, or rather small shrines, must have existed in all the major centres of population, and in later times we know that these were regularly furnished with vessels and other implements of bronze. Thus 'temple bronze' is the more likely interpretation, and this strongly suggests that the king was so short of metal he was demanding the surrender of temple property to help the war effort.

A further clue to the interpretation of the tablets is the possibility of grouping them into series. Very many tablets are exceedingly brief and laconic; in this they resemble single cards extracted from a card index, and they become meaningful only if we can reconstruct the file to which they belong. Some of these series were easily recognisable, especially by the ideograms they use, so that we could group together those listing, for instance, men, women, grain, oil, wine and other goods. But we can go further with this analysis, and here the study of handwriting has proved a valuable clue. As a rule, all the tablets belonging to the same file were written by the same scribe, while another superficially similar file was compiled by a different scribe. We can thus sometimes reconstruct the whole files, or rather baskets, into which the tablets were originally sorted; and the study of a whole file is infinitely more revealing than that of a single brief tablet. Of course tablets may well be missing from the file, and many that we have are damaged, so that our information is inevitably incomplete.

The tablets from Mycenae, Tiryns and Thebes are still too few to yield much useful information, but at least we can verify that they disclose the same sort of organisation as the two major archives, those of Pylos and Knossos. Generally speaking, the Pylos tablets are better organised and thus easier to interpret than those of Knossos; this might be due to their date, if the Knossos ones are really a century or more earlier. But despite differences it is clear that the system of administration was broadly similar in both kingdoms, and such evidence as we have from the other sites fits the picture we can build here.

We need of course to look at the tablets in the light of what we know of the geography of the region, and in some cases we can compare the records with the direct evidence of archaeology. But this has limits: for instance, most agricultural products leave little trace which can be detected archaeologically, and here the tablets can supply crucial information. There is, for example, nothing in the archaeological record of the south-west Peloponnese to suggest that flax was here an important crop. But the Pylos tablets reveal a highly organised textile industry based on flax; and this is strikingly confirmed by the fact that in modern times also much flax has been produced in this area.

The Pylos tablets confirm that Pylos (*pu-ro*) was the Mycenaean name of the site; but among the other place names there are few which can be located on the map. This is because in the period immediately following the destruction of the Palace around 1200 BC, the whole south-western Peloponnese seems to have suffered an abrupt decline in population. Thus many of the sites mentioned on the tablets were probably uninhabited for a time, and if they were later re-occupied, they then acquired new names. But there are a number of clues which enable us to guess the approximate location of the more important names. For instance, a number of names are listed as the location of coastguard units or as supplying rowers for the fleet; such place names must obviously be situated on or near the coast. There is also a standard order in which the major districts are listed; if we can relate that to the geography, we can deduce approximately where some of the areas must be.

We can now determine fairly accurately the limits of the kingdom administered by Pylos. It was divided into a Hither Province; the broad strip of habitable land down the west coast, and a Further Province, across the mountains in the fertile plain of Messenia. Each province was divided into districts, each of which had a governor and his deputy in charge. These sixteen districts are all listed on the tablet illustrated in fig. 17, together with the contributions of bronze required from the governor and deputy governor of each.

At Knossos the situation is a little better. Apart from Knossos itself (*ko-no-so*), we can recognise the names of Amnisos, its harbour, Phaistos, the major site in the south of the island, Lyktos a little further to the east, and Kydonia (the modern Khania) in the far west. There are a number of other names which may be the early form of known Cretan towns. There is a mention of Mount Dikte, already associated with the worship of Zeus. But the picture that has emerged seems to exclude the eastern end of the island, and the kingdom of Knossos seems to have been based on the main central section with some sort of control extending to the western end only.

At neither site is the king mentioned by name; we have only the title 'the king' (*wa-na-ka*). He had an important officer who may have been his second-in-command, perhaps the chief of the army. His court was composed of officers called 'Followers' (*e-qe-ta*), or as we might say 'Companions'.

Some tablets appear to record large quantities of wheat; but it is clear that most of these documents are really lists of persons holding land, which is measured in seed-corn. The holders of land clearly had obligations to fulfil in return for their holding, for we have notes that some of them had not met their obligations; these probably included military service in time of war.

There was no currency in use, but the Palace appears to have paid its workers in kind. Two files of tablets at Pylos list women workers who receive rations of wheat and figs (fig. 18). Some of the women are domestics, such as the 'bath-pourers' already mentioned, who were probably responsible for the functions discharged in modern times by plumbing. But the majority seem to have been workers in the textile industry, producing woollen and linen cloth of various kinds. Other tradesmen are listed as receiving quantities of food and drink.

18   Pylos tablet Ab 573, listing sixteen women of Miletus, with three girls and seven boys, and a ration of wheat and figs

At Knossos something like a third of all the tablets in the archive are concerned with sheep and wool. Each card in the file records the name of the person responsible for the flock, its location, size and in some cases make-up. Other files record the difference between the actual numbers and the nominal strength, most being a round hundred. Yet other tablets record the wool clip, showing deficiencies below the target figure. In Crete at least the production of wool was highly organised; and there too the Palace controlled groups of female workers, who spun the yarn, wove and decorated the cloth. The linen industry was a speciality of the Pylos area.

These women are not specifically called 'slaves', but their status can hardly have been much higher. Other workers are specifically called by this title, but perhaps the distinction between slave and free was not so rigidly drawn as in later Greece. There are also slaves (or servants) of various deities, but some of these seem to have been of higher status.

Wheat and barley both figure prominently on the tablets. Other agricultural produce listed includes figs, olives, olive oil and wine, all still staple items in the diet of the Greek peasant. Apart from sheep, we have records of goats, pigs and oxen; but oxen are not numerous, and seem to have been largely used for traction. This is surely true of the tablets at Knossos which list yokes of oxen, giving not only the name of their driver but actually those of the oxen too.

19   Knossos tablet Ch 897, showing the name of an ox-driver and his two charges

Many series of tablets are concerned with manufactured goods, either listed as in the Palace storerooms or as being produced for the Palace. There was a system by which raw materials were issued to workers, and a careful record was kept of the quantities each received. This is clearly seen at Pylos, where bronze was allotted to groups of smiths, whose names were listed, though what they were required to make with it is not given. The contributions of 'temple bronze' mentioned above are specifically said to be for points for javelins and spears. Weapons as well as tools must have been an important part of the production.

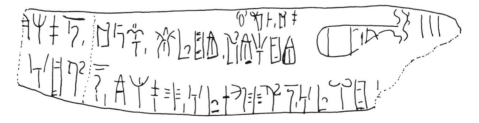

20   Knossos tablet Sd 4403, with a description of three chariot-bodies

At Knossos we have detailed descriptions of chariots, a regular piece of military equipment at that time. Some of them are elaborately decorated, painted red and inlaid with ivory. The wheels are listed separately; they are described as made of elm or willow, but some have bronze or even silver fittings.

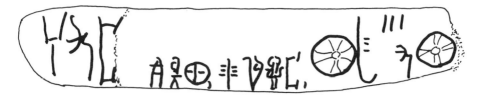

21   Knossos tablet So 4439, listing three pairs and one single wheel made of willow

There are also records of body armour, though the material it is made of is not specified. A complete set of bronze armour has been found in a tomb of Mycenaean date, but it would seem that the type listed at Pylos was made of some material such as linen or leather with bronze plates sewn on to reinforce it. Fig. 22 shows a Pylos tablet recording five pairs of old corslets, each with twenty large and ten small plates, and with four plates for the helmet and two for cheek-pieces. 'Old' probably means no more than 'not newly made'.

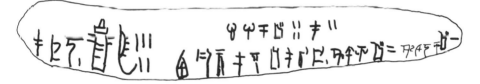

22   Pylos tablet Sh 740, showing armour

There are lists of leather goods mentioning equipment such as harness and trappings for horses, and listing the skins of deer as well as of domestic animals. Some of these were used for making footwear.

In many ways the most interesting document is a set of tablets from Pylos which begins with a heading stating that these objects were inspected when a certain important official was appointed by the king. The list begins with vessels, probably of bronze, which are described by their decoration; among them are six tripod-cauldrons. One of these tablets, where the drawing of a three-legged vessel is clear, was mentioned above as having proved the validity of the decipherment. There are also fire-rakes and tongs, axes and swords. But the list then goes on to describe a collection of furniture. There are 'thrones', i.e. formal chairs of state, decorated with ivory, lapis lazuli and gold, and a larger number of stools, possibly foot-stools, but perhaps also used as seats, equally decorated. Then there is a collection of ten tables, all described in detail and elaborately decorated. The translation of these descriptions is difficult, but there is no doubt that this is a sumptuous collection of precious items. The whole list must be an inventory of a palace storeroom for valuables.

It is surprising that although there was plenty of evidence found in the excavation of the Palace at Pylos to show that no expense had been spared on its construction and decoration, hardly any portable objects of value were found in it. This strongly suggests that before the disastrous fire which destroyed it, the Palace had been deliberately stripped of valuable goods. This would happen if it had been captured by a raiding party, looted and then set on fire. We are therefore justified in asking whether the Pylos tablets give any indication of a state of emergency.

There is no direct evidence, but a number of documents offer indirect evidence, which, taken together, certainly constitute a proof that Pylos was expecting an attack coming from the sea. The most telling is a series of tablets which records the establishment of a coastguard organisation. Some have argued that in default of information about regular practice, this cannot be regarded as proof of an emergency. It would nevertheless be very remarkable if a kingdom of this size could in normal times produce a force of some eight hundred men to keep watch on the coastline. It is clearly not a defensive force, since there are about a hundred miles of coastline, so the force works out at, on average, one man for each 220 yds; and it would be absurd to split the force up into small units, some of only ten men.

Fig. 23 shows the first of five similar tablets dealing with this subject. The first line is a heading which translates: 'As follows the watchers are guarding the coastal

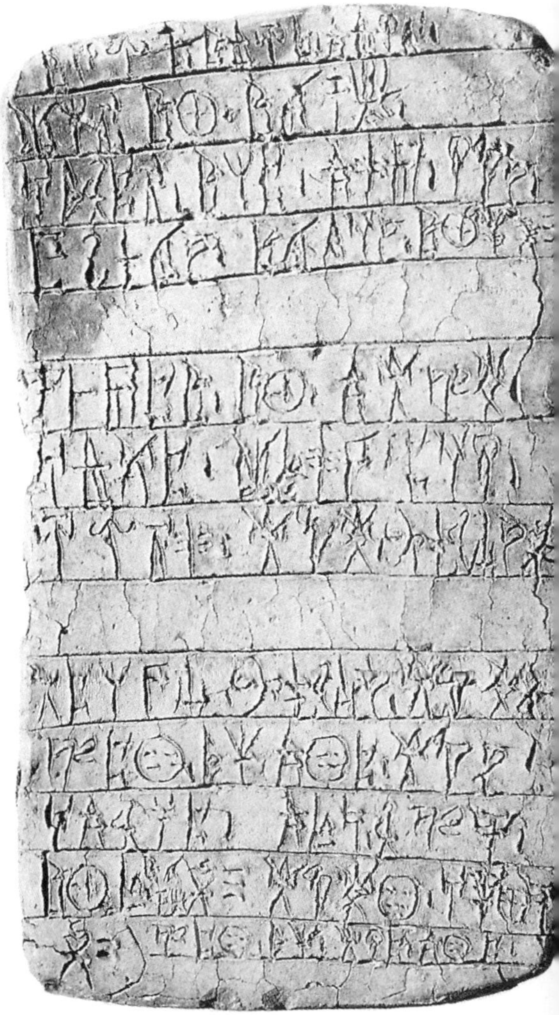

23   Pylos tablet An 657, showing the coastguard organisation

area.' Then the commands of two officers are described, giving the force at their disposal and their location together with the names of their subordinate officers. Eight other commands are listed on the other four tablets of the series. In the case of the second command on this tablet (line 6) it is known that the two men named as the commander and his first subordinate are almost certainly the governor and vice-governor of one of the districts in the north of the kingdom. The men under their command are described partly as natives of a particular town, but also by proper names which sound like non-Greek tribal or ethnic names. The men used for this purpose may therefore not have been full citizens.

area.' Then the commands of two officers are described, giving the force at their disposal and their location together with the names of their subordinate officers. Eight other commands are listed on the other four tablets of the series. In the case of the second command on this tablet (line 6) it is known that the two men named as the commander and his first subordinate are almost certainly the governor and vice-governor of one of the districts in the north of the kingdom. The men under their command are described partly as natives of a particular town, but also by proper names which sound like non-Greek tribal or ethnic names. The men used for this purpose may therefore not have been full citizens.

At the end of the tablet we have an entry stating that a certain 'Follower', an officer of the royal court, was with them. These Followers are rather curiously distributed among the districts, and they seem to be concentrated in the area nearest to the Palace. It is therefore a fair guess that they were in fact in command of the military forces in each area, and the army has been stationed where it is best placed to repel attacks on the main centres of population.

175

A defensive system based on the coast must obviously envisage an attack from the sea, but there is no indication who the expected enemy might be. There are in fact only two reasonable routes by which a land force could attack: either coming down the west coast, where there is a pass which could fairly easily be held, or by a much more difficult route through the mountains of Arcadia. We should therefore expect the Pylians to have manned their fleet, so when we find a document recording about six hundred men who are to serve as rowers, it is reasonable to infer that this is the expected mobilisation of the ships. There is even another tablet which records that small numbers of those due to serve in the fleet have been excused.

Another piece of evidence has already been mentioned, the document (fig. 17) recording the collection of temple bronze from every district in the kingdom. This is specifically said to be 'for points for javelins and spears', that is to say, scrap metal was being requisitioned for the making of armaments. Another document, which is hardly likely to be a normal demand, records the payment of large quantities of gold by local governors and other important officials; the tablet is damaged and some of the figures are lost, but the total comes to the astonishing sum of more than five kg. Wealth on this scale can hardly have been requisitioned annually; it only makes sense if this is a 'one-off' levy for the war.

But the most striking document is that shown in fig. 24. Religious offerings are quite a common type of entry, since the Palace was obviously responsible for maintaining the local shrines. We have lists from Knossos of the issue of olive oil, honey and other goods to various addresses, one of which is the celebrated cave of Eileithyia at Amnisos, well known both from Homer and its archaeological finds. There are similar mentions at Pylos of perfumed oils being sent to addresses, some of which are clearly religious institutions. But the tablet discussed here is unique.

It was, as the illustration shows, written on both sides. This is unusual, though on occasion a scribe, having miscalculated the length of his text, does allow it to run over onto the back or even the edge. Generally, however, a second tablet is written to contain the surplus. What is worse, the scribe here began his draft with blank lines which were never filled. Moreover, there are signs of erasure all over the tablet, and it looks as if it was originally written, then deleted and re-used for the present text. What is now the beginning is written on what was originally the back of the tablet. Even when he wrote the final text, the scribe made obvious mistakes, since in writing formulas that occur several times he omitted signs which are clearly needed. What he wrote is in places exceedingly difficult to read, and this is not entirely due to subsequent damage to the tablet. Altogether the impression given is that of a hasty draft, and had the tablet been stored in the archive room for any length of time, we should have expected a clean copy to have been made, so that this could be destroyed. Since it was not, we may well assume it to have been written in the last days, if not hours, before the Palace was destroyed.

It begins with a date and a place; it is a place name we only know from the tablets, but it is probably the name of the district within which the Palace lay, since the name 'PYLOS' is written six times in large signs at the left. The formula used is not

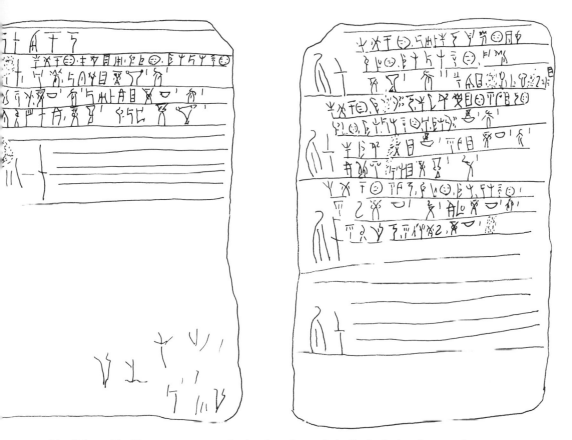

24 Pylos tablet Tn 316, written on both sides, obviously badly drafted and incomplete

wholly clear, but it refers to the bringing of gifts and an unknown word, which seems to mean something like 'victims'. Then after each repetition of the introductory formula we have a list of deities, some familiar such as Zeus, Hera and Hermes, but also including many more obscure names and titles. Each entry ends with a pictogram showing a cup or other vessel, preceded by the ideographic sign for 'gold' and followed by the numeral 1. Each deity is receiving a gold vessel, and since there are no less than thirteen of them, this can hardly be a regular ritual. The scribe began by drawing each cup differently, but as he went on he tired of this and used a simple conventional outline. But in nine of the entries the gold cup is followed by the mention of a human being; most often one woman, but once two women, and twice one man. The women are associated with female deities, the men with male ones. Whether these unlucky people were to be human sacrifices or merely given over to divine service we cannot be sure; but since early Greek legends often refer to human sacrifice, we cannot suppose it was unknown at this period. There is also some archaeological evidence from other sites which points the same way. But if it was a sacrifice of ten human beings at once, it surely suggests an extreme emergency. This ceremony was probably being planned in a last-minute attempt to invoke divine aid, and perhaps the blow fell before it could be carried out.

5
Linear A

Sir Arthur Evans distinguished three types of script used in Crete during the Bronze Age. The latest of these, Linear B, has been deciphered as already shown, but some account must be given of the earlier scripts, although these are not yet fully deciphered. Evans named these 'pictographic' or 'hieroglyphic' from a superficial resemblance to the hieroglyphic script of Egypt, and Linear A, because in this the pictograms of the earlier form had been reduced to simple outlines.

Generally speaking hieroglyphic inscriptions are earlier than the Linear A examples; but there is a much more striking difference in the material on which they usually appear. By far the largest number of hieroglyphic inscriptions are on seal-stones or sealings; only rarely are they found incised with a stylus on clay. Linear A is used either on clay tablets or on objects made of hard materials such as stone or metal. We are probably right in regarding Linear A as a later development of hieroglyphic, but the line between them is sometimes hard to discern.

25   The four faces of a seal from near Lyttos

The number of Linear A inscriptions known is still relatively small, a fraction of the number in Linear B. Moreover, a comparison based upon the number of signs rather than documents increases the disproportion, since so many Linear A documents are short or ill-preserved. It is therefore not surprising that much less progress has been made towards the decipherment of Linear A.

The largest collection of Linear A clay tablets comes from the Minoan palace of Haghia Triada, very close to Phaistos, in the south of Crete. But tablets or fragments of tablets have been found all over the island, and we can assume that this script was in general use for accounting purposes in Crete. So far as the evidence goes, it appears to represent the same language wherever found. Scraps of tablets have also been found in two of the Aegean islands to the north, Melos and Kea.

The same script has been found incised on portable objects of stone, pottery or metal. Here too the distribution is widespread in Crete, and there is a vessel from Thera in the south Aegean. A few inscriptions have been claimed for mainland Greece, or more remote areas; these are all too short for real certainty, and we can safely conclude that Linear A was the script of the Minoan civilisation of Crete and its overseas possessions, thus probably including at least the southern Aegean.

The chronological limits are not easy to define, but 'hieroglyphic' inscriptions are not earlier than the Middle Minoan period (roughly 1900–1600 BC). Towards the end of this period the more simplified forms appear, and Linear A was probably evolved around the eighteenth century. It continued in use until the collapse of the Minoan civilisation in the middle of the fifteenth century. Attempts made to date any Linear A document after this have so far proved vain.

The direction of the script is, so far as can be determined, from left to right. But a few signs are occasionally written reversed as in a mirror, and this suggests that it may perhaps at one time have been used also in the right-to-left direction.

It is immediately obvious that the Linear A script is very closely related to Linear B. The signary is of roughly the same size, and it is used in a similar way. Many of the signs are identifiable with corresponding Linear B ones, though there are some which are unknown to Linear B, and some Linear B signs have no clear ancestors in Linear A. The ideograms too are very similar, so that we can usually form a good idea of the contents of a Linear A tablet. The numerical system is the same, though less formally arranged; the tens may be written as heavy dots as well as bars. There is a major difference in the system of measurement, for although some of the metric signs of Linear B recur, they do not fall into the same patterns. Indeed it is clear the Linear A had a system of fractions, where Linear B uses the next lower unit in the system; but owing to the lack of sufficient well preserved texts, it is still impossible to give values to most of the signs in this class.

There is a certain crudity in presentation to be seen on Linear A tablets which contrasts with the tidier habits of Linear B scribes. Most Linear A tablets are of page shape, but are much smaller than most Linear B tablets of this type. The lines of writing are not usually divided by horizontal lines; and what is worse, separate entries are not tabulated by starting each on a new line. The scribes felt no difficulty in breaking a word at the end of a line, or putting the relevant numeral at the beginning of the next line. It is therefore much more difficult to analyse the pattern of entries, or even to see where one ends and the next begins. But it is clear that the nature and purpose of most tablets was similar to those of the Linear B variety; they are accounts of men and women, animals and produce, of much the same type, even if less detailed.

It is tempting to suppose that we can give the signs the values of the corresponding ones in Linear B. It would after all be perverse to borrow a script, but then to give the signs totally new values. So we should expect most of the signs common to both scripts to have the same, or similar, values. But the analogy of modern alphabets warns us of the danger in taking this approach too far. Some of the letters of the Cyrillic alphabet used for Russian look like English ones; but we know that B, C, P, X and Y, for example, have different values in the Cyrillic script. Since we know the values in both scripts, and we can trace their history over a long period, these differences can be explained. But if we knew nothing of the values in Cyrillic, it would be very difficult to correct the false ideas we should have gained from English.

It was therefore necessary to test the assumption of similar values and see if they could be proved or disproved. There is not enough evidence to complete the proof; but so far as it goes the results are encouraging. The same word seems in certain cases to be spelled either with initial *a-* or initial *ja-*; not only are the sounds very much alike, but we have a similar alternation in Linear B. Many of the entries on the tablets are clearly personal names; if they are decoded on the Linear B model, we find a number which are almost identical with names found on the Knossos Linear B tablets. It might be expected that some of the names in use in Minoan Crete would have survived the Greek conquest. Significantly, those ending in *-u* in Linear A often appear in Linear B ending in *-o*, a change which may well be due to fitting a foreign name into a Greek declensional type. In fact the vowel *o* has a much lower, and *u* a much higher frequency than in Linear B.

Since the structure of most tablets is very similar to that familiar in Linear B, we can apply the same methods to the decipherment. A tablet from the south Cretan site of Haghia Triada will show the possibilities (fig. 26).

The analysis of this tablet is not difficult. The first line is a heading, very likely a place name. The second line begins with a sign identical to the Linear B ideogram for 'wine'. Then follows an isolated sign, which appears to mean something like 'paid out', or 'issued'. After this comes a list of six words, probably personal names, each followed by a numeral, presumably therefore specifying the amout of wine each received. There is a sign after some numerals which must indicate the fraction $\frac{1}{2}$. Some of the figures are slightly damaged, but they can probably be restored as: $5\frac{1}{2}$, 56, $27\frac{1}{2}$, $17\frac{1}{2}$, 19, 5. The last line has a word (made up of two signs) which regularly appears on tablets in this position, followed by the numeral $130\frac{1}{2}$. Since this is the total of the preceding figures, the word before it must effectively mean 'total', 'so much' or the like.

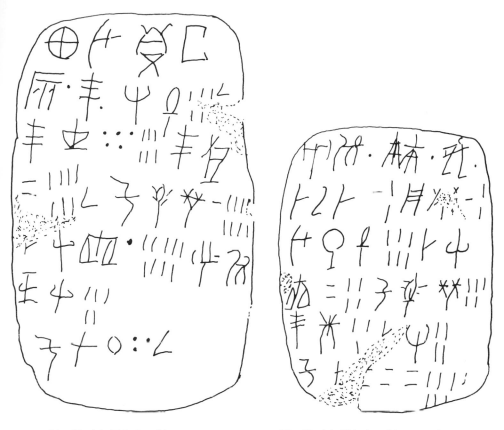

26   Haghia Triada tablet 13   27   Haghia Triada tablet 85, side *a*

In fig. 27 we have a very similar list, but the commodity counted is, apparently, men, since the first line ends with the ideogram for 'man'. The seven separate entries may be place names or descriptive titles, or even persons to whom the groups of men are assigned. Again the total is given with the same formula as in the previous example. Unfortunately many of the tablets are fragmentary or damaged, and their interpretation is thus less certain.

But there is one deduction which is immediately possible: the language cannot be Greek. The word for 'total', if transcribed with the Linear B values, comes out as *ku-ro*, which is not only quite different from the Linear B *to-so*, but cannot be reconstructed as any Greek word of suitable meaning. There are only a few words like this, the meaning of which can be deduced from the context; and although attempts have been made to connect these with words in other languages, especially Semitic, no convincing set of parallels has yet been demonstrated. We need more texts, especially more detailed ones, if we are to make much more progress here.

But we do also have inscriptions of a type not so far found in Linear B, those on movable objects. Many of these are what the archaeologists call 'libation tables', large stone dishes apparently used for offerings to deities. There are also inscriptions on metal objects. These have a quite different structure from the tablets. There are usually no ideograms and no numerals to give a clue to the subject matter. The parallel of classical Greek inscriptions on similar objects suggests that these are religious dedications. They probably record the name of the deity to whom they are offered, that of the donor, and sometimes other details like the reason for making the offering. A number of inscriptions repeat the same words, but which are divine names and which dedicatory formulas is still not clear.

28   Stone ladle from Troullos

A stone ladle from Troullos (fig. 28) is a good example. The first word reappears in various forms at the beginning of inscriptions on other objects, such as libation tables. The right-hand edge begins with a word which, if we apply the Linear B values, reads *ja-sa-sa-ra-me*. The word *a-sa-sa-ra*, with *a-* replacing *ja-*, recurs on a number of such inscriptions, and has been suspected of being a divine name or title.

A silver pin from Platanos also has an inscription of the same votive type, but the newly discovered gold pin (fig. 29) does not repeat any of the regular formulas and therefore remains obsure.

29   A gold pin of unknown origin (now in Haghios Nikolaos Museum)

Lastly we may notice a few incised inscriptions on vessels, the most notable of which is an enormous jar, some five feet high, which has an inscription written in two lines running between the handles. It was found in the Minoan palace of Kato Zakros on the east coast of Crete. The interesting feature here is that the inscription begins with the sign for 'wine' followed by the numeral '32'. If this indicates the capacity and means that it was intended for storing wine, this would certainly provide for a heroic drinking-party, but the second line begins with a variant form of the dedicatory formula, so the meaning of the whole text still remains unclear.

6

The Cypriot Connection

It has long been known that the island of Cyprus, standing on the eastern edge of the Greek world, had a script of its own in use during the classical period. Its decipherment was made easy by the discovery of a number of short inscriptions giving the same text in the local script and in the Greek alphabet. This revealed that the local dialect of the Greek language was written by means of a simple syllabic script, of the same type as that used in Linear B. A connection between it and the 'Minoan' script was suggested by Evans as early as 1894, and he later proposed that the Bronze Age script of Cyprus should be known as Cypro–Minoan. However, only a few short inscriptions of this date were known until fragments of large clay tablets were found at the site of Enkomi, on the east coast of Cyprus, in 1952–3.

The earliest true inscription from Cyprus so far known was discovered at Enkomi in 1955. It is a piece of a large thick clay tablet, containing only three lines of writing. Although some of the signs are unlike anything in Linear A or B, it was immediately obvious that most showed a distinct resemblance. This discovery proved what had already been predicted, that the source of the Cypriot system was Cretan Linear A, not Greek Linear B, for the date of this fragment is around 1500

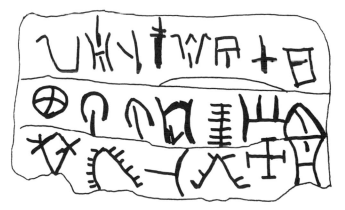

30   Clay tablet from Enkomi, *c*.1500 BC

BC, considerably earlier than anything known in Linear B, but contemporary with Linear A. No progress is possible with this early script so long as evidence for it remains so poor.

The other fragments of clay tablets found at Enkomi belong to a later period, the late thirteenth or twelfth centuries BC. They belong to the large, thick type of tablet used for literary as well as record purposes in the Near East. The script is much changed by this date, and the signs have become simple patterns of lines, probably evolved as the result of habitual use on clay, rather than directly influenced by cuneiform, which had undergone a similar evolution at a much earlier date. There can be no doubt that this script, now generally known as Cypro–Minoan, is descended from a Cretan original; but the equation of signs is often highly problematic, and it is quite impossible to make much progress by means of the clues afforded by Linear A.

In recent times the number of examples of Cypro–Minoan inscriptions has increased, though most of the new discoveries are very short. A frequent type is a small clay ball bearing a few signs. There is also an example of a clay cylinder bearing a longer inscription. What was the function of these objects remains obscure, and without some clue it is impossible to guess the content of such inscriptions.

31 Fragment of a large clay tablet from Enkomi, *c.*1200 BC

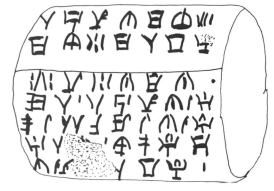

32   Clay cylinder from Enkomi

What has now emerged from the detailed study of this material, especially by Emilia Masson of Paris, is that the tablets use a different variety of the script from the other objects. The significance of this variation is not clear, but the suspicion must arise that the two scripts were used to write different languages. To add to the confusion, a third variety has now appeared on a clay tablet found, not in Cyprus, but at the site of the ancient city of Ugarit on the coast of Syria. This document has been plausibly interpreted as a list of names of Semitic character, which is not suprising since the local language of Ugarit is a Semitic dialect. It does not, however, afford proof that the language of Cypro–Minoan was itself Semitic, and this in fact appears improbable.

Further progress with Cypro–Minoan can be expected, if more examples are found. It would seem likely that more exploration of the important Bronze Age site at Enkomi would yield more tablets of the type already known, and it must be hoped that a solution of the problems that beset the island will soon enable archaeological work to be resumed in areas at present under Turkish occupation.

The Greek colonisation of the island was reported by tradition as beginning after the Trojan War, and there is archaeological evidence for a new people in Cyprus, especially in the west, from about the twelfth century BC. The temple of Aphrodite at Paphos in the south-west was throughout the classical period an important cult site, and Aphrodite was often referred to in Greece as simply 'the Cyprian goddess'. It is from this area that the earliest examples have come of the later Cypriot syllabic script. This remained in use by all the Greek cities of the island throughout the classical period. Although the Greek alphabet was devised, probably in the early eighth century BC, on models derived from Phoenicia, the coast of modern Syria and Lebanon, the Cypriots resisted this innovation, until the spread of the Macedonian empire under Alexander the Great led to the adoption of the standard script of the Greek world.

There can be no doubt about the Minoan origin of this classical script, since not only are some simple signs identical, or almost so, to the Minoan ones, but they have the same values as the corresponding sign in Linear B (fig. 33). In many more cases it is possible to trace some resemblance between signs having the same value and to suggest how they may have evolved. It must be remembered that the script must have been in use over a period of a thousand years, and it is not surprising that many signs show little resemblance.

CYPRIOT
A
B
lo
ro/lo
na
na
pa
pa
po
po
sa
sa
se
se
ta
da
to
to

33 A comparison of classical Cypriot signs with Linear A and Linear B

The syllabary is organised on much the same lines as that of Linear B. The reason for this is not only their common origin, but the fact that they were devised for the same language, even if different dialects of it. Again we have a system with five vowels, since this is what the language demands. The consonants are slightly different: the labio-velar (*q-*) series has disappeared due to changes in the pronunciation of these words; *t* and *d* are no longer distinguished, but *l* and *r* are.

But the main difference is not in the structure of the syllabary, but in its use. No longer is it judged sufficient to write a skeletal notation, which the reader has to fill in for himself; for true inscriptions the script needs to be more complete. The final consonants, *-n*, *-r*, *-s*, are noted by using *ne*, *re* and *se*. All groups of consonants are spelled out using extra vowels as necessary; and equally all diphthongs are spelled out. The only exception is that the nasals (*n* or *m*) are omitted before another consonant. Although a divider is used between groups of signs, this is not always employed at the end of each word, some phrases being treated as a single group. A few examples will illustrate how the system works:

pa-si-le-u-se

basileus

'king'

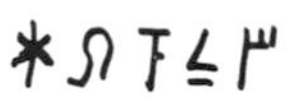

a-po-to-li-se

hā ptolis

'the city'

o-i-e-re-u-se

ho hiereus

'the priest'

sa-ta-si-ku-po-ro-se

Stāsikupros

(man's name)

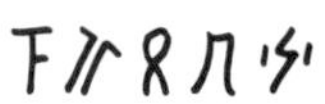

to-no-ro-ko-ne

ton horkon

'the oath'

A further difference concerns the direction of writing. The most common direction is from right-to-left, though there are some examples of left-to-right. This is surprising in view of the left-to-right direction of Cypro–Minoan; it may be that the reverse direction is due to Semitic influence.

There are minor differences in the forms of the signs in use at different sites. The table (fig. 34) gives normalised forms only:

a	e	i	o	u
ja			jo	
ka	ke	ki	ko	ku
la	le	li	lo	lu
ma	me	mi	mo	mu
na	ne	ni	no	nu
pa	pe	pi	po	pu
ra	re	ri	ro	ru
sa	se	si	so	su
ta	te	ti	to	tu
wa	we	wi	wo	
xa	xe		zo	
ga				

34 The Cypriot syllabary; the values *xa*, *xe* and *zo* are not entirely certain; *ga* is only used at certain sites

187

The earliest inscription so far found in this script comes from Palaipaphos in the south-west, where a tomb of the eleventh century BC yielded three bronze spits, one of which bears an inscription. It reads from left to right: *o-pe-le-ta-u*. This makes good sense as *Opheltau*, the genitive of a familiar Greek name *Opheltes*. It is quite common for objects to be inscribed with the owner's name, and this is usually in the genitive case, as we might write *John's*. What is interesting about this inscription, besides the very early date, is that the form of the genitive is characteristic of the Cypriot dialect as known later on, but is slightly different from the Mycenaean. At least it seems to prove the very high antiquity of the Greek colonisation of Cyprus.

There is no other inscription so far known before the eighth century, and they only become at all common in the sixth century. Unfortunately most of these are from funerary monuments and contain nothing but the name of the deceased. There are also a number of dedicatory inscriptions which are not much more informative. In the fifth century, however, we have an important document from the city of Idalion. It is a large bronze tablet (fig. 35) engraved on both sides with a long inscription. It records a contract entered into by 'the king and the city' and gives a reward to a family of physicians who had operated a free health service for the casualties, when the city was besieged by the Persians. It reads from right to left and

35   The Idalion bronze tablet of the fifth century BC

is very well preserved; there are only a few problems caused by the unfamiliar dialect. The following is an extract:

a-no-ko-ne-o-na-si-lo-ne / to-no-na-si-ku-po-ro-ne

anōgon   Onasilon   ton   Onasikuprōn

they ordered Onasilos the (son) of Onasikupros

to-ni-ja-te-ra-ne / ka-se / to-se / ka-si-ke-ne-to-se /

ton iatēran   kas   tos   kasignētos

the physician   and   the   brothers

i-ja-sa-ta-i / to-se / a-to-ro-po-se / to-se / i-ta-i

iasthai   tos   a(n)thrōpos   tos   i(n) tāi

to heal   the   men   those   in   the

ma-ka-i / i-ki-ma-me-no-se / a-ne-u / mi-si-to-ne

makhāi   ikmamenos   aneu   misthōn

battle   wounded   without   fee

This script continued in use down to the Hellenistic period, but at that date obviously many people were unable to read and write it, so inscriptions are found with the text in both Cypriot script in dialect, and in the Greek alphabet in the standard form of the language. An example is given in fig. 36.

36   Cypriot inscription in two scripts, a dedication by Ellowoikos to Demeter and Kore

7

The Phaistos Disk

A book dealing with the pre-alphabetic scripts of the Aegean area cannot avoid mentioning the most famous document so far discovered in Crete. In 1908 an Italian excavator found in the ruins of the first palace at Phaistos in southern Crete a large disk of baked clay, covered on both sides by an inscription. Its date is given by its archaeological context as not later than about 1700 BC. It is therefore contemporary with Linear A, and it has been generally assumed to be a specimen of another script of the same family. While it is certainly an inscription, it is very questionable whether it belongs to the Minoan family, for it is in at least one respect unique.

The disk has the distinction of being the world's first typewritten document. It was made by taking a stamp or punch bearing the sign to be written in a raised pattern, and impressing this on the wet clay. The maker therefore needed to have as many stamps as there were signs in the script. It has the advantage that even complicated signs can be quickly written, and every example of the same sign is identical and easy to read. The disadvantage is that a considerable outlay of time and effort is required to make the set of stamps before any document can be produced. It is therefore evident that the system was not created solely for a single document; its maker must have intended to produce a large number of documents, though it remains some way from being an anticipation of printing.

It is therefore all the more remarkable that after more than eighty years of excavation not another single scrap of clay impressed with these stamps has been found at Phaistos, or at any other site in Crete or elsewhere. It would be very surprising if there were not somewhere more examples of the script waiting to be found, but the disk remains so far unique, and the suspicion must arise that it was an isolated object brought from some other area.

This impression of foreign origin can be supported by two arguments. The work of cutting the stamps, whether made directly or perhaps more likely by making moulds into which metal was poured, is a technique very similar to gem-engraving. We might therefore expect the signs to bear a stylistic resemblance to those engraved on seal-stones. In fact the style of art is noticeably different. Secondly,

37   The Phaistos Disk, side *b*

some of the objects pictured by the signs have a distinctly foreign appearance to those familiar with Minoan art.

38   Signs on the Phaistos Disk

Helmets with crests, as shown in the first sign on fig. 38, are not Minoan, though they were used at a rather later date by the Philistines. The woman sign shows a female dress quite different from that favoured by the Minoans. The third sign is hard to interpret, but it is an object unknown from any Minoan context, though it bears a striking resemblance to a form of sarcophagus, itself probably modelled on a house, in use later among the Lycians, a people of south-west Anatolia.

Comparison with Minoan hieroglyphic and Linear A inscriptions discloses some resemblances between signs; but since both scripts are obviously pictographic in origin, it is not surprising if two pictures of the same object look alike. None of the more complicated and thus distinctive signs can be paralleled. Its Minoan origin must thus rest in doubt until more evidence is available.

Although the origin of the disk is so uncertain, it has the great advantage of being easily legible, since it has suffered very little damage. Both faces of the disk are completely covered with writing arranged in a spiral pattern; the disk was presumably rotated as it was written, so that the bottom of the sign is nearest to the rim. The absence of blank spaces must be the result of practice and careful planning, unless of course this is one of a series of disks containing a long text, and what we have is, so to speak, a page out of a book.

The direction of the script has been hotly disputed, and many people have assumed that it reads from left to right like the other Minoan scripts. But it has now been firmly established that in some places one sign very slightly overlaps that to its right. It follows that the maker worked from right to left, and therefore from the rim towards the centre. It is just possible, but obviously highly improbable, that the reader was expected to read the text in the reverse direction. The signs which represent human beings and animals in profile are shown facing the right, which would be natural with a script running leftwards. It is also clear that the signs round the rim were written first, and there is some irregularity where the spiral leaves the rim and begins to run above the outermost line.

The disk is about 6½ in (160 mm) in diameter and about ½ in (12 mm) thick. There is a total of 242 signs on the two faces. These are arranged into 61 groups, each demarcated by lines drawn freehand to form a series of boxes. The starting point on the rim is indicated by an upright line with heavy dots on it. The number of signs in a group varies from two to seven. In thirteen cases the sign at the left end of a group has an oblique stroke added underneath with a stylus.

The number of different signs is forty-five, but it must not be assumed that this is the total number of signs in the script, since a sample as short as this is unlikely to contain an example of every sign. Statistically it can be shown that the total 'population' of which this is a sample is likely to be at least fifty, and if there are more than a few very rare signs, the total may be sixty or more. This number, combined with the length of the groups of signs, makes it virtually certain that here too we are dealing with a simple syllabic system. The specimen does not appear to contain any ideograms or numerals, and this makes it hard to guess what sort of text it contains. This has allowed would-be decipherers, who are numerous, to propose the most implausible suggestions. The general tendency has been to assume it is some kind of religious text, which has the advantage of permitting the wildest flights of fancy.

The signs with a stroke underneath occur only at the ends of sign groups. This makes it likely that they are some kind of diacritical mark used to modify the reading of the sign to which they are attached. If the signs normally have the values of a consonant followed by a vowel, the strokes might be a means of cancelling the final vowel, so as to write a word ending in a consonant. No script of the Minoan family discussed in this book has such a device, but the *Devanagari* script used for Sanskrit has a similar mark which is used in this way.

It has been observed that a number of the longer sign groups begin with the same two signs. This might suggest that we are dealing with a language which uses prefixes rather than suffixes to modify the meaning of words. But there is a danger in putting much weight on this deduction without a great deal more evidence, for the same effect would be visible in such languages as Greek or French, if they too were written in a syllabic script. This is because the definite article is regularly treated as part of the following noun. Consider for instance the French series: *homme, l'homme, les hommes*. If these were written phonetically, it would appear that we had a word *om* to which the prefixes *l-* and *lez-* could be added.

If we had an adequate sample, such problems might be resolved, but we cannot even identify the type to which the language belongs, much less its linguistic family. We do not know the place of origin of the script, and as shown above there is a fair chance that it is not native to Crete, though this cannot be excluded. We have no means of guessing, even approximately, the nature of the text, for nothing like it has been found written in any known language.

All this could change if more specimens of the script were to be found. No script is in theory undecipherable, even if the language is totally unknown. But in order to make any progress it is essential to have enough texts, and these must be sufficiently variable, not merely repetitions of the same few formulas. Moreover, some of the inscriptions must be found in contexts which allow us to deduce approximately the meaning of some words without reference to their phonetic values. Only a large deposit of similar documents could open the way to a true decipherment of the Phaistos Disk.

This problem has not prevented enthusiastic amateurs all over the world from indulging in wild speculation. The problem is attractive precisely because it is so limited; it is the limitation which prevents certain deductions which also allows scope for misplaced ingenuity. A few decipherments have been proposed using known languages, including a few based upon Greek, despite the obvious improbability of such a solution at this date. What is worse, their authors are rarely aware of what Greek would look like at this period, at least four hundred years before Mycenaean.

But there is an even easier solution, which is to abandon the attempt to make the text fit a known language, and to invent a new language for the purpose. If you have a word which resembles something appropriate in Greek, you can give it that meaning. But if the next word is meaningless in Greek, you look for something suitable in Latin or Sanskrit or Persian, or whatever language takes your fancy. There is of course no way of proving such a language did not exist; there must have been thousands of languages once spoken, which are now totally forgotten. What is always overlooked is that if you abandon the rigour imposed by a known language, you destroy also any means of finding evidence to support your solution.

Others have failed to understand the conclusions to be drawn from the statistics, which establish the type of script, and have assumed that the signs, or some of them, are ideograms. It is then tempting to try to interpret them by looking for the object they represent, and give them values simply by inspection. The history of writing shows unmistakeably that values can hardly ever be guessed by this method. We cannot perhaps rule out the posssibility of a mixed system, part ideographic and part phonetic; but this would require a very large number of different signs, and thus the making of a large set of stamps to be able to write any but the simplest texts. There have even been decipherers who have proposed to regard it not as a script at all, but as some kind of tool or device, and one of my correspondents seriously suggested that it was really a chart for inter-planetary navigation. Science fiction has a lot to answer for.

My own view, shared by all serious scholars, is that the Disk is undecipherable so long as it remains an isolated document. Only a large increase in the number of inscriptions will permit real progress towards a decipherment. Meanwhile, we must curb our impatience, and admit that if King Minos himself were to reveal to someone in a dream the true interpretation, it would be quite impossible for him to convince anyone else that his was the one and only possible solution.

The Location of
the Inscriptions

Specimens of most of the scripts mentioned in this section are to be seen in the Archaeological Museum of Iraklion, Crete. This holds the major collection of Linear B tablets from Knossos, most of the Linear A inscriptions, and the Phaistos Disk. The Linear B tablets from Pylos are all in the National Museum in Athens, together with some from Mycenae. A selection of these is on exhibition. There are small numbers of Linear B tablets in the Archaeological Museums of Thebes and Navplion.

The Ashmolean Museum, Oxford, has a collection of Linear B tablets from Knossos, donated by Evans while he was in charge of the Museum, and a few specimens of Linear A. The British Museum, London, has a few specimens of Linear B, and some classical Cypriot inscriptions. Isolated Linear B tablets are in Cambridge, Manchester and University College, London. Classical Cypriot inscriptions are also to be found in a number of Museums in western Europe.

All the more recent finds from Cyprus are of course still on the island, mostly at the Archaeological Museum in Nicosia. The Cypro–Minoan documents found at Ugarit (Ras Shamra) are in the National Museum of Damascus.

Bibliographical Note

There is now a vast bibliography of Linear B, but most of it is highly technical and to be found in learned journals. For English readers I should like to refer to my own two books, *The Decipherment of Linear B*, (2nd edn. Cambridge, 1967), and for the contents of the tablets, *The Mycenaean World* (Cambridge, 1976). For more advanced study, the major books in English are: Ventris, M. and Chadwick, J., *Documents in Mycenaean Greek* (2nd edn. Cambridge, 1973); and Palmer L. R., *The Interpretation of Mycenaean Greek Texts*, (Oxford, 1963). A useful study of decipherment is Barber, E. J. W., *Archaeological Decipherment*, (Princeton, 1974).

On Linear A and the various Cypriot scripts there is no satisfactory general publication in English. The Linear A texts have been collected and excellently edited by Godart, L. and Olivier, J-P., *Receuil des Inscriptions en Linéaire A*, 5 vols., Paris, 1976–85. The best collection of classical Cypriot inscriptions is Masson, O., *Les Inscriptions Chypriotes Syllabiques* (Paris, 1961). For the Phaistos Disk, there is an excellent photographic edition by Olivier, J-P., *Le Disque de Phaistos*, (École française d' Athènes, 1975), and a full discussion of the problems by Duhoux, Y., *Le Disque de Phaestos*, (Louvain, 1977).

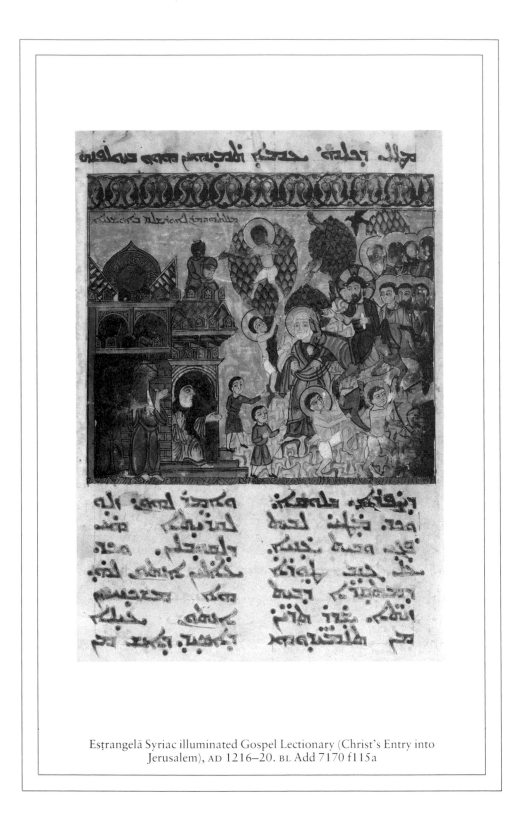

Estrangelā Syriac illuminated Gospel Lectionary (Christ's Entry into Jerusalem), AD 1216–20. BL Add 7170 f115a

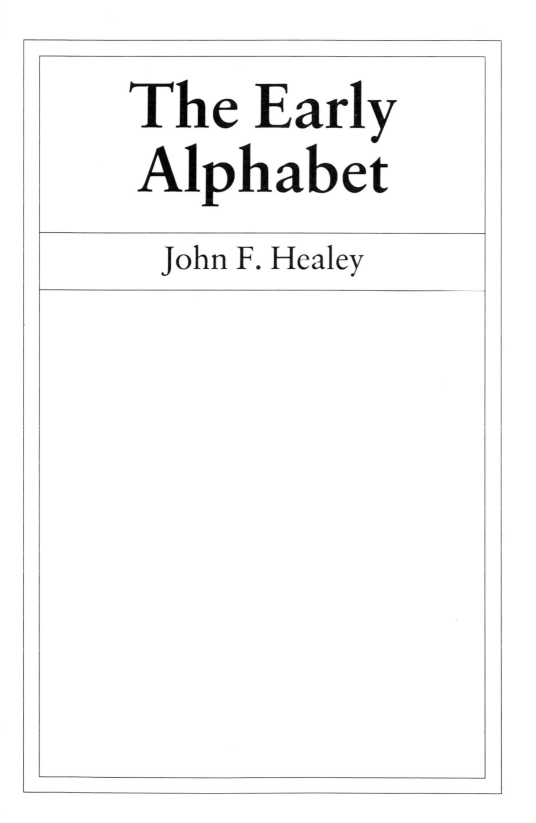

The Early Alphabet

John F. Healey

Note on Transcription

As a general convention within the text, individual *sounds* as part of the language concerned are represented by letters placed between two slashes (e.g. /th/), while *letters* – when the reference is, for example, to their shape in written form or to their position in the alphabet – appear either as capitals (upper case) or as small (lower case) forms *without* slashes (e.g. Latin G/g; Greek Γ/γ). Capitals are often preferred, since the lower case forms arose at a late date and lack significant ancient features which it is often helpful to represent visually.

Acknowledgements

In a survey covering such a wide field the author has been conscious of the need to take advice from various specialists and would in particular like to thank Mr A. R. Millard (University of Liverpool) for many helpful comments and Professor G. R. Smith (University of Manchester) for advice on Arabic and South Arabian. Errors which remain are, of course, entirely the responsibility of the author. Illustrations are reproduced by courtesy of the Trustees of the Chester Beatty Library, Dublin (fig. 21); the Musée du Louvre, Paris (figs. 17, 22, 23, 35); the British Library (figs. 24, 28, 31, 33, 39, 40, frontispiece), and the British Museum (figs. 1, 4, 5, 10, 13, 14, 18, 19, 26, 30); and from the following works by permission of the publishers: D. Pardee, *Les textes para-mythologiques de la 24e campagne*, Éditions Recherche sur les Civilisations, Paris, 1988 (fig. 6); C. Virolleaud, *Le palais royal d'Ugarit* II, Imprimerie Nationale/Librairie C. Klincksieck, Paris, 1957 (fig. 8); *Revue Biblique* 93 (1986) (fig. 9); A. F. L. Beeston, *Sabaic Grammar*, University of Manchester, 1984 (fig. 11); H. Donner and W. Röllig, *Kanaanäische und Aramäische Inschriften* III, Otto Harrassowitz, Wiesbaden, 1969 (fig. 12); K. Jaroš, *Hundert Inschriften aus Kanaan und Israel*, Schweizerisches Katholisches Bibelwerk, Fribourg, 1982 (fig. 20); I. J. Gelb, *A Study of Writing*, University of Chicago Press, 1963 (fig. 25); D. Diringer, *The Alphabet*, Hutchinson, London, 1968 (fig. 27); T. O. Lambdin, *Introduction to Classical Ethiopic (Ge'ez)*, Scholars Press, Missoula, 1978 (fig. 32); *Manuscripts of the Middle East*, Ter Lugt Press, Leiden, 1990 (figs. 36, 37); Y. H. Safadi, *Islamic Calligraphy*, Thames and Hudson, London, 1978 (fig. 38).

Contents

Preface

This section attempts to summarise the general scholarly consensus of views on the early history of alphabetic writing. Inevitably it is necessary to abbreviate and simplify the arguments. Even major issues are often still the subject of dispute. A whole book of over 350 pages has recently been devoted solely to the discussion of early cuneiform alphabets, while in the present volume only a few pages could be given over to this topic!

The origin of alphabetic writing is one of those historical questions which is of interest to all peoples of European, Middle Eastern and Indian origin or educated in the Christian, Jewish or Islamic traditions. For all of us, the alphabet is the first thing we learnt from our parents or our teachers. It is the foundation on which all our subsequent education was based. For many it is also the vehicle of divine revelation, though in fact, as we shall see, the alphabet is one of the many gifts which the great 'book' religions and their associated civilisations owe to the *pagan* world.

The account of the alphabet which follows begins with the discussion of the basic principles involved in alphabetic writing. This is accompanied by a brief description of the characteristics of the Semitic languages for which the alphabet was first used: apart from enabling the reader to understand the problems involved in the devising of the alphabet, this provides a useful reminder that not all languages are alike and that the problems of writing them may vary considerably.

Next, evidence for the earliest attempts at alphabetic writing is outlined. Only one of these attempts was really successful and the third chapter deals with this in detail and with the transmission of this alphabet to the Greeks and ultimately to the Latin West.

The rest of the book is concerned mostly with the ways the alphabet developed later in the Semitic world, leaving behind certain backwaters which continued to exist while the mainstream moved on. The mainstream produced the Jewish (often called the Hebrew) script and the Arabic script. The latter, along with the Latin script, may be regarded as the culmination of a major historical phase in which writing by means of a relatively simple alphabetic system became the foundation of European and Middle Eastern culture, replacing the oral traditions which had existed for millennia before.

Whereas paper and ink may shortly become obsolete, it seems likely that the alphabet, on screen rather than on paper, will remain important for a long time yet. On the other hand, it seems unlikely that our electronic 'writings' are going to survive as long as the earliest alphabetic inscriptions, which were written around 1700 BC and are still today the subject of much lively scholarly interest.

1
Script, Language and the Alphabetic Principle

There is a big difference between script and language, though they tend to be confused. A language consists of a system of sounds. It does not have to be written down. Indeed languages were spoken for millennia before writing was invented and there are still today some unwritten languages (e.g. in India and South America). Any particular language can be represented more or less satisfactorily in any system of writing. One could invent a new system of writing one's own language but one would have to face up to the difficulty of reconciling several conflicting demands on the system. One such demand is the need to keep things simple, so that the new writing system is not so complex as to be unlearnable, but there is also a need to represent all the sounds of the language distinctively, so that the system is unambiguous.

The writing systems of the ancient Near East prior to the invention and spread of the alphabet from c. 1700 BC onwards included a large number of syllabic signs, i.e. with each sign representing a syllable. They were developed from forms of pictographic writing in which small pictures stood for objects and concepts. These had been in use, principally in Egypt and Mesopotamia, since before 3000 BC. Syllabic writing became widespread and new forms of syllabic writing continued to be developed (e.g. Hittite, Cretan, Byblian).

A syllable normally consists of at least two sounds, most commonly a consonant followed by a vowel. Since all languages have far more possible syllables than they have individual sounds (/ba/, /be/, /bi/, /bo/, /bu/, /da/, /de/, /di/, /do/, /du/ are all separate syllables), syllabic systems involved a very large number of signs. The total number of cuneiform signs in the system used in Mesopotamia, for example, is almost six hundred, though some of these retain a pictographic type of function, representing whole words. Many signs had more than one sound-value. Fortunately much smaller repertoires of signs and restricted variations of value were current at any one time and the context would usually show what was intended.

As we will see, the credit for the devising of the alphabetic principle in writing cannot be ascribed to any particular individual, though Greek tradition credited the introduction of the alphabet to Greece to the legendary Kadmos and the Phoenicians. Some scholars would prefer to avoid thinking in terms of an individual inventor, but unless we think of an individual discovering the alphabet, like a Newton or an Einstein, we are in danger of undervaluing the greatness of the achievement.

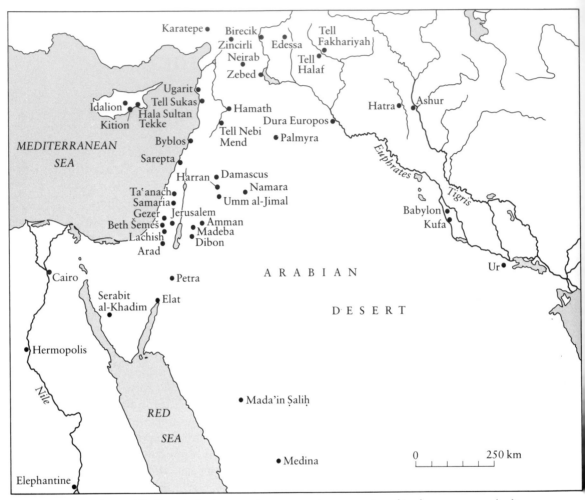

The Middle East (only the more important places mentioned in the text are marked).

This achievement is essentially the insight that writing would be most easily organised if each distinct single sound of a particular language were represented by a single distinctive sign. Since the number of separate sounds is in most languages rather small, the number of signs needed is also rather small – about forty at the most. If we compare this with the writing systems already then in existence (though it seems unlikely that the inventor of the alphabet was an expert in any of these older systems) it implies a glorious simplification. We may note also that the idea of isolating individual sounds has stood the test of time and is still basic to modern linguistics.

Apart from its cumbersomeness, the Akkadian system was unsatisfactory for another reason. It was devised originally not for Akkadian at all but for

Sumerian, and it is often called Sumero-Akkadian. Sumerian is a completely unrelated language lacking some of the distinctive sounds which are essential to Akkadian, so that some of these Akkadian sounds are not properly represented in the script. The inventor of the alphabet on the other hand was able to devise a sign to represent each of the sounds he needed in the (Semitic) language he was intending to write.

Having thus far praised our notional inventor, we must next remark that he did not do quite so thorough a job as he might have done, since he only isolated consonantal sounds and made no allowance at all for vowels. In fact all the ancient Near Eastern alphabets which followed from the first devising of the alphabet are not really alphabets in our modern sense. They are consonantal alphabets and the vowels were only fully represented in these alphabets at a very late date (AD). There were *some* earlier attempts to represent vowels, since in Aramaic and then in Hebrew script certain consonants, particularly **h**, **w** and **y**, came to be used in limited circumstances to represent vowels, i.e. as vowel-letters. Compare English words like 'very' in which y is used as a vowel, though it is normally treated as a consonant as in 'yes'.

In principle it is not unthinkable to write English without vowels. Native speakers of English would be able to add the correct vowels in pronunciation without too much difficulty most of the time. The reader could test this statement by reading it without vowels: Ntv spkrs f nglsh wld b bl t dd th crrct vwls n prnnctn wtht t mch dffclty mst f th tm. In English the main difficulty arises with words *beginning* with a vowel, a difficulty which was less serious in West Semitic scripts since no words began with vowels. Difficulties might well arise also with personal and geographical names, especially names unfamiliar to most readers, but otherwise much would depend on the ability of the reader to apprehend the context of what was being said. It should be remembered that modern newspapers in Hebrew and Arabic are still printed for the most part without vowels and the native speakers of these languages have no difficulty in reading them.

It may be noted that at least one prominent scholar, I. J. Gelb, took the view that this consonantal alphabet is not in fact a true alphabet but should be regarded as a syllabary in which each sign stands for a consonant followed by any vowel. This is a defensible view, but it involves a rather narrow definition of what constitutes an alphabet and it may result in the genius of the consonantal alphabet being undervalued.

However, the true alphabet in our modern sense came into existence when the Greeks, who seem to have got their idea of the alphabet *and* the main letter-forms from the Phoenicians, began to use certain signs, ones which they did not need for consonants in Greek, to represent the vowels. Subsequently the Near Eastern scripts underwent modifications to allow vowels to be expressed either by the addition of special vowel-letters (see above) or by the addition of marks above and below the consonants or, in the case of Ethiopic, by the devising of modifications to the consonants to indicate which particular vowel follows.

There is another aspect of the study of the alphabet which needs brief introduction: the development and fixing of the order of the letters. Surprisingly, perhaps, there is a considerable amount of evidence on this matter even from the earliest times. There are even texts which simply list the letters in the alphabetic order. On the analogy of our ordering of the alphabet as the ABC (pronounced 'ay-bee-cee-dee', etc.), such texts are called 'abecedaries', though the actual ordering may not be the same as ours. (The letter C, as we shall see, was peculiar to Latin and has no real equivalent in the old alphabets.) Information on the alphabetic order is not of purely antiquarian interest: in a number of cases it gives useful information on how the alphabet itself developed. We shall see that the very ordering of both the Ugaritic and the Greek alphabets reveals that certain letters were added secondarily.

Finally, we may note the intrinsic importance of the names of the letters in the different languages. Reflection on the English names of the letters will reveal that this is quite a complicated matter. Why do speakers of British English call Z 'zed', while Americans, apparently with greater logic, call it 'zee', like 'bee' and 'dee'? And why 'el' for L and 'aitch' for H? In the ancient languages the names of the letters can be very important for reconstructing the particular source from which the alphabet was borrowed. For example, the name of the first letter of the Greek alphabet, *alpha* (ἄλφα), is Semitic, like the names of virtually all the letters of the Greek alphabet.

The Semitic Languages

The term 'Semitic' is an accident in the history of scholarship in this field, which arose from an assumed connection with Shem, the son of Noah. It was coined in the eighteenth century AD to refer to a group of languages of which Hebrew and Arabic were the best-known constituents. Today one might prefer a different term, perhaps geographical ('Western Asiatic' or 'Syro-Arabian'), but all other terms have drawbacks and 'Semitic' is convenient and traditional.

Semitic languages were not so widely dispersed as the members of the Indo-European family, but our knowledge of Semitic has great depth in the sense that we possess detailed knowledge of many ancient as well as modern Semitic languages reaching back to the third millennium BC.

The first Semitic language on record is Akkadian which was used in Mesopotamia (basically modern Iraq) under the great empires of the Babylonians and Assyrians. The writing was cuneiform (i.e. with signs formed from patterns of wedges in soft clay) and syllabic. The use of this language in its various dialects continued down to the time of Christ. It had, however, come under strong pressure from Aramaic, another Semitic language, which had its origins in the late second millennium BC and was the language of the Aramaeans.

West Semitic	East Semitic
Eblaite (classification unresolved)	Akkadian:
Ugaritic	*Old Akkadian*
Canaanite: *Phoenician and Punic*	*Babylonian*
Hebrew	*Assyrian*
Moabite, Edomite, etc.	
Aramaic: *Early Aramaic*	
Persian Empire Aramaic	
Nabataean	
Hatran	
Palmyrene	
Jewish Aramaic	
Samaritan Aramaic	
Syriac	
Mandaic	
Modern Aramaic dialects	

South Semitic

Pre-Islamic South Arabian:
  Sabaic, etc.
Pre-Islamic northern dialects:
  Thamudic, Lihyanite, Safaitic, etc.
Arabic
Modern South Arabian:
  Mehrī, etc.
Ethiopian: *Classical Ethiopic (Ge'ez)*
  Amharic, etc.

Table summarising the main divisions of the Semitic language group.

The Aramaean people lived mostly in Syria and upper Mesopotamia and they were using an alphabetic script for their writings. The Aramaic language and script spread rapidly throughout the region. It was used by the great imperial powers of the time and, in the period of the Persian Empire (*c.* 550–323 BC), Aramaic and its script were used by the imperial administration and throughout the western provinces of the Empire as far as Arabia and Egypt.

Aramaic gradually replaced other local languages in Syria/Palestine, languages such as Phoenician (which had an important predecessor in the local language of ancient Ugarit on the Syrian coast *c.* 1500–1200 BC) and Hebrew, which was little used after Old Testament times, though there is some dispute about whether Hebrew became extinct as a spoken language before or after the time of Christ. A number of local dialects of Aramaic became established in important centres. Thus Aramaic became the normal language both of the Jewish communities in the Middle East and of the various 'pagan' kingdoms, like that of the Nabataeans centred on Petra in Jordan. As the pagans were converted and the Christian church spread to the east, Aramaic became its official language, more specifically the dialect of Aramaic known as Syriac (originally the Aramaic dialect of Edessa, modern Urfa/Şanlıurfa in southern Turkey).

After Akkadian and Aramaic, the next great linguistic upheaval in the region came with the dramatic spread of Arabic at the time of the Islamic conquests in the seventh century AD. Arabic remains the main language of the Middle East and the main modern representative of Semitic, though there are also some other living Semitic languages: Amharic (the main Semitic language of Ethiopia), various southern Arabian dialects, remnants of Aramaic (still spoken in parts of Syria, Turkey, Iraq and the USSR) and, of course, modern Israeli Hebrew, which has returned to the Middle East as a spoken language relatively recently.

Since they are relevant to some extent to questions of script, it will be useful to note some major characteristics of the Semitic languages. The first is that all the Semitic languages contain sounds which do not exist in English and other European languages. An example is the so-called emphatic /t/, which is difficult for English-speakers to master. To produce it involves pronouncing the English /t/ but with the tongue flaccid instead of rigid and slightly pressed up towards the roof of the mouth. It is a thickened /t/ of the kind we associate with intoxication or a dental anaesthetic. Since this sound does not exist in English or in our script (which is really the Latin script with a few modifications), linguists have to represent this consonant with a conventional sign to make it clear that it is not the ordinary /t/ which is in question. The convention widely accepted is to place a dot under the ordinary /t/, i.e. /ṭ/. There are other special sounds which need not be explained here, but the variety of signs likely to be encountered in studying the alphabets used for the Semitic languages include such extras as / ḍ/, / ṣ/, / ṭ/, /ġ/, /ʾ/, /ʿ/ and /š/. The Semitic scripts also often distinguish long from short vowels and this distinction is usually represented by the placing of a line over the vowel in our Latin script to mark the long variety: /ā/, /ī/, /ū/. When we give the equivalent in our own script for the letters in a word of one of the other scripts (for example, Hebrew שָׁלוֹם = šālōm), the process is called transliteration.

The other relevant point is that consonants in verbal roots have a special role in all Semitic languages. They are not more important than vowels, as is often quite erroneously stated, but in many words the vowels carry out the grammatical job of giving precise meaning to a form, while the consonants are the 'root' and have attached to them the basic notion which is common to all the words based on that particular set of consonants. Thus there is an Arabic root *KTB*. *KTB* does not mean anything as it stands. Indeed it is totally unpronounceable. But by adding vowels in different patterns (and sometimes special prefixes), the root *KTB* comes to life and takes on meaning as a real word in the language: *kātib* means 'writer', *kataba* 'he wrote', *kitāb* 'book', *kutub* 'books', *kutubī* 'bookseller', *kitāba* 'writing', *maktab* 'office', and *maktaba* 'library, bookshop'. Observing these words we can confirm that there is a root *KTB* and deduce that it has to do with 'writing'. Thus the consonants are the bones which convey the basic meaning, while the vowels add flesh to the skeleton.

From this it is clear why some scholars connect the consonantal alphabet with the distinctive role played by consonants in Semitic word-formation. One should not, however, conclude that the ancient Semitic peoples used a consonantal alphabet because vowels were unimportant to them. They were *very* important. Indeed, the best-attested ancient Semitic language, Akkadian, is written in a syllabic script taken over from Sumerian which *does* indicate vowels, while the other important literary languages – Hebrew, Syriac, Arabic and Ethiopic – all eventually developed ways of expressing vowels in writing.

What one could, perhaps, say of the early consonantal alphabet is that it handled the root aspect of word-formation well, but was defective in that it failed to account satisfactorily for vowels, the other important ingredient in word-formation. The separation of consonants and vowels in the alphabet could, therefore, be said to correspond to the separation of function of vowels and consonants in the Semitic languages.

Writing Materials and Types of Script
The basic data for our study of the early alphabet are very varied. There are large public monumental inscriptions, burial inscriptions, private letters, coins, seals, casual graffiti, legal documents, literary works and, of course, Bibles and Qur'āns. The material on which the writing was executed also varied considerably and it could have an important influence on the development of the script. Much depended on local availability of materials. In Egypt papyrus was the typical material for most purposes. In Mesopotamia soft clay was used and subsequently dried or baked. Public monuments in both areas were usually of stone.

It is clear that the cuneiform writing system, using signs formed by patterns of wedge-shaped marks (Latin *cuneus* 'wedge'), was particularly suited to impression on soft clay. This style of writing could be imitated in stone but would be very difficult to use on papyrus. It is angular and sharp because of the type of stylus which was used, a cut reed. Cuneiform did spread westwards to Anatolia, Syria and Egypt and was used, as we shall see, for writing one of the earliest alphabets, but the major developments in alphabetic writing occurred not on clay tablets, but on the smooth dry surface of papyrus, dressed stone and pot.

Ancient papyrus is rarely preserved since, unlike dried clay tablets, which are very durable when buried in the earth, in most climatic conditions papyrus tends to rot and so disappear. Thus, although it is likely that papyrus was used extensively for writing in Phoenicia, Syria and Palestine, little has survived from those areas. Egypt, however, is one of the places where the climate sometimes allows preservation of papyrus (away from the river Nile itself) and we are fortunate in having some important collections of documents from there. Writing material produced from animal skins also is rarely preserved, though it *was* used, as were wax writing-boards. Inscriptions on stone are more durable, though vulnerable to shattering, grinding and weathering, and the same is true of writing on pieces of broken pot, commonly used in Palestine and elsewhere. An inscribed potsherd is called an ostracon (plural ostraca). Papyrus and pot were probably used side by side in Palestine as they were in Egypt, where papyrus was used, for example, for Aramaic legal and literary documents. Pot tended to be used as a cheap substitute for papyrus in writing ephemeral documents such as lists, notes, etc.

Epigraphy is the term generally used for the study of inscriptions carved or scratched on hard materials. In the study of regions where there are a lot of papyri preserved, the term palaeography tends to be restricted to the study of papyri only, though the distinction between writing on papyrus and writing on hard materials is really artificial. Both are part and parcel of a community's 'epigraphic' remains. In relation to Semitic inscriptions, it is common to use the term palaeography for a particular aspect of the study of writing on all materials, i.e. the study of the progressive developments and changes in the forms of the letters or signs. In the early history of writing, a fundamental development is the step from pictographic to linear forms in which the original pictographic intention has been forgotten or is very secondary. Forms thus become stylised and take on a life of their own, unrelated to the need to represent a pictured object.

Another broad distinction which should be noted is that between formal and cursive forms of writing. Normally the primary form of a writing system is that used for accounts, letters and lists, even if these are carefully produced by civil servants. The making of great public inscriptions is a secondary affair and would hardly happen without the prior existence of a strong tradition of 'normal' writing. The standardised, formal and decorative forms used especially for public monuments are usually called 'monumental'. A monumental script often gains a life of its own, becoming a separate script.

By contrast, the term 'cursive' is used for the type of script which is typically written at great speed. It is rounded rather than square, flowing and joined up (ligatured). The most cursive forms of script generally appear in the most casual pieces of writing. At its extreme this might be a traveller scratching his name on a rock-face while sitting to rest. This is called a graffito (plural graffiti). But we have to be careful. If this traveller has visited places where he has seen formal inscriptions, he might introduce monumental features into his graffito in order to make it look more impressive. Often monumental features are archaising features, which might deceive us in our attempt to date the text on palaeographic grounds. We see informal scripts particularly in letters and practical documents, though again there may be a degree of formality even within the cursive tradition.

It is also often possible to see the influence of the cursive style on the monumental style. Developments in the cursive style eventually cause changes in the monumental style. Thus even in the 'monumental' style of our own alphabet (e.g. on foundation stones and in print) the old-fashioned g with a closed loop hanging from the left of the upper circle is disappearing, just as it has mostly disappeared in handwriting. Nobody actually writes postcards to friends in the letter-style used in a printed book or on a foundation stone. Very few people, for example, reproduce the 'printed' form of lower-case a in their handwriting, or write without joining any of the letters.

The question of the direction of writing – right to left v. left to right, etc. – will be discussed where it arises, but it should at least be noted here that scripts can follow different conventions and may go through periods of uncertainty, using several methods side by side. Also, our convention of separating words with spaces is not found in all the traditions discussed here. Some separate words with special markers. Greek tended not to separate words at all. Most of the scripts we shall deal with habitually join certain words together. The word 'and' and also some prepositions are thus attached directly to the following word. And only at a rather late stage did the convention creep in of marking the ends of sentences.

2
First Attempts at Alphabetic Writing

There is evidence of attempts to write early West Semitic languages in a *local* syllabic script, i.e. neither in Mesopotamian cuneiform nor in Egyptian hieroglyphs. Such attempts have been identified in very early, second-millennium BC, inscriptions from Byblos in Lebanon and from Jordan. Unfortunately, the evidence is not very extensive and the interpretation of the material extremely uncertain.

The first steps towards *alphabetic* writing appear also to have been taken in the early second millennium BC. There is uncertainty about the order of events and precise dating, but a number of inscriptions have been discovered in Sinai and Palestine (and called Proto-Sinaitic or Proto-Canaanite) in which it appears that the Egyptian way of writing has been converted into an alphabetic system.

The Invention of the Consonantal Alphabet

The Egyptian system is essentially syllabic though, unlike Akkadian cuneiform, the vowel in any syllable is not defined. Thus there were, in Egyptian, signs representing **b** plus any vowel, **d** plus any vowel, etc. It appears that ultimately the signs used for these single-consonant signs derived from pictographs, though through the course of time the 'picture' came to represent not the object concerned but the first consonant of the Egyptian word for this object. Thus the sign for 'mouth', $\bigcirc$, originally pronounced as the word for 'mouth', *r* or *r'i*, came to be used for **r** plus any vowel or none. The principle of using a sign to represent the first letter of the word it stands for is called acrophony ('initial sound'). This gave the Egyptians the ready possibility of alphabetic writing, since in essence this kind of consonant-only system was all that was used for the alphabetic scripts which *did* develop. However, the Egyptians themselves did not take this step, and multi-consonant signs continued to be the basis of the Egyptian script.

The writers of the Proto-Sinaitic or Proto-Canaanite inscriptions apparently *did* take this step in the early to middle second millennium BC. The evidence is difficult and scholars do not agree on all points. The texts in question first became well known through a series of short inscriptions of *c.* 1700 BC onwards,

1   carved by miners at the turquoise mines at Serabit al-Khadim in Sinai. Because the number of signs in these inscriptions was so small (less than thirty), it quickly became clear that this script was an alphabet and not a syllabary.

1 Sandstone sphinx with Proto-Sinaitic alphabetic inscription on its base. From Serabit al-Khadim, *c.* 1700 BC. BM WA 41748

Subsequently, other examples have been found in Palestine (Shechem, Gezer, Lachish), so we can be certain that we are dealing with a fairly widespread phenomenon. While we can never hope to know who invented the new so-called linear alphabet, two things seem clear. Firstly, there is clearly an Egyptian inspiration behind the invention, since there are some similarities of signs and the basic acrophonic principle (which has no parallel in cuneiform) must have come from knowledge of the Egyptian script. Secondly, the texts are in Canaanite West Semitic, not Egyptian, so we can be fairly sure of an origin of the script in the Semitic area which had close cultural contact with Egypt. Palestine is currently the strongest candidate, though the importance of the Phoenician coast (especially cosmopolitan Byblos) in the script traditions leads one to suspect that that region may have played a major role, just as it had produced a syllabic script of its own and eventually produced Ugaritic and Phoenician.

Basically the new script, which has been deciphered with a fair degree of 2,3 certainty (though the texts are not always understood), uses the *Semitic* (not the Egyptian) word for the object of the original pictograph as the starting

2 Examples of Proto-Sinaitic: each group of letters reads (*l*)*b'lt*, 'for the goddess Ba'alat'.

3 Some Proto-Sinaitic forms.

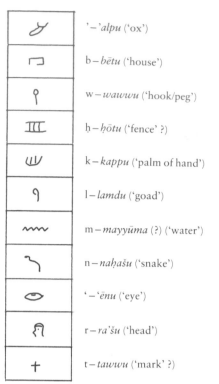

ʾ	ʾ – ʾalpu ('ox')
	b – bētu ('house')
	w – wawwu ('hook/peg')
	ḥ – ḥōtu ('fence' ?)
	k – kappu ('palm of hand')
	l – lamdu ('goad')
	m – mayyūma (?) ('water')
	n – naḥašu ('snake')
	ʿ – ʿēnu ('eye')
	r – raʾšu ('head')
	t – tawwu ('mark' ?)

point and uses the first letter of *that* word as the value of the sign. Thus the drawing of a house stood for 'house'. 'House' in West Semitic was *bēt*. Hence the 'house' pictograph was used for the consonant **b**. The acrophonic principle may not explain all the signs, but the following are clear: ' from *ʾalpu*, 'ox'; **b** from *baytu/bētu*, 'house'; **w** from *wawwu*, 'hook/peg'(?); **y** from *yadu* 'hand/arm'; **k** from *kappu*, 'palm of hand'; **l** from *lamdu*, 'goad'; **m** from *mayyūma* (?), 'water'; **n** from *naḥašu*, 'snake'; ' from *ʿaynu/ʿēnu* 'eye'; and **r** from *raʾšu*, 'head' (original pronunciations partially conjectural).

While the Proto-Sinaitic/Proto-Canaanite inscriptions are quite obscure, there are some later Proto-Canaanite texts which are better understood (e.g. the thirteenth-century BC Lachish ewer, an ostracon of the twelfth century BC from Beth Šemeš, and the ʿIzbet Ṣarṭah inscription, also of the twelfth century) and, although the material we have in this type of writing is very limited, it is clear from comparison of many of the letters with the much better known Phoenician script that the Phoenician is the direct descendant of the Proto-Sinaitic/Proto-Canaanite. Intermediate forms are found in a variety of small inscriptions from Palestine (the el-Khader arrowheads, twelfth century BC) and Lebanon (two in Proto-Canaanite and two in Phoenician). There are even fragments from as far away as Crete and Sardinia (eleventh century BC),

4 Phoenician inscribed arrowhead (front and back), 11th century BC. BM WA 136753

which should be especially noted in connection with the spread of the Semitic alphabet to the Greeks (discussed below).

As we shall see, the Hebrew, Aramaic and Greek scripts depend, at least according to the common view, on the Phoenician. From the Greek came our Latin alphabet and the Cyrillic (Russian) script, and from the Aramaic came the Arabic script and most of the scripts used in India. Thus from the Proto-Sinaitic/Proto-Canaanite alphabet came the writing systems of a large proportion of the modern world's population, Chinese being the main exception. Although we do not know who invented the new alphabet, the cultural advance it constituted is enormously significant.

The Ugaritic and Similar Alphabets

Other experiments in alphabet creation were going on at roughly the same time in northern Syria and Palestine; we know this from a number of finds, but principally from the archives of the ancient city of Ugarit, modern Ras Shamra (see map p. 202). From 1929 onwards, large numbers of inscribed clay tablets were found in excavations at the site. These are dated to the Late Bronze Age c. 1400–1200 BC and, while many were written in the familiar syllabic cuneiform of Akkadian and Hittite, some were written in a previously unknown   5,6

5 Ugaritic literary tablet.
BM loan 84 (AO 17.325) reverse

cuneiform script (i.e. based, like the Sumero-Akkadian script, on wedge shapes) written from left to right. H. Bauer, E. Dhorme and C. Virolleaud worked on its decipherment at the same time, the first two having been engaged (on opposite sides!) in cipher work during World War I.

The decipherers worked in different ways, but what follows will give a basic idea of the kinds of logic used. It was quickly realised that the new script, despite being cuneiform, was alphabetic, since it clearly had only thirty signs in all. This was the basic working assumption. A second assumption, derived from knowledge of the linguistic history of the region, was that the language was probably West Semitic, akin to Phoenician and Hebrew, using like them a consonantal alphabet. These assumptions lead one to expect certain typical West Semitic prefixes and suffixes as well as, for example, traditional West Semitic ways of writing introductory formulae. Also it was noticed that a special sign was frequently used as a word-separator, just as we separate words by leaving a space between them.

Several texts and some brief inscriptions began with the same sign – [sign]. Thus we find [signs] and [signs]. Since there is a well-known West Semitic formula of using the preposition /l/, 'for, concerning', in the titles of texts and in ownership marks, it was guessed that [sign] stood for **l**. Similarly /-m/ and /-t/ are very common West Semitic endings used to mark plurals and feminine gender. Signs [sign] and [sign] seemed to fit the bill, since they occurred frequently at the ends of words. The group [signs] occurred a number of times. This is a very rare pattern in West Semitic (i.e. initial and final consonants of a word identical). The only likely candidate was the word for 'three', *šlš*, so it was supposed that [sign] represented /š/ (a supposition which was later refined to /t̠/, a sound not preserved in Phoenician and Hebrew, where it merged with /š/). Further guesswork led to the identification of [signs] as *lbʿl*, 'to (the god) Baʿal', and [signs] ([sign]) as *mlk(m)*, 'king(s)'. By this kind of procedure and with little delay, all the signs were identified and the language was confirmed to be a West Semitic one related to the later Phoenician and Hebrew languages.

The hypothetical decipherment was regarded as successful because it actually worked: the texts could be read and understood (on the basis of comparison with other Semitic languages) and they proved to include extremely important myths, rituals and administrative documents. However, the decipherment received its definitive seal of certainty when in 1955 a new tablet was found at Ugarit which, though it was broken, listed the majority of the letters and gave alongside each one the consonantal equivalent as represented in the Akkadian cuneiform script (with vowel attached, since the Sumero-Akkadian system cannot express consonants alone).

The remarkable thing about the Ugaritic alphabet, apart from its early date, was the fact that it was a *cuneiform* alphabet. This makes it look superficially like Akkadian

ʾa	[sign]	k	[sign]
ʾi	[sign]	l	[sign]
ʾu	[sign]	m	[sign]
b	[sign]	n	[sign]
g	[sign]	s	[sign]
d	[sign]	ṣ̀	[sign]
ḏ	[sign]	ʿ	[sign]
h	[sign]	ġ	[sign]
w	[sign]	p	[sign]
z	[sign]	ṣ	[sign]
ḥ	[sign]	q	[sign]
ḫ	[sign]	r	[sign]
ṭ	[sign]	š	[sign]
ṯ	[sign]	t	[sign]
y	[sign]	t̠	[sign]

7 The Ugaritic cuneiform alphabet.

cuneiform, but the individual signs are different from the Akkadian signs. No doubt the basic technology of writing followed a Mesopotamian model (Akkadian texts were well known in the West at this time), but the actual forms of the letters seem to have been inspired at least in part by the linear alphabet of the Proto-Canaanite/Proto-Sinaitic inscriptions.

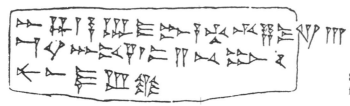

8 Ugaritic abecedary found in 1948.

8   Ugarit also gives us our first glimpse of an established ordering of the letters of the alphabet, since an abecedary text was found in 1948 which simply lists the letters in order: 'a, b, g, ḫ, d, h, w, z, ḥ, ṭ, y, k, š, l, m, ḏ, n, ṯ, s, ʿ, p, ṣ, q, r, ṱ, ġ, t, 'i, 'u, ś. The last three appear to be additional and so we have basically a twenty-seven-letter system which has been expanded by the addition of 'i, 'u and ś, a special s-sound used outside literary texts in words of Hurrian origin and in texts actually *in* Hurrian, since the Ugaritic cuneiform alphabet was also used at Ugarit for this language. This cuneiform alphabet is a 'long' alphabet by comparison with the 'short' twenty-two-letter alphabet used for Phoenician and Hebrew.

   The sound represented as ' in transliteration is the glottal stop between two vowels, heard today in Glasgow and Cockney dialects of English in the pronunciation of words such as 'bottle' as /bo'el/, and between the /e/ and the /o/ of modern German *beobachten*. In the Ugaritic script there are three varieties of this letter *aleph* (as it is called in Hebrew). Apparently the two extra forms of *aleph*, 'i and 'u, were devised as aids to help indicate the vowel following the *aleph* (or sometimes in front of it), though without any distinction in vowel length. Occasionally these signs seem to be used as pure vowel signs without the glottal stop, though this is not normal. It is best to regard the emergence of the three *aleph*s as an intrusion of syllabic writing into an otherwise consonantal system. The Ugaritic scribes who developed the long cuneiform alphabet may have been inspired in this regard by the existence of certain syllabic cuneiform signs which were sometimes used simply to indicate a vowel. The Ugaritic forms of 'i and 'u may actually be derived from the Akkadian signs for i and ú. Like the letter ś, they may have been devised especially to assist with the writing of non-Semitic words.

   There are other cuneiform alphabetic inscriptions of similar date, perhaps a little later, from the area to the south of Ugarit. These appear at various sites including Taʿanach, Nahal Tavor and Beth Šemeš in Palestine, Tell Nebi Mend in Syria and Sarepta in Lebanon. There is even an inscription from Cyprus (Hala Sultan Tekke), though the silver dish on which it is found may be an import from the Levantine coast.

Some of these other inscriptions, as well as a small number of texts from Ugarit itself, are in the shorter alphabet. This shorter repertoire was more or less adequate for the later languages of the area, such as Phoenician and Hebrew, though it may be noted that at least one of the Hebrew letters was pronounced in two different ways which later had to be distinguished by the use of additional marks (on this see below). Indeed one of the inscriptions in alphabetic cuneiform, the one from Sarepta in Lebanon, seems to be in the Phoenician language.

It is not easy to explain the complex history of the alphabet in this period. According to a widespread view, the alphabet was being shortened because linguistic changes were taking place which involved the loss of certain sounds. Thus Hebrew did not need to represent /ḫ/, /t̲/, /ṭ/, /ġ/ or /t̲/, while /š/ *was* needed, but came to be represented by the otherwise unwanted sign for /t̲/, so that the old letter š was dropped. The shorter cuneiform alphabet is usually seen as a step in this direction. At the same time the sporadic nature of the finds has been taken to suggest that the idea of a cuneiform alphabet did not really catch on and become popular. It is essentially medium-related and depends upon the local availability of suitable clay. More importantly, the southern area of Syria/Palestine was under considerable Egyptian influence at this time and it appears that writing, using a descendant of the Proto-Sinaitic/Proto-Canaanite script, was normally done on papyrus, which rarely survives in this area.

Recently another theory has been put forward which, while attractive, as yet lacks sufficient proof. It is, however, worthy of being recorded here. There is some evidence to support the view that the Ugaritic alphabet is an expanded version of the shorter cuneiform alphabet which must, therefore, have preceded it, rather than a longer prototype of the later shortened alphabet. On this view there would have been in the area of Syria/Palestine in the middle of the second millennium BC two alphabets, a linear one and a cuneiform one, side by side. The cuneiform version was widespread but much less used. It was expanded to allow for extra sounds which were needed as a result of southern Semitic – Arabian – influence. The Ugaritic language has a full range of consonantal sounds, as do South Arabian and the much later Arabic. There are other signs of an Arabian connection in Ugaritic culture.

A key piece of evidence would be the cuneiform alphabetic text from Beth Šemeš, which is in fact an abecedary, though instead of following the established West Semitic order (beginning ', b, g, d ...), it follows the South Arabian order (h, l, ḥ, m ...). (On letter-ordering, see the next section.) This would suggest that what we know as the South Arabian letter-order (though only from a later date) intruded into Palestine, perhaps with an incoming ethnic group, at a very early date. However, there is much that is unproved in this neat schema.

9

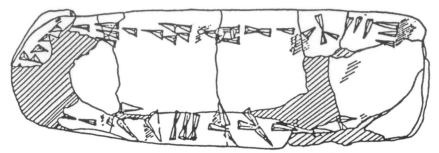

9 The Beth Šemeš abecedary: cuneiform alphabet with South Arabian letter-order.

The Ugaritic cuneiform is the only well-known alphabetic cuneiform. There is no doubt that the cuneiform alphabets disappeared and the other branch of alphabetic tradition, that of the forms descended from the Proto-Sinaitic/Proto-Canaanite script, replaced it. Ugarit itself was destroyed by the Sea Peoples *c.* 1200 BC, and with it disappeared the Ugaritic alphabet.

Direction of Writing and Abecedaries

Since the cuneiform alphabets give us our first coherent evidence on the subject, it is appropriate here to add some comments on the direction of writing and on the ordering of letters to form the complete alphabet.

West Semitic texts before the emergence of the Phoenician script are not uniform in their direction of writing. The Ugaritic alphabet is written from left to right like classical Greek, Latin and English, but there are a few Ugaritic texts which follow the opposite pattern, right to left. The earlier Proto-Sinaitic/Proto-Canaanite scripts are very irregular: writing could be in either direction or vertical. Some early Greek and South Arabian texts are written boustro-phedon (βουστροφηδόν) – like an ox ploughing a field: from left to right in the first line, right to left in the second, left to right in the third and so on (or starting on the right in the first line). In such inscriptions the letters are often reversed to face the direction of writing.

With the settling down of the Phoenician alphabet *c.* 1100–1050 BC, the right-to-left order became fixed and so it has remained for the main Semitic scripts which survive to the present day. It may be noted that this fact is of some significance in the discussion of the date at which the Greeks received the alphabet from the Phoenicians, since in the earliest Greek inscriptions the direction is still *not* fixed (see below).

The ordering of the alphabet is best established from abecedaries, school or practice texts in which a trainee lists the letters of the alphabet in the order in which he has learnt them. The complete Ugaritic abecedary, referred to earlier, clearly established the Ugaritic letter-order. This order is interesting not only in itself but, as we have seen, because of what it reveals about the development of the Ugaritic alphabet. It seems that the three letters at the end, 'i, 'u, s̀, were added at a secondary stage of development. Apparently 'i and 'u, the additional forms of the letter 'a, were added at the end before š was finally attached. This avoided disrupting the traditional order.

The ordering of the Phoenician and Hebrew alphabets is the same as that of the basic Ugaritic twenty-seven-letter alphabet, after the removal of ḫ, š (replaced by the sign formerly used for /t/), ḏ, ṯ and ġ: ', b, g, d, h, w, z, ḥ, ṭ, y, k, l, m, n, s, ', p, ṣ, q, r, š (old ṯ), t. Hence Ugarit's claim to have established the first alphabet so far known to history, though as we have seen, its is not the first alphabetic writing. Reference to another major traditional Semitic letter-ordering pattern is found in the next section.

Also of interest are the names of the letters. Many of these correspond to the object depicted in the original pictograph from which the letter developed. Thus the letter b is called bēt in Hebrew, i.e. 'house', and the original pictograph was a picture of a house. These names go back to the very beginnings of the alphabet. Letters added later tended not to have proper names of this kind, while the names for the original letters were fixed to such a degree that when the Greeks took over the Phoenician alphabet (see below) they retained the old names, alpha, bēta (ἄλφα, βῆτα) etc., despite the fact that the names were absolutely meaningless in Greek.

The South Arabian Alphabet

Directly related to the linear proto-alphabet is the alphabetic system adopted in southern Arabia. The inscriptions in this script come from ancient South Arabian kingdoms such as those of the Sabaeans and the Minaeans, and the earliest may date to c. 500 BC or earlier, though the script did not die out until c. AD 600. Despite all efforts, these inscriptions are notoriously difficult to date.

It is thought that another small group of inscriptions represents the link between the Proto-Canaanite and the South Arabian scripts. These come not from southern Arabia but from Babylonia (seventh century BC) and from near Elath on the Gulf of Aqaba (eighth to seventh centuries BC). There are also

10

10 South Arabian inscription from Saba, 2nd century BC. BM WA 103021

other inscriptions of an intermediary type from Arabia. These materials are called Proto-Arabian and this Proto-Arabian script seems to have branched off from Proto-Canaanite *c.* 1300 BC.

In the north of Arabia there are also well-known relatives of the South Arabian script, more or less contemporary with it, including the scripts used for such languages as Lihyanite, Thamudic and Safaitic. The dating of these texts is again difficult. They probably run from several centuries BC right down to the Islamic period. One precisely dated example in this category of script is a bilingual in Thamudic script and Nabataean script (though the *language* of the Nabataean part seems in fact to be early Arabic). The Nabataean text contains a date which fixes the text at AD 267–8.

An offshoot of this script was exported to Ethiopia and forms the basis of the classical Ethiopic (Ge'ez) and modern Amharic scripts (see below). The first Ge'ez inscriptions were actually written in the monumental South Arabian script.

11   By careful reconstruction of rather fragmentary evidence, it has been concluded that the order of the twenty-nine South Arabian letters was as follows: **h, l, ḥ, m, q, w, š, r, b** (or **ǵ**), **t, s, k, n, ḫ, ś, f, ', ', ḍ, g, d, ǵ** (or **b**), **ṭ, z, ḏ, y, ṯ, ṣ/ẓ.** As has been noted above, it has been discovered recently that the ordering of the alphabet in southern Arabia has a precedent in one of the cuneiform alphabetic texts *not* from Ugarit, i.e. the Beth Šemeš tablet, which gives the alphabet in the South Arabian order. It is therefore likely that the South Arabian alphabetic tradition goes right back into the second millennium BC.

Y	h	𐩵	s	𐩵	d
𐩡	l	𐩫	k	𐩴	ǵ
𐩲	ḥ	𐩬	n	𐩷	ṭ
𐩣	m	𐩭	ḫ	𐩸	z
𐩤	q	𐩦	ś	𐩹	ḏ
⊕	w	◇	f	𐩺	y
𐩦	š	𐩠	'	𐩻	ṯ
)	r	o	'	𐩼	ṣ
𐩨	b	𐩵	ḍ	𐩽	ẓ
X	t	𐩴	g		

11 The South Arabian alphabet.

3
Consolidation of the Alphabet and Export to the West

Although the main evidence of the Proto-Sinaitic/Proto-Canaanite and even cuneiform alphabets is in the south – Palestine, Sinai, etc., with Ugarit an outpost of the cuneiform alphabet in the north – some early and much later evidence suggests that the Phoenician coast and specifically Byblos may have been a major focus of script development.

The Phoenician, Hebrew and Aramaic Alphabets

The twenty two-letter Byblian alphabet (the Phoenician alphabet) evolved *c.* 1050 BC in a direct line of descent from the earlier linear alphabets. As we have seen, the right-to-left orientation of writing and the stylised linear character of the letters became fixed at about this time. The inscription of the Ahiram sarcophagus, dated *c.* 1000 BC, finds the script already in a classic form. Other inscriptions, also from Byblos, follow soon after.

12

12 Phoenician inscription of Ahiram. From Byblos, late 11th century BC.

A little later the Phoenician script spread and came to be used by kingdoms to the north, as is evidenced by ninth-century BC inscriptions from Zincirli (Ya'udi/Sam'al) in modern Turkey and from Karatepe (also in Turkey, eighth century BC). The latter are especially important since they are in fact bilingual in Phoenician and Hieroglyphic Hittite.

Within the Phoenician orbit, the script was later used in the so-called Punic colonies of the Phoenicians around the Mediterranean. Other Phoenician materials have been found, for example, at Ur in Mesopotamia and in Cyprus. Most of these inscriptions are carved on stone, but a few are in ink and there are some signs of a tendency towards more cursive forms. Phoenician and Punic inscriptions continued to be produced until the second to third centuries AD.

13,14

13 Phoenician inscription on obelisk from Kition (Cyprus), 4th century BC. BM WA 125082

14 Phoenician votive inscription from Idalion (Cyprus), 390 BC. BM WA 125315

The Phoenician alphabet spread south to the Hebrews and was adopted by the Aramaeans to the east. Both the Hebrews and the Aramaeans were at this time establishing kingdoms. The Aramaeans have left a number of monumental inscriptions, while the Hebrew material is mostly of a less dramatic kind, though extensive in the quantity (letters, seals, etc.) which has come to light, partly as a result of the intensive archaeological exploration of Palestine.

15   Thus three main West Semitic scripts emerged from the earlier Byblian linear alphabet. The primary one was the Phoenician, from which the Aramaic and Hebrew scripts are usually thought to be derived. The twenty-two-letter Phoenician script, which had become stabilised *c.* 1050 BC, remained essentially unchanged during most of its long life; Phoenician bears the great distinction of having been the probable source used by the Greeks for their adoption of the alphabet.

The Phoenician script was at first used unchanged by the Hebrews, who

	Early Phoenician	Moabite	Hebrew Ostraca (sixth century BC)	Early Aramaic	Late Aramaic Papyri	Palmyrene Aramaic	Monumental Nabataean Aramaic	'Square' Jewish/ Hebrew Printed
'	𐤀	𐤀	𐤀	𐤀	א	א	ﭏ	א
b	𐤁	𐤁	𐤁	𐤁	⸾	𐤁	ﭏ	ב
g	𐤂	𐤂	𐤂	𐤂	⸾	⸾	⸾	ג
d	𐤃	𐤃	𐤃	𐤃	⸾	⸾	⸾	ד
h	𐤄	𐤄	𐤄	𐤄	⸾	⸾	⸾	ה
w	𐤅	𐤅	𐤅	𐤅	⸾	⸾	⸾	ו
z	𐤆	𐤆	𐤆	𐤆	⸾	⸾	⸾	ז
ḥ	𐤇	𐤇	𐤇	𐤇	⸾	⸾	⸾	ח
ṭ	𐤈	𐤈	𐤈	𐤈	⸾	⸾	⸾	ט
y	𐤉	𐤉	𐤉	𐤉	⸾	⸾	⸾	י
k	𐤊	𐤊	𐤊	𐤊	⸾	⸾	⸾	כ
l	𐤋	𐤋	𐤋	𐤋	⸾	⸾	⸾	ל
m	𐤌	𐤌	𐤌	𐤌	⸾	⸾	⸾	מ
n	𐤍	𐤍	𐤍	𐤍	⸾	⸾	⸾	נ
s	𐤎	𐤎	𐤎	𐤎	⸾	⸾	⸾	ס
'	𐤏	𐤏	𐤏	𐤏	⸾	⸾	⸾	ע
p	𐤐	𐤐	𐤐	𐤐	⸾	⸾	⸾	פ
ṣ	𐤑	𐤑	𐤑	𐤑	⸾	⸾	⸾	צ
q	𐤒	𐤒	𐤒	𐤒	⸾	⸾	⸾	ק
r	𐤓	𐤓	𐤓	𐤓	⸾	⸾	⸾	ר
š	𐤔	𐤔	𐤔	𐤔	⸾	⸾	⸾	ש
t	𐤕	𐤕	𐤕	𐤕	⸾	⸾	⸾	ת

15 Phoenician, Hebrew and Aramaic scripts.

16 The Hebrew Gezer 'Calendar', 10th century BC.

17 Moabite inscription of King Mesha from Dibon (Jordan), *c.* 850 BC. Louvre AO 5066

accepted the script along with a whole cluster of other cultural traditions from the peoples they met when they settled in Palestine. Thus the very earliest Hebrew inscription is in the Phoenician script. This is the so-called Gezer Calen-

16 dar, a small tenth-century BC stone tablet bearing a brief catalogue of the agricultural activities of the year. In fact, it cannot be easily decided linguistically whether this text is actually Hebrew or Phoenician. Surprisingly, the best witness to the earliest distinctively Hebrew script-form is the ninth-century BC

17 Moabite inscription of King Mesha, the Moabites having used the Hebrew script. Y. Aharoni, it may be noted, attempted to identify in a tenth-century BC inscription from Arad a transitional script between the Phoenician and the Hebrew.

However, the Phoenician script was not entirely satisfactory from the Hebrew point of view. Hebrew has some sounds not represented in Phoenician. At least in later periods, one of the letters taken by Hebrew from Phoenician, the letter we transliterate as š, was in fact pronounced in Hebrew in two different ways, as /š/ (i.e. /sh/) and /ś/; the precise manner of articulation of the latter is uncertain, but it was different from the other Hebrew s-sounds and may have resembled the Welsh /ll/ as in *llan*. Later Hebrew came to distinguish the two by placing a dot on the right or left of the letter. It would have been feasible to invent a new letter, but writing systems are extraordinarily conservative once established and the Phoenician model was dominant. Hence no such radical innovation was undertaken.

224

18 Hebrew tomb inscription from Jerusalem, 8th–7th century BC. BM WA 125205

19 Hebrew ostracon from Lachish, early 6th century BC. BM WA 125702

Other Hebrew inscriptions follow in a long series throughout the first millennium BC. These include, for example, the inscription of the royal steward Shebaniah from Siloam (eighth to seventh centuries BC) and ostraca from Samaria (eighth century), Arad (seventh to sixth centuries), Yavneh-Yam (seventh century) and Lachish (sixth century). There are also clay sealings, *bullae*, from Lachish, Arad and Jerusalem, which were originally attached to

18

19

225

papyrus documents. These show the importance of the writing of Hebrew on papyrus at this period, though sadly virtually all of it has perished.

Politically and culturally, ancient Israel was somewhat isolated and as a result the developments in the script during this long period are limited. There are certain tendencies to a more cursive style, but almost all our sources are inscribed on stone and pot and we have very little information about writing on soft materials. A good example of a stone inscription is the Siloam tunnel

20 Hebrew inscription from the Siloam tunnel, Jerusalem, *c.* 700 BC.

inscription (eighth century BC), which is probably meant to be a formal monumental inscription but actually contains many cursive features, with downstrokes curving to the left. The cursive form seems to have been normal and there may have been no Hebrew tradition of royal inscriptions requiring a monumental script.

The Hebrew script, having been in decline from the time of the Babylonian exile (sixth century BC), when Aramaic was in the ascendant, was eventually abandoned by the Jewish community in favour of the Aramaic script. The old script, called in later Jewish tradition $k^e t\bar{a}b$ *'ibrī*, 'Hebrew script', did not, however, disappear immediately. Among the Dead Sea Scrolls there are Bible fragments in the old script (Leviticus) and there are also coins from the Hasmonaean period (135–37 BC) and the first and second Jewish Revolts AD 66–70 and 132–5 bearing legends written in it. The retention of the old script may have had an element of nationalism about it. It was also favoured by certain Jewish sects, certainly by the Samaritans, who retained it throughout the ages. By contrast, the orthodox tradition of mainstream rabbinic Judaism came to be rather hostile to the old script and gave legitimacy to the newly adopted Aramaic script by ascribing its introduction to Ezra who, it was claimed, brought it with him on

21 Samaritan Bible manuscript (Gen 21: 4–14), 13th century AD. Chester Beatty Library (Dublin) Ms 751 27v

the return from exile in Babylon. According to the Mishnah, a collection of Jewish legal judgements compiled *c*. AD 200, the Law scroll (Torah), when written in the old Hebrew script (as it was by the Samaritans), did not have about it the same sanctity as adhered to a normal scroll in the Jewish Aramaic script.

The Aramaic script, derived from the Phoenician in about the eleventh to tenth centuries BC, was the most vibrant of the three scripts. Not only did it ultimately supplant the other two, it also spread far beyond the area of the Aramaean people and became a script of convenience for Assyrians, Persians and others and was used in Egypt, Arabia, Cilicia, Anatolia, Afghanistan, etc. At first Aramaic basically used the Phoenician script, as evidenced by Aramaic inscriptions from Zincirli, Hamath and Damascus

22

in the ninth to eighth centuries BC. But, as a result of its international currency under the Assyrians and the powers which succeeded them, it developed extremely rapidly, diverging from Phoenician from the eighth century BC onwards and becoming increasingly cursive and more and more simplified. The Aramaic language

23

22 Aramaic inscription on stele of King Zakkur of Hamath, *c*. 780–775 BC. Louvre AO 8185

23 Aramaic funerary stele from Neirab (Syria), 7th century BC. Louvre AO 3027

24 Aramaic papyrus from Elephantine (Egypt), 5th century BC. BL Or Pap cvi AB

and a rather cursive form of the script were used, for example, by Adon, the king of a city-state in Phoenicia in *c.* 600 BC in his letter, fortunately preserved on papyrus, to the Pharaoh. Gradually a difference between formal and cursive styles developed. The cursive is better known and is attested mainly on

24 papyrus and leather from Egypt (sixth to third centuries BC), including papyri from Hermopolis and Elephantine and the Arsham documents, and from Wadi Daliyeh near Jericho (fourth-century BC documents of Samaritan families). However, despite the rapid cursivisation which took place (almost a shorthand developed), the

15 Aramaic script retained, as a result of international use, a virtually complete homogeneity until about a century after the collapse of the Persian Empire, the last cohesive force holding it together.

Again there were sounds which were inadequately represented by the Phoenician script, but no new signs were added. Indeed, to some extent developments in the Aramaic language, such as the disappearance of the sounds /ḏ/ and /ṯ/, relieved the problem of the absence of signs for these.

It is worth noting a recent discovery which could have a profound effect on our perception of the way (outlined in the previous paragraphs) in which the Aramaic script relates to the Phoenician script. This is the long inscription, a bilingual in Aramaic and in Assyrian cuneiform, from Tell Fakhariyah (ancient Sikanu) found in 1979 near Tell Halaf in north-east Syria. The date of this inscription, while not precisely known, is certainly not earlier than the ninth century BC, yet the script is peculiar by comparison with other, slightly later, Aramaic inscriptions which are probably more strongly under Phoenician influence. Awareness of this influence is the basis of the traditional view outlined above, that the Aramaic script derived from the Phoenician.

However, some of the peculiarities of script of the new inscription are shared with earlier forms of the linear script. For example, the letter 'ayin appears with a dot in the centre: ⊙. The dot had disappeared from the Phoenician form of 'ayin much earlier. Therefore, it is possible that there existed in the East an early offshoot of the Proto-Canaanite script which developed independently before being replaced by the more dominant script-form of the Aramaic of the West. At the time of writing, however, this view has not yet found wide acceptance – it is quite revolutionary and will take some time to evaluate.

There are other minor scripts worth noting which are derived from Phoenician either directly or via Hebrew or Aramaic. The Moabite script, attested

principally in the Mesha inscription of *c.* 850 BC, derives from Hebrew (though   17
it predates most of our evidence for Hebrew). It was used in central Jordan,
south of Amman. By the sixth century BC it had come under Aramaic influence.
The Ammonite script further north (around Amman) may derive from Aramaic
(the Aramaic of Damascus) or show strong Aramaic influence. The evidence
of an Edomite script tradition in southern Jordan is meagre. Edomite is represented in the seventh to sixth centuries BC by seals, weights, fragmentary ostraca
and fragmentary writings on stone. L. G. Herr identified a southern Palestinian/
Transjordanian grouping of scripts, including Moabite and Edomite with
Hebrew, while J. Naveh emphasises the Aramaic influence on the Edomite
script (from the seventh century BC onwards). There is virtually no evidence
of a Philistine script and none of these minor scripts had any long-term significance.

Gradually, then, from as early as the ninth to eighth centuries BC, the Phoenician, Hebrew and Aramaic scripts had begun to diverge to some extent, forming   15
national script-traditions, though the Aramaic one would have to be called
an international rather than a national script.

Finally, before moving on, we may note one other feature, the use initially
by Aramaic and then also by Hebrew (and the minor scripts) of vowel-letters,
i.e. the occasional use of certain consonants, particularly **h**, **w** and **y**, to represent
vowels. Aramaic from an early date used them for vowels within words as
well as at the end of words. Hebrew at first used them only at the ends of
words, but gradually extended this use to the internal vowels. Thus the Hebrew
h could stand for /o/, /a/ or /e/ at the end of a word. The letters **w** and
y were typically used to represent /u/ and /i/, normally /u/ and /ī/. Not all
the vowels could be represented in this way even when the system, which
was never used totally consistently, was fully operational, but this development
does show that the lack of vowels was seen as a problem.

The Export of the Alphabet to Greece

There is a widely accepted view that the Greeks learned the alphabet from
the peoples of the Phoenician coast (see B.F. Cook, *Greek Inscriptions*, pp.
264–7). This can be clearly demonstrated by a comparison of the Phoenician
and early Greek letters. Some of the letters – **A** is a good example – even
retain an element of the pictograph, in this case the drawing of a bull's head
(ⱶ), now upside down and without eyes! The Greek name for this letter
is *alpha* (ἄλφα), a word which is meaningless in Greek (apart from referring
to this particular letter) but which means 'bull' in West Semitic languages
(e.g. Ugaritic *'alpu*, Hebrew *'elef*). This is true of almost all the Greek letter-
names. The letter-order in Phoenician and Greek is basically the same, though
some supplementary letters were developed and added to the alphabetic order:
Υ, Φ, Χ, Ψ, Ω. The ascription of the alphabet to the Phoenicians was firmly
embedded in Greek historical tradition as found in the works of the fifth-century

BC Greek historian Herodotus. The letters are called *phoinikeia grammata* (Φοινιχήια Γράμματα), 'Phoenician letters', and were supposed to have been brought to Greece by the legendary Kadmos.

Much less certain are the date and the route of the transmission of the alphabet to the Greeks. The arguments are complex. On the question of date, we should first note the *varieties* of the earliest Greek script, which is first known to us in the eighth century BC. Forms of letters vary considerably and the earliest Greek inscriptions are sometimes written from left to right, sometimes right to left and sometimes boustrophedon (see p. 218). On the other hand, the similarities between the Greek scripts, including the use of certain letters to represent vowels (below), clearly indicate a single common origin. The need to allow time for the diversification of the Greek scripts suggests a date for the import of the alphabet well before the eighth century BC.

25,26,27

25 Early Greek inscriptions from Athens and Thera.

26 Early Greek inscription from Ephesus, 6th century BC. BM GR 1867. 11–12. 441

Early Greek Alphabets: 8th–7th centuries BC

Athens	Thera	Crete	Naxos	Corcyra	Boeotia

27 Early Greek alphabets, 8th–7th centuries BC.

Further, it can be argued that certain of the forms of letters taken over by the Greeks, for example the short o with a dot in it (⊙) reflecting the pictograph of an eye (the corresponding Semitic letter is called 'ayin, meaning 'eye'), are quite early forms, also indicating a very early date. Again, by the eighth century BC, the right-to-left direction of writing was already the rule in the scripts derived from Phoenician, so that it is hard to imagine the Greeks borrowing the script at that late date and still being uncertain on direction. The likeliest earlier date would be c. 1100–1050 BC. Against this, however, we have to place the fact that at the moment our earliest Greek evidence is of *c.* 740–730 BC. Further, some of the evidence may be uncertain; as we have seen, the supposedly very early dotted **o** is now found in an Aramaic inscription of the ninth century BC. Hence suggestions of an earlier date for the Greek alphabet remain speculative and are a matter of heated debate among scholars.

As to the route by which the alphabet passed to the Greeks, there is almost universal agreement that Phoenicia was the starting point. We have seen that native Greek tradition supposed this. There is, however, room for debate about where the encounter with the Phoenician alphabet took place. It need not have been in mainland Greece and the context may well have been commercial activity. The point of contact might have been in the Ugaritic region, since there were Greek settlements there in the late ninth century BC (e.g. Tell Sukas), though we may note also the occurrence of Phoenician inscriptions in Cyprus and Sardinia. But much of this is speculation and we cannot absolutely exclude another possible route. We have seen that there is evidence in the ninth century BC of an independent, eastern Aramaic script-tradition with affinities with early Greek script. Further, the names of many of the Greek letters (*alpha, bēta, gamma, delta*) have an /-a/ suffix which is a distinctive feature of Aramaic of all types (though it could have other explanations in these Greek letter-names). North-east Syria, the Aramaean homeland, had its own routes of contact with the Greek world which ran through Anatolia and did not involve Phoenicia. This could be a source for the early Greek script and would eliminate some of the arguments for an eleventh-century borrowing of the script, bringing us back to the traditional date of the ninth or eighth centuries BC.

Although the Greeks basically played a secondary role to the western Semitic peoples, they added a new dimension to alphabetic writing. A number of the Phoenician letters which were not needed for consonants in particular Greek dialects were put to use to represent vowels. The Phoenician letter '*ayin*, written as a circle and representing a guttural not found in Greek, came to be used for the vowel /o/. The Phoenician letter *he* ultimately came to be used for /e/ (**E**) and *yod* for /i/ (**I**). Similarly, the sign for the glottal stop, *aleph* ('), was used as **A**. The sign for fricative (dotted) /ḥ/ (pronounced as a roughly breathed aitch, as in a stage whisper) came to be used for /ē/ as Greek **H**. Another originally Phoenician sign was adapted for use as /u/ü/, the latter as in German *über*, French *sur* (Greek **Y**), and finally ordinary **O** was modified by being opened at the bottom to produce **Ω**, long /ō/. Some of these developments were at first confined to the Ionic dialect of Greek, but eventually they spread and Greek had letters to represent /a/, /e/, /ē/, /i/, /o/, /ō/ and /u/ü/ (**A, E, H, I, O, Ω, Y**): a full range of essential vowels. This meant that a true alphabet was for the first time in operation, an alphabet in which not only consonants but vowels too were represented. This was, of course, an enormous advance on the Phoenician and other Semitic systems, though, as we have seen, certain consonant-signs (especially in Aramaic) *were* adapted for use also as vowels. The Semitic scripts eventually introduced alphabetic vowel-notation by adding signs above and below the consonants. One of the Syriac scripts, ironically, made the transition to representing vowels by re-importing the Greek vowel-signs and adding them above and below the line!

Greek also invented, in addition to the sign for /ō/ (Ω), special signs for /ph/, /kh/ and /ps/ (Φ, X, Ψ), adding them with Y and Ω to the end of its alphabet.

Some archaic dialects of Greek included letters derived from Phoenician (or Proto-Canaanite) which did not survive with their original value – for example, *digamma*, pronounced /w/, from Phoenician *wāw*, shaped roughly like our F (and, in fact, the source of our F). There seem to have been eastern and western variants of the Greek alphabet. The most important eastern variant was the Ionic form, including various other scripts of Asia Minor and eastern Greece. An example of the variation is the different treatment of the signs for Phoenician /h/ and /ḥ/. In the East these were used for /e/ and /ē/ (Greek E and H), but in the West the Phoenician H was used for both /e/ and /ē/, while the Phoenician Ḥ was used for a breathy version of aitch – a sound similar to its original Phoenician sound. After several twists and turns of development, the Ionic alphabet of Miletus was officially adopted in Athens in 403/2 BC and comes to us as the 'classical' Greek alphabet, in which the direction of writing – left to right – had become invariable. The other, variant, alphabets gradually died out. The classical Greek alphabet runs as follows: A, B, Γ, Δ, E, Z, H, Θ, I, K, Λ, M, N, Ξ, O, Π, P, Σ, T, Y, Φ, X, Ψ, Ω (i.e. A, B, G, D, E, Z, Ē, Th, I, K, L, M, N, Ks, O, P, R, S, T, U, Ü, Ph, Kh, Ps, Ō).

A number of offshoots of the Greek alphabet developed for other languages, and such offshoots had to adapt to the repertoires of sounds used in those languages. We may note Lycian (in southern Asia Minor), Coptic (in Egypt) and Etruscan (in Italy, where there were Greek colonies, for example, on the island of Pithecusa from c. 775 BC). Etruscan inscriptions are found from very early on; the Etruscans must have received the alphabet in about the eighth century BC. The Etruscan alphabet at first had twenty-six letters (written from right to left or boustrophedon), perhaps borrowed from Greek colonists from Chalcis in Euboea, though this number had been reduced by the end of the fifth century BC to a standard form representing twenty letters: /a/, /e/, /i/, /u/, /g~k/, /v/ (i.e. *digamma*), /z/, /h/, /th/, /l/, /m/, /n/, /p/, *san* (an extra **s** derived ultimately from Phoenician), /r/, /s/, /t/, /ph/, /kh/, /f/. The latest dated Etruscan inscription comes from the first century AD; the Etruscan script was completely superseded, one could say swamped, by the Latin script as it spread with the Roman Empire. It is possible that the Etruscan script is the ancestor of the various runic scripts of northern Europe.

Other later derivatives of the Greek script (with some Latin elements) may be noted, particularly the Cyrillic script (ninth century AD) and its associated scripts used for various Slavic languages. Other Slavs, including the Poles and the Czechs, were to adopt the Latin script with modifications. For further discussion of these important scripts see D. Diringer, *Writing*, pp. 156 ff.

The Latin Alphabet

Our own alphabet is, of course, derived – though not directly – from that of the Greeks. The mediators were the Etruscans, whose script was transmitted to the Romans. The Roman or Latin script (Latin being the name of the Romans' language) is very similar to our own, apart from certain minor modifications introduced in the Middle Ages. Early Latin inscriptions go back to the seventh to sixth centuries BC, a date at which the direction of writing was still from right to left (or even boustrophedon as in the early Greek inscriptions).

The procedure of transmission to the Romans was complex but can be explained as follows (note that capitals or upper-case letters are used consistently in this section to refer to letter-forms, and small or lower-case letters between slashes to refer to sounds, as the lower-case Latin forms did not actually emerge until later).

The Etruscans had no distinct /g/ sound and used the G-sign (like a modern C) for /k/. The old K-sign thus ceased to be of use, being replaced by C (pronounced as in 'cat'), and it was basically without any K that the alphabet came to the Romans, though for obscure reasons they did retain K for a very few specific words. The Romans, unlike the Etruscans, *did* need to represent /g/ and, since the old G-sign had already been used to represent /k/, which they also needed, they invented a new sign for /g/ by adding a stroke to the existing C, thereby producing G. In the letter-order it took the place of the Greek Z, which was not essential for Latin, though Z was secondarily reintroduced into the Latin alphabet to help with the writing of words of Greek origin and thus came to stand at the end of the alphabet. The Romans did not need to represent /th/ or /ks/ (Θ, Ξ), or the sounds /ph/, /kh/, /ps/ and /ō/, for which Greek had added letters at the end of the alphabet (Φ, in practice replaced by F, a derivative of the archaic Greek *digamma* and ultimately derived from Phoenician *wāw*, X, Ψ and Ω). They did need to represent /u/ü/, Greek Y, which, in the form of V, was used for both /v/ and /u/, while I stood for /i/ and the consonant /y/. At a secondary stage Y was reintroduced as a separate letter, like Z, though added to the letter-order before Z. It, too, was used in words of Greek origin. Thus the Roman alphabet was as follows: A, B, C (=/k/), D, E, F, G, H, I, K, L, M, N, O, P, Q (derived from an archaic Greek letter), R (originally in its Greek form P, identical with the sign we use for /p/), S, T, V, X (a derivative of Greek Ξ /ks/, not the Greek X [/kh/]), Y, Z. Other differences between the Greek and Latin scripts (e.g. in the forms of Latin D *v*. Greek Δ, C/G *v*. Γ, L *v*. Λ and S *v*. Σ) are explained by the fact that the Latin forms are western variants transmitted via Euboean colonies. Much later, in the Middle Ages, U was distinguished from V and consonantal **J** from **I**, and finally, in the eleventh century AD, **W** (double-U) came into existence, though it is still not used in all European languages. It is pronounced as /v/ in German, while the German **V** normally stands for /f/.

From the Latin alphabet came all the western European scripts. Gradually a distinction developed between different styles of writing, notably between upper-case and lower-case letters, also called majuscules and minuscules; the latter were particularly characteristic of normal handwriting. In the Middle Ages, *national* handwriting styles developed. What we call 'Italic' is one of these. In Britain and Ireland there developed the Anglian/Irish script characteristic of some of the great monastic manuscripts of the Middle Ages such as the Book of Kells (*c.* AD 800). The Irish national script has been abandoned relatively recently, as has the 'Gothic' script formerly used by German printers. As we have noted, some of the eastern European peoples adopted a modified form of the Greek script (Russian, etc.). Others have used a version of the Latin script modified by the use of special 'accents', as in č, ł, ø.

A relatively modern case of adaptation is that of Turkish. Ottoman Turkish used the Arabic alphabet for the Turkish language, which is totally unrelated structurally to Arabic despite strong cultural links through Islam and many Arabic loan-words into Turkish. In 1928, as part of a Europeanisation programme, Atatürk replaced the Arabic script with the Latin script, modified by the addition of the following: ç/Ç (/ch/), ğ/Ğ (soft /g/y/), i/İ, ı/I (neutral short vowel similar to the second vowel of 'cousin'), ö/Ö (as in German), ş/Ş (/sh/), ü/Ü (also as in German); c/C is used for /j/ as in 'jam'.

4
Alphabetic Scripts in the Late Antique Middle East

From the eighth century BC onwards, the newly developed alphabet had considerable success not only among the Greeks but also with the Assyrians, the Babylonians and then the Persians. This success is closely bound up with the importance of the Aramaic language, which became a *lingua franca* for diplomacy and trade. Aramaic and the Aramaic variety of the alphabet were thus dispersed over a wide area from Egypt to northern India. As in the case of Greek, non-Semitic languages made use of the alphabet.

It may have been under the inspiration of the Aramaic alphabet that the Persians attempted to invent a cuneiform alphabet for Old Persian, though all that was achieved was a much simplified syllabic script.

We have seen that Aramaic was used as an official language by the Assyrians, Babylonians and Persians. After the collapse of the Persian Empire, the Imperial Aramaic language and script, which had been more or less unified across the Empire, began to break up, and local dialects and scripts developed. The main local variants were Jewish, Nabataean, Palmyrene, Hatran and Syriac. In addition there is the Mandaic script, which is attested later but actually goes back to a script contemporary with those already mentioned. It may be noted, although there is no need to go into the details, that the increasing use of joined-up, cursive forms in some of these scripts – the Jewish script, the Syriac and the Nabataean (along with Arabic, derived from the same script tradition) – led, first, to the emergence of 'final' forms of letters (i.e. forms taken by particular letters at the end of a word, resulting basically from the fact that there was no need to join up with what followed), and, second, to the development of special conventions about *how* to make joins, if any, on the right and left of each letter.

The so-called Jewish script is the form of the western Aramaic script which developed in Palestine in the service of the Jewish community. At first it existed alongside the Hebrew script, which was a continuation of the old Hebrew script discussed earlier. Gradually, however, the old Hebrew script fell into general disuse and the Aramaic script began to be used even for writing the Hebrew language. It was used for manuscripts of the Hebrew Bible from as early as the third century BC (Dead Sea Scrolls text of the Book of Exodus). In the inter-testamental period, the majority of the Dead Sea Scrolls texts are in this script, which is also attested in early papyri (e.g. the Nash papyrus of the second century BC) and inscriptions, some in mosaic, including synagogue inscriptions.

28 Jewish (Square Hebrew) script: Pentateuch with Tiberian vowel signs, early 10th century AD. BL Or 4445 f98r

The early history of the script can be divided into three phases: Old Jewish (250–150 BC); Hasmonaean (after the Hasmonaean dynasty, 150–30 BC); and Herodian (30 BC – AD 70). Spread throughout the Jewish diaspora, this newly adopted script in due course became the so-called square script – in Hebrew *kᵉtāb mᵉrubbā'*, 'square script', or *kᵉtāb 'aššūrī*, 'Assyrian script', referring to its approximate place of origin – the standard Jewish book-hand used for all formal purposes. The modern printed forms are as follows (right to left):

א ב ג ד ה ו ז ח ט י כ ל מ נ ס ע פ צ ק ר ש ת

' b g d h w z ḥ ṭ y k l m n s ' p ṣ q r š t

This is known today, somewhat inaccurately, as the Hebrew script. It was used even for Babylonian Jewish Aramaic (i.e. an Aramaic script adopted for Hebrew, naturalised as the 'Hebrew' script and then used once more for Aramaic!). Throughout the Middle Ages it was the standard form of the Jewish/Hebrew script. Alongside there developed a cursive hand, one version of which is seen in the Rashi script (associated with the scholar of that name who died in AD 1105), while another ultimately produced the modern Hebrew cursive.

At a rather uncertain date, probably from the fifth to sixth centuries AD, to which time belong some of the materials recovered at the end of the last century from a Cairo synagogue, Hebrew began to develop systems for adding the vowels and other signs to the consonantal alphabetic texts. The only mark needed to distinguish confusable consonants was that used to distinguish /š/ and /ś/, which for centuries used the same sign. A dot was placed on the left above the letter to indicate /ś/ and a dot on the right to indicate /š/.

(Some earlier traditions use a dot within the letter, or a second small š -sign above the letter, to indicate pronunciation of the sign as /š/, with a small s to indicate pronunciation as /ś/.) Other dots were used (as in Syriac, below) to distinguish variations in pronunciation of certain consonants, notably b, g, d, k, p, t, which could in certain circumstances be pronounced as 'aspirates' (/p/ > /ph/, /t/ > /th/, etc.), and also to indicate doubling of consonants (which is not properly indicated in any of the scripts we have dealt with thus far).

For vowels, the problem was much greater. Earlier, the consonants w, y, h and, to a certain extent, ' had sometimes been used to represent vowels rather than consonants; but now, especially in view of the decline of the Hebrew language and consequent uncertainties about correct pronunciation (particularly of vowels), scholars began to add marks to the text – in the first place to the Biblical text – to clarify the pronunciation. Several systems emerged. The Jewish community in Mesopotamia during the fifth to sixth centuries AD, probably influenced by the use of dots for this purpose in Nestorian Syriac (see below), developed a system of supralinear marks, i.e. marks placed above the line of consonants. This is called the Babylonian system. In Palestine, an earlier so-called Palestinian system gave way in the eighth to ninth centuries AD to a complex and fairly comprehensive system of supralinear and sublinear dots and strokes representing a rather elaborate series of distinctions between vowels. This is the Tiberian system, which subsequently became totally domi-

28 nant and is used in the later manuscript tradition, especially of Biblical texts.

The other major western script form is that of the Nabataeans, the people of the Arab kingdom of Petra, which flourished in the first century BC and the

15 first century AD. The Arab peoples of the area had been using a northern version of the South Arabian script for some time, but the Nabataeans used the Aramaic language and script for public purposes from the fourth century BC

29 onwards. Most of the formal inscriptions come from Petra in Jordan, Madā'in Ṣāliḥ, the Nabataean outpost in Saudi Arabia, and southern Syria, though there are a few from as far afield as Rome, where there was a Nabataean merchant colony. The dates of the main inscriptions, many of them tomb-inscriptions, extend from the second century BC to the annexation of the Naba-taean state by the Romans in AD 105–6. Thereafter, literally thousands of short Nabataean inscriptions and graffiti exist, especially from Sinai and south-ern Jordan/northern Saudi Arabia. Even in formal inscriptions on stone, the Nabataean script is notably cursive in character. Letters are frequently joined

29 Nabataean formal inscription from Petra, 1st century AD.

and many of the letters have a very rounded shape. A few examples of Nabataean, written in ink on papyrus and on wall-plaster (c. AD 100 onwards)
have survived. These show that there was a cursive Nabataean alongside the
monumental or formal script. (We will return to Nabataean in connection
with Arabic.)

In the East, a whole variety of Aramaic scripts developed. The interrelation
between these is a matter of dispute. J. Naveh would trace their origin back
to an ancestor in the Seleucid period (c. 300 BC onwards).

Palmyrene is the very widely attested Aramaic dialect and script of Palmyra/
Tadmūr in the Syrian desert. The texts date from the mid-first century BC   15,30
to the destruction of Palmyra by the Romans in AD 272. Palmyra in the Roman
period was a major trading centre; the longest of the Palmyrene texts, a bilingual
in Palmyrene Aramaic and Greek, is a taxation tariff. Trade connections took
the Palmyrene script to other places, some not far away, such as Dura Europos
on the Euphrates, but others at a great distance. Of particular interest is the

30 Limestone bust with
Palmyrene inscription. Palmyra,
late 2nd century AD. BM WA
102612

Palmyrene inscription from South Shields, Roman Arbeia, in the north-east of England, carved on behalf of a Palmyrene merchant for his deceased British wife. It probably dates to the early third century AD.

The Palmyrene script existed in two main varieties, a monumental and a cursive one, though the latter is little known and the evidence mostly from materials found outside Palmyra itself. The Syriac script of Edessa in southern Turkey, dealt with in more detail below, is often regarded as derived from or closely related to the Palmyrene – similarities are found in the following letters: ', b, g, d, w, ḥ, y, k, l, m, n, ', r and t – though a strong case can also be made for connecting Syriac closely with a northern Mesopotamian script-family represented principally in texts from Hatra, a city more or less contemporary with Palmyra in Upper Mesopotamia. The Hatran Aramaic inscriptions (approximately four hundred in number) extend in date from the late first century to the third century AD. Closely related inscriptions have been found at Ashur and in south-east Turkey (second century AD). Hatra was under the influence of the Romans' great eastern rival, the Parthians, and provides a link with more easterly regions which also adopted the Aramaic language and/or script.

A southern Mesopotamian group of scripts is represented by Mandaic, used by the Mandaeans of southern Iraq, a religious community with Gnostic and Jewish-Christian characteristics. The Mandaic script is unique as an Aramaic offshoot in that it took the use of vowel-letters to a logical conclusion: *all* vowels are represented in this way, so that the vowels are incorporated into the main line of writing and no additional markings are needed to indicate their existence. Its basic letter-forms seem to belong to a southern Mesopotamian group of Aramaic scripts. The Mandaic may be related to the Elymaic script (Elymais, Khuzistan, at the head of the Arabian Gulf). The latter is known from coins and rock-inscriptions of the second to third centuries AD. There are, however, strong resemblances also between Mandaic and Nabataean, and it may be suspected that there is some western influence involved. The Mandaean sect, which still survives in southern Iraq, claimed to have come from Palestine, and there is much internal evidence from the Mandaean religious literature to support this claim.

There are Aramaic inscriptions from as far afield as Afghanistan and Pakistan, while the Aramaic script was later used for the writing of various non-Semitic languages such as Middle Iranian (Pahlavi) and Uighūr (which is Turkic). In India, too, offshoots of the Aramaic script developed. We may note the Brahmi script (seventh century BC) from which most of the scripts used in India developed and the Kharoṣṭhī script (fifth century BC). Minor derivatives of the Aramaic script were used for inscriptions found at Nisa in Turkmenistan (Parthian ostraca) and Armazi in Georgia (second century AD). The Armenian and Georgian scripts were created in the fifth century AD and also have an Aramaic origin.

31 Ethiopic Gospels (Christ healing two blind men), AD 1664–5. BL Or 510 f51a

While the development of the Aramaic scripts continued, older script forms survived in a very few places and underwent their own developments. As we have seen, the old Hebrew script was for the most part replaced by the Aramaic script, but it did not disappear completely. It survived, right down to the modern period, in use among the Jews' Samaritan neighbours, both for Samaritan Hebrew and for Samaritan Aramaic.   21

A much more important backwater from the point of view of script – no denigration of the culture or literature is implied – is Ethiopia. The classical Ethiopian script is closely connected with the old South Arabian script (above, p. 219), which disappeared from southern Arabia when the Arabic language and script took over. The first Ethiopic inscriptions were written in the monumental South Arabian script. For Ethiopic use, the South Arabian alphabet was first reduced from twenty-nine to twenty-four letters and these were then expanded with new inventions to twenty-six. In addition there are labialised forms of certain letters (q, ẖ, k, g) representing /qu/ (as in 'quick'), /gw/ (as in 'Gwent'), etc. The Ethiopian script, written from left to right, continues in use to the present day, though seven extra letters are used for the modern official language of Ethiopia, which is called Amharic.   31

The Ethiopian script is unique among the Semitic scripts in that it has adapted a consonantal script by adding extra strokes to each consonant in a more or less regular pattern to indicate the vowel following that consonant. This development took place in about the fourth century AD. In theory, the twenty-six consonants could have markers added to them so as to indicate the following   32

Consonant + Vowel	a	u	i	ā	ē	e/no vowel	o
h	ሀ	ሁ	ሂ	ሃ	ሄ	ህ	ሆ
l	ለ	ሉ	ሊ	ላ	ሌ	ል	ሎ
ḥ	ሐ	ሑ	ሒ	ሓ	ሔ	ሕ	ሖ
m	መ	ሙ	ሚ	ማ	ሜ	ም	ሞ
š	ሠ	ሡ	ሢ	ሣ	ሤ	ሥ	ሦ
r	ረ	ሩ	ሪ	ራ	ሬ	ር	ሮ
s	ሰ	ሱ	ሲ	ሳ	ሴ	ስ	ሶ
q	ቀ	ቁ	ቂ	ቃ	ቄ	ቅ	ቆ
b	በ	ቡ	ቢ	ባ	ቤ	ብ	ቦ
t	ተ	ቱ	ቲ	ታ	ቴ	ት	ቶ
ḫ	ኀ	ኁ	ኂ	ኃ	ኄ	ኅ	ኆ
n	ነ	ኑ	ኒ	ና	ኔ	ን	ኖ
ʼ	አ	ኡ	ኢ	ኣ	ኤ	እ	ኦ
k	ከ	ኩ	ኪ	ካ	ኬ	ክ	ኮ
w	ወ	ዉ	ዊ	ዋ	ዌ	ው	ዎ
ʿ	ዐ	ዑ	ዒ	ዓ	ዔ	ዕ	ዖ
z	ዘ	ዙ	ዚ	ዛ	ዜ	ዝ	ዞ
y	የ	ዩ	ዪ	ያ	ዬ	ይ	ዮ
d	ደ	ዱ	ዲ	ዳ	ዴ	ድ	ዶ
g	ገ	ጉ	ጊ	ጋ	ጌ	ግ	ጎ
ṭ	ጠ	ጡ	ጢ	ጣ	ጤ	ጥ	ጦ
p	ጰ	ጱ	ጲ	ጳ	ጴ	ጵ	ጶ
ṣ	ጸ	ጹ	ጺ	ጻ	ጼ	ጽ	ጾ
ḍ	ፀ	ፁ	ፂ	ፃ	ፄ	ፅ	ፆ
f	ፈ	ፉ	ፊ	ፋ	ፌ	ፍ	ፎ
p̣	ፐ	ፑ	ፒ	ፓ	ፔ	ፕ	ፖ

32 The Ethiopic alphabet: the 26 basic letters with their vowel-markers.

vowel as /a/, /u/, /i/, /ā/, /ē/, /o/ and /e/ or no vowel, producing 182 different syllables, each consisting of consonant plus vowel. To these are to be added five forms of each of the labialised consonants (i.e. a further twenty syllables). Adding the seven Amharic consonants (multiplied by seven for the vowels), we have a grand total of 251 syllabic signs. The basic characteristic features of the form of each vowel remain just about recognisable, but in practice the vowel-markers came to be incorporated into the form of the consonants in a variety of ways, so that the student of this script really has to learn all 251 forms as if they were a syllabary. As a writing system this is almost as cumbersome as syllabic cuneiform, but the Ethiopic script has survived well and boasts an unrivalled beauty and elegance, despite the fact that the letters are never joined. Like ancient South Arabian (and some northern scripts), it uses a word-separator (in the form of two dots, one above the other).

The alphabetic order of Ethiopic is similar to that of South Arabian (**h, l, ḥ, m** ...) and the names of the letters, thought until recently to be modern intrusions from the Hebrew tradition, may in fact be very ancient. It can be argued that their form is such as to suggest an origin before 1000 BC, which might bring these names right back to the origins of the alphabet itself.

31

5
Towards the Arabic Alphabet

Among the various forms of the Aramaic script, one which had particularly widespread success was the local form of the script which developed in Edessa (modern Urfa/Şanlıurfa) in the first centuries AD. It is attested at this early date in a number of short inscriptions. The earliest is dated AD 6 (from Birecik, west of Edessa), while a particularly important and unusual text is a long parchment bill of sale from Dura Europos dated AD 243. In its early stages this script was very similar to Palmyrene, but it quickly developed and then received an unexpected boost from the fact that Edessa (Semitic name ʾUrhoy) became the focus of the spread of Christianity in the Semitic-speaking world. As a result, by about AD 200 the Bible was translated into the local Aramaic dialect, which became known as Syriac, and the dissemination of the Syriac Bible and the works of Syriac-speaking and -writing theologians led to the use of the Syriac language and script from Palestine to the ends of the Silk Road. Another epigraphic oddity, like the Palmyrene inscription from South Shields, is the bilingual Chinese and Syriac text from Sian in China!

The early Syriac form of writing, known to us in many superb manuscripts from the fifth century AD onwards, is the elegant *estrangelā* script. The word is derived from Greek *strongulos* (στρογγύλος) and means 'rounded'. A rather crude version of this script is found in the very earliest Syriac inscriptions of the first century AD from the area of Edessa. As a result of sectarian strife among the Syriac-speaking Christians, there developed western and eastern script variants called respectively Jacobite (after the supposed founder of the western Syrian church, which the orthodox regarded as heretical) and Nestorian (after the supposed heresy of the eastern Syrians). The correct name of the Jacobite script is *serṭā* or *serṭā pᵉšīṭā*, '(script of) the (simple) character', and it is the most cursive of the three. It emerged in the eighth century AD or a little earlier, the earliest dated manuscript coming from AD 731–2. The Nestorian or East Syrian script developed fully later (twelfth to thirteenth centuries AD), but its features appear as early as the sixth century AD, at which point it is still very similar to *estrangelā*. It continued to bear close resemblance to the *estrangelā* script, which itself enjoyed something of a revival in the tenth century AD.

Note may also be made of two minor varieties of Syriac script, the Melkite, derived from *serṭā* and used by Christians loyal to Constantinople, and that used in Palestine for Christian Palestinian Aramaic. The latter is a crude version of *estrangelā* and rather similar to cursive Palmyrene. The Maronites have traditionally used the *serṭā* script.

All three principal forms of Syriac script – *estrangelā*, Jacobite and Nestorian

frontispiece
33

34

33 Esṭrangelā Old Syriac Gospels (John 6.53–64), 5th century AD. BL Add 14451 f49b

34 The Syriac scripts.

	Serṭā	Esṭrangelā	Nestorian
'			
b			
g			
d			
h			
w			
z			
ḥ			
ṭ			
y			
k			
l			
m			
n			
s			
'			
p			
ṣ			
q			
r			
š			
t			

– are extensively preserved in manuscripts and inscriptions and are still in use today. The earliest dated literary manuscript, showing an already mature calligraphic *esṭrangelā* hand, is dated AD 411.

There are two important innovations associated with (though not unique to) the Syriac scripts: the use of diacritics and the use of vowel-signs. Diacritics are distinguishing marks added to letters or words to differentiate forms which could be confused. The simplest example is the case of letters which, through a long process of development involving strong cursive tendencies, become indistinguishable. The problem is well known to teachers trying to read their pupils' handwriting! In several of the late Aramaic scripts, the letters **d** and **r** had become indistinguishable. Even in Nabataean and in Palmyrene sporadic attempts were made to use diacritics to solve the problem. In Syriac, a simple solution was universally used from a very early period: **d** had a dot added below it, **r** had a dot added above it.

In the Syriac script this is the only pair of letters which presented a serious problem. Other potential confusions are resolved by the fact that the method of joining letters together

33
34

is very strict. Thus **q** and **w** are very similar, but the rules about joining and about final forms mean that it is always clear which is meant. But there are other types of potential confusion in Syriac. In a text without any vowels marked, it is usually impossible to distinguish, except by context, a singular from a plural noun, since the difference lies in the vocalisation (the vowels). Thus Syriac developed a double-dot mark, placed above nouns and occasionally verbal forms, to indicate a plural. Similarly, diacritic dots were used to distinguish the Syriac words for 'his' and 'her' and to distinguish the past tense of the verb from the participle, again because the differences lay in the vocalisation alone.

The real solution to problems of this kind had to lie in the invention of a system of marking vowels. The introduction of vowel-signs rendered most of the diacritics redundant, though not the diacritics for **d** and **r**, and diacritic dots were used to distinguish ordinary from aspirated pronunciation of /b/, /g/, /d/, /k/, /p/, /t/ (see Hebrew above).

Syriac ended up with two systems of vowel-notation. The one used in the East, which developed from as early as the fourth to fifth centuries AD, was an extension of the use of diacritic dots and consisted of patterns of dots (single and double) above and below consonants to indicate the vowel following the consonant. The consonants **w**, **y**, and **'** had already come to be used to indicate /ū/ō/, /ī/ē/ and /ā/ē/. This covered a wide range of distinctions between vowels, and it was this system which seems to have inspired the Hebrew vocalisation systems (see above).

In the West there emerged a system – traditionally attributed to Jacob of Edessa (d. AD 708), fragments of whose grammatical works survive, and definitely in use from *c.* AD 700 – in which the Greek letters **A, E** (in the form ε), **H** (/ē/, in later Greek /ī/), **O** and the combination **OU** (Greek OY, pronounced /oo/) were used to represent the vowels /a/, /e/, /i/, /o/ (pronounced like the vowel in 'raw') and /u/. They were written in very small script above or below the consonant after which the vowel was to be pronounced. While not perfect in that it does not make all necessary distinctions (so that certain of the older dot-signs remained in use), it *is* as good as the system used for English, in which it is equally true that not all necessary distinctions are seen in spelling (compare the different pronunciations of the letter **e** in 'the cat', 'the apple', 'then, 'they').

Syriac has the distinction of being the probable originator of vowel-notation by supralinear and sublinear markings. Both Hebrew and Arabic owe to Syriac their inspiration in this regard.

Syriac-speaking communities have survived in large numbers in the area around the point where the borders of Syria, Turkey and Iraq meet, and there are also *emigré* communities in Europe and the United States. Books, magazines and newspapers are still produced in the Syriac scripts.

A small number of scholars have argued that the Arabic script, which is quite unrelated to the older South Arabian script (above), was derived from the Syriac. In fact, it seems that there are a number of influences at work in the development of the Arabic script. One of these may well be awareness by the Arabs in the great cultural centres such as Damascus of the strong Syriac tradition of calligraphy, i.e. decorative writing, especially in fine copies of literary works. Syriac influence is also likely in the development of the Arabic diacritics and the vowel-system – a mixture of direct influence and analogical formation. It seems, however, that the origins of the Arabic script do not lie in Syriac alone.

Although the Arabs are known to have been present as an identifiable group from as early as the Assyrian period (in the ninth to seventh centuries BC), they did not become prominent historically until about the time of Christ. In this later period there was a strong Arab presence in the Hellenised cities of the Middle East such as Edessa and Palmyra (see map p. 202), where both Greek and Aramaic scripts were in use.

The first independent and clearly defined northern Arab kingdom known to us is that of the Nabataeans, centred on Petra in modern Jordan. Although known by their local tribal names (Nabaṭu and Šalamu), the Nabataeans were certainly Arabs, and they spoke a form of the Arabic language. For their inscriptions, however, they used the Aramaic which had become established as a language of colonial administration under the Assyrians and Persians. The fact that the Nabataeans normally spoke Arabic is reflected in the intrusion of certain distinctively Arabic forms and words into the Aramaic of their inscriptions. When eventually the Arabs in the region began to experiment for the first time with writing Arabic, they used the Nabataean Aramaic script which was familiar to them.

The Nabataean Aramaic script, derived ultimately from the earlier Aramaic script in use under the Persian Empire, is best known (as we have seen) from the first century AD. It is found in two forms. The formal script was used 29,35 for monumental inscriptions, quite common on tombs, especially at Petra and at Madā'in Ṣāliḥ in Saudi Arabia. Alongside this formal script is a cursive 36 script used principally on papyrus, of which we have a few precious surviving examples. The cursive script is continuous and flowing, with a regular pattern of joining of letters. The difference between the cursive and formal scripts is analogous to the difference between normal handwriting and the careful 'book-hand' one might use for a public notice. The cursive style tended to influence the formal script more and more in the first four centuries AD, and the Nabataean script developed into a cursive forerunner of the Arabic script.

However, some of the forms closest to Arabic already appear in the texts 37 of the first century AD, so it is likely that there was a continuous tradition of writing on papyrus or parchment leading to the writing of Arabic texts, though little has survived. During this period, the first half of the first millennium AD, the Arabic language was spreading into the area of Palestine, Jordan

35 Nabataean tomb inscription from Madeba, 1st century AD. Louvre AO 4454

36 Early monumental and cursive Nabataean.

Dates AD	4/5	72/3	90/100	125		146/7	
ʾ							
b							
g							
d							
h							
w							
z							
ḥ							
ṭ							
y							
k							
l							
m							
n							
s							
ʿ							
p							
ṣ							
q							
r			ь = br				
š							
t							

247

Dates AD	Monumental 1st century	Cursive 1st/2nd century	211/2	265/6	266/8	305/7	328/9	Arabic
,								ا
h								ـه ة
w								و
ṭ								ط
y								ـى ي
m								ـم
ʿ								ـع ع
p								ف
š								ـش ش
t								ـت ت

37 Typical Nabataean forms approximating to Arabic.

38 The Namāra inscription (Arabic language, Nabataean script), AD 328–9.

and Syria, replacing the older (Arabian) languages of the area as well as Aramaic, which had become traditional. The early surviving Arabic texts were carved on stone. The very earliest to use the Nabataean Aramaic script – setting aside a short and disputed first-century AD inscription – comes from the mid-third century AD (AD 267–8), though the most famous example, the text from **38** Namāra in southern Syria, is dated to AD 328–9. The latest dated Nabataean text comes from AD 355–6.

It seems that the Nabataean script lies at the origin of the Arabic script, but there are still some unresolved problems about the early development of the latter. Firstly, there is the chronological gap between the fourth century AD (the Namāra inscription and the last-dated Nabataean inscription) and the seventh, when papyri and inscriptions in Arabic proper become common. This can be partly bridged by the evidence of further transitional scripts in a group of short Arabic inscriptions from Zebed (AD 512), Ḥarrān, south of Damascus (AD 568) and Umm al-Jimāl (earlier a quite important Nabataean centre). Though rather scattered, these help to provide a link.

Secondly, there seem to have been from the beginning of the Islamic period several forms of the Arabic script. The so-called 'western cursive' script is the one most closely connected with Nabataean. The similarities are also ref-

39 Qur'ān in Naskhī script, 14th century AD.
BL Or 12809 f214a

lected in the more developed *naskhī* (Meccan-Medinan) script used in many
fine manuscripts. This form of Arabic script must represent the outcome of
a continuous tradition of writing in Nabataeo-Arabic in the Ḥijāz-Jordan-Syria
area. In the East a slightly different script came to be called Kūfic (named
after, though not directly linked with, Kūfa in Iraq); this may have arisen
from an offshoot of the Nabataean script and may have been more strongly
influenced by Syriac models.

    We have noted earlier the development of diacritics in Syriac. There were
also early attempts at diacritics in Palmyrene, Nabataean and other late Aramaic
scripts. Thus the latest dated Nabataean inscription has a diacritic to distinguish
d and **r**. It was especially in the cursive ligatured scripts that problems of
differentiating between letters arose. In Nabataean, the following pairs came
to be hard to distinguish: **b/n, g/ḥ, z/r, y/t, p/q.**

39

40

40 Qur'ān in Kūfic
script, 9th century AD.
BL Or 1397 f18b

As the earlier script began to be used for Arabic, another problem was added to this. Arabic has a richer variety of consonantal sounds and needed twenty-eight consonants instead of the existing twenty-two. Hence, probably inspired by Nabataean and/or Syriac, Arabic used diacritic dots, firstly to distinguish certain letters (for example, z and r – z with a dot above, r without dot), and secondly to create new consonants; for example, a dot was added above the basic shape of 'ayn, ', in order to create a further letter ġayn, ġ, since the sound /ġ/ did not exist in Aramaic and had no letter to represent it. A new ordering of the consonantal alphabet was also established, largely on the basis of the shapes of the letters (right to left):

ا ب ت ث ج ح خ د ذ ر ز س ش ص ض ط ظ ع غ ف ق ك ل م ن ه و ي

y w h n m l k q f ġ ' ẓ ṭ ḍ ṣ š s z r ḏ d ḫ ḥ j ṯ t b '

It may be noted that the exact forms differ according to whether the letter is in initial, final or medial position in a word.

Finally, like Syriac, Arabic developed a system of marking vowels by the use of supralinear and sublinear marks. The three basic signs used, ˘ , ˘ and ۇ , are probably derived from letters of the Arabic alphabet. This is obvious for ۇ , from the Arabic w (و), though the other two forms are stylised. The three signs stand for short /a/, /i/ and /u/. The sign for /i/ is sublinear and the other two are supralinear. They could be lengthened if combined with the 'vowel-letters' ', y and w to produce /ā/, /ī/ and /ū/. In addition, special signs were devised to indicate the doubling of a consonant (represented only by dots in Hebrew and Syriac) and to indicate the absence of any vowel after a consonant (ambiguously represented in Hebrew, and not in Syriac at all).

The Arabic script was, of course, widely used among the non-Arab peoples who accepted Islam. The most important offshoots of the script are the Persian and Ottoman Turkish varieties. Extra diacritics were devised to represent sounds which Arabic did not need to represent (i.e. for Persian /p/, /ch/, /j/ [as in French *jour*], /g/; for Turkish the same four plus /ng[n]/).

Arabic, Persian and Turkish manuscripts are notable for their use of calligraphy ('beautiful writing'), though the calligraphic tradition extends back to the Greco-Roman period. Sometimes there is evidence of calligraphy even in inscriptions on stone. The Nabataean tomb-inscriptions provide a good example. The earliest and best-attested calligraphic manuscripts in the Semitic languages are the ones in Syriac. Islam, however, took up the calligraphic tradition and made it its own in a special way. In some Muslim circles there was a reluctance to paint pictures of religious themes. As a result the artistic spirit of the Arabs was poured into abstract decoration and calligraphy.

29,35
33

Examples of Letters

Having surveyed the developments leading to the formation of the Greek and Latin alphabets on the one hand and the Hebrew and Arabic alphabets on the other, we have in the process also touched on the roles played by a number of 'minor' alphabets. In the light of this general survey it may be useful to look in some detail at a few of the individual letters of our own alphabet, tracing their origin back to the beginnings of alphabetic writing. There is only space here for a few examples and these have been chosen primarily for the relative simplicity of their history. Some letters are much more complex, and some letters of our alphabet have a relatively short history (i.e. **J** and **W**).

B

The pictograph derived from Egyptian was the picture of a house: ⬜ . In the transmission of the sign to the Proto-Sinaitic/Proto-Canaanite alphabet, the sign stood for **b**, the first letter of the West Semitic word for 'house', *bēt*. The box-like shape is best preserved in the South Arabian script, in which **b** is ⊓ , and this is reflected in the Ethiopic ⋔ , the Ethiopic script having been derived directly from the South Arabian. In the system of vowel-markings devised for Ethiopic, the different forms of this letter are ⋔ ⋔ ⋔ ⋔ ⋔ ⋔ ⋔ . In Ugaritic, **b** is 𒑲 and this may be a cuneiform version, turned upside down, of the ⊓ ⋔ found in South Arabian and Ethiopic. It is also quite similar to the original pictograph.

In later Proto-Canaanite and in Phoenician, the letter changed to ⊓ then ⅃ , and stabilised as 𝈋 , the form which is standard in Phoenician, Hebrew, Moabite etc. This is the form taken over by Greek, though with a number of variations such as 𝈈 and 𝈉 . Eventually it settled, with the fixing of the direction of writing, to become **B**, which has persisted into Latin and the European alphabets.

Within the West Semitic tradition the letter continued to evolve and in the Aramaic script it began to change quite dramatically. As in the case of a number of other letters, Aramaic began to open the closed loop at the top of the letter. This tendency may be related to the speed of writing in a highly cursivised form and to the materials used, especially papyrus. Whatever the cause, the opening of the top of the letter produced 𝈓 , then 𝈓 , then 𝈓 , then 𝈓 . The **b** in the Jewish (Hebrew) script was eventually formalised as ב , while in the other Aramaic scripts a variety of forms emerged. In Syriac (in all three types of script) we find ܒ and in formal Nabataean ܒ and in the cursive ܒ (final ܒ). The classic form of the letter in the cursive Arabic script is ب , the dot being added to distinguish it from other letters. The dot was essential when the letter was joined to others: e.g. ـبـ = **b**: ـنـ = **n**!

N

N is derived from a pictograph of a snake (*nahaš*), basically a wiggly line: ⌐. This is still reflected in Ugaritic ▷▷◁ and as the scripts developed this became in Phoenician ⌐, in Hebrew ⌐ and in Aramaic ⌐ . The same basic shape is retained by South Arabian ⌐ and Ethiopic ⌐ ⌐ ⌐ ⌐ ⌐ ⌐ ⌐ .

In Greek we have the forms ⌐ and ⌐ , eventually levelled or balanced as **N**.

In the Aramaic tradition there are completely different developments: ⌐ became ⌐ (Jewish: J) and then ⌐ (final ⌐). In Syriac and Nabataean it became a single short vertical stroke (⌐ / ⌐), which, when joined (⌐) was identical with several other letters including **B**. In Arabic it was distinguished by the addition of a single diacritic above it: ⌐ .

R

R is more complex. It originally depicted a human head (*rā'š/rō'š*) – in pictographic form ⌐ . This was stylised as ⌐ . Thus in Phoenician and Hebrew we find ⌐ , with gradual opening of the head in Phoenician to produce ⌐ (Ugaritic ⌐ ; South Arabian ⌐).

The letter entered the Greek alphabet as **P**, with a minor variant ⌐ . Latin adopted and developed the variant form.

Aramaic opened the loop at the top, producing ⌐ , then ⌐ , then ⌐ (Jewish ⌐). **R** and **D** ended up virtually identical, for example in Nabataean (⌐) and Syriac (⌐ , *serṭā* ⌐). Diacritics were added, at first irregularly, but then in Syriac systematically to distinguish r (⌐ / ⌐) from d (⌐ / ⌐). In cursive Nabataean ⌐ became ⌐ , then ⌐ , which is the Arabic form (⌐ when joined). In Arabic it had to be differentiated from z: a dot was added to z (⌐).

O

O is an even more complicated case, since its origin is a West Semitic *consonant* called (in Hebrew) '*ayin*. The name '*ayin* means 'eye' and the first letter of the Semitic word, transliterated as ', was pronounced as a constricted, almost strangulated, version of the glottal stop (/'/, see above). The original pictograph is, as might be expected, the picture of an eye: ⌐ , gradually rounded to ⊙ and eventually losing its dot (as the pictographic aspect was forgotten). The Ugaritic ⌐ is a cuneiform attempt to reproduce the circle and the circular shape is retained in South Arabian (O) and in Ethiopic, where the forms with vowels are ⌐ ⌐ ⌐ ⌐ ⌐ ⌐ ⌐ . The Ethiopic series illustrates well how the addition of the vowel-marker in that script could lead to fairly complicated variations in the basic letter.

In Greek, too, the circle is retained. Some archaic scripts have the dot in the middle, reflecting a very early form of the letter (though note that the dotted form was still in use in the eastern Aramaic script as late as the ninth century BC). But Greek had no /'/-sound and used O as a vowel, as we still do in the Latin alphabet. At a second stage Greek modified the O to produce Ω, representing long /ō/.

Meanwhile, in the Semitic area, O continued to be used for /'/. It is again in Aramaic that the changes occurred. As in other cases, Aramaic opened the closed loop at the top producing ○ . When this was written in two strokes it became ५ , then ५ , then ५ (the form in the Jewish script). In later Aramaic dialects two forms were prevalent, the Syriac ┴ and the Nabataean ५ , which became ५ , then ५ , then Arabic ५ .

H

In the case of **H**, as in several other cases in the transmission of the alphabet between languages (notably in the case of the various Semitic /s/-sounds), there has been some switching of usage. The sign from which **H** developed is ∭ , probably originally depicting a fence. In the Phoenician tradition the form changed to 目 , then 目 . The sound it represented – transcribed as /ḥ/ – is a roughly breathed aitch.

Some archaic Greek scripts used for dialects which preserved an /h/-sound used the sign as **H** for the so-called rough breathing, a breathy aitch found at the beginning of many Greek words. But it was not used for this in Ionic Greek (which lacked this sound) or in the later Greek script (in which a reversed apostrophe, ', came to be used for the rough breathing). Instead, **H** was used to represent the long vowel /ē/ (later /ī/). In Latin it again reverted to use as a consonant.

In the Aramaic tradition the letter became П (Jewish script П) and in later Aramaic we find Syriac ᴧ (through reduction of size and joining up) and Nabataean ⴳ , which became ⴰ and in cursive forms ⴰ and ⴰ . The Arabic is close to this with ᴧ (final ح), but at first this sign had to do duty for both /ḥ/ and for /ḫ/, a consonantal sound which Arabic has but none of the Aramaic scripts represent. Its sound is more rasping than /ḥ/, more like the /ch/ in the Scottish 'loch'. In due course Arabic devised a diacritic above the letter to indicate /ḫ/, leaving /ḥ/ unmarked. (In a separate development, g also ended up with the same basic shape and was given a sublinear diacritic).

It may be noted that both /ḥ/ and /ḫ/ did exist in Ugaritic, South Arabian and Ethiopic, though the relation of the forms to the tradition described above is hard to explain. Thus /ḥ/ is ⴰ in Ugaritic, Ψ in South Arabian and ⴰ in Ethiopic, while for /ḫ/ we have ⴰ , ⴰ and ⴰ .

Excursus: Use of the Alphabet for Numerals

The older, syllabic writing systems of the ancient Near East had their own methods of using various signs to indicate numerals without having to write the words out in full. In the common West Semitic tradition, a single vertical stroke represented **1** and other strokes were added to produce the numbers up to **9**. **10** has a sign of its own (usually ⌐ originally a horizontal line) and so does **20** (⌐̣ originally two horizontal lines). The larger numbers are simply formed by placing the numbers side by side: **14** = ⅢⅠⅠ ⌐ .

It appears that the Greeks used two systems. The older one, dating to the seventh century BC, is acrophonic – i.e. the first letter of the word used for the numeral was used as a sign for that numeral. Thus 'ten' is in Greek *deka* (Δέχα) and the sign for **10** is Δ. For 'one' a simple vertical stroke was used. The other system, traditionally connected with Miletus and in use at least from the second century BC, gives numerical values to each of the letters of the alphabet; **a** to **th** (α – θ, including the archaic *digamma*) are used for **1 – 9**, **i – r** (ι – ρ, including the archaic **q**) for **10, 20, 30**, etc. to **100** and **s** to archaic *san* (σ – ⋋) for **200, 300**, etc. to **900**. Use of *digamma*, the old **q** and *san* (of Phoenician origin) suggest an origin where these three survived in use.

The Roman numerals are still in use and current usage needs no introduction. It should, however, be noted that the origins of **M, D, C, L**, etc. are very complex. For example, **D** (**500**) is actually not a letter but half of an old sign for **1000**, ⊂⊃ . These signs gradually became assimilated to letters of the alphabet though they are not alphabetic in origin.

It was from Greek influence in the Hellenistic period that the alphabetic numeral system was adopted by Hebrew and Aramaic. In Hebrew, **' – ṭ = 1 – 9, y – ṣ = 10, 20, ...90**, and **q – t = 100, 200, 300, 400** (**tq = 500** and so on). Thus **y' = 11** and **qy' = 111**. Diacritic dots were put over the unit letters to turn them into thousands: א̈ = **1000**. Similarly Syriac, also under Greek influence, began to use the equivalent letters, abandoning the older system (see above). In Arabic, prior to the import from India of the system we call the Arabic numerals (since we got them from the Arabs), the same alphabetic system was used, exactly as in Hebrew and Syriac. Arabic even adopted the alphabetic order of these other scripts for this purpose, despite the fact that this did not correspond to the new Arabic alphabetic order based on letter-shape. The Ethiopic script also used the same system, but retained the Greek letters for this purpose, so clearly the alphabetic character of the numerals had ceased to be significant.

Relationship between Main Scripts

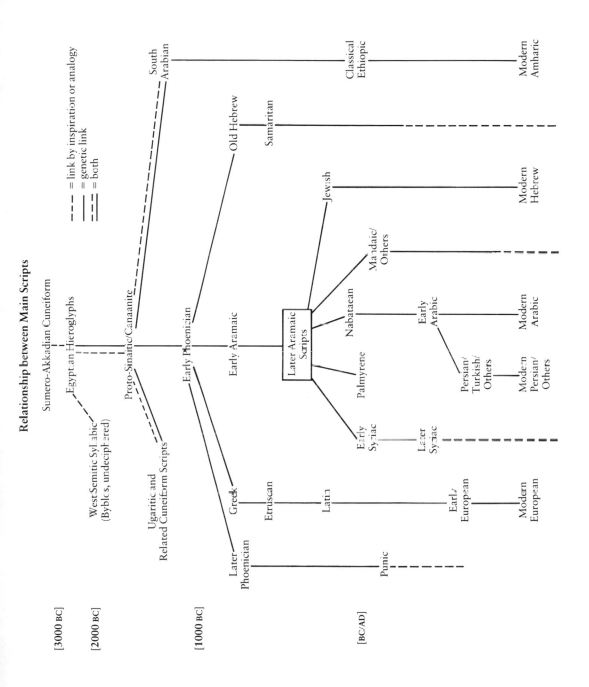

- - - - = link by inspiration or analogy
—— = genetic link
═══ = both

[3000 BC]

Sumero-Akkadian Cuneiform

[2000 BC]

Egyptian Hieroglyphs

West Semitic Syllabic
(Byblos, undeciphered)

Ugaritic and
Related Cuneiform Scripts

Proto-Sinaitic/Canaanite

[1000 BC]

Early Phoenician

Early Aramaic

Later Aramaic Scripts

Later Phoenician

Greek

Etruscan

South Arabian

Classical Ethiopic

Modern Amharic

Old Hebrew

Samaritan

Modern Hebrew

Jewish

Mandaic/Others

Nabataean

Early Arabic

Modern Arabic

Palmyrene

Persian/Turkish/Others

Modern Persian/Others

Early Syriac

Later Syriac

Latin

Early European

Modern European

Punic

[BC/AD]

255

Summary and Conclusions

In the short space available here we have covered a wide range of topics, concentrating on the earliest attempts at alphabetic writing, the development of the West Semitic scripts and the transmission of the alphabet to the Greeks, the later Semitic scripts and the origins of the Arabic script. A number of general points have been made in the process.

The two great pivotal moments in this story are the devising of the consonantal alphabet on an acrophonic basis in the early second millennium BC, and the addition of the vowels to the consonantal repertoire in the earlier part of the first millennium BC. The first of these steps forward we owe to some uncertain group of inventors, possibly in a scribal school in Palestine, Phoenicia or Syria. The second we owe to the Greeks. The only other invention in this field which is more important than either of these is the invention of writing itself, probably in Mesopotamia in the late fourth millennium BC.

From these developments have come enormous benefits for mankind. We are ourselves still using a developed form of the same alphabet tradition. But it is not only the long-standing character of this invention which should be noted, nor its wide distribution and its adaptability to languages which have only recently been written down. After all, cuneiform was widespread, lasted three thousand years and was used for such diverse languages as Sumerian, Akkadian and Hittite. Rather, the great contribution of the development of the alphabet was the fact that its simplicity was the first and necessary prerequisite of universal literacy.

Once the alphabet was available, virtually anyone could learn to read and write. It was no longer necessary to undergo a lengthy training, and literacy could therefore no longer easily be controlled by a scribal élite. In ancient times, holy books and books of philosophy were at last open to all. In more recent times, before the advent of sound media such as radio and television, ideas disseminated through books, pamphlets, posters and newspapers led to major political changes including the American War of Independence and the French and Russian Revolutions. Indeed, the immense possibilities inherent in each individual's being able to read and write – to transmit and receive information at will – have yet to be exhausted even now, four thousand years later.

Further Reading

P. C. Craigie, *Ugarit and the Old Testament* (Grand Rapids, 1983)

M. Dietrich and O. Loretz, *Die Keilalphabete: die phönizisch-kanaanäischen und altarabischen Alphabete in Ugarit* (Münster, 1988)

D. Diringer, *The Alphabet: A Key to the History of Mankind*, (London, 3rd edn 1968)

D. Diringer, *Writing* (London, 1962)

G. R. Driver, *Semitic Writing from Pictograph to Alphabet* (London, 3rd edn 1976)

A. Gaur, *A History of Writing* (London, 1984)

I. J. Gelb, *A Study of Writing* (Chicago/London, 2nd edn 1963)

S. A. Kaufmann, 'The Pitfalls of Typology: On the Early History of the Alphabet', *Hebrew Union College Annual* 57 (1986), pp. 1–14

A. G. Loundine, 'L'abécédaire de Beth Shemesh', *Le Muséon* 100 (1987), pp. 243–50

A. R. Millard, 'The Canaanite Linear Alphabet and its Passage to the Greeks', *Kadmos* 15 (1976), pp. 130–44

J. Naveh, *The Development of the Aramaic Script* (Jerusalem, 1970)

J. Naveh, *Early History of the Alphabet: An Introduction to West Semitic Epigraphy and Palaeography* (Jerusalem/Leiden, 1982)

J. Naveh, 'Proto-Canaanite, Archaic Greek, and the Script of the Aramaic Text on the Tell Fakhariyah Statue' in *Ancient Israelite Religion: Essays in Honor of Frank Moore Cross*, ed. P. D. Miller *et al.* (Philadephia, 1987), pp. 101–13

E. Puech, 'Origine de l'alphabet', *Revue Biblique* 93 (1986), pp. 161–213

J. Ryckmans, 'L'ordre alphabétique sud-sémitique et ses origines', in *Mélanges linguistiques offerts à Maxime Rodinson* (Paris, 1985), pp. 343–59.

J. Ryckmans, 'A. G. Lundin's Interpretation of the Beth Shemesh Abecedary: A Presentation and Commentary', *Proceedings of the Seminar for Arabian Studies* 18 (1988), pp. 123–29

Y. H. Safadi, *Islamic Calligraphy* (London, 1978)

B. Sass, *The Genesis of the Alphabet and its Development in the Second Millennium BC* (Wiesbaden, 1988)

1   Psykter (wine cooler) attributed to Oltos, made in Athens *c.* 520–510 BC.
MMA 10.210.18.

Greek Inscriptions

B. F. Cook

Preface

This section is intended to make accessible to the non-specialised reader some idea of what epigraphers do, and why and how they do it. It is not a systematic textbook of Greek epigraphy, although it may be useful in various ways to beginners in the subject. In order to make any progress, serious students will need at least a working knowledge of Greek and also of Latin, which is still used for commentaries in more learned publications. Here translations have been provided, and the inscriptions have been arranged not according to traditional classifications nor in regional or chronological sequences. Instead they have been divided into two main groups – first inscriptions cut in stone, then those written on other materials – and within each group they have been arranged roughly in order of increasing difficulty, with examples consisting wholly or largely of names at the beginning and those with problems of script or dialect at the end.

Thanks are due to Professor Stephen G. Miller, Director of the American School of Classical Studies at Athens, for permission to reproduce fig. 2; and to the Metropolitan Museum of Art for figs 1, 4, 10, 29, 30, 48 and 54 (Rogers Fund), 45, 47, 51 (Fletcher Fund), 40 (Museum Purchase), 53 (Purchase, Joseph Pulitzer Bequest) and 9 (Hewitt Fund, Munsey Fund and Anonymous Gift).

Contents

1
Introduction to Greek Inscriptions

The use of inscriptions in antiquity

Literacy, the ability to read and write, has long been one of the hallmarks of civilisation. The lack of writing deprives men of the ability to keep records not only for immediate use but also for posterity. In studying and interpreting the past the absence of records leaves the historian helpless: the prehistorian has to rely for his evidence on excavation. Fortunately the Greeks were literate from a fairly early stage in their development, so that only the earliest Greek culture belongs to the prehistoric period.

In ancient Greece inscriptions on stone slabs and bronze plaques served many purposes for which today we would use printed documents. They were particularly important for spreading and recording information in the Greek democracies, where all citizens were entitled to play an active part in government. In Athens, where the democratic form of government was particularly highly developed, there was a corresponding need for extensive public records, and inscriptions carved on stone slabs have survived in considerable quantity. These include laws, decrees passed by the Assembly, treaties with other cities, war memorials, lists of objects dedicated in temples, lists of the names of Archons and the winners of competitions, records of the sale at auction of confiscated property, and the accounts of income and expenditure of public funds. Similar inscriptions on stone are known from many other Greek cities, but they are not so numerous as those from Athens.

Even in Athens it was not the custom to record everything on stone. Temporary notices like drafts of proposed legislation and lists of men required for military service were written on whitened boards and displayed in the Agora, or Civic Centre. Other records were kept on papyrus and stored in the Metroon, the sanctuary of the

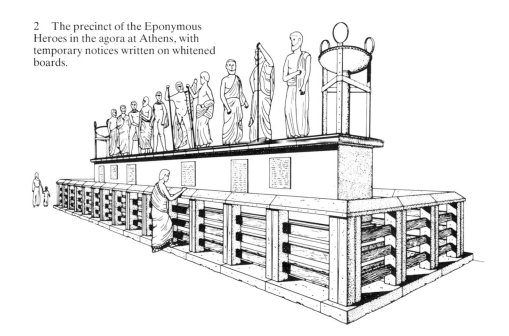

2 The precinct of the Eponymous Heroes in the agora at Athens, with temporary notices written on whitened boards.

Mother of the Gods. This stood next to the Council Chamber in the Agora and so was conveniently placed to serve as a public record office.

Athens was fortunate enough to have quarries of high-quality white marble close at hand. This was used not only for inscriptions but also for sculpture and eventually even for whole buildings like the Parthenon. In some other cities, where there was no local supply of suitable marble, inscriptions were cut on bronze plaques, often provided with holes to make it easy to nail them up in some public place. The long-lasting quality of bronze was almost proverbial, and the Roman poet Horace was to describe his own verse as 'a monument more permanent than bronze'.

Inscriptions were also used by private citizens, for example, to mark their property and especially to make dedications to the gods. Potters and vase-painters sometimes signed their vases or gave the names of the mythological figures they portrayed. The Greeks also preserved the memory of the dead, as we do, by inscriptions on tombstones (epitaphs).

Why study Greek inscriptions?

Inscriptions can be very useful in the study of ancient history, for they are original documents, contemporary with the events that they record, and they tell us many things that we cannot learn from other sources. Some inscriptions provide valuable information about events that the ancient historians described only briefly. Thucydides, writing in the fifth century BC, gives a short account of events between the Persian invasion of 480–79 BC and the outbreak of war between Athens and Sparta in 431. One of the most important things that happened in this period was the foundation of a league of independent states in alliance with the Athenians against the Persians, and its gradual transformation into an empire ruled by Athens. Thucydides describes the process only briefly, and many details of the story are now known only from inscriptions.

The allies all contributed to the resources of the League, some by providing ships and crews for the fleet, others substituting payments in cash. After 454, when the Treasury of the League was transferred from Delos to Athens, one sixtieth of the annual payments was made over to Athena and the amounts were recorded on marble slabs, many fragments of which still survive. Intensive study of the accounts and related inscriptions has yielded much information about the composition of the League and the means employed by the Athenians to gain domination of it. Most of the surviving fragments of the Tribute lists, as they are called, are preserved in the Epigraphic Museum in Athens, but a small fragment in the British Museum records   3 part of the payments in the year 448/7 BC.

Many events were not recorded by the ancient historians, at least not in those texts that have survived, and our knowledge of them is entirely derived from inscriptions. Such events include the treaties made in 433/2 BC between Athens and two Greek cities in Italy, 5 Rhegion and Leontini, and between the Eleans and the 58 Heraeans about 500 BC.

3   Fragment of the Athenian tribute-lists, 448/7 BC.
BM GR 1863.5–16.1.

263

Inscriptions also provide details of public administration or social life that the ancient historians could omit because their readers were already familiar with them. The preambles of Athenian decrees include details of procedure in the assembly, and the methods used to administer public funds can be seen in accounts of income and expenditure and in the records of the stewards of the Treasury of Athena.

In other cities lists of magistrates reveal their precise titles, which varied from place to place. In Thessalonika the title Politarchs ('Rulers of the citizens') corresponded to the Archons ('Rulers') of Athens; in Rhegion the magistrates were still using the Greek title Prytanis ('President') when as individuals they had adopted Roman names after the city came under Roman rule in the first century BC.

			Ionia	Athens	Corinth	Argos	Euboea (cf. Etruscan)
A	α	a	AA	AA	AA	AA	AA
B	β	b	B	B	⊔	Ɔ	B
Γ	γ	g	Γ	Λ	C<	ΓΛ	<C
Δ	δ	d	Δ	Δ	Δ	D	DᐳD
E	ε	e	ᴙE	ᴙE	B	ᴙE	ᴙE
F	Ϝ	w	—	Ϝ	Ϝ	ᴙF	Ϝ
Z	ζ	z	I	I	I	I	I
H	η	ē	⊟H	—	—	—	—
	[h]	h	—	⊟H	⊟H	⊟H	⊟H
Θ	θ	th	⊗⊕⊙	⊗⊕⊙	⊗⊕⊙	⊗⊕⊙	⊗⊕⊙
I	ι	1	I	I	ξ	I	I
K	κ	k	K	K	K	K	K
Λ	λ	l	ΓΛ	Ⳑ	ΓΛ	Ⱶ	Ⳑ
M	μ	m	ᴍM	ᴍM	ᴍM	ᴍM	ᴍᴍM
N	ν	n	ᴎN	ᴎN	ᴎN	ᴎN	ᴎN
Ξ	ξ	x	Ⱦ	(ΧϹ)	Ⱦ	ⱦH	X
O	o	o	O	O	O	O	O
Π	π	p	Γ	Γ	Γ	Γ	ΓΓ
Ϻ	—	s	—	—	M	M	M(?)
Ϙ	ρ	q	Ϙ	Ϙ	Ϙ	Ϙ	Ϙ
P	ρ	r	PD	PR	PR	PR	P
Σ	σ ς	s	ξ	Ϟ	—	ξ	Ϟ
T	τ	t	T	T	T	T	T
Y	υ	u	VY	ᴦYV	ᴦYV	ᴦYV	ᴦYV
Φ	φ	ph	φ	φⳊ	φⳊ	φⳊ	φⳊ
X	χ	kh	X	X	X	X	Ɏᴪ
Ψ	ψ	ps	ᴪᴪ	(φϹ)	ᴪᴪ	ᴪ	(φϹ)
Ω	ω	ō	ᴖΩ	—	—	—	—

Table 1. Some archaic alphabets

Origin and development of the Greek alphabet

The Greeks themselves told various stories about the origin of writing. The historian Herodotus, who lived in the latter part of the fifth century BC, records a tradition that the Greeks learnt to write from the Phoenicians, although he was probably wrong, as we shall see, to suggest that it was from a group of Phoenicians who had settled in Boeotia. The Greeks did, however, call letters *phoinikeia* ('Phoenician things'), as he says, and the derivation of Greek letters from Phoenician is confirmed by similarities in their names, by the way in which they were written, and by their order from *alpha* to *tau.*

As Herodotus himself was aware, the Greeks made some changes in the pronunciation and form of the letters. The Phoenicians had used ordinary words for the names of the letters, and the shapes of the letters themselves recalled the meanings of the words: *aleph* means 'ox', *beth* means 'house', and so on. When the Greeks took over the Phoenician script, they learnt the names of the letters by rote. In a different language the meanings of the names were inevitably lost, and the pronunciation was changed slightly. *Aleph* and *beth* became *alpha* and *beta*: the combination of the names for these first two letters gives the word 'alphabet'.

The Greeks found that their language required fewer consonants than Phoenician, in particular fewer sibilants, and they adapted some Phoenician consonants for use as vowels, which were unwritten in Phoenician, as in other Semitic languages like Hebrew. They also invented new signs for *upsilon* and for the double consonants *phi, chi* and *psi,* adding them at the end after *tau.*

As the Phoenician letters were adapted to fit the various dialects spoken in different parts of Greece, a number of local variations on the alphabet arose. All of them, however, perpetuated the same mistake with regard to the Phoenician sibilants. The Greek letters kept the same place in the sequence as the Phoenician signs from which they were derived, but each acquired the same wrong name. Thus the Phoenician *zayin* (I) acquired the Greek name *zeta*, derived from *tsade*, and gave its own name to the Greek *san* (M), which took a sign derived from *tsade* (M); and the Phoenician sign *samekh* (Ⱦ) was written as Ⱦ and called *xi* in Greek (the name coming from *shin*), while its name was altered to *sigma*, which in turn borrowed *shin*'s zig-zag sign, tilting it from ᴡ to Ϩ or Ϩ. Most local Greek alphabets used either *sigma* or *san* but not both. The uniformity in the errors with the names of the Phoenician sibilants suggests a common origin for all Greek alphabets. Where and when the original Greek alphabet came into existence remains uncertain, but there are some clues.

The earliest Greek inscriptions yet known are scratched on pottery. They can be dated about 730 BC, but it is likely that the Greeks were already writing a generation or two earlier, perhaps on more perishable materials like leather or wood. Some of the earliest inscriptions come from Euboea, and it can hardly be a coincidence that the Euboean pottery of around 800 BC is among the earliest found at the Greek trading-post of Al Mina on the north Syrian coast. Indeed, as recent (1981–3) excavations at Lefkandi in Euboea have shown, luxury goods from the East reached Euboea in the tenth century BC, when the rest of Greece is still believed to have been isolated from foreign contacts.

Clues about the place where the Greeks learnt to write can be gleaned from variations in the local alphabets in use in various cities around the Aegean, especially in the writing of composite letters representing consonants, when different sound-values may be allocated to the same character. Most local alphabets fall into two types, known for convenience as 'red' and 'blue'. In the 'blue' alphabets Y stands for 'ps', 'kh' is represented by X and 'ks' by Ⱦ. In the 'red' alphabets, however, Y stands for 'kh' and X (or +) may be transferred to 'ks'; in the absence of a single character for 'ps' two letters are used, usually ΦϨ but sometimes ΠϨ, depending on local pronunciation. There is a further clue in the use of sibilants, for some early alphabets used *san* (M) for 's' rather than *sigma* (Ϩ, Ϩ), which later became universal. Thus local forms of the alphabet appear to fall into cohesive groups that reflect the distribution of dialects and likely trade routes across the Aegean.

The Euboeans, for example, who were Ionian, have a 'red' alphabet and use *sigma*. The same is true of the Boeotians and several other Doric-speaking communities in central Greece, and also of various parts of the Peloponnese including the eastern Argolid, Arcadia and Elis as well as Sparta and her Italian colony Taras (modern Taranto). A similar alphabet seems to connect Rhodes with the Sicilian colonies Gela and Acragas (Agrigento). Achaea, however, in the northern Peloponnese, and Epirus in north-western Greece combine a 'red' alphabet with *san* instead of *sigma*. Doric-speaking Corinth and Argos also use *san* but with a 'blue' alphabet. Megara passed on its 'blue' alphabet with *sigma* to Byzantium. In Athens and Aegina, where a dialect akin to Dorian was spoken, X represents *chi* as in the 'blue' alphabets, but *psi* is at first written as ΦS and 'ks' as XS. Surviving inscriptions suggest that literacy came to Athens early. This may account for the initial absence there of the composite characters, which were perhaps invented only after the Greek alphabet began to develop variations in different areas.

Although certainty is not possible since the evidence is incomplete, it seems likely that the Greeks learnt the alphabet from the Phoenicians before 750 BC in a single place, probably in northern Syria, and that literacy spread along the trade routes to various parts of Greece, reaching Euboea and Athens early. Some scholars, especially experts in the ancient Semitic languages, doubt these conjectures and in particular favour an earlier date.

Local variations in the forms and meanings of the characters lasted for centuries, but eventually the Ionic alphabet prevailed. An early Ionic development was the provision of separate characters for the 'long' and 'short' forms of the vowels 'e' and 'o'. In most local alphabets O was standard for *omicron* ('little O'), and it was the Ionians who first opened the circle at the bottom to produce Ω for *omega* ('big O'). Outside Ionia the Phoenician letter ⊟ (*heth*) was called *heta* by many Greeks. Written as ⊟ and later as H, it was used as an aspirate (h). In Ionia, as in some parts of England, the local dialect did not have an aspirate. The character H was therefore called *eta* and was used as the long form of 'e'.

Among variations in the forms of letters *gamma*, *lamda* and *sigma* deserve special mention. The Athenians, the Euboeans and some others wrote *lamda* as ᴸ, but elsewhere the character was inverted to Γ and eventually the form Λ prevailed. In Athens, however, Λ was long used for *gamma*, elsewhere usually written Γ but as Ϲ in some places, including Euboea. For a long time the Athenians continued to write *sigma* as S with three strokes or 'bars', while in many other places, including Ionia, *sigma* had four bars: Σ. After about 450 BC the four-barred *sigma* gradually came into use in Athens, and in 403/2 the Athenians passed a law to make the use of the Ionian alphabet compulsory in official documents.

The Ionian alphabet eventually superseded all other local alphabets and is still in use in Greece today. At a very early period, however, the Euboeans transmitted their own version of the alphabet to their colonies in Italy. There it was taken over by the Etruscans, again with some modifications to suit the needs of their own language, and was later adopted by the Romans, who spread it around the

4   Etruscan bucchero jug inscribed with the alphabet. 6th century BC. MMA 24.97.21.

non-Greek provinces of the Empire. The differences between modern European and Greek letter-forms can be traced to the use in Italy of the Euboean alphabet, which eventually fell out of use in Greece itself. For example, although the first two letters, A and B, are the same, for the second and third letters we use the Euboean forms C and D, while the alternative forms Γ and Δ have survived in Greece.

Even after the Ionic alphabet became standard a number of variant letter-forms came into use, especially during the Hellenistic and Roman periods. They included a rounded form of *epsilon* (Є), a similar lunate, or moon-shaped, *sigma* (C), and cursive forms of *mu* (ᴎ) and *omega* (ɯ).

Some features of Greek inscriptions

Boustrophedon

Like the Phoenicians the Greeks at first wrote from right to left (as is still the practice in Arabic and Hebrew), but they soon began to write from left to right if this was more convenient. Vase-painters sometimes wrote in both directions on the same vase. In some early Greek inscriptions on stone each line begins under the last letter of the previous line and runs in the opposite direction. Even the letters are turned round to face the other way. Since it recalled the method of ploughing a field in alternate furrows up and down, turning the ox-drawn plough at the end of each furrow, this method of writing was called 'ox-turning', or *boustrophedon*. It may be seen in two 29 early Athenian epitaphs and in the inscription from Sigeion. In the printed text arrows 30 indicate the direction of the lines on the stone. 32

Stoichedon

Many official inscriptions of the Classical period, especially at Athens, were carefully carved on stone slabs with the letters aligned vertically in columns as well as horizontally in lines. Since the letters were arranged almost like soldiers on parade, such inscriptions were said to be written 'in files', or *stoichedon*. The same effect is produced by a typewriter, which allots an equal space to each letter, irrespective of its actual width.

Ligatures

In order to save space in Latin inscriptions the Romans often combined two or more letters, making a single stroke do duty as part of each. This practice was sometimes followed in Greek inscriptions during the Roman period. Many ligatures are used in the Pontarch inscription – for example, ᴎ for *HN* in the middle of the ninth line. 23 Earlier in the same line is a ligature of three letters, ᴎ for *THN*, and in the line above four letters are combined, ᴎ for *HNΩN*, using a straight-lined version of the cursive *omega*.

Numerals

The Greeks used two systems of numerals, the alphabetic and the acrophonic. The acrophonic or initial-letter system used as numerals the first letters of the Greek 3 words for five, ten, hundred and thousand, either singly or in combination. Thus 5 27 (*pente*) was represented by Γ, 10 (*deka*) by Δ, 100 (*hekaton*) by the early aspirate H, and 1,000 (*khilion*) by X. For 50 a tiny *delta* was placed inside the *pi* (Ᵽ), and for 500 Γ and H were combined to form Ᵽ. Units were represented by single strokes, and the numerals were repeated as often as necessary to represent particular numbers. Thus ΔΔΓⅠⅠⅠ is 28 and ᵽHᵽΔΔΓⅠⅠⅠⅠ is 679.

The alphabetic system allocates numerical values to the letters of the alphabet, the
38 units from 1 to 9 being represented by *alpha* to *theta*, the tens to 90 by *iota* to *qoppa*,
40 and the hundreds by *rho* to *sanpi* (λ). In printing alphabetic numerals it is customary
to distinguish them from ordinary letters, usually by adding a mark like an acute
accent ′ above the line after numbers up to 999. A similar mark below the line
precedes the numbers from 1,000. Thus 522 is represented by $\phi\kappa\beta'$, and 5,522 by
$,\varepsilon\phi\kappa\beta'$.

$\alpha = 1$	$\iota = 10$	$\rho = 100$
$\beta = 2$	$\kappa = 20$	$\sigma = 200$
$\gamma = 3$	$\lambda = 30$	$\tau = 300$
$\delta = 4$	$\mu = 40$	$\upsilon = 400$
$\varepsilon = 5$	$\nu = 50$	$\phi = 500$
$F = 6$	$\xi = 60$	$\chi = 600$
$\zeta = 7$	$o = 70$	$\psi = 700$
$\eta = 8$	$\pi = 80$	$\lambda = 800$
$\theta = 9$	$\rho = 90$	$\lambda = 900$

Table 2.   Alphabetic numerals

The use of acrophonic numerals may have begun as early as the seventh century
BC, but is best known in Attica from about the middle of the fifth century BC. Like
Roman numerals they were only really suitable for recording calculations made with
counters, and they are hardly ever seen in inscriptions datable after 100 BC, as the less
cumbersome alphabetic numerals gained favour. The alphabetic system was not
introduced until the second century BC and survived beyond the Roman period into
the Byzantine era.

Dating of inscriptions
The date of an inscription is of primary importance for its interpretation, but it is
seldom possible to assign a date that is both accurate and certain. Often it is only possible to suggest a fairly wide bracket, such as 'fourth century BC' or 'Roman imperial
period'. Usually the epigrapher must seek out and interpret various kinds of information that point towards a date. Sometimes the date is actually included in the text.
It was the custom in many Greek cities to identify each year by the name of the
principal magistrate for that year. In Athens this was the Archon, and the names of
successive Archons were listed in inscriptions. These Archon lists, first compiled
about 425 BC, are recorded in part by the historians Diodorus and Dionysios of
Halicarnassus, and fragments of the slabs themselves survive in Athens. It is therefore
often possible to assign an inscription to a particular year if the Archon's name is
quoted. When the treaty between Athens and Rhegion was renewed, the first eight
lines were recut to give an up-to-date preamble, while the terms of the treaty
remained the same. In the new preamble the name of the Archon for that year is given
as Apseudes, legible in part at the beginning of the fourth line. Since the Athenian
Archons took office on the first day of the month Hekatombaion, which normally fell
in July according to our calendar, each Athenian year overlaps two of our years and is
therefore designated by a double date. In this way the renewal-date of the treaty with
5 Rhegion is written 433/2 BC, because Apseudes is known to have been Archon from
July 433 to July 432 BC. Sometimes, although not in this case, additional evidence
dates an event in one year or the other, and it is then conventional to underline the
appropriate figure: thus 433/2 would mean the actual date was 432 BC.

268

5 Fragment of a treaty between Athens and Rhegion, renewed in 433/2 BC, when the upper part was recut; the lower part was cut *c.* 448 BC. BM GR 1816.6–10.206.

Inscriptions may also include the regnal years of kings and emperors, and a series of inscriptions on cinerary urns found at Alexandria can be dated precisely by the regnal years of the Ptolemies. The symbol ∟ stands for the Greek ἔτους, 'in the year...'. Although the particular Ptolemy is not named, some inscriptions in the series can be dated with certainty for example, because the figure for the year is so large that only one Ptolemy's reign was long enough to accommodate it, or because the day of the month is given according to both the Greek and the Egyptian calendar and only one year has that particular double date.

Other inscriptions can be dated accurately because they refer to events recorded by ancient historians. The inscription on an Etruscan helmet dedicated to Zeus at Olympia tells us that it was captured by the Syracusans at the Battle of Cumae. This battle, which is mentioned by the contemporary poet Pindar and the later historian Diodorus Siculus, was fought in 474 BC, and the inscription must have been put on the helmet soon afterwards. An epitaph in verse commemorating the Athenians who fell in battle at Potidaea was carved on a wall-block from their tomb, which was built at public expense. Since this engagement was described by the historian Thucydides, the inscription can be dated 432 BC.

A less precise but still reliable date can sometimes be derived from references to a historical personage, such as Alexander the Great, or to less famous people whose genealogies and family histories can be reconstructed to some extent from a series of related inscriptions. The study of individuals, or prosopography, is particularly rewarding for cities like Athens, where a great mass of material still survives. About 30,000 Athenian citizens are known by name. Epitaphs of different members of the same family can sometimes be linked to build a family tree extending several generations, but other kinds of inscriptions can yield similar results.

From about 332 BC lists were compiled annually in Athens of youths undergoing military training (*epheboi*). After 305 BC, when this training was no longer compulsory, it gradually became a form of higher education for the rich, including rich foreigners, but the custom of publishing the lists continued into the Roman period. One such list, carved on a marble shield, names Alkamenes as trainer. The same man is known to have held the office of Strategos ('General') in AD 209/10, his father appears on an ephebe list of about AD 160, and his son, who according to the inscription served as assistant on this occasion, himself appears in an ephebe list that belongs to the reign of the Emperor Commodus (AD 180/1-191/2). The inscribed shield can therefore be dated within a few years of AD 200.

An archaeological or historical context can provide at least an indication of a date. If the foundation date of a city is known, it follows that all inscriptions from the site must be later. Similarly, in cases of total or partial destruction of a city the inscriptions must be earlier. Some inscriptions have been found in the wall built by the Athenians on the advice of Themistocles immediately after the expulsion of the Persians: these inscriptions must all antedate the Persian sack of Athens in 480 BC. A similar argument could be applied to all fragments of the inscriptions recording payment to Athena's treasury of a quota from the contributions of the members of the Delian League, even if these inscriptions could not be dated by other methods, since all are later than the transfer of the League's treasury to Athens in 454 BC.

Approximate dates can be assigned to inscriptions that show changes in standard phraseology or the forms of the preambles, if these changes can be identified in inscriptions dated by other means. The forms of names and constitutional arrangements can also provide clues. The use of Roman-style names for officials in an inscription from the Greek city of Rhegion points to a date after the grant of Roman citizenship throughout Italy about 89 BC.

Some inscriptions are associated with buildings or works of art to which dates can be assigned on stylistic grounds. The style of the relief sculpture on the grave-stele of Xanthippos points to a date around 430 BC. The epitaph of Rhoumas is inscribed on a herm that incorporates a portrait-head, the style of which suggests a date between about AD 100 and AD 150. This is consistent with the letter-forms, including the lunate *epsilon* and *sigma*, and the cursive *mu* and *omega*.

Letter-forms alone may in the last resort be used to indicate the date of an inscription, although this method of dating is notoriously unreliable, especially outside Athens after about 400 BC. Even in Athens there are traps for the unwary. Although a decree passed in the Archonship of Euclides (403/2 BC) made the use of the 'Ionic' alphabet compulsory in official documents after that date, Ionic forms had made occasional appearances in official inscriptions earlier, so their presence does not indicate a date after 403/2. The replacement of the Attic three-barred *sigma* by the Ionic four-barred version (ϲ) is particularly erratic. In private inscriptions the change to the Ionic alphabet is even less reliable for dating: the Ionic *xi*, for example, already occurs along with the four-barred *sigma* in the epitaph of Xanthippos about 430 BC.

The following changes of letter-forms are fairly reliable: from the third century BC *xi* may be written Ξ instead of Ξ; before the third century *alpha* with a broken crossbar (Λ) seldom occurs; during the third and second centuries BC the forms of *sigma*

6 Grave-relief of
Xanthippos, *c.* 430 BC.
BM GR 1805.7–3.183.

and *mu* become rectangular (Σ for ξ and M for M), and in the first centuries BC and AD *pi* changes from Π to π. In the Roman period *alpha*, *delta* and *lamda* sometimes acquire elongated forms (A to A, Δ to Δ and Λ to Λ), and rounded forms derived from cursive script become popular for *epsilon* (ε), *mu* (H), *sigma* (c) and *omega* (ω). It is always necessary to remember that while the introduction of new styles of lettering may be dated approximately from inscriptions securely dated by other means the older styles tend to persist: inscriptions are sometimes later than they appear at first sight. Letter styles also vary considerably from place to place, so that changes attested in one place are not reliable for dating inscriptions from another.

The restoration of inscriptions

Very few Greek inscriptions, apart from short texts, have survived complete. Most of the stones on which they are cut have been damaged in some way, by the accidents of time, through deliberate destruction, or by later use for other purposes. An inscribed base honouring a successful athelete from Didyma near Miletus was recut to serve as 21 a building block. The whole of the left side, including the decorative moulding at the top, has been reworked. In consequence the letters at the beginning of each line are damaged and difficult to read. The large slab from Sigeion with duplicate inscriptions 32 in Ionic and Attic dialect and script suffered a more bizarre fate. For many years it served as a bench outside the local church, and the inscription was thought to have special properties since no one could understand it. The sick were brought there and rolled on it in the hope of a miraculous cure. Fortunately travellers from Europe copied the text before the middles of the lines were worn away by this practice, and the restored text is based on these early records.

Various methods are used by editors of inscriptions to indicate the restorations they have made. Certain or probable restorations of letters no longer legible on the stone are placed in square brackets [ ]. Round brackets ( ) are used to complete abbreviations, and in this book they are also used for words that are not present in the Greek text but are needed to complete the sense of the English translation. For example, the inscription translated 'Smikylion (son) of Eualkides' says only 'Smikylion of Eualkides' in the Greek. Brackets of other shapes are also used by epigraphers: angled brackets ⟨ ⟩ to denote letters missing in error, and corrections of the stone-cutter's mistakes; hooked brackets { } for duplicated letters; and double square brackets [[ ]] for letters or words that have been erased. It is one of the first duties of an epigrapher to be scrupulously careful in the use of these conventional signs.

Where a letter that is only partially preserved is ambiguous, that is, where the surviving traces do not make it possible to exclude other interpretations, it is necessary to warn the reader of the printed text by placing a dot underneath. When the missing letters cannot be restored, a dot is placed on the line for each one if the total can be calculated. If the number of missing letters is not known for certain, the gap is indicated by a series of dashes. If there is an actual blank space on the stone, the letter 'v' (for the Latin *vacat*, 'it is empty') is used to denote each uninscribed letter space. A single upright stroke | is used at the start of each new line on the stone if the printed text runs on, without regard to the original arrangement. A pair of strokes ‖ may be used at the start of every fifth line.

Epigraphers have a number of techniques to help in restoring gaps in inscriptions. When an inscription is written *stoichedon*, the exact number of missing letters can be determined by counting those in the line above or in the line below, or by measuring the spacing in the same line. Even when the inscription is not *stoichedon* it is possible to estimate fairly accurately how many letters are missing. Of course, a restoration must never contain too many letters to fit on the stone nor too few to fill the lacuna.

An inscription now in the British Museum may serve as a warning. The slab, which consists of eight lines of verse commemorating a fountain house, was found in the eighteenth century. The text of the inscription was published in 1752, but the slab itself was lost to view before a detailed epigraphic examination could be made. The text is quite well-preserved, apart from a damaged area near the beginning of the first line, where a few letters are missing. This gap proved a standing invitation to editors, and several ingenious restorations were proposed in anthologies of Greek verse published in the eighteenth and nineteenth centuries. After the stone was rediscovered in 1970, it soon became obvious that many of these restorations contained too many letters to fit in the available space on the stone, and when the inscription was republished they were simply rejected as being 'epigraphically impossible'. No scholar, however eminent, could escape the limitations imposed by the stone.

An editor's freedom to suggest restorations is also limited in other ways. Proposed restorations must complete the sense and the grammatical structure of the Greek text; the wording must be appropriate to the period of the original; and account must be taken of the shape and size of the stone itself. The last point is particularly important when dealing with inscriptions so fragmentary that none of the original edges of the slab are preserved. Since marble is of limited strength, the thickness of a fragment will give an indication of the maximum possible width and height of the slab.

7 Metrical inscription from a fountain-house on Lesbos, Roman period, perhaps 2nd century AD. BM GR 1070.9–25.1.

Even very fragmentary texts can sometimes be restored with near certainty if the editor can recognise that the surviving letters form part of a standard word or phrase that occurs in other inscriptions. One of the commonest of such epigraphic formulas is the dedication 'So-and-so dedicated (this)', sometimes adding the name of the god to whom the offering was made. The key word is 'dedicated' ($\dot{\alpha}\nu\acute{\epsilon}\theta\eta\kappa\epsilon$).

On occasion historical evidence helps in the restoration. For example, Herodotus tells us that King Crocsus of Lydia paid for some of the columns of the temple of Artemis at Ephesus. When the temple was excavated a number of fragments of column bases were found, each having no more than two or three letters: *BA*, *KP*, *AN*, *ΘHK*, *EN*. Variations in the dimensions of the fragments indicated that they belong to at least three separate column drums, but it is almost certain that all of them

8

8 Fragments of the columns of the archaic temple of Artemis at Ephesus, dedicated by Croesus between 560 and 546 BC. BM GR 1872.4–5.19.

bore the same inscription: 'King Croesus dedicated (this)' (Βασιλεὺς Κροῖσος ἀνέθηκεν).

Decrees of the Athenian democracy were frequently inscribed on stone slabs for public display on the Acropolis or in other parts of the city. The preambles of the decrees, including the names of that year's Archon and other officials, follow standard formulas that lend themselves to comparison with other inscriptions, so that detailed and accurate restoration is sometimes possible. For example, only the upper right-hand corner is preserved of the slab on which the Athenian decree confirming the treaty with Rhegion in 433/2 BC was inscribed. By a fortunate coincidence a delegation from Leontini was in Athens at the same time, and the preamble of the decree confirming the treaty with Leontini is so similar to that of the Rhegion decree that it was probably passed by the same session of the Assembly. Comparison with the Leontini decree makes it possible to restore the preamble of the Rhegion decree with some confidence. Little is preserved of the treaty itself except a provision for the Athenians to take an oath to observe it.

Three features distinguish the preamble from the main text: it is cut in an area slightly recessed from the face of the slab, there are more letters in each line, and the lines themselves are closer together. It may therefore be inferred that the slab was originally inscribed when a treaty was made earlier than 433/2. In that year the treaty was renewed in the same terms, and while the slab itself was reused for economy the old preamble was erased and replaced. The new preamble, however, was slightly longer than the old one, and could be accommodated only by squeezing in an extra line and by making each line contain more letters. At the end of this recut section ten spaces were left over, perhaps because the stone-cutter miscalculated, so that there is a long gap between the first five letters of the proposer's name and the last two, which began the next line and are now lost. The name Kalli[as] can be restored with certainty from the Leontini treaty, where it is completely preserved. (The Leontini treaty too was recut in this way, but there it had been the word 'proposed' that was divided between the end of the new preamble and the beginning of the old text, and the gap was equivalent to only two letters.)

Among other inscriptions that show the Athenian democracy at work are financial records, including not only statements of income and expenditure but also inventories of the valuable contents of official treasuries, such as the objects in precious metal dedicated to the goddess Athena and kept in the *pronaos* ('front porch') of the Parthenon. These were entrusted to commissions of citizens and were subject to audit when each commission handed over its responsibilities to its successor. The inventories are very repetitive, with each year's acquisitions added at the end of the previous year's list. Even though damage to the various marble slabs has left individual inscriptions in a fragmentary state, careful comparison of the comissioners' names and the lists of objects for successive years has made it possible to restore missing letters and words with considerable accuracy.

Most restorations, however convincing, are doomed to remain untested, but sometimes further fragments of an incomplete restoration come to light, to confirm or confound the restorations of previous editors. The dedication on the base of an archaic sculptured grave-stele from Attica, now in the Metropolitan Museum, may serve as an example. Of the seven fragments comprising the inscription the first four to come to light included three that join, while the fourth was a 'floating' fragment. Incomplete letters could be restored with some confidence from the surrounding traces, but editors have disagreed on the restoration of the missing parts. Since the epitaph is in verse, restorations must fit the metrical form as well as complete the sense and the grammar in the available space.

In the first state John Marshall read the surviving letters correctly and proposed to place the floating fragment in the second line:　9a

μνῆμα φίλōι Με[γακλεῖ με or ὁ]
πατὲρ ἐπέ[θēκε θα]νόν[τι]
χοῦν δὲ φ...

He was also the first to suggest that *Με* in the first line might be the beginning of the name of Megakles, a member of the wealthy Alcmaeonid family. This suggested reading has been widely but not universally accepted.

Some years later Hiller von Gaertringen proposed to read χοῦν δὲ φ[ίλē μέτēρ] in the third line and suggested a different reading in the second, introducing the name of Onetor: πατὲρ ἐπέ[θēκε]ν ᾽Ον[έτōρ]. Meanwhile, unknown to Hiller von Gaertringen, another fragment had been added. This confirmed his conjectural φ[ίλē] in the third line and the reading ἐπέθēκε in the second. Various other proposals followed, including an attempt by Gisela Richter to restore the whole verse making　9b
Megakles the dedicator and introducing the name of Menon for the dead youth.

μνῆμα φίλōι Με[γακλὲς με]
πατὲρ ἐπέθēκε [Μέ]νōν[ι]
χοῦν δὲ φίλē[κεῖται
Φαιναρέτē θυγάτēρ]

Me(gakles), his father, dedicated (me), a memorial to dear Menon; with him (lies buried) dear (Phainarete, the daughter)

When the next two fragments were added it became clear that Hiller von Gaertringen's emendations were correct only in the third line. The second line contains no name: John Marshall had been right from the beginning. The text may now be　9c
restored:

μνῆμα φίλōι με[_ ca. 8 _]
πατὲρ ἐπέθēκε θανόντ[ι]
χοῦν δὲ φίλē μέτēρ
1.　Με[γακλεῖ με?] is restored by some editors.

The last line remains a problem. Dietrich von Bothmer has proposed the insertion of a sculptor's signature in a metrical form that occurs elsewhere: ἔργον ᾽Αριστοκλέος ('the work of Aristokles'). Although this completes the elegaic couplet, the comment seems intrusive in a funerary epigram and leaves the word 'mother' hanging without a verb, 'dedicated' being in the singular, not the plural form. Unless more fragments turn up to complete the text, the last line seems likely to remain a mystery.

275

2
Inscriptions on Stone

Although many Greek inscriptions cannot be read and understood without a working knowledge of the language, a knowledge of the Greek alphabet alone is enough for those inscriptions that consist only of proper names. These can be read simply by substituting English letters for the corresponding Greek letters. Epitaphs, that is,

6 inscriptions on gravestones, often consist only of names. An Athenian gravestone of about 430 BC is inscribed simply with the name Xanthippos (Ξάνθιππος).

The full name of an Athenian citizen consisted of his personal name, his father's name and the name of the *deme* or district in which they were registered. The

11 patronymic, or father's name, is in the genitive case meaning '(son) of ...': Σμικυλίων | Εὐαλκίδου | ἐκ Κεραμέων ('Smikylion, (son) of Eualkides, from Kerameis').

On a marble slab in New York a successful athlete is commemorated by an inscrip-

10 tion with illustrations of the prizes he had won. The slab is unfortunately incomplete so the man's name is lost, but he was of the deme of Rhamnous in Attica, and his father's name may be restored as Alexander:

Παναθή - "Ισθμια ἐξ "Αργους Νέμ[εα]
 ναια   ἀσπίς

[_ _ _ʼΑλε]ξάνδρου ʽΡαμνούσιος ἀνη[_ _ _]

Panathenaia   Isthmia   The shield from Argos   Nemea
[... son of Ale]xander of Rhamnous...

The surviving illustrations show a Panathenaic prize amphora, the pine crown from Isthmia, the Argive shield and the crown of wild celery from Nemea. On the left, above the man's name, there would have been an illustration of another prize, perhaps the laurel crown from Delphi or even the crown of wild olive from Olympia.

10 Prizes won by an athlete from Rhamnous. Roman imperial period. MMA 59.11.19.

11   Epitaph of Smikylion, mid-4th century BC. BM GR 1850.7–24.1.

Other types of inscriptions could consist chiefly of names – in particular, dedications to deities. It was a common practice to dedicate offerings either in support of petitions or in thanksgiving for favours granted. Strictly speaking, 'votive' offerings are those made in fulfilment of a vow (Latin *votum*), but the term is also applied to dedications in general, including petitions and thank-offerings. In practice it is often impossible to assign an individual offering to a particular category. Such offerings were frequently made to the deities who were believed to be responsible for curing diseases, particularly Asklepios and Hygieia. Asklepios, the patron of medical centres at Epidauros, Kos and various other places in the Greek world, was believed to have been a human physician who received heroic or divine honours after his death. Hygieia was the personification of Health (her name is the root of the English word 'hygiene').

A marble slab, which was found in the sanctuary of Asklepios on Melos, has a relief showing a leg from just above the knee together with an inscription Ἀσκλη|πιῷ | καὶ | hυγεία ‖ Τύχη | εὐχαρισ|τήριον ('Tyche (dedicated this) to Asklepios and Hygieia (as a) thank-offering') The aspirate is represented by two dots over the *upsilon*. Note that the *iotas*, which form part of the case-ending for the dative case, are printed beneath the *omega* and the *alpha* ('subscript'), as they would be in a literary text, since they do not appear on the stone. When the *iota* is cut on the stone, this is indicated by printing it beside the relevant letter ('adscript'), as in no. 9. Tyche had evidently suffered from some kind of leg trouble and presented this slab in thanksgiving for a cure. This practice of dedicating representations of parts of the body that have been healed survives to this day in Greece and other countries of southern Europe. The inscription has modern parallels too: the personal columns of religious newspapers occasionally include items like the following: 'Thanksgiving to St Jude for favours received.' — cover

Alexander the Great made a more imposing dedication to the goddess Athena, an entire temple at Priene in Asia Minor. The first part of his long journey of conquest took him through Asia Minor, where he liberated the Greek cities from Persian rule. The historian Strabo records that Alexander offered to defray the entire cost of rebuilding the Temple of Artemis at Ephesus, which had been burnt down in 356 BC, on condition that the gift should be recorded by an inscription on the Temple. There was a precedent for this since King Croesus had dedicated many of the columns of the previous temple. The Ephesians, however, declined Alexander's offer on the grounds that it was not fitting for one god to dedicate a temple to another. No ancient historian records that Alexander made a similar offer to the people of Priene, but the dedicatory inscription on the temple indicates that the offer was both made and accepted; Βασιλεὺς Ἀλέξανδρος | ἀνέθηκε τὸν ναὸν | Ἀθηναίηι Πολιάδι ('King Alexander dedicated the temple to Athena Polias'). After the temple was excavated in 1869–70 by the Society of Dilettanti, this block and several others from the adjacent wall were removed to London. Immediately below the dedication was inscribed a letter from Alexander granting Priene various privileges including exemption from taxes, while the rest of the wall was used for other records, forming a kind of permanent civic archive. — 12, 8

12   Alexander the Great's dedication of the temple of Athena Polias at Priene, 334 BC.
BM GR 1870.3-20.88.

Inscriptions recording the dedication of buildings could include a list of the officials involved in the construction. An example from Iasos records work on the Council Chamber and the Archeion. The Archeion, the residence or office of the principal Magistrate, was also the place where public records were preserved. It probably stood alongside the Council Chamber like the corresponding record office (the Metroon) at Athens.

> οἱ αἱρεθέντες τοῦ τε βουλευτηρίου καὶ τοῦ ἀρχείου ἐπιμεληταὶ
> Λύσανδρος Ἀριστοκρίτου, Μενοίτιος Εὐκράτου, Ἱεροκλῆς Ἰάσωνος,
> Ἱεροκλῆς Λέοντος, Ἀρκτῖνος Ποσειδίππου, καὶ ὁ ἀρχιτέκτων
> Ἀναξαγόρας Ἀπελλικῶντος Ὁμονοίαι καὶ τῶι δήμωι.
> The elected commissioners of the Council Chamber and the Archeion Lysandros
> (son) of Aristokritos, Menoitios (son) of Eukratos, Hierokles (son) of Jason,
> Hierokles (son) of Leon, Arktinos (son) of Poseidippos, and the architect
> Anaxagoras (son) of Apellikon (dedicated the buildings) to Concord and the
> People.

Other inscriptions of Iasos and an account by the Roman historian Livy of relations between King Antiochos and the people of Iasos suggest that political concord was achieved in the city during the second century BC by driving into exile those citizens who favoured alliance with Rome rather than with Antiochos. The city's loyalty to Antiochos was secured by generous gifts, and it is possible that he provided the money that was spent restoring the Council Chamber and the Archeion. These funds were administered by an *ad hoc* commission of five citizens.

An inscription from a Roman arch at Thessalonika consists of the names of those who held public office at the time of its construction:

> πολειταρχούντων · Σωσιπάτρου · τοῦ · Κλ[εο]‖πάτρας · καὶ · Λουκίου ·
> Ποντίου Σεκούνδο[υ]‖ υἱοῦ · Αὔλου · Ἀονίου · Σαβείνου · Δημητρίου · τ[οῦ]
> | Φαύστου · Δημητρίου · τοῦ · Νεικοπόλεως Ζω[ίλου]‖ τοῦ Παρμενίωνος ·
> τοῦ καὶ Μενίσκου · Γαΐου · Ἀγιλλήΐο[υ]‖ Ποτείτου · ταμίου[·] τῆς πόλε⟨ω⟩ς
> Ταύρου · τοῦ · Ἀμμίας | τοῦ καὶ Ῥήγλου · γυμνασιαρχοῦντος · Ταύρου τοῦ
> Ταύρο[υ]‖ τοῦ καὶ Ῥήγλου.

13   Building-inscription from Iasos, 2nd century BC. BM GR 1872.6-10.43.

14   Woodcut showing the inscription on the Roman arch at Thessalonica before its demolition in 1876. 2nd century AD. BM GR 1877.5–11.1.

Sosipatros (son) of Kleopatra and Lucius Pontius Secundus, Aulus Avius Sabinus, Demetrios (son) of Faustus, Demetrios (son) of Nikopolis, Zoilos (son) of Parmenion, also known as Meniskos, (and) Gaius Agilleius Potitus as Politarchs, Tauros also known as Reglus (son) of Ammia as City Treasurer, and Tauros also known as Reglus (son) of Tauros as Gymnasiarch.

The date can no longer be given in absolute terms since we do not have the annual list of the principal magistrates, or Politarchs, corresponding to the list of Athenian Archons. The title 'Politarchs' (literally,'rulers of the citizens') was used in several Greek cities and its occurrence at Thessalonika is also known from the Acts of the Apostles (XVII, 6:8). Although St Luke quotes the title correctly, this has disappeared in many English versions of Acts either by attempts to translate the term (Authorised Version: 'rulers of the city') or by vague periphrases (Revised Standard Version: 'city authorities').

When the arch was demolished in 1876, a slab containing most of the text was taken to the British Consulate in Thessalonika, and it was presented to the British Museum in 1877 by J. E. Blunt, HM Consul General. The ends of lines three to four were carved on the next slab, which was unfortunately not preserved, but the whole text can be read in a woodcut showing the inscription before demolition.

Two of the Politarchs, Aulus Avius Sabinus and Gaius Agilleius Potitus, together with Lucius Pontius Secundus who was father of another, have Roman names, which have been transliterated into Greek. The names of the other Politarchs are Greek in form. A similar mixture of Latin and Greek names can be seen in an inscription from 15 Rhegion (now Reggio Calabria in southern Italy), which consists of a list of municipal officials and sacrificial assistants. Rhegion was founded as a Greek colony about 720 BC, and Greek continued to be spoken there long after the city came under Roman rule. The illustration shows a 'squeeze', an impression of the inscription made by forcing a sheet of moist, soft paper into the letters with a brush. When the paper has dried it may be removed from the stone, allowing the epigrapher to take away a light-weight and exact copy for study.

πρύτανις ἐκ τοῦ · ἰδίου · καὶ · ἄρχων · πεντα|ετηρικὸς · Σέξ(τος) ·
Νουμώνιος Σέξ(του) · υ(ἰὸς) · Ματοῦρος | συνπρυτάνεις · Κ(οίντος) ·

15 Cult-officials at Rhegion in the Roman period, late 1st century BC or 1st century AD.
BM GR 1970.6–2.1.

Ὀρτώριος · Κ(οίντου) · υ(ἱὸς) · Βάλβιλλος · Μ(άρκος) Πετρώ | νιος ·
Μ(άρκου) · υ(ἱὸς) · Ποῦλχερ · Μ(άρκος) · Κορνήλιος · Μ(άρκου) · υ(ἱὸς) ·
Μαρτιᾶλις ‖ ἱεροσκόποι · Μάνιος · Κορνήλιος · Οὐῆρος · Γ(άϊος) Ἀντώνιος
| Θύτης · ἱεροσαλπιστὴς · Γ(άϊος) · Ἰούλιος · Ῥηγῖνος ·
ἱεροκῆ(ρυξ) | Γ(άϊος) · Καλπούρνιος · Οὐῆρος · ἱεροπαρέκτης · Κ(οίντος) ·
Καικίλιος · | Ῥηγῖνος · τ(α)μίας · Μελίφθονγος · Ματούρου · σπονδαύλης |
Ναταλις καπναύγης · Ἑλικὼν Ματούρου μάγιρος Ζώσιμος.

Prytanis-in-chief and Quinquennial Archon, Sextus Numonius Maturus, son of
Sextus; Co-prytaneis, Quintus Ortorius Balbillius, son of Quintus, Marcus
Petronius Pulcher, son of Marcus, Marcus Cornelius Martialis, son of Marcus.
Haruspices, Manius Cornelius Verus, Caius Antonius Thytes; sacrificial
trumpeter, Caius Iulius Reginus; sacrificial herald, Caius Calpurnius Verus; priest's
attendant, Quintus Caecilius Reginus. Steward, Meliphthongos, (slave) of Maturus;
ceremonial piper, Natalis; smoke-observer, Helicon, (slave) of Maturus; cook,
Zosimos.

It should be noted that although the inscription is in Greek most of the names are
Latin in form. The difference between Latin and Greek names may reflect a distinction between citizens and slaves, especially since the steward appears to be on the
staff of the chief official. There is also a clear difference in status between those with
religious titles (Haruspex, etc.) and those with municipal office, who add their patronymics. Each of the latter follows the Latin convention. In a Latin inscription the first
name would appear as SEX(TUS) NUMONIUS SEX(TI) F(ILIUS) MATURUS.

The heading of a list of youths undergoing military training (epheboi), which was
16 carved on a marble shield about AD 200, includes the name of the trainer (kosmetes)
in large letters: Ἀλκαμένους κοσμη|τεύοντος ἔφηβοι ('Epheboi, Alkamenes being
trainer'). There is a ligature between eta and beta in 'epheboi'. The names of the
epheboi are listed by tribes, beginning as usual with the tribe of Erechtheis. The sign
ﾉ is used to mark the start of each new tribe, and a curved line ⊃ indicates that the
youth's father's name was the same as his own. Abbreviations are identified by a sign
like an acute accent (').

Ἐρεχθεῖδος	Tribe of Erechtheis
Αὐρ(ήλιος) Δημήτριος	Aurelius Demetrios
Ἰσίτυχος Ζωπύ(ρου)	Isitychos (son) of Zopyros
Ζώπυρος ⊃	Zopyros (son of Zopyros)
Ζωσιμιανὸς Σοφ	Zosimianus (son) of Soph(...)
Φανίας Μυστικοῦ	Phanias (son) of Mystikos
Ἡρακλείδης ⊃	Herakleides (son of Herakleides)

16 List of Ephebes at Athens, *c.* AD 200.
BM GR 1805.7–3.232.

The names of the foreigners who had come to Athens to complete their education are given at the bottom under the heading ἐπένγραφοι ('enrolled in addition'), and Alkamenes adds a comment in the fourth column:

ἀντικοσμήτῃ δὲ οὐ|κ ἐχρησάμην διὰ τὸ | ἐν τῷ νόμῳ περὶ τοῦ|του μηδὲν γεγρά‖φθαι ἄλλως τε καὶ | τῷ υἱῷ ἐχρησάμην | εἰς ταύτην τὴν | ἐπιμέλιαν | Μ(άρκῳ) Αὐρηλίῳ ‖ Ἀλκαμένει Λαμ|πτρεῖ.

I did not use a deputy Kosmetes because nothing is written in the law about this, and especially because I used my son M. Aurelius Alkamenes of Lamptrai for this duty.

To read this comment by Alkamenes on the actual stone requires some knowledge of Greek beyond the mere alphabet. The same is true of most inscriptions, including epitaphs that are not confined to the names of the dead. A grave-stele from Smyrna commemorates two men, both of whom were awarded an honorary crown by their fellow citizens. The crowns are shown at the top of the stele and ὁ δῆ|μος ('the People'), is written in each. The men's names follow, in the accusative case instead of the nominative that is more usual on grave reliefs, as if they were quoted from the text of an honorary decree passed by the People:

Δημοκλῆν   Δημοκλῆν
Δημοκλῆους   Ἀμφιλόχου

281

The men themselves are represented in low relief, and below are eight lines of verse:

τὸν πινυτὸν κατὰ πάντα καὶ ἔξοχον ἐν πολιήταις
  ἀνέρα, γηραλήου τέρματ᾽ ἔχοντα βίου,
Ἀΐδεω νυχίοιο μέλας ὑπεδέξατο κόλπος,
  εὐσεβέων θ᾽ ὁσίην εὔνασεν ἐς κλισίην.
μνῆμα δ᾽ ἀποφθιμένοιο παρὰ τρηχῆαν ἀταρπὸν
  τοῦτο πάϊς κεδνῆι τεῦξε σὺν εὐνέτιδι.
ξεῖνε, σὺ δ᾽ ἀείσας Δημοκλέος υἱέα χαίρειν
  Δημοκλέα στείχοις ἀβλαβὲς ἴχνος ἔχων.

The man (who was) wise in all things and eminent among the citizens, reaching the end of a long life, the black bosom of gloomy Hades welcomed (him) and laid (him) on the hallowed couch of the pious. This memorial of (one who) perished along a rough path his son set up, together with his wedded wife. Stranger, having bidden farewell to Demokles (son) of Demokles, may you travel with safe footsteps.

18   The epitaph of a man called Rhoummas is also in three lines of verse, carved in a recessed panel on the front of a herm, a rectangular pillar surmounted by a man's head. Herms with the head of Hermes or Dionysos were often placed near doorways or crossroads, but this one may have served as a grave-marker and appears to be a portrait. It was made by cutting down a statue, which had perhaps been broken previously. The legs no longer exist, the arms have been reduced to projections, and the trunk has been squared off. A notch about half-way down his left side shows where the rib cage ended, and there are traces of the buttocks at the back. The shapes of the letters, including a tendency to serifs, the lunate *sigma* and *epsilon*, and the cursive *mu* and *omega*, are consistent with the date between AD 100 and 150 suggested by the style of the sculpture. Only one of the eyes has an engraved circle for the pupil: perhaps Rhoummas was partially blind.

The inscription is again cut without regard for word endings, but the ends of the lines of verse correspond with the ends of the fifth, ninth and fourteenth (last) lines of the text. An ivy wreath is used as a space filler at the end of the fifth line.

Ῥουμμᾶν | ἄνδρα βλέπον|τες ἐν εἰκό|νι μαρμαρο‖παίστῳ |
γνωρίσατε | μεγάλας πί|στεις ἀνύσαν|τα δι᾽ εὐχῆς ‖
οὐκ ἔθανέν | γε θανών, | ἀγαθῆς γὰρ | ἐτύγχανε | γνώμης.

Recognise Rhoummas when you look at him in a portrait carved in marble, a man who performed great (deeds of) faith through prayer; dying he did not indeed die, for he came by a good repute.

19   An ivy wreath is also used to separate two lines of verse on another grave stone with a slightly gruesome but moralising tone. A representation of a skeleton is carved in relief below the inscription, which reads·

εἰπεῖν τίς δύναται | σκῆνος λιπόσαρκον | ἀθρήσας
εἴπερ Ὕλας | ἢ Θερσείτης ἦν, ὦ ‖ παροδεῖτα;

Who can say, having looked at a fleshless corpse, whether it was Hylas or Thersites, passer-by?

Hylas was a beautiful youth who set off with Herakles to accompany the Argonauts. He disappeared *en route* for, having been sent off to get water, he was seized by the nymphs on account of his beauty' (Apollodorus 1. 9.19). Thersites on the other hand was 'the ugliest man who went to Troy', according to Homer (*Iliad* 2. 216). The implication of the epigram is that the fair and the ugly were equal in death.

17 *Above and below (detail)* Epitaph
of Demokles, 2nd or 1st century BC.
BM GR 1772.7–3.2.

18 *Above* Epitaph of
Rhoummas, *c.* AD 100–150.
BM GR 1948.10–19.1.

ΕΙΠΕΙΝ ΤΙΣ ΔΥΝΑΤΑΙ
ΣΚΗΝΟΣ ΛΙΠΟΣΑΡΚΟΝ
ΑΘΡΗΣΑΣ ΕΙΠΕΡ ΥΛΑΣ
ΗΘΕΡΣΕΙΠΗΣΗΝ Ω
ΠΑΡΟΔΕΙΤΑ

19   *Left* Funerary epigram
illustrated by a skeleton, Roman
period. BM GR 1805.7–3.211.

ΓΑΘΗ ΤΥΧΗ
ΛΕΥΚΙΟΝ ΛΕΥΚΙ
ΟΥ ΝΙΚΗΣΑΝΤΑ
ΑΜΕΓΑΛΑ ΔΙΟΥ
ΠΕΙΑ ΑΓΩΝΙΣΑ
ΙΕΝΟΝ ΔΕ ΚΑΙΟ
ΥΜΠΙΑΤΑ ΕΠΠΕΙ
ΗΠΕΡΙ ΤΟΥΣ ΤΕΡΑ
ΙΟΥ ΑΓΩΝΙΣΑΙ ΕΠΙ
ΕΚΑ ΤΟΥΣ ΑΛΛΟΥΣ
ΑΝΤΑΣ ΑΓΩΝΑΣ
ΞΙΟΝ ΕΚΩ ΣΗ ΒΟΥ
ΗΚΑΙ Ο ΔΗΜΟΣ

ΛΒΕΙΤΑΣ ΖΗΣΑ ΔΕ ΤΗ
ΜΗΝΑΣ ΔΥΟ
ΧΑΙΡΕΤΕ

T 187

21   *Above* Honours for the
athlete Loukios of Miletus,
Roman period.
BM GR 1859.12–26.91.

20   *Left* Epitaph of Avita,
Roman period.
BM GR 1805.7–3.187.

22 A curse for the misuse of a tomb at Halicarnassus, 2nd or 3rd century AD.
BM GR 1847.12–20.3.

Death came early to Avita, a child of ten, whose grave relief shows her seated with a scroll on her lap. The object in front of her is probably a reading-stand with another scroll on it. Her pet dog sits behind her chair. Ἀβεῖτα · ζήσασα · ἔτη · ι′ · | μῆνας δύω | χαίρετε ('Avita, having lived 10 years 2 months. Farewell'). Her name was Avita in Latin, transliterated into Greek as Ἀβεῖτα in accordance with the pronunciation of the time. Epitaphs of children, especially in the Roman world, often gave their ages very accurately in terms of years and months, sometimes in days, and even occasionally in hours.

In the Greek cities of Asia Minor it was customary for those who could afford it to have a tomb for themselves and members of their families built during their own lifetime. Many of the inscriptions from such built tombs include a prohibition on unauthorised burial there. The prohibition was sometimes backed by the threat of a fine, or, as in an inscription from Halicarnassus, by a formidable curse.

[τ]ὸ μνημεῖον κατεσκ[εύα]σαν Ἑρμῆς καὶ Θοιοδότη Ἀπολλοδώρου· μὴ
ἐξέστω δὲ | ἕτερον τεθῆναι μηδένα, εἰ μὴ Ἑρμην πάπαν καὶ Θοιοδότην καὶ
Ἑρμην | τὸ ὄνομα τὸ Ἑρμῆδος, θρεπτὸν αὐτῶν·εἰ δέ τις ἐπιχειρήσι θειναί
τινα μηδὲ | γῆ καρποφορήσοιτο αὐτῷ μηδὲ θάλασσα πλωτὴ μηδὲ τέκνων
ὄνησ(ι)ς ‖ μηδὲ βίου κράτησις ἀλλὰ ὠληπανώλη εἴ τις δὲ ἐπιχειρήσι λίθον
ἆμαι ἢ λῦ|σαι αὐτὸ, ἧιω ἐπικατάρατος ταῖς προγεγραμμέναις ἀραῖς, οὐδὲ
ἐξέ|στω ἐκχωρῆσαί τινι τὸ μνημῖον· ἐπιμελήσονται δὲ οἱ διακατέχοντες | τὸ
οἰκίδιον τὸ ἐξέναντι τοῦ μνημίου.

Hermes and Thoiodote (daughter) of Apollodoros set up the memorial. It is not allowed for anyone else to be buried except Hermes the father and Thoiodote and Hermes their slave (given) the name of Hermes. But if anyone attempts to bury anyone, may the land not be fruitful for him nor the sea navigable, may he have no profit from his children nor a hold on life but may he encounter utter destruction; and if anyone attempts to remove a stone or loosen it, let him be cursed by the curses inscribed above; and it is not allowed to transfer the memorial to anyone; and those who occupy the cottage opposite the tomb shall take care of it.

A very large number of surviving inscriptions both from Athens and elsewhere record the honours awarded to men during their own lifetime for various reasons. These often took the form of decrees passed either by the Council in the name of the entire citizen body or by the Council and People together. At Miletus the Council and People honoured a successful local athlete with an inscription set up in the precinct of Apollo at Didyma where the Didymaean Games were held. The steps of the temple itself served as a grandstand for the races, and they are still covered with the names of spectators.

Ἀγαθῇ Τύχῃ | Λεύκιον Λευκί|ου νικήσαντα | τὰ μεγάλα Διδύ‖μεια,
ἀγωνισά|μενον δὲ καὶ Ὀ|λύμπια τὰ ἐν Πεί|[σ]ῃ περὶ τοῦ στεφά|νου,

ἀγωνισάμενον ‖ δὲ καὶ τοὺς ἄλλους | ἅπαντας ἀγῶνας | ἀξιονείκως
ἡ βου|λὴ καὶ ὁ δῆμος.

(With) Good Fortune! The Council and the People (honour) Lucius (son) of Lucius
for his victory in the Great Didymaean Games and for having competed for the
crown in the Olympic Games at Pisa and for having competed in all the other
competitions in a manner worthy of victory.

Even to take part in the Olympic Games, which were controlled by the citizens of
Pisa in whose territory Olympia lay, was evidently considered to bring honour to the
city from which Lucius came.

    A very large number of decrees simply give praise and honour, rather like a
modern 'vote of thanks', no more tangible reward being thought necessary. A striking
example was found at Tomis (modern Constanţa), which in antiquity was the principal
city, or metropolis, of a federation (*koinon*) of Greek cities, including Histria and
Odessos. They were all on the west coast of the Black Sea, south of the Danube, and
the senior official of the Federation was known as the Pontarch ('ruler of Pontos', that
is, of the Black Sea). While it is not certain when the Federation was founded, it is
clear from inscriptions found at Tomis that the Romans made use of it as an instrument of imperial rule. The Pontarch also served as Chief Priest in the cult of the
emperor and in this capacity he was entitled – and therefore expected – to provide
public displays of gladiatorial combats and the slaughter of wild beasts. These spec-
tacular events, although disgusting to modern sensibilities, were highly popular in
Rome, and the taste for them was deliberately spread around the cities of the empire
to foster the dissemination of Roman culture. The inscription, which dates from the
second century, records a decree congratulating Aurelius Priscius Annianus for
carrying out the duties of Pontarch and Chief Priest, in particular for not failing to
provide displays of gladiators and wild beasts. As often, the Pontarch's wife had
served as Chief Priestess and shared her husband's honours. Under Roman influence
many adjacent letters in this inscription have been linked as 'ligatures'.

23   Honours for Aur.
Priscius Annianus, Pontarch at
Tomis, 2nd century AD.
BM GR 1864.3–31.6.

Ἀγαθῆ · Τύχη
κατὰ τὰ δόξαντα τῆ κρατίστη
βουλῆ · καὶ τῷ λαμπροτάτῳ · δήμῳ τῆς λαμ -
προτάτης · μητροπόλεως καὶ
α' · τοῦ εὐωνύμου Πόντου · Τόμεως τὸν
ποντάρχην · Αὐρ(ήλιον) · Πρείσκιον
Ἀννιανὸν
ἄρξαντα τοῦ κοινοῦ τῶν Ἑλλήνων καὶ τῆς μητρ[ο] -
πόλεως τὴν · α' · ἀρχὴν ἁγνῶς καὶ ἀρχιερασά -
μενον τὴν δι' ὅπλων καὶ κυνηγεσιῶν ἐνδόξως
φιλοτειμίαν μὴ διαλιπόντα, ἀλλὰ καὶ βουλευ -
τὴν καὶ τῶν πρωτευόντων Φλαβίας Νεαπό -
λεως καὶ τὴν ἀρχιέρειαν σύμβιον αὐτοῦ,
    Ἰουλίαν Ἀπολαύστην,
    πάσης τειμῆς χάριν.

With Good Fortune.
In accordance with the decree of the most puissant Council and the most illustrious People of Tomis, the most illustrious Metropolis and the first (city) on the west of the Black Sea: All honour to the Pontarch Aur(elius) Priscius Annianus,
who held with distinction the highest office of the Confederacy of the Hellenes and of the Metropolis, and who served as Chief Priest, nobly missing no opportunity to present spectacles of armed men and wild animal hunters, being in addition a member of the Council and one of the leading citizens of Flavia Neapolis, and to the Chief Priestess, his wife Julia Apolausta.

After 403/2 BC the Ionic alphabet was used in all official Athenian inscriptions, including not only those dealing with the government of the city as a whole but also those relating to individual demes, which had a corporate life of their own. The office of Demarch ('ruler of the deme') was very important locally, and the Demarch's name therefore appears alongside that of the Archon in an inscription of the deme of Piraeus publishing the regulations governing the lease of public land to private individuals. Provision was made to guarantee the payment of rents, restrictions were placed on the removal of soil and timber, and cultivation was forbidden during the last six months of a ten-year lease to allow the next leaseholder to plough immediately. The Archon's name is Archippos, but since the archonship was held by men of that name in both 321/0 and 318/7 BC it is uncertain to which year this document belongs.

24

ἐπὶ Ἀρχίππου ἄρχοντος Φρυνίωνος δημαρχοῦ[ντος]‖[κ]ατὰ τάδε
μισθοῦσιν Πειραιεῖς Παραλίαν καὶ Ἁλμυρί‖[δ]α καὶ τὸ Θησεῖον καὶ τἆλλα
τεμένη ἅπαντα· τοὺς μισ⟨θω⟩‖[σ]αμένους ὑπὲρ: Δ': δραχμὰς καθιστάναι
ἀποτίμημα της μ‖[ι]σθώσεως ἀξιόχρεων τοὺς δὲ ἐντὸς Δ' δραχμ⟨ῶ⟩ν
ἐγγυητὴ‖[ν] ἀποδιδόμενον τὰ ἑαυτοῦ τῆς μισθώσεως. ἐπὶ τοῖσδε μ‖[ι]σθοῦσιν
ἀνεπιτίμητα καὶ ἀτελῆ. ἐὰν δέ τις εἰσφορὰ γ‖[ί]γνηται ἀπὸ τῶν χωρίων τοῦ
τιμήματος, τοὺς δημότας ε‖[ἰ]σφέρειν. τὴν δὲ ὕλιν καὶ τὴν γῆν μὴ ἐξέστω
ἐξάγειν το‖[ὺ]ς μισθωσαμένους, μήτε ἐκ τοῦ Θησείου μήτε ἐκ τῶν ἄλλ‖ων
τεμενῶν μηδὲ τὴν ὕλην ⟨ἄ⟩λλοσ· ἢ τῶι χωρίωι. οἱ μισ⟨θω⟩‖σάμενοι τὸ
Θεσμοφόριον καὶ τὸ τοῦ Σχοινοῦντος καὶ⟨ὅ⟩σ'‖ ἄλλα ἐννόμια τὴν
μίσθω⟨σ⟩ιν καταθήσουσι τὴμ μὲν ἡμισ‖έαν ἐν τῶι Ἑκατομβαιῶνι, τὴν δὲ
ἡμισέαν ἐν τῶι Ποσιδε‖ῶνι. οἱ μισθωσάμενοι Παραλίαν καὶ Ἁλμυρίδα καὶ

287

24   Regulations for the lease of public land by the deme Piraeus, 321/0 BC.
BM GR 1785.5–27.9.

τὸ Θη|σεῖον καὶ τἆλλα εἴ πού τι ἐστίν, ὅσα οἷόν τε καὶ θεμιτόν | ἐστιν
ἐργάσιμα ποεῖν, κατὰ τάδε ἐργάσονται, τὰ μὲν ἐ|ννέα ἔτη ὅπως ἄν
βούλωνται, τῶι δὲ δεκάτωι ἔτ⟨ε⟩ι τὴν ἡ|μισέαν ἀροῦν καὶ μὴ πλεί⟨ω⟩, ὅπως
ἄν τῶι μισθωσαμένωι | μετὰ ταῦτα ἐξῆι ὑπεργάζεσθαι ἀπὸ τῆς ἕκτης ἐπὶ
δέκ|α τοῦ Ἀνθεστηριῶνος· ἐὰν δὲ πλείω ἀρόσηι ἢ τὴν ἡμισέ|αν, τῶν
δημοτῶν ἔστω ὁ καρπὸς ὁ πλείων. τὴν οἰκίαν τὴ[ν] | ἐν Ἁλμυπ]ίδι
στέγουσαν παραλαβὼν καὶ ὀρθὴν κατὰ τ[..] | [_ _ _ _ _ _ _ _^ca. 30^ _ _ _ _ _ _ _ _]
τ. ονορθαι [...]

In the time of Archippos as Archon, Phrynion as Demarch. In accordance with the
following terms the people of Piraeus lease Paralia and Halmyris and the Theseion
and all the other precincts; those leasing for more than 10 drachmas are to
provide a security of a value equivalent to the rent; for those leasing for less than
10 drachmas, the guarantor is to give his own property as security for the loan.
Under these conditions they lease without rates and without taxes; but if any War
Tax is levied on the valuation of the property, the demesmen are to contribute.
And the Lessors shall not be permitted to remove the mud (?wood) or the soil,
neither from the Theseion nor from the other precincts, nor (to carry off) the
wood elsewhere than to the property. Those leasing the Thesmophorion and the
(place) of the reed-growing and any other (places) covered by legislation shall pay
the rent half in the (month of) Hekatombaion and half in the (month of)
Poseideion. Those leasing Paralia and Halmyris and the Theseion and the other
places if there are any, so far as it is possible and proper to bring (them) into
cultivation, shall cultivate them as follows: for nine years however they wish, but in

the tenth year (they are) to till for half the year and no more, so that it shall be possible for the one who leases subsequently to plough up from the 16th of (the month of the) Anthesteria. And if he tills for more than the half year, the excess crop shall belong to the deme[smen]. Taking over the roofed house in Halmyris … (he shall maintain it?) upright …

It is possible that ὕλιν ('mud') in the ninth line was an error by the stonecutter for ὕλην ('wood'). The stonecutter certainly made several other errors, including *alpha* and *lamda* for *omega* in the fifth and nineteenth lines, *lamda* for *alpha* in the eleventh, *eta* for *epsilon* in the eighteenth, *omicron* omitted near the end of the twelfth, and blank spaces for *sigma* in the middle of the thirteenth and for *theta omega* at the end of the eleventh.

The next group of inscriptions from Athens date from before 403/2 BC and make use of the Attic alphabet. The chief difference among the consonants is that Λ represents *gamma*, not (as in the Ionic alphabet) *lamda*, which in Attic is written L. The sign H (*heta*) is still used as the aspirate (and is transliterated as *h*) rather than as the 'long' form of the vowel 'e'. In the Attic alphabet both 'long' and 'short' forms as well as the diphthong 'ei' are represented by *epsilon*, and *omicron* stands not only for the 'long' and 'short' forms of 'o' but also for most cases of the diphthong 'ou'. Since the double consonants *xi* and *psi* have not yet been introduced, the sounds they represent are written as *chi sigma* (ΧΣ) and *phi sigma* (ΦΣ). *Sigma* itself was often written with four bars (Ϻ) in the Ionic fashion before the use of the Ionic alphabet became mandatory. A few scattered examples occur even before 500 BC, and after about the middle of the fifth century the old three-barred sigma (Ϻ) gradually dropped out of use.

The attractive appearance of so many of the official inscriptions of the Athenian democracy in the later fifth century BC is largely achieved by a combination of a classically simple style of lettering with a strict adherence to the discipline of the *stoichedon* arrangement. Although the work of particular stonecutters can sometimes be recognised in groups of inscriptions, in the absence of signatures or other records not one of these men is known to us by name.

It was the Athenian custom in time of war to commemorate each year the men who fell on active service. The famous funeral oration, which Thucydides puts into the mouth of Perikles at the end of the first year of the Peloponnesian War, is a model of a speech for such an occasion. A memorial was also provided at public expense. In 432 BC, shortly before the Peloponnesian War itself broke out, the Athenians saw action at Potidaea. Thucydides tells us that the Athenian victory came quickly, whereupon some of the Potidaeans fled to the walls. 'After the battle', he goes on, 'the Athenians set up a trophy and they surrendered the dead under truce to the Potidaeans. Of the Potidaeans and their allies not far short of 300 were killed, of the Athenians themselves 150 men and Kallias the General.' A single slab survives from the monument built in Athens to commemorate Kallias and his men. The inscription includes twelve lines of verse that evidently comprised three epigrams of four lines each. The first is very fragmentary, but the other two may be restored with some confidence. In one the flight of some of the Potidaeans, which was described by Thucydides, is contrasted with the honourable fate of the dead. A small fragment of the same inscription, which was found in the Athenian agora in 1935, preserves a few letters from the ends of the last three lines, so confirming the restorations proposed in earlier publications.

25

αἰθὲρ μὲμ φσυχὰς ὑπεδέχσατο σόμ[ατα δὲ χθὸν]
   τōνδε Ποτειδαίας δ' ἀμφὶ πύλας ἐλ[ύθεν].
ἐχθρōν δ' οἱ μὲν ἔχοσι τάφο μέρος, h[οι δὲ φυγόντες]

τεῖχος πιστοτάτεν ηελπίδ᾽ ἔθεντο [βίου].
ἄνδρας μὲμ πόλις ηέδε ποθεῖ καὶ δε͂[μος Ἐρεχθε͂ος]
πρόσθε Ποτειδαίας ηοὶ θά\νον ἐμ προ[ο]μάχοις,
παῖδες Ἀθεναίον, φσυχὰς δ᾽ ἀντίρρο[π]α θέντες
ἐ[λλ]άχσαντ᾽ ἀρετὲν καὶ πατρ[ίδ᾽] εὐκλ[έ]ϊσαν.

The air received the spirits and [the earth] the bodies of these men, and [they were undone] around the gates of Potidaea; of their enemies some attained the destiny of the grave, others [fled and] made the wall their surest hope [of life].

This city and the people [of Erechtheus] mourn the men who died in [battle] before Potidaea, sons of Athenians; [placing] their lives as a counterpoise they received glory in exchange and brought honour to their native land.

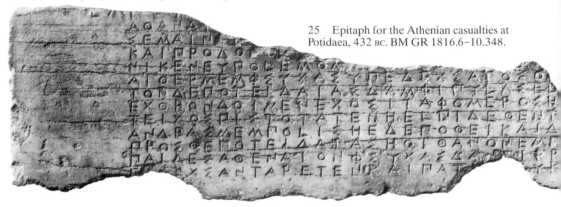

25 Epitaph for the Athenian casualties at Potidaea, 432 BC. BM GR 1816.6–10.348.

The inscription for the men who fell at Potidaea in 432 doubtless included a list of their names, which has not survived. Among related inscriptions that have survived is a list of Athenians who were killed on active service in a single year during the Peloponnesian War. Some parts of the list are difficult to read since the surface of the stone has been damaged and a number of letters are illegible. A fairly easy section appears about half-way down the first column.

Ἀντιοχίδος	of (the tribe) Antiochis
Ἀριστομέδες	Aristomedes
Ἀμεινοκλε͂ς	Ameinokles
Αἰσχίνες	Aischines
Παντακλε͂ς	Pantakles
Χαρίδεμος	Charidemos
Τιμόχσενος	Timoxenos
Ανιιφάνης	Antiphanes
ἐμ Ποτειδαίαι	in Potidaea
Παντακλε͂ς	Pantakles
Ἀγνόδεμος	Hagnodemos
Ἀρχίας	Archias
ἐν Ἀμφιπόλει	in Amphipolis
Φιλόφρον	Philophron

The men's names are grouped according to their tribes, and the first word in each section is the name of the tribe. There is a blank line at the end of each section before the next heading. The name of Antiphanes was added later in this space: the letters do

26　List of Athenian casualties, 425/4 or 424/3 BC. BM GR 1816.6–10.173.

not conform to the *stoichedon* pattern, and the stonecutter has used H for *eta*. Since the names of the tribes recur in each column, it seems likely that the casualties of two major engagements head the list, but the exact locations are not known since the upper part of the slab is missing. At the foot of the first column are the names of those who fell at Potidaea and Amphipolis, in Thrace and at Pylos, Sermylia and Singos. It has been suggested that most of these campaigns can be placed in 424 BC, and that the casualty from Pylos died of wounds received there in the previous year. Non-citizens who gave their lives are listed at the end of the second column under three headings: *engraphoi* ('enrolled men'), *toxotai* ('archers') and *xenoi* ('aliens').

　　To the historian the records of the valuable gifts presented from time to time to the goddess Athena provide an insight into the working of the Athenian democracy. Commissions of citizens, including a chairman and a secretary, were appointed annually to be responsible for the treasures. An inventory was taken each year when responsibility was handed over from one commission to the next, and the lists seem to have been recorded permanently on stone every four years on the occasion of the Great Panathenaia. To the epigrapher the repetitive nature of the lists provides an opportunity to restore with almost complete certainty the gaps in the text caused by damage to the surviving slabs. The texts themselves provide many examples of the acrophonic system of numerals. One drachma is represented by ⊢ and one obol by I. The account of the treasures kept in the *pronaos* ('front porch') of the Parthenon for the year 414/3 BC, for the first year of a four-yearly cycle, begins as follows:

27

[τάδ]ε [παρέδο]σαν hαι τέτταρες ἀρχ[αί, hαὶ ἐδίδοσαν τὸν λόγον ἐκ
Παναθēναίōν ἐς Παναθέναια ᵛᵛᵛ] | [τοῖ]ς ταμίαις Τεισαμενōι Παιαν[ιεῖ καὶ
χσυνάρχοσι hοῖς Πολυμέδες Κēφισίōνος Ἀτēνεὺς ἐγρα]|[μμά]τευε· hοι δὲ
ταμίαι, hοῖς Πολυ[μέδες Κēφισίōνος Ἀτēνεὺς ἐγραμμάτευε, παρέδοσαν
τοῖς ταμ ᵛ]|[ίαις] Πολυχσενίδēι Ἀχαρνεῖ καὶ χ[συνάρχοσι, hοῖς Λευκαῖος

291

27   Inventory of treasurers in the Parthenon, 414/13 and 413/12 BC. BM GR 1816.6–10.282.

Κōμάρχο Ἀφιδναῖος ἐγραμμάτευε, ʹ] ‖ [ἐν τōι] πρόνεōι· φιάλē χρυσē ἐχς ἑ̃ς
ἁ[ποραίνονται, ἄσταθμος· φιάλαι ἀργυραῖ ΗΔΔΙ, σταθμὸν τού ʹʹ]‖[τ̄ὸν
ΤΤ]ΗΗΗΗΔΔΔΗΗ· κέρατα ἀργυρᾶ ΙΙΙ, [σταθμὸν τούτōν ΓΔΔΓΗΗ·
ποτέρια ἀργυρᾶ Γ, σταθμὸν τούτōν ʹ] ‖ [ΗΓΔΓΗΗ·] λύχνος ἀργυρὸς,
σταθμὸν τ[ούτο ΔΔΔΓΗΗ·

These (are the) things (that) the four commissions who rendered the account from
Panathenaia to Panathenaia handed over to the stewards Teisamenos of Paiania
and his colleagues for whom Polymedes (son) of Kephision of Atene was secretary;
and (the things that) the stewards for whom Polymedes (son) of Kephision was
secretary handed over to the stewards Polyxenides of Acharnai and his colleagues,
for whom Leukaios (son) of Komarchos of Aphidnai was secretary, in the *pronaos*:
a golden libation bowl, from which they sprinkle themselves, unweighed; 121
silver libation bowls, the weight of these 2 Talents 432 Drachmas; 3 silver drinking
horns, the weight of these 528 Drachmas; 5 silver cups, the weight of these 167
Drachmas; a silver lamp, the weight of this 38 Drachmas...

In the three remaining years of the cycle the preamble is different. The account for
413/2 BC begins:

[τάδε ηοι] ταμίαι τὸν ηιερὸν χρέμ[άτōν] τ̄ες Ἀθēναίας Πο[λυχσενίδ̄ες
Ἀχαρνεὺς καὶ χσυνάρχοντες,] ‖ [ηοῖς Λευ]καῖος Κōμάρχο Ἀφιδνα[ῖος
ἐ]γραμμάτευε, παρ[έδοσαν τοῖς ταμίαις, ηοῖς Αὐτοκλείδ̄ες ʹʹ] ‖ [Σōστράτ]ο
Φρεάρριος ἐγραμμάτ[ευε, Κ]αλλαίσχρōι Εὐπ[υρίδει καὶ χσυνάρχοσι
παραδεχσάμενοι ʹ] ‖ [παρὰ τὸν] προτέρōν ταμιōν, ηοῖς [Πολυ]μέδ̄ες
Κēφισίōν[ος Ἀτēνεὺς ἐγραμμάτευε, ἐν τōι πρόνεōι· ʹʹ]

These (are the) things the stewards of the sacred monies of Athena, Polyxenides of
Acharnai and his colleagues, for whom Leukaios (son) of Komarchos of Aphidnai
was secretary, handed over to the stewards for whom Autokleides (son) of
Sostratos of Phrearoi was secretary, Kallaischros of Eupyridai and his colleagues
having received (them) from the previous stewards, for whom Polymedes (son) of
Kephision of Atene was secretary, in the *pronaos* ...

It is not known for certain when construction began on the temple on the Athenian
acropolis now known as the Erechtheion. It was probably some time after 421 BC, but
work was later postponed at a date that is also not recorded. In the late summer of
409 BC the Athenian Assembly passed a decree proposed by Epigenes appointing a

28   Report of the Building Commission for the Erechtheion at Athens, 409/8 BC.
BM GR 1785.5–27.1.

Commission to complete the temple. The date is given in the prescript of a long   28
inscription, in which the Commission recorded its progress during the first year: the
decree was passed during the first session of the Council in the archonship of Diokles,
who took office in 409 BC. The three commissioners included Chariades from Agryle,
who was one of the Treasurers of the Delian League (Hellenotamias) in 408/7 BC, and
was evidently a man of some standing. Assisted by an architect and a secretary, the
Commissioners began by carrying out a detailed survey of the building so far as it had
been completed and by compiling an inventory of the blocks, both finished and un-
finished, that were lying around the site. Their first report also includes details of
blocks set in place that year.

[ἐ]πιστάται τô νεô τô ἐμ πόλει ἐν hôι τô ἀρχαῖον ἄγαλμα, Βροσυν[ί]-
[δ]ēς Κēφισιεύς, Χαριάδēς Ἀγρυλēθεν, Διόδēς Κēφισιεύς, ἀρχιτέκτō[ν]
[Φι]λοκλês Ἀχαρνεύς, γραμματεύς Ἐτέαρχος Κυδαθēναιεύς,
[τά]δε ἀνέγραφσαν ἔργα τô νεô hôς κατέλαβον ἔχοντα κατὰ τὸ φσέ-
[φισ]μα τô δέμο hὸ Ἐπιγένēς εἶπεν ἐχσεργασμένα καὶ hēμίεργα ἐπὶ Διο-
[κ]λέος ἄρχοντος, Κεκροπίδος πρυτανευόσēς πρότēς ἐπὶ τês βολês
[h]êι Νικοφάνēς Μαραθόνιος πρôτος ἐγραμμάτευσεν.

τô νεô τάδε κατελάβομεν hēμίεργα·
ἐπὶ τêι γονίαι τêι πρὸς τô Κεκροπίο·
    πλίνθος ἄθετος μêκος τετρά-
IIII ποδας, πλάτος δίποδας, πάχος
    τριhēμιποδίος.
    μασχαλιαίαν μêκος τετράποδα,
I   πλάτος τρίποδα, πάχος τριôν
    hēμιποδίôν.
    ἐπικρανίτιδας μêκος τετράπο-

293

Γ   δας, πλάτος τρίποδας, πάχος
τριῶν ἡμιποδίōν.
γονιαίαν μêκος ἡεπτάποδα,
[1]   πλάτος τετράποδα, πάχος
τριῶν ἡμιποδίōν.
γογγύλος λίθος ἄθετος, ἀντίμο-
[1]   ρος ταῖς ἐπικρανίτισιν μêκος
δεκάπος, ἡύφσος τριῶν
ἡμιποδίōν.

The Commissioners of the temple on the Acropolis, in which (there is) the ancient image: Brosyn...es [Brysonides?] of Kephisia, Chariades from Agryle, Diodes [Dioudes?] of Kephisia, architect [Phi]lokles of Acharnai, secretary Etearchos of Kydathenaion, recorded as follows the work on the temple in the state in which they found it completed or half-finished, in accordance with the decree of the People, which Epigenes proposed in the archonship of Dio[k]les, while the tribe of Kekropis held the first prytany, during (the session of) the Council in which Nikophanes of Marathon was the first to serve as secretary.

We found the following parts of the temple half-finished: at the corner towards the Kekropion:
4 wall-blocks unplaced, length four feet, width two feet, thickness one foot and a half;
1 *maschaliaia*, length four feet, width three feet, thickness one foot and a half;
5 blocks of wall-crown, length four feet, width three feet, thickness one foot and a half;
1 angle-block, length seven feet, width four feet, thickness one foot and a half;
1 moulded block unplaced, backing for the wall-crown, length ten feet, height one foot and a half.

The term *maschaliaia* has not been convincingly explained.

Fragments are preserved in the Epigraphic Museum in Athens of the lower part of this stele and also of related inscriptions that give details of expenditure on the Erech-theion in subsequent years. The account for 408/7 BC names a different architect (Archilochos) from Agryle. Neither he nor Philokles actually designed the building, but they were responsible for supervising the construction.

An earlier inscription with the Attic three-barred *sigma* is carved on three sides of a slab presented to the British Museum in 1781 by the Society of Dilettanti, having been found in a house in Athens by Richard Chandler. The slab is incomplete, and the inscriptions on the principal faces are very fragmentary. They appear to deal with the regulations for various festivals celebrated by the deme Skambonidai. On one occasion the skin of the sacrificial victim is to be the perquisite of the Demarch, perhaps because he had to provide the beast in the first place. The flesh is to be distributed to the people raw.

On the narrow end of the slab is an extract from the deme's financial regulations. The text is well preserved as far as it goes. It includes the end of the oath to be taken on assuming office and the beginning of the regulations for the financial examination normal at the end of a term in public office in Athens.

[.] κêρυχ[θ]‖êι:ἐπαγγ|ελθêι:κα|ἰ τὰ κοιν‖[ὰ] τὰ Σκαμ|βōνιδōν | σōō̄:καὶ
ἀ|ποδόσō̄:π|αρὰ τὸν ε‖ΰθυνον:τ|ὸ καθêκο|ν:ταῦτα ἐ|πομνύνα|ι̣:τὸς τρê‖ς
θεός:ἡό|τι ἄν τō[ν] | κοινōν:μ|ὲ̀ ἀποδιδ|όσιν:παρ‖ὰ τὸν εΰθ|υνο[ν π]ρό| _ _ _

31

294

29 Epitaph of Chairedemos, *c.* 550 BC. MMA 16.174.6.

... as it may] be heralded (and) announced. I shall both safeguard the common
(property) of the Skambonidai, and I shall return to the Public Examiner what is
due. These things (they are) to swear (by) the three gods. Whatever of the common
(property) they do not give back to the Public Examiner ...

The inscription from Skambonidai already has an *epsilon* with vertical and horizontal
strokes and a *theta* in the form of a dot in a circle. At an earlier stage of the development of the Athenian alphabet *epsilon* was written with oblique strokes and the
upright had an extension below the lowest bar; *theta* had a cross rather than a dot in
the circle; and *chi* was sometimes written + rather than X. The two following inscriptions are both written *boustrophedon*. A metrical epitaph on the base of a stele in   29
New York consists of an elegiac couplet (a dactylic hexameter followed by a penta-
meter). The layout of the inscription ignores the verse form, but punctuation is used
to separate some of the words. At the end is an additional comment in prose about
the sculptor, perhaps an actual signature:

$\overline{X}αιρεδέμο$: $τόδε$ $σῆμα$: $πατὲρ$ $ἔστε̄[σε$ | $\overline{θ}]ανόντος$:
'$Aνφιχάρ\langle ε̄\rangle ς$: $ἀγαθὸν$ $παῖδα$ $ὀ|\overline{λ}οφυρόμενο[ς]$
    $Φαίδιμος$ $ἐποίε$

On the death of Chairedemos his father Amphichares set up this monument
mourning a good son. Phaidimos made it.

In the name of Chairedemos the third syllable should be 'long', but it has been treated
as 'short' in order to force the name into the metre.
   A second Athenian gravestone in New York has a simpler epitaph: '$Aντιγένει$:   30
$Παναίσχε̄ς$ $ἐπ|έθε̄κεν$ ('To Antigenes Panaisches set up (this monument)).

30 Epitaph of Antigenes, *c.* 510–500 BC. MMA 15.167.

32 Another early inscription, also written *boustrophedon*, records the presentation of a wine-bowl and strainer for civic use in the town hall (*prytaneion*) at Sigeion in north-western Asia Minor. The text is given twice, first in the Ionic dialect and alphabet, then in Attic with smaller letters and a more detailed text:

$\overrightarrow{\Phi\alpha\nu\omicron\delta\acute{\iota}\kappa\omicron}|\ \overleftarrow{\acute{\epsilon}\mu\grave{\iota}}\ \tau\acute{\omicron}\varrho\mu\omicron\kappa|\overrightarrow{\varrho\acute{\alpha}\tau\epsilon\omicron\varsigma}\ \tau\tilde{\omicron}\ |\ \overleftarrow{\Pi\varrho\omicron\kappa\omicron\nu\nu\eta}|\overrightarrow{\sigma\acute{\iota}\omicron}\ \kappa\varrho\eta\tau\tilde{\eta}\varrho|\overleftarrow{\bar{\alpha}}\ \delta\grave{\epsilon}:\kappa\alpha\grave{\iota}$
$\acute{\upsilon}\pi\omicron\kappa|\overrightarrow{\varrho\eta\tau\acute{\eta}\varrho\iota\omicron\nu}:\kappa|\overleftarrow{\alpha\grave{\iota}}\ \mathring{\eta}\theta\mu\grave{\omicron}\nu:\acute{\epsilon}\varsigma\ \pi|\overrightarrow{\varrho\upsilon\tau\alpha\nu\acute{\eta}\iota\omicron\nu}\ |\ \overleftarrow{\acute{\epsilon}\delta\omega\kappa\epsilon\nu}:\Sigma\upsilon\kappa\epsilon|\overrightarrow{\tilde{\epsilon}\upsilon\sigma\iota\nu}.$

$\overrightarrow{\Phi\alpha\nu\omicron\delta\acute{\iota}\kappa\omicron}:\epsilon\grave{\iota}\mu\grave{\iota}:\tau\tilde{\omicron}\ h|\overleftarrow{\acute{\epsilon}\varrho\mu\omicron\kappa\varrho\acute{\alpha}\tau\omicron\varsigma}:\tau\tilde{\omicron}\ \Pi\varrho\omicron\kappa\omicron|\overrightarrow{\nu\tilde{\epsilon}\sigma\acute{\iota}\omicron}:\kappa\mathring{\alpha}\gamma\grave{\omicron}:\kappa\varrho\alpha\tau\tilde{\epsilon}\varrho\alpha\ |$
$\overleftarrow{\kappa\mathring{\alpha}\pi\acute{\iota}\sigma\tau\alpha\tau\omicron\nu}:\kappa\alpha\grave{\iota}\ h\bar{\epsilon}\theta\mu|\overrightarrow{\grave{\omicron}\nu}:\acute{\epsilon}\varsigma\ \pi\varrho\upsilon\tau\alpha\nu\epsilon\tilde{\iota}\omicron\nu:\overleftarrow{\check{\epsilon}\delta\omicron\kappa\alpha}:\mu\nu\tilde{\epsilon}\mu\alpha:\Sigma\iota\gamma\epsilon\langle\iota\rangle|\overrightarrow{\tilde{\epsilon}\upsilon\sigma\iota}:$
$\acute{\epsilon}\grave{\alpha}\nu\ \delta\acute{\epsilon}\ \tau\iota\ \pi\acute{\alpha}\sigma\chi|\overleftarrow{\tilde{\bar{o}}\ \mu\epsilon\lambda\epsilon\delta\alpha\acute{\iota}\nu\epsilon\nu}:\mu\epsilon\ \hat{o}\ |\ \overrightarrow{\Sigma\iota\gamma\epsilon\iota\tilde{\epsilon}\varsigma}:\kappa\alpha\acute{\iota}\ \mu'\ \acute{\epsilon}\pi\omicron|\overleftarrow{\langle\tilde{\iota}\tilde{\epsilon}\rangle\sigma\epsilon\nu}:h\alpha\acute{\iota}\sigma\tilde{o}\pi\omicron\varsigma:$
$\kappa\alpha\grave{\iota}\ |:\overrightarrow{h\mathring{\alpha}\delta\epsilon\lambda\phi\omicron\acute{\iota}}.$

I am (the stele) of Phanodikos (son) of Hermokrates of Prokonnesos; and he gave a wine-bowl and a stand and a strainer to the Sigeans for the town hall.

I am (the stele) of Phanodikos (son) of Hermokrates of Prokonnesos; and I gave a wine-bowl and a stand and a strainer to the Sigeans for the town hall as a memorial; and if I suffer anything, care for me, O Sigeans; and Haisopos and his brothers made me.

Since Ionic was the dialect of the Sigeans themselves, repetition of the text in Attic suggests that the stele was set up after the Athenian conquest of the area, which according to Herodotus took place while Pisistratus was tyrant of Athens. The precise date of the stele has been the subject of much scholarly controversy, but a date just after the middle of the sixth century seems to fit both the historical circumstances and the style of the inscription.

33 Another Ionic inscription was brought to London from Ephesos by J. T. Wood, the discoverer of the temple of Artemis. It was part of a long text originally carved on a wall in columns, twenty-one letters wide, which were separated by vertical lines. In the adjacent column too few letters survive to permit restoration of the text. The surviving portion deals with the interpretation of lucky and unlucky signs in the flight of birds:

$[\acute{\epsilon}\kappa\ \mu\grave{\epsilon}\nu\ \tau\tilde{\eta}\varsigma\ \delta\epsilon\xi\iota\tilde{\eta}]\varsigma\ \epsilon\grave{\iota}\varsigma\ \tau\grave{\eta}\nu\ \grave{\alpha}\varrho\iota\sigma\tau\epsilon\varrho\grave{\eta}\nu\ \pi\epsilon\tau|\acute{\omicron}\mu\epsilon\nu]\omicron\varsigma:\mathring{\eta}\mu\ \mu\grave{\epsilon}\nu:\grave{\alpha}\pi\omicron\kappa\varrho\acute{\upsilon}\psi\epsilon\|[\iota$
$\delta\epsilon]\xi\iota\grave{\omicron}\varsigma,:\mathring{\eta}\nu\ \delta\grave{\epsilon}:\acute{\epsilon}\pi\acute{\alpha}\varrho\epsilon\iota:\tau\mathring{\eta}\|[\nu\ \epsilon]\mathring{\upsilon}\acute{\omega}\nu\upsilon\mu\omicron\nu:\pi\tau\acute{\epsilon}\varrho\upsilon\gamma\alpha:\kappa\mathring{\alpha}\nu\ \|\ [\acute{\epsilon}\pi\acute{\alpha}]\varrho\epsilon\iota:\kappa\mathring{\alpha}\nu$
$\grave{\alpha}\pi\omicron\kappa\varrho\acute{\upsilon}[\psi]\epsilon\iota:\epsilon\|[\upsilon\acute{\omega}\nu]\upsilon\mu\omicron\varsigma,:\acute{\epsilon}\gamma\ \delta\grave{\epsilon}:\tau\tilde{\eta}\varsigma\ \grave{\alpha}\varrho\iota\sigma\tau[\epsilon\varrho\tilde{\eta}\varsigma]:\acute{\epsilon}\varsigma\ \tau\grave{\eta}\nu\ \delta\epsilon\xi\iota\grave{\eta}\nu:$
$\pi\epsilon\tau\acute{o}\|[\mu\epsilon]\nu\omicron\varsigma:\mathring{\eta}\mu\ \mu\grave{\epsilon}\nu:\iota\theta\grave{\upsilon}\varsigma:\grave{\alpha}\pi\omicron\kappa\varrho\|[\acute{\upsilon}]\psi\epsilon\iota:\epsilon\mathring{\upsilon}\acute{\omega}\nu\upsilon\mu\omicron\varsigma,:\mathring{\eta}\nu\ \delta\grave{\epsilon}:\tau\grave{\eta}\nu\ \|$
$[\delta\epsilon\xi]\iota\grave{\eta}\nu:\pi\tau\acute{\epsilon}\varrho\upsilon\gamma\alpha:\acute{\epsilon}\pi\acute{\alpha}\varrho\alpha\varsigma\ \_\ \_\ \_$

[...flying from right to left], if it goes out of sight, it is lucky; but if it raises its left wing, whether it rises or goes out of sight, it is unlucky; but flying from the left to the right, if it goes straight out of sight, it is unlucky, but if raising the right wing...

The beginning of the sentence is missing but the first few words can be restored with some certainty by comparison with what follows in this rather repetitive text. In antiquity the left wing was clearly ill-omened.

Although the letter-forms of the Ionic alphabet gradually became standard throughout Greece from the late fifth century BC, the use of local dialects survived
34 rather longer. An inscription of the later third century from Orchomenos is still in the Boeotian dialect that was spoken there. It records a contract between the city (called Erchomenos in Boeotian) and Euboulos (written Eubolos, reflecting Boeotian pronunciation) of Elateia. Euboulos had lent the city a large sum of money, and the

31 *Left* Extract from the financial regulations of the deme Skambonidai at Athens, *c.* 460 BC. BM GR 1785.5–27.2.

32 *Right* Inscription from Sigeion in Ionic and Attic script and dialect, *c.* 550–540 BC. BM GR 1816.6–10.107.

33 *Below* Rules for taking omens from the flight of birds, *c.* 500–475 BC. BM GR 1867.11–22.441.

297

34   *Left* Loan-agreement between Euboulos of Elateia and the city of Orchomenos, 3rd century BC. BM GR 1816.6–10.377.
35   *Right* Three proxeny-decrees awarding privileges to foreigners at Kalymna, 4th century BC. BM GR 1856.8–26.6.

first two sections of the inscription record two repayments, the second of which liqui-
dated the entire loan. The third section reads:

ἄρχοντος ἐν Ἐρχομενῦ Θυνάρχω, μει|νὸς Ἀλαλκομενίω, ἐν δὲ Ϝελατίῃ
Με|νοίταο Ἀρχελάω, μεινὸς πράτω, ὁμο|λογ⟨ί⟩α Εὐβώλυ Ϝελατιῆϋ κῆ τῇ
πόλι Ἐρ‖χομενίων· ἐπιδεὶ κεκόμιστη Εὔβω|λος πὰρ τὰς πόλιος τὸ δάνειον
ἅπαν | καττὰς ὁμολογίας τὰς τεθεῖσας Θυ|νάρχω ἄρχοντος, μεινὸς
Θειλουθίω, | κῆ οὔτ' ὀφείλετη αὐτῦ ἔτι οὐθὲν πὰρ τὰν ‖ πόλιν ἀλλ' ἀπέχι
πάντα περὶ παντὸς | κῆ ἀποδεδόανθι τῇ πόλι τὺ ἔχοντες | τὰς ὁμολογίας,
εἶμεν ποτιδεδομέ|νον χρόνον Εὐβώλυ ἐπινομίας ϝέτια | πέτταρα βόεσσι
σοὺν ἵππυς διακα‖τίης ϝίκατι προβάτυς σοὺν ἤγυς χει|λίης· ἄρχι τῶ χρόνω
ὁ ἐνιαυτὸς ὁ μετὰ | Θύναρχον ἄρχοντα Ἐρχομενίυς· ἀπ[ο]‖γράφεσθη δὲ
Εὔβωλον κατ' ἐνιαυτὸν | ἕκαστον πὰρ τὸν ταμίαν κῆ τὸν νομώ‖ναν τά τε
καύματα τῶν προβάτων κῆ | τᾶν ἠγων κῆ τᾶν βουῶν κῆ τᾶν ἵππων κ[ῆ] | κά
τινα ἄσαμα ἴωνθι κῆ τὸ πλεῖθος, με[ὶ] | ἀπογραφέσθω δὲ πλίονα τῶν
γεγραμ|μένων ἐν τῇ σουγχωρείσι. ἠ δέ κά τις ‖ [πράτ]τη τὸ ἐννόμιον
Εὔβωλον, ὀφειλέ‖[τω ἁ πό]λις τῶν Ἐρχομενίων ἀργουρίω | [μνᾶς]
πεττεράκοντα Εὐβώλυ καθ' ἕκα‖[στον ἐ]νιαυτὸν, κ[ῆ] τόκον φερέτω δρά Ⅲ |
[κατὰ] ἰᾶς μνᾶς ἑκάυτας κατὰ μεῖνα ‖[ἕκαυ]τον κῆ ἔμπρακτος ἔστω
Εὐβ[ώλυ | ἁ πόλις] τῶν Ἐρχ[ο]μεν[ίων]

During the archonship of Thunarchos in Orchomenos, month of Alalkomenios,
and of Menoitas (son) of Archelaos in Elateia, first month; an agreement between
Euboulos of Elateia and the city of Orchomenos: whereas Euboulos has recovered
from the city the whole loan according to the agreements made during the
archonship of Thunarchos, month of Theilouthios, and nothing is still owed to him
by the city, but he has received everything in full, and those having the contracts
have restored (them) to the city, there shall be an additional period for Euboulos of
right of free pasturage for four years for 220 oxen and horses and 1,000 sheep and
goats; the year after the archonship of Thunarchos at Orchomenos begins the
period; and Euboulos shall register every year with the Treasurer and the Land
Agent the brands of the sheep and the goats and the oxen and the horses, and any
that go without a brand, and the total; and he shall not register more than written
in the agreement. And if anyone imposes dues for pasture on Euboulos, the city of
Orchomenos shall owe Euboulos 40 minas of silver each year, and it shall bear
interest of 3 drachmas for each mina every month, and the city of Orchomenos
shall be under bond to Euboulos…

Since there is no mention of interest on the loan, it seems likely that in lieu of interest
Euboulos was allowed to graze his animals on the common land of Orchomenos without charge. The size of the payments suggests that the loan was repaid earlier than
had originally been stipulated. Euboulos, having expected to have a longer period of
free pasturage under the original contract, is thus compensated by a grant of free
pasturage for four years, beginning at the end of the year in which repayments were
made (the archonship of Thunarchos). Provision is made to indemnify Euboulos if
anyone imposes charges for pasturage, to which under the contract he is entitled free
of charge.

The use of the Doric dialect also survives in inscriptions from the island of
Kalymna. A single stele found at the temple of Apollo records three decrees conferring the title of Proxenos and various privileges on foreigners. A *proxenos* performed
some of the functions of a modern Vice-Consul, helping foreign citizens, for example,
by representing them in the law courts, to which as foreigners they had no right of

35

299

access. Such services could be provided for each other by private citizens of different cities, but if a man regularly assisted visitors (usually merchants) from a particular city, it was customary to recognise this officially. The first two decrees also confer the title of Euergetes ('Benefactor') and are dated by the month and the year (the year specified as usual by the name of the chief magistrate):

ἔδοξε τᾶι ἐκκλησίαι τᾶι Καλυ|μνίων, μηνὸς Ἀρταμιτίου ἐπ᾽ Ἀ|ριστολαΐδα, Παρμενίσκον τὸν Ἀ|λεξιδίκου ἦμεν εὐεργέταν κα[ὶ] ‖ πρόξενον Καλυμνίων καὶ αὐτὸ[ν] | καὶ γένος ἀεὶ καὶ ἦμεν αὐτοῖς ἔγ|κτησιν ἐγ Καλύμναι καὶ ἀτέλεια[ν] | τῶν ἐξαγομένων καὶ ἐσαγομένων | καὶ ἐμ πολέμωι καὶ ἐν ἰράναι. ‖

   Θεός

ἔδοξε τᾶι ἐκκλησίαι τᾶι Καλυμνί|ων, μηνὸς Καρνείου, ἐπὶ Λευκάρου, | Διοσκουρίδαν τὸν Δελφὸν καὶ Ἀλε|ξίδικον εὐεργέτας καὶ προξένους ‖ ἦμεν Καλυμνίων καὶ αὐτοὺς καὶ ἐκγό|νους καὶ ἦμεν αὐτοῖς ἐγ Καλύμναι | ἀτέλειαν τῶν ἐσαγομένων καὶ ἐξα|γομένων καὶ ἔσπλον καὶ ἔκπλον καὶ | ἐμ πολέμωι καὶ ἐν ἰράναι.

Decreed by the Assembly of Kalymna, in the month of Artemitios, under Aristolaidas: Parmeniskos son of Alexidikos to be a benefactor and a *proxenos* of Kalymna, both himself and his family in perpetuity, and to have the right to own property in Kalymna and immunity from taxation on exports and imports both in war and in peace.

   God (grant good fortune)

Decreed by the Assembly of Kalymna, in the month of Karneios, under Leukaros: Dioskourides of Delphi and Alexidikos to be benefactors and *proxenoi* of Kalymna, both themselves and their descendants, and to have in Kalymna immunity from taxation on imports and exports and the right to sail in and out in war and in peace.

The decrees vary slightly in particulars and even in vocabulary, presumably because they were framed in the meeting of the assembly rather than drafted in detail first. Thus, although all three make the titles hereditary, no particular significance should be attached to the use of the word for 'family' (*genos*) rather than 'descendants' (*ekogonoi*) in the decree for Parmeniskos, no for the omission in his case of the right of sailing in and out, which may be taken as implied by the tax-exemption on imports and exports. The right to own real property (*egktesis*), however, was a very valuable privilege rarely conferred on foreigners.

36   The most famous Greek inscription in the British Museum is probably the Rosetta Stone, which derives its importance not from the intrinsic interest of the text but from the presence on the same slab of translations into ancient Egyptian in both the hieroglyphic and demotic scripts. Study of the Rosetta Stone was crucial for the decipherment of Egyptian writing. The text records a long and rather sycophantic decree passed by the general council of Egyptian priests, in which honours are bestowed on Ptolemy V Epiphanes in recognition of his services to Egypt both at home and abroad. The Greek text abounds in errors. The first line begins: βασιλεύοντος τοῦ νέου καὶ παραλ⟨α⟩βόντος τὴν β⟨α⟩σιλείαν παρὰ τοῦ πατρὸς ('In the reign of the young one, who has taken over the kingdom from his father...'). The stonecutter has twice written Λ (*lamda*) for Α (*alpha*), the correct readings being given in angled brackets in the transcription. Other errors elsewhere in the text include Ξ (*xi*) for Σ

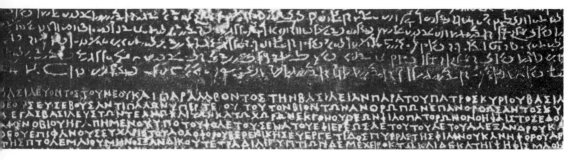

36   Part of the Rosetta Stone, 27 March 196 BC. BM EA 24.

(*sigma*), Η (*eta*) for ΙΙ (*iota* twice, at the end of one word and the beginning of the next) and ΙΙ for Η (that is, *eta* with the bar missing), as well as letters left out altogether: *Πτομαίου* for *Πτο⟨λε⟩μαίου*. The text concludes with a provision that has many parallels in earlier Greek inscriptions: '[This decree shall be inscribed on a slab] of hard stone in hieroglyphic, demotic and Greek characters and set up in each of the first, second [and third (rank) temples beside the image of the ever-living King].' The restorations are based on the demotic text.

3
Inscriptions on Other Objects

Apart from epitaphs and votives most inscriptions on stone slabs are public rather than private in character. Inscriptions on other objects, however, are usually private. Dedications and statements of ownership are particularly frequent on bronzes and pottery. They are regularly added after the manufacture of the object itself, cut or scratched into the surface. Scratched inscriptions on pottery are known as *graffiti*, while inscriptions painted on pottery after manufacture are called *dipinti*. *Dipinti* referring to trade, often painted on the underside of figured vases, are usually faint and difficult to interpret. Other *dipinti* include the epitaphs written in ink with a reed pen on cinerary urns from Alexandria. Inscriptions applied to vases during manufacture include signatures of potters and painters, the names of the figures and other comments. Pottery and bronze vessels given as prizes in competitions were appropriately inscribed during manufacture. These may be classified as public inscriptions, which were not confined to stone slabs.

As with inscriptions on stone slabs, the simpler inscriptions on other objects can be read with little or no knowledge of Greek beyond the alphabet. For example, the first

37 twenty letters of the alphabet (*alpha* to *upsilon*) are inscribed in sequence on a stone *eikosahedron* (a geometrically regular solid object with twenty triangular faces). It is likely to have been used as a die in a game of chance: the ancients also used six-sided dice marked in the same way as their modern counterparts, but on the *eikosahedron* the absence of *digamma*, the alphabetic numeral for six, shows that the letters are not used here as numerals but have a purely alphabetic value. The relatively late date is shown by the broken crossbar on the *alpha* and the lunate *sigma*.

In order to ensure fair trading many Greek cities maintained official standards of

38 volume and weight, appointing *agoranomoi*, market-clerks or, as we might call them, Inspectors of Weights and Measures, to enforce the regulations. A lead weight of one mina (100 drachmai), issued in the fourth year of an unnamed ruler, bears around its edge the names of Zenobios, who was perhaps the *agoranomos*: ἔτους δ′ | δημόσια | μνᾶ | Ζηνοβίου ('Year 4. Official mina. (Of) Zenobios').

The name of an Athenian citizen with his father's name (patronymic) and their

39 deme (demotic) is clearly inscribed on a small rectangular bronze plate about 11.6 cm long, 2.0 cm wide and 2 mm thick: Ἀριστοφῶν ⦂ Ἀρισ|τοδήμου ⦂ Κοθω(κίδης) ('Aristophon (son) of Aristodemos (of the deme) Kotho(kidai)'). Aristophon and other members of his family are known also from other inscriptions, including grave-stelae. His brother Exekestides was wealthy enough to fit out a trireme in 353/2 BC.

Bronze plates like this were used to identify jurymen, or dikasts, and to assign them to particular cases in the courts. In order to ensure a fair trial and prevent bribery Athenian juries were very large, and the selection of jurymen took place just before cases were heard. Prospective jurymen inserted their tickets according to their allocated section letter (in this case *gamma*) in slots in a marble slab that stood at the entrance to the law courts. The slots were arranged in columns and rows, and at the side was a tube into which black and white balls were poured at random. Men whose tickets were in rows opposite white balls were selected for the jury. The procedure is described by Aristotle (*Constitution of Athens* 63.4), although by his day boxwood had replaced bronze as the material of dikasts' tickets.

Dikasts' tickets were issued by the state and authenticated with official stamps. The owl at the lower left served also as the design of the three-obol coin, an allusion to the juryman's pay of three obols a day, after 424 BC. The *gorgoneion* has been interpreted as signifying that the holder was also eligible to participate in the annual allotment of magistracies.

In order to prevent unauthorised transfer of tickets holes were bored through the plate in patterns appropriate to the letters. When tickets were officially reissued to other citizens, the old holes were allowed to remain and provide clues to the previous name, even when the actual lines of the letters had been obliterated. In this case the previous owner's name has been read as: *Φιλοχάρης | 'Αλαι(εύς)* ('Philochares of Halaï').

The lunate *sigma* (C), the similar *epsilon* (Є) and the cursive forms of *mu* (ᄊ) and *omega* (Ѡ) are more suitable than angular letters for writing in ink on papyrus and parchment or on harder surfaces like wood and pottery. From the third century BC onwards the style of handwriting diverged increasingly from that of monumental lettering in stone. The third- and second-century BC cemeteries at Alexandria in Egypt have yielded large numbers of hydriai used as urns for the ashes of the dead. They are known as Hadra vases after an Alexandrian suburb where they were first found in quantity during the nineteenth century. Some of them carry commemorative

37   *Left* Stone eikosahedron with part of the alphabet, Roman period. BM GR 1891.6–24.38.
38   *Right* Lead weight of 1 mina, 2nd or 1st century BC. BM GR 1925.7–20.1.

39   *Below* Bronze juryman's ticket from Athens, mid-4th century . BM GR 1873.8–20.129.

40 Dated Hadra vase, 19 May 213 BC. MMA 90.9.29.

inscriptions, usually written in ink. When the dead man was an official visitor, an ambassador or the like, the inscription may include the signature of the Alexandrian official who arranged the funeral, as well as the date. In addition to the regnal year dates may include the month according to either the Egyptian or the Macedonian calendar. One Hadra vase in New York is dated by both calendars, the Greek month being given first:

Ⳑ θ′ Ὑπερβερεταίου λ′ | Φαρμουθὶ ζ′ | Τιμασιθέου τοῦ | Διονισίου Ῥοδίου ‖ πρεσβευτοῦ | διὰ Θεοδότου ἀγοραστοῦ.

Year 9, Hyperberetaios 30, Pharmouthi 7; Timasitheos (son) of Dionysios of Rhodes, an Ambassador; by Theodotos, agent.

Theodotos, who was active in the reign of Ptolemy IV, signs himself as *agorastes*, which literally means 'buyer': it is here translated as 'agent' by analogy with the Crown Agents, who act as financial agents for nearly 100 governments overseas and for many other official bodies. From other inscriptions, especially on papyri, scholars have been able to prepare a table of the relationship between the Egyptian and the Julian calendars, from which it has been calculated Pharmouthi 7 in the ninth year of Ptolemy IV was the equivalent of 19 May 213 BC.

Also from Egypt comes a wooden board in London with an extract from the first book of Homer's *Iliad* (lines 467–73) written on it in ink. It has an iron handle at the top for carrying or suspension, perhaps in a schoolroom. The wood has cracked along the grain, and the lower part has not survived. The text is written on a thin layer of kaolinite clay, and where this has been abraded the letters have also of course been lost. The losses include the whole of the top line (467) and parts of most others, especially at the right-hand side.

41   Wooden board with a quotation from Homer's *Iliad*, from Egypt, Roman period.
BM GR 1906.10-20.2.

[αὐτὰρ ἐπεὶ παύσαντο πόνου τετύκοντό τε δαῖτα,]
δαίννυθ᾿ / οὐδέ τι / θυμὸ[ς ἐδεύετο δαιτὸς ἐΐσης.]
αὐτὰρ / ἐπεὶ / πόσυος / καὶ / ἐδ[ητύος] ἐξ ἔρον ἔντο,
κοῦροι / μὲν [...] κρητῆρας / ἐπεστέψαντο / ποτοῖο,
νώμησαν δ᾿ / ἄρα / πᾶσιν / ἐπαρξάμενοι / [δ]επάεσσιν·
οἱ δὲ / πανημέριοι / μολπῇ / θεὸ[ν ἱλάσκοντο,]
καλὸν / ἀείδοντες / παιήον[α, κοῦροι Ἀχαιῶν.]

[But when they had ceased from labour and had prepared the banquet,] they feasted, nor did their appetite [lack anything of the shared feast.] But when of drink and [food they had satisfied their desire,] youths filled the bowls with wine and served it to everyone, pouring the first drops in the cups for a libation. So all day long with song [they appeased the gods,] singing the beautiful paean…

In addition to the usual cursive letters (including ⱳ for *omega*, which does not occur on the Hadra vase) there is a new way of writing *alpha* (ⱥ), a forerunner of the miniscule or lower-case form. The extended right-hand strokes of both *delta* and *lamda* also anticipate the lower-case forms of these letters. The divisions between words are marked by oblique strokes, and breathings and accents appear sporadically, not always in the form that the grammarians would consider 'correct' – for example, θῦμος not θυμός. In the last line but one παναμέριοι has been corrected to πανημέριοι. The first surviving word, δαίννυθ᾿, is more usually written δαίννντ᾿: it is not clear whether the aspirate *theta* represents a local pronunciation where the non-aspirated *tau* is normal, or is simply another mistake. The same is true of πόσυος for πόσιος in line 469.

Although individual letter-forms from the Ionic alphabet gradually came into use in Athens in private inscriptions before their use became obligatory for official inscriptions in 403/2 BC, texts on Athenian vases and bronzes are mainly in the Attic alphabet before that date. Many thousands of Athenian vases, both black-figured and red-figured, have been attributed to individual artists whose particular style of drawing can be recognised and distinguished from others. Since none of these potters and painters are mentioned in ancient literature, most are unknown to us by name and have been given nicknames like the Painter of London B 46. Their real names are known to us only if they actually signed their work, as did Tleson: Τλέσον ho Νεάρχο ἐποίεσεν ('Tleson the (son) of Nearchos made (me)'). Tleson is rare among potters in including his patronymic, perhaps because his father, Nearchos, was also a 42

distinguished potter who used to sign his works. Most potters and vase-painters
43 signed with their own name only: *Ἐχσεκίας ἐποίεσε* ('Exekias made (me)'). The
signature is written retrograde (right to left).

Exekias has decorated his amphora with a picture of a Greek slaying an Amazon,
and has thoughtfully included their names – Achilles (*Ἀχιλεύ[ς]*) and Penthesilea
(*Πενθεσιλέα*). He has also added a comment on one of the elegant youths of his day:
'Onetorides (is) fair' (*Ὀνετορίδες καλός*). Such comments are fairly common on
Attic vases, and since some of the youths referred to later became distinguished in
public life, their names can provide useful clues to the dates of the vases that mention
them.

Although Exekias signed the amphora with Achilles and Penthesilea only as potter,
the painting too can be attributed to his hand since he also signed two other vases as
painter, and the style is evidently the same. Among other Athenian vase-painters who
44 signed their works the earliest to do so was Sophilos, who decorated an elaborate
wine-bowl with a scene of guests arriving for the wedding of Peleus and Thetis. Peleus
(*Πēλεύς*) is standing at the door of his house to welcome the guests as they arrive. Iris
(*Ῑρις*), the messenger, leads the procession, followed by Hestia (*hεστία*) and
Demeter (*Δēμέτē[ρ]*). The names of Peleus and Iris are written retrograde, as is the
signature on the wall of the house: *Σόφιλος ⫶ μ' ἔγραφσεν* ('Sophilos painted me').
Since the composite letter *psi* did not exist in the Attic alphabet, Sophilos wrote the
sound as *phi sigma* (**φＳ**). He also used the early closed form of the aspirate (**Ꮚ**),
whereas a generation or so later Tleson used the open form (**H**).

Names can also be added to scenes from daily life to give them a personal quality.
1 The vase-painter Oltos identified all the figures in a scene in the *palaestra*
('gymnasium') on a *psykter* ('wine-cooler') now in New York. On the left in fig. 1 is a
javelin-thrower named Batrachos (**Β Ρ · · Α ✕ Ο Ꙅ** *Βά[τρ]αχος*).
The jumper's name is Dorotheos (**ᗡ Ο Ꭰ Ⴘ Ꙅ Ε Ο Ꙅ** *Δōρόθεος*),
and Oltos has added a comment: **ι Ꙅ ι ᗝ Ꙅ Ο н Ǝ ꟼ ꓦ Ο ꓦ Ꭺ Η**
hαλούμενος εἶσι ('he is about to jump'). Between the two athletes a pipe-player
called Smikythos (**Ꙅ м ι ᴋ ꓴ** *Σμίκυ[θος]*) provides the rhythm for their movements. On the other side of the vase are a discus-thrower called Antiphanes (**Ꭺ Ν Τ ι Φ Ꭺ Ν Ｅ Ꙅ** *Ἀντιφάνες*) and his trainer
(**Ꙅ Ǝ · ᒐ · ι · Ꭺ**, perhaps *Ἀντιμένες*, Antimenes), as well as
another trainer (**Ꭺ ᒐ ᴋ Ｅ Τ Ｅ Ꙅ** *Ἀλκέτες*, Alketes), and a boy
victor, Epainetos, who is praised for his beauty (*Ἐπαίνετος καλός*, 'Epainetos is
fair'). A judge called Kleainetos (**ᴋ ᒐ Ｅ Ꭺ ι Ν Ｅ Τ Ο Ꙅ** *Κλεαίνετος*) is just
visible on the right in the frontispiece.

Some of the inscriptions run from right to left because they start near the person to
whom they refer. Oltos adds two comments in which the vase itself addresses the
viewer: **ꓣ ꓳ ꓯ Ƅ** (*πô μc*, 'drink me') and **ο · ι Ꙅ Ꭺ Ӿ** (*χάυκυ*, 'I open
my mouth wide').

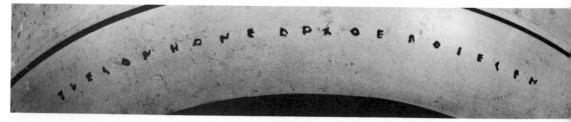

42 Signature of Tleson the potter, *c.* 550 BC. BM GR 1867.5–8.946.

43   Amphora signed by Exekias as potter, *c.* 540–530 BC. BM GR 1836.2–24.127.

44   Wedding-reception of Peleus and Thetis on a bowl signed by Sophilos as painter, *c.* 580 BC. BM GR 1971.11–1.1.

An important series of vases are those made to contain the olive oil given as prizes in the Panathenaic Games at Athens. One side shows the event in which the prize was won, the other shows the goddess Athena, whose birthday the festival celebrated, and
45 bears the inscription τὸν Ἀθένεθεν ἄθλον ('(one) of the prizes from Athens'). On an example in New York the painter did not allow quite enough space for the inscription.

The black-figure technique of vase-painting survived on Panathenaic prize amphorae long after red-figure was invented (and even after it was eventually abandoned) because it was traditional. During the fourth century BC the name of the Archon is often added, and the inscriptions instead of being written sideways down the vase are written in a vertical column, like the 'down' lights in a crossword puzzle.
46 An example in London, commissioned in the archonship of Pythodelos (336/5), retains the Attic alphabet for the traditional prize formula but employs Ionic forms including *eta* and *omega* in the Archon inscription Πυθόδηλος ἄρχων.

A black-figured amphora in New York has a puzzling inscription that seems to
47 have no connection with the painted decoration, a warrior wearing greaves and

45 Prize amphora from the Panathenaic games, *c.* 530 BC. MMA 56.171.4.

46 Inscriptions from a Panathenaic prize-amphora, 336/5 BC. BM GR 1873.8–20.371.

carrying a helmet, spear and shield. The first problem is to decide whether the second and third *epsilons* should be read as 'short' or 'long' (that is, standing for *eta*). If short, the text would read δυ' ὀβέλō καὶ μ' ἔθιγες ('Two obols and you touch me', that is, 'You can have me for two obols'). In general scholars prefer to read δυ' ὀβέλō καὶ μὲ θίγξς ('Two obols – and hands off', that is, 'Do not touch: I am worth more than two obols'). The inscription may well be a joke by the vase-painter. It is actually written from right to left.

The inscription on a bronze statuette in New York, originally dedicated as a votive offering, is in an early form of the Attic alphabet, but relatively easy to interpret. The statuette is of a lyre-player, barely 8 cm high, with an inscription on the back of his tunic: Δόλιχος μ' ἀνέθēκεν ('Dolichos dedicated me'). The letters include an early form of *chi* (+) and a very unusual *sigma* with no fewer than five bars. *Theta* is written simply as a circle with a dot in it, and the lowest bar of *epsilon* is placed high on the stem, giving the letter a tail rather like our F.

Of the alphabets used in other parts of Greece during the archaic period the Ionic

48

47   *Above* Amphora with a price-inscription, *c.* 540 BC. MMA 56.171.13.

48   *Right* Bronze statuette of a lyre-player, *c.* 500 BC. MMA 08.258.5.

49   Bowl dedicated by Sostratos to Aphrodite at Naukratis, *c.* 600–500 BC.
BM GR 1888.6–1.456.

50   Dedication by Rhoikos to Aphrodite at Naukratis, *c.* 600–550 BC. BM GR 1888.6–1.392.

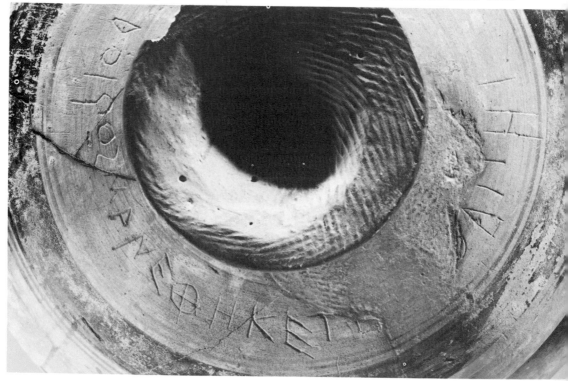

is perhaps the easiest for the modern reader since the characters are close in shape to those in use today. A bowl from Naucratis in Egypt has a votive inscription incised inside the rim: Σώστρατος μ' ἀνέ[θ]ηκεν τῆ' φροδίτηι ('Sostratos dedicated me to Aphrodite'). The 'long' vowels *eta* (already in the open form H) and *omega* (Ω) are distinguished from the 'short' *epsilon* (E) and *omicron* (O), and *sigma* is of the familiar four-barred type.

Another vase from Naucratis with a *graffito* ('incised inscription') was dedicated to Aphrodite by a man from Samos: Ῥοῖρος μ' ἀνέθηκε τ[ῆι Ἀφρ]οδίτηι ('Rhoikos dedicated me to Aphrodite'). It has been suggested that the dedicator may be identified with Rhoikos of Samos, an early sculptor credited with the invention of casting bronze statues. Rhoikos spells his name not with *kappa* (K) but with the guttural *qoppa* (Ϙ), a character that was widespread in early alphabets but gradually fell out of use in the sixth century BC. The form of the initial *rho* without a leg is typical of the Samian alphabet.

A different form of *rho* with a tail (Ρ), which as we have seen was transmitted to the west by the Euboeans, is also found in most of the local alphabets of the Greek mainland. A bronze spear-butt in New York appears to have been part of the spoils of a battle dedicated by the victors to Castor and Polydeuces: ἱερὸς Τυνδαρίδαιυς ἀπ' Ἐραέōν ('Sacred to the Tyndaridai from the Heraeans'). Although the *sigma* is of the four-barred type that we have seen in Ionic script, separate forms for *eta* and *omega* are lacking in Arcadian. The case-ending for the dative form 'to the Tyndaridai' is characteristic of the Arcadian dialect.

49
50
51

51   Bronze spear-butt dedicated to the Dioscuri, *c.* 500–480 BC. MMA 38.11.7.

The tailed *rho* is prominent in the dedicatory inscription on another item of spoil, a bronze helmet found at Olympia in 1817: hιάρον ὁ Λεινομένεος | καὶ τοὶ Συρα-κόσιοι | τõι Δὶ Τυράν⟨õν⟩ ἀπὸ Κύμας. ('Hieron (son) of Deinomenes and the Syracusans (dedicated me) to Zeus, Etruscan (spoils) from Cumae'). Hieron's victory over the Etruscans in a naval battle off Cumae in 474 BC is recorded by the historian Diodorus, so this inscription is quite closely dated. It is one of several by Hieron and his brother Gelon that provide evidence for the Syracusan alphabet during this period. Another typical feature is the late survival of the closed form of *heta* (Ⴖ) as an aspirate. The origin of the alphabets used by Syracuse and other Doric colonies in Sicily is not fully understood. Syracuse itself was a colony of Corinth but does not use the Corinthian alphabet, perhaps because when the first Syracusan colonists left Corinth the alphabet was not yet in use there.

52

52   Etruscan bronze helmet dedicated by the Syracusans to Zeus at Olympia, 474 BC.
BM GR 1823.6–10.1.

Although it shares the tailed *rho* and the closed form of the aspirate (Ƌ), the
alphabet used in Argos is not closely connected to the Syracusan. In its earliest form
Argive has much in common with Corinthian, including the use of the sibilant *san*.
Around 500 BC, however, *san* in Argive gave way to the four-barred *sigma* seen on a
53   prize hydria of about 470–60 BC, together with a distinctive form of *lamda* (Ⱶ): πὰρ
ℎέρας ⋮ Ἀργείας ⋮ ℎαϝέθλὸν ('(One) of the prizes from Argive Hera'). The most
famous prizes from Argos were the bronze shields mentioned by an ancient commentator on the poet Pindar, one of which appears on the Rhamnousian relief, but
bronze vessels like bowls and hydriai were also given as prizes, as inscriptions like this
one show.
    The Argive dialect was one of those that long retained a sound similar to the
Semitic *waw* and represented by (Ϝ), usually called *digamma* because it resembles two
gammas, one above the other. Here it appears near the beginning of 'prizes', separating the *alpha* and *epsilon*. The prize inscriptions on Attic Panathenaic amphorae
show that this sound had already disappeared from the Attic dialect.
    Prizes were awarded not only for athletic successes. Around 540–30 BC a young
54   woman called Melousa, who lived in Taras (modern Taranto in the 'heel' of Italy), won
a prize for her skill in working wool, a splendid black-figured cup imported from
Athens. Her success was recorded in a *graffito* underneath the foot: Μελόσας · ἐμὶ ·
νικατέριον · ξαίνοσα τὰς κόρας ἐνίκε ('I am Melousa's prize; she won the
maidens' carding contest'). The cup, now in New York, is said to have been found in
Taranto, and this is confirmed by the use of Laconian letter-forms, including Χ for *xi*.
The dialect is Doric, with *alpha* in νικατέριον where other dialects including Attic
would have *eta*.

53   Bronze prize-hydria from the games at Argos, *c.* 470–460 BC. MMA 26.50.

54   Melousa's prize for her skill in wool-carding, *c.* 540–530 BC. MMA 44.11.1.

55 Aineta's aryballos, with her portrait and the names of her lovers, *c.* 625 BC. Reproduced over actual size. BM GR 1865.12–13.1.

The same Doric pronunciation is reflected in the spelling of the names on a Corinthian *aryballos* ('perfume-pot') that once belonged to Aineta: Αἰνέτα | ἐμί. | Μενέας | Θέρōν ‖ Μυρμίδας | Εὔδιϙος | Λυσανδρίδας | Χαρικλίδας | Δεξίλος ‖ Ξένϝōν | Φρύξ. ('I am Aineta (*or* Aineta's). Meneas, Theron, Myrmides, Eudikos, Lysandrides, Chariklides, Dexilos, Xenon, Phryx').

The inscription ought to be easy to read since it consists almost entirely of personal names in the nominative, presumably a list of Aineta's lovers. It is made more difficult not so much by the Doric spelling as by the use of the archaic Corinthian alphabet, in which several characters resemble those alloted to different letters in other alphabets. So Ɓ is not *beta* but *epsilon*, and ⟨ is *iota*, not *sigma*. *Sigma* in fact, does not exist in the Corinthian alphabet, which uses *san* (Μ) as the sibilant: this in turn must be distinguished from *mu*, written ᛘ. The use of *qoppa* and the presence of *digamma* should by now cause no more difficulty than the absence of the 'long' vowels *eta* and *omega*. Experts have disagreed since the nineteenth century whether Αἰνέτα is the nominative form of the name or a Doric genitive, that is, whether the 'portrait' is saying 'I am Aineta' or the pot itself, like many others, is announcing ownership: 'I belong to Aineta.'

314

A plate from Kamiros in Rhodes is hardly more difficult to read than Aineta's 56
aryballos but poses problems of its own. It shows an episode from the *Iliad*
(17.59–113), with Menelaus (Μενέλας) and Hector ("Εκτōρ) fighting over the body
of Euphorbos (Εὔφορβος). Hector's name is written retrograde, and the *rho* has no
tail. Menelaus (here 'Menelas') again exemplifies the difference between *mu* at the
beginning and *san* at the end, and has *lamda* in the Argive form (Ͱ) that we saw on the
bronze hydria. The *beta* in Euphorbos, however, is of the normal type, not the idio-
syncratic Argive form (ᕍ). Since the plate itself is East Greek, that is, was made in one
of the Greek settlements in the eastern Aegean, on the coast of Asia Minor or on one
of the offshore islands, it implies that a modified version of the Argive alphabet was in
use in one of the Doric-speaking cities on or near Rhodes. Kalymna has been
suggested.

56   Plate showing the death of Euphorbos, *c.* 600 BC. BM GR 1860.4–4.1.

An island at the other end of the Greek world, Kephallenia off the north-western coast of Greece, is the likely source of a bronze discus dedicated to the Dioscuri:

> Ἐχσοΐδα μ' ἀνέθēκε Διϝὸς ϙόροιν μεγάλοιο ⋮
> χάλκεον hōι νίκασε Κεφαλᾶνας μεγαθύμος.

Exoidas dedicated me to the sons of mighty Zeus, (the) bronze with which he overcame the great-hearted Kephallenians.

The inscription consists of two lines of verse, Homeric in metre and diction: the last two words are quoted from the *Iliad*, and the end of the first line is adapted from the 'Homeric Hymn to the Dioscuri' with only the case-ending of 'sons' changed. It is written retrograde in a single spiral line that begins around the circumference of the discus. The alphabet, like others in the west, belongs to the 'red' group, with Ѱ for *chi*; it uses *san* (M) rather than *sigma* as the sibilant, and has *qoppa* as well as *kappa*. The aspirate is the normal closed form (Ⴃ), but *gamma* is of an unusual lunate form found also on nearby Ithaka.

A similar 'red' alphabet, related also to Arcadian and Laconian, was in use at Olympia, where a bronze tablet recording an alliance between the people of Elis and the Heraeans was found in 1813. Similar inscriptions have been found at Olympia more recently. All the tablets have holes so that they could be nailed up, probably in a temple.

57   Bronze discus dedicated to the Dioscuri, *c.* 550–525. BM GR 1898.7–16.3.

ἀ ϝράτρα τοῖρ Ϝαλείοις : καὶ τοῖς Ἐρ|ϝαδίοις : συνμαχία κ᾿ ἔα ἑκατὸν
ϝέτεα : | ἄρχοι δέ κα τοῖ : αἰ δέ τι δέοι : αἴτε ϝέπος αἴτε ϝ|άργον : συνέαν
κ᾿ ἀλάλοις : τά τ᾿ ἄλ⟨α⟩ καὶ πὰ‖ρ πολέμο : αἰ δὲ μὰ συνέαν : τάλαντόν κ᾿|
ἀργύρο : ἀποτίνοιαν : τῶι Δὶ Ὀλυνπίōι : τοὶ κα|δαλέμενοι : λατρειόμενον :
αἰ δέ τιρ τὰ γ|ράφεα : ταὶ καδαλέοιτο : αἴτε ϝέτας αἴτε τ|ελεστὰ : αἴτε
δᾶμος : ἔν τὲπιάρōι κ᾿ ἐνέχ‖οιτο τōι ᾿νταῦτ᾿ ἐγραμένōι.

The treaty between the Eleans and the Heraeans: let there be an alliance for 100
years; and let this (year) begin (it); and if there be any need, either of word or of
deed, let them stand by each other in other matters and in war; but if they do not
stand by (each other), let the defaulters pay to Olympian Zeus a talent of silver for
his service; and if anyone damages this inscription, whether private citizen or
magistrate or community, let him be liable to the sacred penalty written herein.

The inscription is probably to be dated around 500 BC. In addition to the use of
digamma features of the local dialect include 'rhotacism', that is, the substitution of
rho for *sigma*, for example, at the end of the third word, and the pronunciation
ai instead of *ei* for 'if'.

This inscription was bequeathed to the British Museum by Richard Payne Knight
(1750–1824), a wealthy landowner and antiquary, who was also a distinguished
amateur scholar. His attempt to transcribe the text into the common Greek dialect
and script of the Roman period was remarkably successful. He took account of
digamma, recognised the 'red' Ѵ as *chi*, and correctly interpreted various features of
the dialect including rhotacism. His failure to recognise τοῖ as the dialect form of
τόδε ('this') is entirely understandable, given the state of knowledge of Greek dialects
in the early nineteenth century. His modest disclaimer of total certainty might well be
taken as a motto by modern epigraphers: *Judicent tamen doctiores, et siquid
probabilius habuerint, proferant* ('Let the more learned sit in judgement, and if they
have a more probable (reading), propose it').

58   Treaty between the Eleans and the Heraeans, *c.* 500 BC. BM GR 1824.4–99.17.

Further Reading

A. G. Woodhead, *The Study of Greek Inscriptions* (1959): the indispensable textbook.

Sterling Dow, *Conventions in Editing (Greek, Roman and Byzantine Scholarly Aids* 2, 1969): essential reading for professional epigraphers.

R. Meiggs and D. Lewis (eds), *A Selection of Greek Historical Inscriptions to the End of the Fifth Century BC* (1969: revised edn, 1988), abbr. Meiggs and Lewis, updates and largely replaces:

M. N. Tod, *A Selection of Greek Historical Inscriptions to the End of the Fifth Century BC* (2nd edn, 1946), abbr. Tod i².

id., A Selection of Greek Historical Inscriptions, Vol. II from 403 to 328 BC (1949), abbr. Tod ii.

L. H. Jeffery, *The Local Scripts of Archaic Greece* (1961: new impression forthcoming), abbr. *LSAG,* a monumental study of the early Greek alphabets: not for beginners.

F. Millar, 'Epigraphy' in M. Crawford (ed), *Sources for Ancient History* (1983): a useful survey of the value and limitations of epigraphic evidence for historians.

R. Meiggs, *The Athenian Empire* (1972), makes much use of epigraphic evidence.

Alan E. Samuel, *Greek and Roman Chronology* (1972), is invaluable for ancient calendars.

Abbreviations and References

Museum Catalogues

BM Cat. Bronzes	H. B. Walters, *Catalogue of the Bronzes, Greek, Roman and Etruscan in the Department of Greek and Roman Antiquities, British Museum* (1899)
BM Cat. Sculpture i, iii	A. H. Smith, *A Catalogue of Sculpture in the Department of Greek and Roman Antiquities, British Museum,* Vols i and iii (1892, 1904)
BM Cat. Sculpture i, 1	F. N. Pryce, *Catalogue of Sculpture in the Department of Greek and Roman Antiquities, British Museum,* Vol. i, part 1, *Prehellenic and Early Greek* (1928)
BM Cat. Vases	H. B. Walters, *Catalogue of the Greek and Etruscan Vases in the British Museum,* Vol. ii *Black-figured Vases* (1893)
MMA Cat. Bronzes	G. M. A. Richter, *The Metropolitan Museum of Art: Greek, Etruscan and Roman Bronzes* (1915)
MMA Cat. Sculpture	G. M. A. Richter, *Catalogue of Greek Sculptures in The Metropolitan Museum of Art* (1954)

Epigraphic Publications

CIG	*Corpus Inscriptionum Graecarum* (4 vols 1828–77)
GIBM	*The Collection of Ancient Greek Inscriptions in the British Museum* (4 vols 1874–1916)
IG	*Inscriptiones Graecae* (many vols 1873–)
SEG	*Supplementum Epigraphicum Graecum* (serial publication, i, 1923–)

References

Cover (right) BM GR 1867.5–8.117. *BM Cat. Sculpture* i, 809. *CIG* 2429. *GIBM* 365.

1 MMA 10.210.18. Beazley, J. D., *Attic Red-figure Vase-painters,* 2nd edn (1963), p. 54, no. 7.

2 The precinct of the Eponymous Heroes at Athens. *The Athenian Agora: A Guide* (1976), p. 69, fig. 26.

3 BM GR 1863.5–16.1. *IG* i³.264, 272. Meritt, B. D., Wade-Gery, H. T., and McGregor, M. F., *The Athenian Tribute Lists* i (1939), pp. 3 and 33–4, no. 60, figs 38–9, pls VII, XV.

4 MMA 24.97.21. Jeffery, L. H., *LSAG,* p. 241, no. 22, pl. 48.

5 BM GR 1816.6–10.206. *GIBM* 5. *IG* i³.53. Meiggs and Lewis, pp. 171–5, no. 63.

6 BM GR 1805.7–3.183. *BM Cat. Sculpture* i, 628. *GIBM* 123. *IG* ii².12332.

7 BM GR 1970.9–25.1. *IG* xii.2, 129. Cook, B. F., *Antiquaries Journal* li (1971), pp. 263–6, pls XLIII(b) and XLV.

8 BM GR 1872.4–5.19. *BM Cat. Sculpture* B 16. *GIBM* 518. Tod i², pp. 9–10, no. 6.

9 MMA 11.185. *MMA Cat. Sculpture* 15. *IG* i². 981. Guarducci, M., in Richter, G. M. A., *The Archaic Gravestones of Attica* (1961), pp. 159–65, no. 37. Jeffery, L. H., *LSAG* p. 78, no. 32, pl. 4. *Id., Annual of the British School at Athens* lxvii (1962), pp. 146–7, no. 63, pl. 41a. Clairmont, C. W., *Gravestone and Epigram* (1970), pp. 13–15, no. 1, pl. 1.

10 MMA 59.11.19. *CIG* 234. *IG* ii².3145. *SEG* xxi.698. Bothmer, D. von, *Metropolitan Museum of Art Bulletin* n.s. xix (1960/1), pp. 181–3, fig. 1. Robert, J. and L., *Revue des Etudes Grecques* lxxiii (1960), p. 157, no. 144; lxxvi (1963), p. 132, no. 80.

11 BM GR 1850.7–24.1. *BM Cat. Sculpture* i, 599. *GIBM* 86. *IG* ii².6338.

12 BM GR 1870.3–20.88 *CIG* 2904. *GIBM* 399. Hiller von Gaertringen, F., *Inschriften von Priene* (1906), p. 129, no. 156. Tod ii, pp. 241–2, no. 184.

13 BM GR 1872.6–10.43. *GIBM* 443.

14 BM GR 1877.5–11.1. *GIBM* 171.

15 BM GR 1970.6–2.1. *CIG* 5763. *IG* xiv.617. Cook, B. F., *Antiquaries Journal* li (1971), pp. 260–3, pls xli iii(a) and xli iv. To the references there cited add: F. Poulsen in *Photographische Einzelaufnahmen antiker Sculpturen* (ed. P. Arndt and G. Lippold), xi (1929), p. 25, no. 3098.

16 BM GR 1805.7–3.232. *GIBM* 44. *IG* ii².2191.

17 BM GR 1772.7–3.2. *BM Cat. Sculpture* i, 703. *CIG* 3256. *GIBM* 1024.

18 BM GR 1948.10–19.1. Haynes, D. E. L., and Tod, M.N., *Journal of Hellenic Studies* lxxiii (1953), pp. 138–40, pl. v. *SEG* xii.561.

19 BM GR 1805.7–3.211. *BM Cat. Sculpture* iii, 2391. *GIBM* 1114. *IG* xiv.2131.

20 BM GR 1805.7–3.187. *BM Cat. Sculpture* i, 649. *CIG* 6866. *GIBM* 1127.

21 BM GR 1859.12–26.19. *GIBM* 928.

22 BM GR 1847.12–20.3. *CIG* 2664. *GIBM* 918.

23 BM GR 1864.3–31.6. *GIBM* 175.

24 BM GR 1785.5–27.9. *GIBM* 13. *IG* ii².2498. *SEG* xxxii.226.

25 BM GR 1816.6–10.348. *GIBM* 37. *IG* i².945. *SEG* x.414, xxi.125, xxii.64. Tod i², pp. 127–8, no. 59. P. A. Hansen, *Carmina epigraphica saeculorum VIII–V a.Chr.n.* (1983), pp. 8–10, no. 10.

26 BM GR 1816.6–10.173. *GIBM* 38. *IG* i².949.

27 BM GR 1816.6–10.282. *GIBM* 26. *IG* i³.309–10.

28 BM GR 1785.5–27.1. *GIBM* 35. *IG* i³.474.

29 MMA 16.174.6. *MMA Cat. Sculpture* 14. *SEG* iii.55. Guarducci, M., in Richter, G. M. A., *The Archaic Gravestones of Attica* (1961), p. 156, no. 34. Jeffery, L. H., *LSAG*, p. 77, no. 20, pl. 3. *Id., Annual of the British School at Athens* lxvii (1962), p. 118, no. 2, pl. 32(c).

30 MMA 15.167. *MMA Cat. Sculpture* 20. *SEG* x.460. Guarducci, M. in Richter, G. M. A., *The Archaic Gravestones of Attica* (1961), pp. 169–70, no. 61. Jeffery, L. H., *LSAG*, p. 78, no. 34, pl. 4. *Id., Annual of the British School at Athens* lxvii (1962), p. 147, no. 65, pl. 41(b).

31 BM GR 1785.5–27.2. *GIBM* 1. *IG* i³.244.

32 BM GR 1816.6–10.107. *GIBM* 1002. *SEG* iv.667. Guarducci, M. in Richter, G.M.A., *The Archaic Gravestones of Attica* (1961), pp. 165–8, no. 53. Jeffery, L. H., *LSAG*, p. 371, nos 43–4, pl. 71.

33 BM GR 1867.11–22.441. *GIBM* 678. Jeffery, L. H., *LSAG*, p. 344, no. 55(a).

34 BM GR 1816.6–10.377. *GIBM* 158. *IG* vii. 3171.

35 BM GR 1856.8–26.6. *GIBM* 245. Segre, M., *Tituli Calymnii (Annuario della Scuola Archeologica di Atene* n.s. v–vii [1944–5]), p. 43, no. 1, pl. VII.

36 *BM EA* 24. *GIBM* 1065. Andrews, C., *The Rosetta Stone* (1981).

37 BM GR 1891.6–24.38. British Museum, *A Guide to the Exhibition Illustrating Greek and Roman Life*, 2nd edn (1920), p. 205.

38 BM GR 1925 7–20.1. Previously unpublished.

39 BM GR 1873.8–20.129. *BM Cat. Bronzes* 331. *IG* ii². 1849. Kroll, J., *Athenian Bronze Allotment Plates* (1972), pp. 183–4, no. 83.

40 MMA 90.9.29. B. F. Cook, *Inscribed Hadra Vases in The Metropolitan Museum of Art* (1966), p. 24, no. 9, pls III and XI.

41 BM GR 1906.10–20.2. British Museum, *A Guide to the Exhibition Illustrating Greek and Roman Life*, 2nd edn (1920), p. 198.

42 BM GR 1867.5–8.946. *BM Cat. Vases* B 421. *CIG* 8301. Beazley, J. D., *Attic Black-figure Vase-painters* (1956), p. 181, no. 1.

43 BM GR 1836.2–24.127. *BM Cat. Vases* B 210. Beazley, J.D., *Attic Black figure Vase painters* (1956), p. 144, no. 7.

44 BM GR 1971.11–1.1. Williams, D., J. Paul Getty Museum, *Occasional Papers on Antiquities* i (1983), pp. 9–34.

45 MMA 56.171.4. Beazley, J. D., *Paralipomena* (1971), p. 127, no. 1.

46 BM GR 1873.8–20.371. *BM Cat. Vases* B 607. Beazley, J. D., *Attic Black-figure Vase-painters* (1956), p. 415, no. 4.

47 MMA 56.171.13. Beazley, J. D., *Paralipomena* (1971), p. 55, no. 50. Webster, T. B. L., *Potter and Patron in Classical Athens* (1972), pl. 77–8, pl. 10.

48 MMA 08.258.5. *MMA Cat. Bronzes* 59. Richter, G. M. A., *Handbook of the Greek Collection* (1953), p. 67, pl. 48c.

49 BM GR 1888.6–1.456. Gardner, E. A., *Naukratis* ii (1888), p. 62, no. 701, pls VI and XXI.

50 BM GR 1888.6–1.392. Gardner, E.A., *Naukratis* ii (1888), p. 65, no. 778, pls VII and XXI. Jeffery, L. H., *LSAG*, p. 341, no. 3(b).

51 MMA 38.11.7. *SEG* xi.1045. Jeffery, L. H., *LSAG*, p. 215, no. 11, pl. 40.

52 BM GR 1823.6–10.1. *BM Cat. Bronzes* 250. *GIBM* 1155. *SEG* xi.1206. Jeffery, L. H., *LSAG*, p. 275, no. 7, pl. 51. Meiggs and Lewis, p. 62, no. 29.

53 MMA 26.50. *SEG* xi.355. Jeffery, L. H., *LSAG*, p. 169, no. 26, pl. 29.

54 MMA 44.11.1. Jeffery, L.H., *LSAG*, p. 283, no. 1, pl. 53.

55 BM GR 1865.12–13.1. *IG* iv.348. Jeffery, L. H., *LSAG*, p. 131, no. 9, pl. 19. Guarducci, M., *Epigrafia Greca* iii (1974), p. 462, fig. 181.

56 BM GR 1860.4–4.1. Jeffery, L. H., *LSAG*, p. 358, no. 47, pl. 69.

57 BM GR 1898.7–16.3. *BM Cat. Bronzes* 3207. *GIBM* 952. *IG* xi.1.649. *SEG* xiv.470. Jeffery, L. H., *LSAG*, p. 234, no. 5, pl. 45.

58 BM GR 1824.4–99.17. *BM Cat. Bronzes* 264. *GIBM* 157. *SEG* xi.1182. Jeffery, L. H., *LSAG*, p. 220, no. 6, pl. 42. Meiggs and Lewis, pp. 31–3, no. 17.

Bronze mirror with a scene from the underworld, late 4th century BC. A winged Lasa holds out a scroll inscribed with the names of the figures: Lasa, Aivas (Ajax) and Hamphiare (Amphiaraos, the Greek diviner and seer). Diam. 16.5 cm (BM Br 622, 1847.9–9.4).

Etruscan

Larissa Bonfante

Acknowledgements

I am deeply grateful to the following for help, suggestions and encouragement: Vittoria and Giuliano Bonfante, Marie-Françoise Briguet, Andrew Burnett, Eirene Christodoulou, Brian Cook, Stefania Del Papa, Adriana Emiliozzi, Nancy de Grummond, Alessandro Morandi, Lorenzo Smerillo, Judith Swaddling, David Tripp. Special thanks go to Ellen Macnamara, to my editor Teresa Francis, and to Massimo Pallottino.

All mirrors, gems and alphabets are drawn by Sue Bird. Figs. 1, 2 and 3 are drawn by Sue Bird and Sue Goddard: Fig. 2 is adapted from Banti, 3, and Fig. 3 from L. Bonfante (ed.), *Etruscan Life and Afterlife*, Detroit 1986, map 5. Fig. 4: Pallottino, *Etruscans*, Fig. 9. Fig. 5: M. Pallottino, *Saggi di Antichità*, Rome 1979, 629–30. Fig. 6: *Thesaurus* 421. Fig. 7: drawn by Eva Wilson and reproduced by courtesy of B.T. Batsford Ltd. Fig. 8: E. Macnamara. Fig. 9: Paris, Bibliothèque Nationale. Fig. 10: A. Morandi, *MEFRA* 100 (1988), Fig. 3. Fig. 38: Morandi, *Epigrafia Italica*, 66. The numerals on p. 340 are from *Thesaurus* 422.

Contents

1

Introduction

The Etruscans lived in central Italy, in an area bounded by the Arno and the Tiber rivers, from at least 700 BC (and probably earlier) to the first century BC. The Greeks knew them as Tyrrhenians, and gave this name to the sea which the Etruscans controlled to the west of the Italian peninsula, including some of the best harbours in the Mediterranean. The Romans called them Tusci or Etrusci. They evidently called themselves Rasna, or, according to Dionysius of Halicarnassus (first century BC), Rasenna.

New discoveries and new studies are allowing us to trace the lively commercial, cultural and political relations of the Etruscans and their contacts with the Greeks, Phoenicians, Latins and other inhabitants of Italy and Europe, from the beginning of their history as a people until the death of the Etruscan language. Like the ancient Greek cities or the Tuscan cities of the Renaissance, each Etruscan city had its own character, style and independence. There was never an Etruscan empire; there was, however, an Etruscan people who shared a language, religion, geographical location, customs and costumes which made them recognisably different from other peoples in Italy and the Mediterranean. They also shared a name; and, long before the Romans, they almost succeeded in uniting Italy.

The Etruscans brought 'civilisation', that is the culture of cities, including writing, to
1   the peoples of Italy and much of Europe, acting as the principal intermediaries between the Greeks and the non-Greeks, or 'barbarians', of the west. Their political rule and direct colonisation extended over much of the Italian peninsula; their commercial
2   activities and cultural influence reached much farther. The Etruscan cities were rivalled only by those of Sicily and Southern Italy, founded by Greek settlers who brought culture to the west. The first of these Western Greeks, the Euboeans, settled in Pithekoussai (modern Ischia) in about 775 BC. The third great power in Italy, that of Carthage, was limited to western Sicily and Sardinia, but Phoenicians and Etruscans were commercially and politically allied and Phoenician influence was important for Etruscan art, religion and culture. It was Greek culture, however, which had the most visible impact on the Etruscans and, through them and the Romans, on Europe and the Mediterranean.

Etruscan history and civilisation and their influence are known to us from three types of evidence: Greek and Roman literary sources, archaeology and the Etruscan language – the subject of this section.

No Etruscan literature has come down to us, so the only ancient sources available are the writings of Greek and Roman authors. They describe the Etruscans as 'pirates', sea-going folk who traded and, when the occasion arose, raided rival ships and settlements. The maritime Etruscans in fact competed with Greek and Phoenician traders in the eighth and seventh centuries BC. During this international period, appropriately known as 'Orientalising' because of the influence from the east, the Greeks began their westward colonisation, attracted by Italy's rich mineral resources – iron and copper – which were controlled by the Etruscans.

1   Ancient Italy and its peoples, 8th–6th centuries BC.

When Greek historians turned their attention to this wealthy western people, they discussed the problem of their 'origins'. Herodotus (c.450 BC) quoted the Lydians, who claimed their ancestors had founded the Etruscan cities when they emigrated from Asia Minor, under the leadership of a certain Tyrrhenus. This theory was widely accepted in antiquity. In the first century BC Virgil could simply refer to the Etruscans as 'Lydians', and everyone understood him. Dionysius of Halicarnassus, a Greek historian writing at the time of Augustus, questioned this theory, though no one paid much attention in his own time. He argued that the Etruscans were in fact native to Italy. Not only did they call

2   The Etruscan cities.

themselves Rasenna, and not Tyrrhenians, but, as he says, 'this most ancient nation does not resemble any other cities in their language or in their way of life, or customs' (1.30.2). Dionysius shrewdly related the problem of Etruscan origins to the nature of their language, and anticipated much of the modern discussion on the subject. The Lydian language is not at all close to Etruscan; nor has any archaeological evidence come forth, in the course of modern excavations of ancient Lydian cities, to confirm Herodotus' theory about an eastern origin. A third theory, wholly modern, suggesting that the Etruscans came down into Italy from the north, was based on nineteenth-century archaeological discoveries and theories, now known to be incorrect. The Etruscan presence in the Po Valley in fact resulted from conquest from the south.

3 The languages of ancient Italy.

Scholars today agree that, whatever the origins of the Etruscan people or the Etruscan language, the Etruscan civilisation as we know it developed on Italian soil. We must think in terms of a gradual transformation of groups in central Italy, in the prehistoric period from the end of the Bronze Age and throughout the Iron Age, into the historical people we know as the Etruscans, with their own special culture, social structure and economy.

Archaeological evidence is absolutely fundamental to our knowledge of Etruscan history. It allows us to situate the Etruscans in time and place and to recognise their foreign contacts, and provides reliable information about various phases of their art, culture and the extent of their influence. Furthermore, since we have no continuous narrative history, the dating system we use is based on the archaeological record.

The phases of Etruscan art do not correspond exactly to those of the art of their neighbours, the Greeks. For the sake of convenience, however, we use the same chronological terminology. The Iron Age period in the area of ancient Etruria (ninth to eighth centuries BC) is generally known as Villanovan (from the name of a site near Bologna where tombs from this phase have been excavated and dated). One does not, however, refer to the 'Villanovans', only to a 'Villanovan period'. The people of this period are now recognised by many scholars as 'proto-Etruscans'.

3   Writing does not appear in Etruria until about 700 BC, thus we have no direct evidence as to the languages spoken in central Italy at this time. But archaeology shows that there was continuity between Villanovan centres and those of the Orientalising period (seventh century BC) and that it is very likely that the Etruscans were already living in this area and speaking the Etruscan language for some time before they began to write it down. They learned to write using the Greek alphabet adopted from their recently arrived neighbours at Pithekoussai and Cumae; and they began to record their language.

The Orientalising and Archaic (c. 600–400 BC) periods were the high point of Etruscan culture, art, power and influence. As the Roman historian Livy says, nearly all Italy, from the Alps to the straits of Sicily, rang to the fame of the Etruscan nation. The Po Valley, with its centre at Bologna (Felsina), was clearly Etruscanised by this time. Livy reports that twelve cities were founded there, to match the loose organisation of 'Twelve Peoples' in Etruria proper. In the south, Etruscan influence – and no doubt power – reached as far as Campania, to Capua and elsewhere. Rome's neighbour Praeneste (modern Palestrina) has yielded some of the most important tombs of the Orientalising period, the Barberini and Bernardini tombs, with Etruscan-style luxury articles and Etruscan inscriptions.

The most important city to show the effects of Etruscan 'civilising' was Rome itself. According to Roman tradition, Etruscan kings ruled in Rome from the end of the seventh century BC until 510/509 BC, when the Republic was established. Archaeology confirms the importance of Etruscan art and culture in Rome: temples were built in the Etruscan style and Etruscan inscriptions have been found. The name of one of the streets of ancient Rome, the Vicus Tuscus near the Capitoline Hill, long preserved the memory of their residence in the city. The Etruscans brought many innovations: writing, monumental architecture, the depiction of the human figure in art, luxurious customs, music, processions, chariots and games. But the Romans continued to speak Latin, beginning now to write it down using the Greek alphabet they learned from the Etruscans.

The fifth and fourth centuries saw a decline in Etruscan power. The loss of Rome as a base in the south and invasions of the Gauls from the north mark the end of its expansion. The coastal cities especially declined, although the cities of the interior – Volsinii (modern Orvieto), Chiusi, Volterra, Arezzo, Perugia and Fiesole – experienced a rise to prominence. In the final, Hellenistic, phase of Etruscan history (third century BC onwards) came the triumph of Roman prestige and power, the Romanisation of the oligarchic Etruscan noble families and the demise of the Etruscan language. Some of the longest inscriptions in Etruscan which survive from this period – sacred texts, mostly from the central Etruscan area around Lake Bolsena, rich in sanctuaries – constitute the latest recension of traditional texts originating from earlier periods. Whatever there may have been of Etruscan literature – drama, poetry, historical works – has perished. The Etruscans themselves stopped speaking their native language, became Romans, and abandoned, with their language, their tradition. There was thus no reason to preserve their texts by copying them in other books or volumes. A number of bilingual inscriptions, many of them epitaphs from the second and first centuries BC, testify to the change-over from Etruscan to Latin.

Although the Etruscans had ceased to exist as a separate people by the first century BC and certainly by the time of Augustus, Etruscan families and traditions survived in Rome. Maecenas, Augustus' friend and adviser, was a descendant of a noble Etruscan family. The emperor Claudius wrote a history of the Etruscans, in twenty volumes, which regrettably has not come down to us. His first wife, Urgulanilla, was Etruscan. In AD 408, when Alaric, king of the Goths, threatened to destroy Rome, some Etruscan priests went to the emperor, offering to perform certain magic rites and recite Etruscan prayers and incantations to ward off the enemy. But they were unsuccessful, for Rome was sacked, and it was the last time the Etruscan language was spoken.

The Etruscan language

The problem of Etruscan origins is encapsulated in the peculiarity of their language, which is different from any other in Italy or in Europe. Unlike all the other languages of Europe, except for Basque, Hungarian and Finnish, Etruscan does not belong to the great Indo-European family of languages spoken from around 4000 BC by groups of people migrating from a region in central Europe around the Baltic area, as far east as India and as far west as Ireland. The only known related language is that preserved in a remarkable inscription, written in an alphabet and language akin to Etruscan on a stele with the figure of a warrior, found in 1885 at Kaminia on the northern Aegean island of

4

Lemnos and dated to the late sixth century BC. It has 98 letters, forming 33 words. In 1928 Italian archaeologists in Lemnos found similar fragmentary inscriptions on sherds of locally made pottery. These were of vital importance, for they showed that the language was actually spoken in Lemnos: the stele had not been imported from elsewhere in the Mediterranean. We know, therefore, that a dialect close to Etruscan was spoken at Lemnos before the Athenian conquest of the island in the second half of the sixth century BC. This dialect was different from all

4 Stone stele from Lemnos, 6th century BC. Athens, National Museum.

other languages spoken in the area. We do not know, however, how and when it came to be spoken there.

The Etruscan language which we read on the earliest inscriptions in Etruria had evidently already been spoken in the area for a long time, and it provides proof of the Etruscans' relationship with their neighbours. For instance, the commercial and cultural contacts they had with the Greeks are reflected in their vocabulary: Greek names for drinking vessels were taken into the language (e.g. *culichna,* from *kylix,* 'cup'). A very large number of Greek mythological figures are depicted and named in Etruscan art and inscriptions. We find Etruscan words in Umbrian, and most of the so-called Iguvine Tablets from Gubbio, in the Umbrian dialect, are written in the Etruscan alphabet. We also find, on the other hand, Umbrian and Latin words in Etruscan. For example, Etruscan *nefts* is certainly of Latin origin: it comes from Latin *nepos,* 'nephew'. The Latin word was adopted by the Etruscans, just as the word *cousin* was adopted from French into English. *Vinum*, 'wine', also comes from Latin. Conversely, Etruscan influence in Rome left clear traces in the Latin language. A close study of Latin vocabulary reveals many words which were originally Etruscan, most of them connected with luxurious living and higher culture, including writing. Four words dealing with writing came into Latin by way of the Etruscan language, confirming the Etruscan transmission of the Greek alphabet to the Romans: *elementum,* whose earlier meaning was 'letter of the alphabet', *litterae,* 'writing' (originally derived from Greek *diphthera,* 'skin', a material on which people wrote); *stilus,* 'writing implement', and *cera,* 'wax' (for wax tablets on which to take notes).

The main problems confronting scholars studying the Etruscan language are, first, that it resembles no other language in Europe or elsewhere: in direct contrast with Linear B, which turned out to be an unknown script used for a known language, Etruscan is an unknown language written in a known script – the alphabet. Secondly, no literature survives: we have no narrative texts, no history, poetry or drama. Thirdly, the 13,000 Etruscan inscriptions that have come down to us are mostly short: dedications or epitaphs, with names, human and divine, titles, and a few common nouns, numbers and verbs. The few longer ones are technical: religious texts, prayers, rites and contracts. Attempting to solve these difficulties, scholars have studied the Etruscan language in a variety of ways, using bilingual inscriptions and glosses as well as linguistic and cultural-archaeological methods.

5 Bilingual texts include three gold tablets written in Phoenician and Etruscan, found in 1964 at Pyrgi, the port of Caere, as well as some thirty Etruscan-Latin inscriptions. There are also numerous 'picture bilinguals', in which labels or captions identify pictures on wall-paintings, gems and engraved mirrors. Particularly promising is the comparison of Etruscan religious inscriptions with those of their neighbours. The Iguvine Tablets, for example, in the Umbrian language, are 'quasi-bilinguals', written partly in the Etruscan and partly in a Latin alphabet, and resemble religious inscriptions of Etruria in both structure and content.

Glosses comprise the only non-archaeological epigraphical evidence available to us concerning the Etruscan language. They are definitions or marginal notes, intended by ancient authors to explain Etruscan words which appeared in Greek or Latin texts, including many words which referred to the *etrusca disciplina,* the religious sphere of divination which the Romans imported from their neighbours. They refer to birds, plants

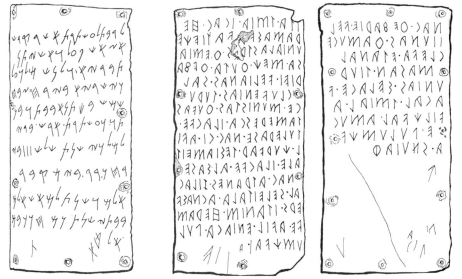

5   Gold tablets from Pyrgi, c. 500 BC. Inscribed in Etruscan (centre and right) and Phoenician (left) (*TLE* 874, *CIE* 6314).

and rituals: for example *capys*, 'eagle'. Other glosses explain *atrium*, the 'entrance' of the typical Roman house; *ais*, 'god'; *lucumo*, 'king', and *clan*, 'son'.

Important contributions have also been made by the study of names and syntax and of the transformation of Greek words brought into Etruscan, such as the names of Greek gods and heroes inscribed on Etruscan gems and mirrors. Etruscan pronunciation, and the changes it underwent during the approximately seven centuries when Etruscan was spoken and written, can be reconstructed because these changes were regularly reflected in the spelling, which remained, it seems, strictly phonetic. The Etruscans never developed an 'historical' spelling as in English, where for example the *oo* of 'spoon', once pronounced with a long *o*, as in 'whole', now has the same sound as *u* in 'rule'.

Etruscan cannot be interpreted through any kind of 'etymological' method which claims connections, for example, with Albanian and Basque, Hebrew, Turkish, etc. Such connections are based on accidental, superficial resemblances with other languages or language families, not on any real relationship. As a language, Etruscan is in fact isolated. For this reason, the most fruitful method has been the cultural-archaeological approach, in which an inscription is considered in its historical context and in close relation to the monument or object on which it appears. A good example of inscriptions studied in such a manner is the Etruscan book reconstructed from linen bands later used to wrap a mummy, now in Zagreb (see p. 345). These were originally part of a ritual book, a liturgical calendar listing names of gods, dates, and types of offerings to be made.

The discovery of the Pyrgi tablets, hailed as the long-sought-after 'bilingual' in 1964, marked a turning-point in Etruscan studies. It coincided with, and was in part responsible for, a new focus in the study of the Etruscan language, which can be summarised as follows:

1. A view of the historical and geographical context of the inscriptions as having been made in Italy at a specific time is in keeping with the growing consciousness of the Etruscans as deeply involved in ancient Italy as well as in the ancient Mediterranean.

2. A new study of monuments which have been in museums and collections for a

hundred years or more has resulted in discoveries as important as those from newly excavated material, restoring archaeological and historical contexts of objects uprooted from their original environment by 'treasure hunting' excavations.

3. Collections of all known inscriptions have been made or are in progress. Such *Corpora*, begun in the nineteenth century, have been started up again and new ones inaugurated in a remarkable wave of international collaboration: these include the *Corpus of Etruscan Inscriptions (CIE)*; the *Thesaurus*, listing all Etruscan words to be found in inscriptions and glosses; and the *Corpus of Etruscan Mirrors (CSE)*, containing many interesting names of mythological figures. The guiding spirit behind all these projects has been Massimo Pallottino, who was also responsible for the *Testimonia Linguae Etruscae (TLE)* a selection of the most important inscriptions, listed according to their provenance. The appearance of a fully-fledged grammar of Etruscan (Pfiffig 1975) – though criticised by some scholars as over optimistic – has helped to stimulate further study.

Note on the transcription
of Etruscan letters

(all these are rough equivalents)

Υ = *ch* (*kh*), aspirate: as in English *kin*.

$\odot\ O$ = *th*, aspirate: as in English *ten*.

ϕ = *ph*, aspirate: as in English *pan*.

$\xi\ \boxplus\ X$ = *s*, sibilant: as in English *sin*.

M = *ś*, sibilant: perhaps pronounced as in English *shin*.

Note. Aspirate consonants, for which there are no signs in English, were pronounced with an audible breath puff, or 'h' sound, following a *k*, *p* or *t* sound. Initial *k*, *p* and *t* have a somewhat similar sound in English. In Etruscan, as in Greek, ϕ was pronounced with such a plosive sound, not like an *f*; that is why a new letter had to be found for the sound of *f*, which the Greeks did not have.

Etruscan had voiceless consonants or stops, *k* (and *c* and *q*), *p* and *t*; but not the voiced (sonant) consonants *g*, *b* and *d* (these are so called because their pronunciation involves the use of the vocal cords).

Etruscan sounds are here transcribed in lower-case italics, and letters in italic capitals.

2
The Etruscan Language

The Alphabet

Since a historical people is usually defined by its language, strictly speaking we can only identify these inhabitants of central Italy as 'Etruscans' from the moment when we first begin to see texts written in the Etruscan language, around 700 BC. These were written in the same script we use today, the alphabet, in which each sign originally represented a different sound. From the alphabetic script of the Phoenicians, without vowels, was derived the Greek alphabet, in which certain consonantal sounds were adapted to signify vowels: A, E (H = long *e*), I, O (Ω = *omega*, 'large o' or long *o*) and Y. An impressive sign of historical conservation is the fact that schoolchildren today still recite the alphabet in roughly the same order in which the Greeks first received it, almost 3,000 years ago.

As a prestigious sign of the new Orientalising style and as a status symbol, the alphabet decorates a number of Etruscan objects placed in rich tombs of the seventh century BC. These 'model' alphabets, taken directly from the Greek alphabet as brought west by the Euboeans, bear witness to the speed with which this new development was adopted. The Etruscans considered the letters of the alphabet decorative, perhaps even magical, and copied them on various objects. They wrote from right to left, like the Phoenicians and other ancient Semitic peoples.

Writing implements decorated with these letters were placed in the tombs of wealthy, important people. Examples include an ivory writing tablet from Marsiliana d'Albegna (Archaeological Museum, Florence), originally decorated with gold leaf, meant to be worn as a pendant; a bucchero (shiny black pottery) container in the shape of a rooster, with a crested lid, which may once have held a coloured liquid like ink (Metropolitan Museum, New York); and a tall, slender bucchero vase, a brush or pen holder, from the Regolini-Galassi tomb in Cerveteri, now in the Vatican Museum, covered not only with the letters of the alphabet but with syllables as well.

The alphabet of twenty-six signs displayed on all these objects is called a 'model' alphabet. Some of its letters – ß, Γ, ⟩, O – are never used in Etruscan inscriptions (so, too, Italian children learn the signs *k*, *j*, *w* and *y*, which never appear in Italian words). Etruscan has no *b*, *d*, or *g* (voiced stops), and no *o*, but these signs are included in the alphabet, which faithfully reproduces the Greek model from which the Etruscan derived. Of the four signs for *s*, only two were regularly used at any one time or place.

There are, to date, seventy-five known Etruscan inscriptions from the seventh century BC, a very respectable quantity when compared with Greek inscriptions from this period. These and later examples show the steps in the adaptation of the alphabet to the Etruscan language. The sound *u* (written ∨ or Υ) was regularly substituted for *o*. The Greek Φ, an aspirate, was pronounced as a *p* followed by the sound of 'h': it was not an *f* sound, as it is today. A new sign, 8, represented the sound *f*, unknown in Greek. In fact we owe the sound *f* to the Etruscans, who passed it on to the Latins, Oscans, Umbrians and

Model alphabet	Archaic inscriptions (7th–5th century BC)	Later inscriptions (4th–1st century BC)	Transcriptions and phonetic values
A	A	A	a
𐌁			(b)
𐌂	)	⊃	c (= k)
𐌃			(d)
𐌄	𐌄	𐌄	e
𐌅	𐌅	𐌅	v
I	I	ⱶ	z (= ts)
𐌇	𐌇	⊟⊘	h
⊗	⊗○	⊙○	θ (= th)
I	I	I	i
𐌊	𐌊		k
𐌋	𐌋	𐌋	l
𐌌	𐌌	𐌌	m
𐌍	𐌍	𐌍	n
⊞			(s)
○			(o)
𐌐	𐌐	𐌐	p
M	M	M	ś
𐌒	𐌒		q
𐌓	𐌓	𐌓	r
𐌔	𐌔	𐌔	s
T	T	𐌕	t
Y	Y	V	u
X	X		ś
Φ	Φ	Φ	φ (= ph)
Ψ	Ψ	Ψ	χ (= kh)
	(𐌚8)	8	f

6 Etruscan alphabets.

Veneti in Italy, and beyond to Northern Europe. In reading Etruscan transcriptions of Greek names, it is important to remember that the Etruscans changed the voiced stops *g*, *b* and *d* to *k*, *p* and *t* (voiceless) whenever these appeared in foreign words – Greek, Latin or Umbrian. Thus from the Greek word *thriambos* came the Latin word *triumpus* or *triumphus*, 'victory celebration', by way of Etruscan.

All alphabets, when first used, are strictly phonetic, and Etruscan spelling remained so. The alphabetic system changed twice, first when the Greek model alphabet was adapted to the needs of the Etruscan language, then some time around 400 BC various other changes culminated in the creation of the so-called 'neo-Etruscan' alphabet. Several letters disappeared. *K* continued to be used in the northern cities, as did the sibilant M (*ś*). An inscription can accordingly be dated, not absolutely, but in general terms, as belonging to the Archaic period or to the later period (fourth to first centuries BC).

The loss of vowels in Etruscan spelling after the first syllable, resulting in clusters of consonants, was due to an intensive stress accent which around 500 BC affected Etruscan as well as other languages of Italy (Latin, Umbrian, Oscan, Sabellian). The first syllable was heavily accented, with the result that following vowels weakened ($a > e > i$), and eventually dropped out. This abbreviation, or syncope, is most obvious in the later, neo-Etruscan inscriptions of the fourth century BC and the Hellenistic period. On Etruscan mirrors, for example, we find the Greek name Alexandros written in the abbreviated form Alcsentre, and even Elcsntre. Ramutha (a woman's name) becomes Ramtha; Rasenna (the name of the Etruscans) Rasna; Klytaimestra (Clytemnestra) becomes Clutumsta, then Clutmsta; *turice*, 'gave', becomes *turce*. (The pronunciation of English also provides example of this: both 'Leicester' and 'Worcester' are pronounced in a 'syncopated' way.) This loss of vowels was only partly compensated for by nasal liquids (the 'l' in Atlnta, for the Greek name of the female athlete Atalanta, was pronounced something like the final syllable of English 'castle'). Conversely, sometimes in the internal syllables extra vowels were inserted in consonant clusters to make words easier to pronounce. This tendency accounts for the transformation of the Greek name of the goddess Artemis into Aritimi, of the Etruscan name for Herakles (Hercle) into Herecele and of Menrva (Minerva) into Menerva.

As stated above, the direction of Etruscan writing normally goes from right to left, the reverse of classical Greek, Latin or English. In the Archaic period inscriptions are occasionally written *boustrophedon*, 'as the ox ploughs' – one line going from left to right, the next from right to left, and so on. This was the system used by the early Greeks, before they settled on writing left to right (*c.*550 BC). Examples of Etruscan writing from left to right do occur on some mirrors, where they are clearly dictated by a desire for symmetry or to keep the label close to the figure. Inscriptions of the third century BC or later, under Latin influence, also read from left to right. In this late period some inscriptions in the Etruscan language were written in the Latin alphabet, and some, in the Latin language, with Etruscan letters.

In the earliest inscriptions the words are not separated at all, the letters running on one after the other (*scriptio continua*). From the sixth century BC, words are often divided from each other by one, two or more dots placed vertically above each other. Sometimes this 'punctuation' separates groups of letters or syllables within a word: such syllabic punctuation constitutes a peculiar feature of Etruscan writing in certain periods.

Pronunciation

Consonants

Since they could not pronounce the voiced stop *g*, the Etruscans used the third letter of the Greek alphabet, *gamma* Γ, ⟨ or ⟨, with the value of *k*. Thus for the sound *k* (English *think*) they used three signs: K (K) before *a (ka)*; C (⟨) before *e* and *i (ce, ci)* ; and Q (Q) before *u (qu)*. The same system was used by the early Latins, who imitated the Etruscan. The K of early Latin survived before *a* in a few words, such as *Kalendae*, from which 'calendar' derives. (In English the same three letters survive with the sound of *k: ke, ca, qu.*)

The influence of Etruscan on the Latin alphabet is shown by the fact that the Latins followed the Etruscan use of the Greek *gamma*, written as a C, to represent the sound of *k (cena, cura, catena, civis, corium)*. Originally in Latin the letter C could be pronounced as *k (Caesar*, from which comes the German word *Kaiser)* and also as *g (Caius*, pronounced *Gaius)*. It was not until about 250 BC that the Romans introduced a new letter, G (which was merely a slightly changed C), specifically for the voiced stop *g*. In order to avoid changing the order of the alphabet, this new letter G took the place of the Greek letter Z, which the Latins had inherited but did not use; the 'slot' was therefore available. Later, in the first century BC, when more intimate contact with the Greeks made it necessary to write Greek words, the Latins reinstated the letter Z, which, having lost its place, was put at the end – where it still is today.

In general, pronunciation was harsh. We have seen that the voiced stops *b, d, g* were substituted by *p, t, k*. The aspirated sounds *(ph, th, ch, ts)* also gave a rough texture to speech. The letter Z (𐌆) in Etruscan had a voiceless sound, as for example in English *gets, eats,* and not as in *zeal*. Some scholars have suggested that the modern *gorgia toscana* so obvious in Florence and Siena today (Coca Cola = 'hola hola') derives from Etruscan.

The Etruscans had a sound *f* (pronounced more or less as in English *find, stuff)*. The Greeks did not have this sound, nor did they have a sign for it. At first the Etruscans approximated the sound with the two sounds *w* and *h*, written as Ϝ𐌇. Later they adopted a new sign, 𐌚 (its origin is obscure). The Latins, however, kept the first element of *vh*, Ϝ: F, the letter familiar to us with the sound of *f*.

The Etruscan Ϝ *(digamma*, here transcribed as *v)* was bilabial, like English *w* or Latin *v* in *vincit*. Diphthongs like *au* are frequently spelled *av: lautni > lavtni; aule > avle*.

Vowels

The Etruscan vowel system is simple. There are only four vowels: *a, e, i, u*. In Etruscan the letter A is always pronounced *ah*, as in *father; I* is always *ee*, as in *machine;* U is *oo*, as in *rule* or *moon*. U always substitutes for *o*, which does not exist, as we have seen. E is *eh*, as in *elf;* it was a very closed vowel, almost like *i*, with which it was in fact often interchanged. So we see both *ica* and *eca, mini* and *mine, cliniiaras* and *clenar*, etc. The Greek name Iason (Jason) becomes Easun; and the Etruscan genitive form *-ial* often becomes *-eal*. Etruscan had only short vowels, like several modern languages, for example Spanish and Romanian. There were no long vowels like Greek *eta* (H) or *omega* (Ω). Since the letter *H* or 𐌇 was not needed to represent a long *e*, as in Greek, it was therefore available to represent the sound of *h*, as in English *hat* today. It already had the value of *h* in some Greek dialects.

Greek diphthongs are usually preserved, except of course that *oi* becomes *ui*. In later inscriptions (fifth to first centuries BC), *ai* often becomes *ei* or even *e*: thus the Greek name Aias (Ajax) is written as Aivas, Eivas or Evas in Etruscan. *Graikos,* 'Greek', written *Graecus* in Latin, becomes *creice* in Etruscan. There is a general trend toward the simplification of two different vowels, forming a diphthong, into a simple vowel. *Eu* sometimes becomes *u* in Etruscan: for example, the name of Castor's brother Pollux, Polydeukes in Greek, in Etruscan becomes Pultuce.

Grammar

Etruscan is an inflected language. There are different endings, or inflections, for nouns, pronouns and verbs. Though the limited amount of materials at our disposal precludes the systematic setting out of an Etruscan 'grammar', and even the use of conventional grammatical terms is anything but certain, there are certain forms we can recognise.

Note: For Etruscan personal names and other words cited in the text, see the Appendices.

Nouns
Here is an example of a declension.

	Singular	Plural
Nominative and Accusative	*clan,* 'son'	*clenar,* 'the sons'
Genitive, 'of'	*clens,* 'of the son'	*clenaraśi* ⎫ 'to the sons'
Dative, 'to'	*clensi,* 'to the son'	*cliniiaras* ⎭
Locative, 'in'	**clenthi,* 'in the son'	

(* this form is not attested, only hypothetical)

Common nouns have no special endings for masculine, feminine or neuter.

Only personal names have gender in Etruscan. Many masculine names end in *e* (Greek and Latin equivalents are given where known):
   Hercle (Gk Herakles; Lat. Hercules), Menle (Gk Menelaos), Achle (Gk Achilles), Zimite (Gk Diomedes), Tite Cale (Lat. Titus Calus), Aule (Lat. Aulus), Taitle (Gk Daidalos; Lat. Daedalus), Sime, Artile.

Others end in a consonant:
   Evas (Gk Aias; Lat. Ajax), Arnth (Lat. Arruns), Larth (Lat. Lars), Velthur, Laran.

Feminine names end in -*i* or -*a:*
   Uni (Lat. Juno), Menrva (Lat. Minerva), Clutmsta (Gk Klytemnestra, Klytaimestra), Ati, Seianti, Lasa

and sometimes in -*u:*
   Zipu, Thanchvilu.

Names of gods often have the nominative in *-s:*
> Fufluns (no precise equivalent; Gk Dionysos; Lat. Bacchus), Sethlans (no precise equivalent; Gk Hephaistos), Tins (no precise equivalent; Gk Zeus), Selvans (Lat. Silvanus).

Otherwise male and female gods' names may have the same endings, whether consonant:
> Turan (no precise equivalent; Gk Aphrodite), Thanr (f), Malavisch (f), Laran (m)

or vowel:
> Pacha (Lat. Bacchus), Aplu (Gk Apollo).

The genitive is formed by adding *-s* or *-l* to the stem, often inserting a vowel between the stem and the ending. After a liquid consonant (*l, r*), *-us* is used:
> Velthur > Velthurus, Vel > Velus, Thanchvil > Tanchvilus.

The genitive ending in *-al* is added to feminine names ending in *-i:*
> Uni > Unial, Ati > Atial

and to masculine names ending in *-s:*
> Laris > Larisal

or ending in a dental:
> Arnth > Arnthal.

Sometimes a special ending in *-sa* or *-isa* designates the patronymic, 'son of'.
> *aule velimna larthal clan = aule velimna larthalisa*, 'Aules Velimna, son of Larth'.

Thus the genitive expresses possession (*arnthal clan*, 'son of Arnth'). It also expresses dedication (as does the dative in Latin):
> *ecn turce ... selvansl*, 'this [she] gave to Selvans'.

There is also a dative form in *-si:*
> *mi titasi cver menache*, 'I was offered to Tita as a gift'.

The plural is formed by adding *-r (-ar, -er, -ur)*. An uncommon shift of the stem vowel in the plural occurs in *clan > clenar*, 'son' > 'sons'.

The locative ending is *-thi.*

Pronouns
1. Personal pronouns
First person: Nom. *mi*, 'I'
   Acc. *mini*, 'me'
No other case forms are known.

   Third person: (animate, male and female) *an*, 'he', 'she'
   (inanimate, neuter) *in*, 'it'
No other case forms are known.

2. Demonstrative pronouns
Nom. *ita, eta, ta*, 'this'; or *ika, eca, ca*, 'this'
Acc. *etan, tn*, 'this'; or *can, cn, ecn*, 'this'
Loc. *calti*, 'in this'; or *eclthi, clthi*, 'in this'

Adjectives
A variety of forms denote adjectives:

1. Of quality
    aisiu, 'divine' (from *ais,* 'god')
    hinthiu, 'infernal' (from *hintha*, 'underworld')

2. Possession or reference
    aisna, eisna, 'pertaining to god', 'divine'
    pachana 'of or pertaining to Bacchus' (from Pacha, 'Bacchus')
    śuthina, 'of or pertaining to the tomb' (from *śuthi,* 'tomb').

    Family names in *-na* belong to this type. But in southern Etruscan cities the family name (equivalent to our last name) ends in *-s: aule vipiiennas.* This may derive from a genitive form (*-s*), 'of the Vipiienna', etc., a formation similar to della Robbia, di Giovanni, etc. in Italian, and names with *de* in French, *von* in German and *van* in Dutch. (In fact, when an inscription gives a name in the genitive we often cannot tell whether the nominative ends in *s* or not: Atnas, Pulenas, Vipinanas, etc.)

3. Collective
    math, mathcva, 'full of drink' (from *math* 'honeyed wine')
    srencva, 'full of ornament' (from *sren,* 'picture' or 'figure')
    flerchva, 'group of sacred statues, offerings' (from *fler,* 'offering, sacrifice').

Adverbs and Conjunctions
The conjunction *-c* is equivalent to Latin *-que,* meaning 'and'. *Um,* enclitic *-m,* also means 'and'.
    Alpan or *alpnu* is an adverb, 'gladly', 'willingly'; it can also mean 'as a gift', 'offering'.

Verbs
The present active form consists of the root, *ar, zich, tur.* Another form ends in *-a*:
    ara, tva, as in *eca sren tva,* 'this picture shows'.

The best-known form is the third person singular past (aorist). In the active form the ending is *-ce*:
    turce, 'he/she gave'
    svalce, 'he/she lived'
    lupuce, 'he/she died'
    muluvanice, 'he/she made/built'.

This can be distinguished from the passive form, *-che,* for the first person singular:
    mi . . . zichuche, 'I was written'
    mi titasi cver menache, 'I was offered to Tita as a gift'.

The text of the Zagreb mummy (see p. 345 below) gives examples of imperatives. One type of imperative consists of the simple verbal root (as in the Indo-European languages):
    vacl ar, 'make (*ar*) the libation (*vacl*).

Another imperative, ending in *-ti, -th* or *-thi,* is used for the second person singular:
    racth tura, 'prepare the incense'.

Another form seems to be a passive participle of obligation, ending in *-ri* or *-eri*:
huthiś zathrumiś flerchva nathunsl . . . thezeri-c, 'and on the 26th the sacrifices for Neptune are to be made'.

Numerals

Etruscan numerals are known from funerary inscriptions recording the age of the deceased and from the 'Tuscania dice', on which the first six numbers are written out in words rather than shown by dots, as usual. We therefore know the first six numbers:
thu, zal, ci, śa, mach, huth

Their order was recognised because in antiquity the sum of each of the two opposite sides of the die added up to seven: *mach* + *zal* = seven; *thu* + *huth* = seven; *ci* + *śa* = seven. Other clues led to the identification of each particular number, so that the order given above is generally accepted today.

What these numerals show, beyond any shadow of a doubt, is the non-Indo-European nature of the Etruscan language. Basic words like numbers and names of relationships are often similar in the Indo-European languages, for they derive from the same root.

Another peculiarity of Etruscan is the formation of numbers by subtraction, a system found also in Latin. Given the cultural influence of the Etruscans in Rome, Latin may have derived it from Etruscan. In Etruscan, 17 = 20 − 3, 18 = 20 − 2, 19 = 20 − 1. In Latin we have *duodeviginti, undeviginti.* Multiples of 10 are formed with the addition of *-alc* or *-alch.* (An asterisk indicates forms not attested in inscriptions.)

1	*thu*	10	*śar*	30	*ci-alch (ce-alch)*
2	*zal, es(a)l*	16	*huth-zar*	40	*śe-alch*
3	*ci*	17	*ci-em zathrum*	50	*muv-alch (*mach-alch)*
4	*śa*	18	*esl-em zathrum*	60	**huth-alch*
5	*mach*	19	*thun-em zathrum*	70	*semph-alch(?)*
6	*huth*	20	*zathrum*	80	*cezp-alch(?)*
7	*semph(?)*	27	*ci-em-ce-alch*	90	**nurph-alch(?)*
8	*cezp(?)*	28	*esl-em-ce-alch*	100	?
9	*nurph(?)*	29	*thun-em-ce-alch*	1000	?

Etruscan	Roman	Arabic
|	I	1
∧	V	5
×	X	10
↑	L	50
⊂ ✳	C	100
☺	C or M?	100 or 1000?
⊕	M or M̄?	1000 or 10,000?

Etruscan numerals

3
Writing Materials and Methods

Books and writing were very important to the Etruscans throughout their history: Pallottino has even called them the 'People of the Book'. They wrote on a variety of materials: bronze, clay, plaster, stone, gold, lead, cloth, wax, and perhaps papyrus. We know from Roman historians that books made of linen, *libri lintei,* were used in Rome, and Etruscan ritual texts were also written on linen. It was imported from Egypt by the seventh century BC and was also woven in Etruria. In Etruscan art such books are usually shown as attributes of priests or *haruspices* (diviners), and are sometimes folded, not rolled up like scrolls. For example, a folded linen book appears on the lid of a funerary urn from Chiusi, on the bed or couch of the deceased, under the characteristic pointed hat of the Etruscan *haruspex.* Perhaps a similar book is represented by the folded cloth at the bedside of the owners of the Tomb of the Reliefs in Cerveteri, where the furnishings of a normal upper-class household – including plates, ropes, a gaming-board, dishes and pets – were all shown in brightly painted relief on the walls of their house-like tomb.

The most famous linen book, and the only one to have come down to us in anything like its original form, is the cloth recycled as wrappings for an Egyptian mummy, now in Zagreb (see also p. 345). This book was a liturgical calendar, and the cloth – of which almost 3.5 m in length and 35 cm in width is preserved – was compact and tightly woven, clearly meant to be written on. The surface may have been treated in a special way so that the ink, which was probably applied with a brush, would not be absorbed. Two types of ink were used: black ('ivory black') for the text, and red (cinnabar, 100 per cent HgS) for the vertical lines dividing the columns. Red was also used to underline special sections in the text, evidently to help the officiating priest find his place in the ritual by unfolding the book gradually and turning to the appropriate section. The right-hand end of the cloth is much more worn than the left: this was perhaps the beginning of the book (it would of course have been at the back, as in Hebrew books).

Scrolls are represented on several monuments. We cannot be certain what material was actually used; perhaps papyrus imported from Egypt, or possibly linen, like the folded books.

Wax tablets were used for memos, letters, tallies and other records. Bronze styli used to
7 incise the letters in the wax have been preserved, many of them decorated with attractive bronze figurines. The frames of these wax tablets were usually made of wood, though some especially precious ones might have been made from ivory or bone. They were in two parts hinged together as a diptych, so they could be closed and the message, inscribed on the wax surface with a stylus, protected from wear as well as prying eyes. The date of the Marsiliana ivory tablet with a 'model' alphabet, mid-seventh century BC, puts it in the period when the alphabet was still a novelty, in Greece as well as in Etruria. On a relief
8 from Chiusi, a man is shown recording something, probably the prizes won in a competition. The date of this relief, about 500 BC, is contemporary with a story recorded by the historian Livy (2.12): Caius Mucius Scaevola's attempt to kill the Etruscan king – or

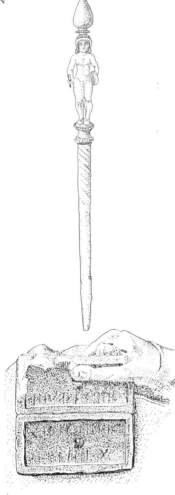

8   Detail of a stone relief from Chiusi, *c.* 500 BC: a secretary recording prizes on a hinged tablet. Palermo Archaeological Museum.

7   *Left*   Writing implements: bronze stylus, and relief showing wax tablets.

'tyrant' – Porsenna, who was besieging Rome. Porsenna's secretary, who was seated writing next to the king, was dressed so elegantly that Scaevola mistook him for Porsenna: evidently the secretary played an important role in Etruscan society. Yet there was nothing like a 'scribal' caste or group. The awkwardness of many inscriptions, such as those denoting ownership, shows that literacy was widespread – at least as much as in other ancient societies in the same historical period.

A large number of inscriptions in Etruria have been preserved on terracotta. On a tile from Capua (see p. 345) an inscription was incised in the clay while it was still wet: this is the easiest way of writing on clay. A seventh-century vase in Villa Giulia in Rome has the letters 'embossed' in relief, in a decorative pattern below the neck. The sarcophagus of Seianti Hanunia Tlesnasa has its handsome letters cut into the clay. Terracotta urns of the later period have the inscription either incised or painted on. On vases, 'labels' identifying the figures depicted were often painted on the clay, before or after firing. In the Archaic period the following Etruscan inscription was scratched on the foot of a handsome imported Greek vase, an Attic cup by the painter Oltos (*c.*500 BC):

itun turuce venel atelinas tinas cliniiaras

'This gave (*turuce*) Venel Atelinas to Tina's sons', or 'Venel Atelinas gave this to the sons of Zeus' (i.e. the Dioskouroi).

The Etruscan owner of a Greek vase often wrote a dedication to a god in this way.

Bronze was a material widely used in Italy for inscriptions. The Umbrian Iguvine tablets, the Oscan Agnone plaque (see Chapter 6) and the *Monumentum Ancyranum*, a Greek translation of Augustus' testament, are outstanding examples of this type of document. (For the Etruscans, terracotta and bronze were not secondary materials; they were what they worked best, in contrast to the Greeks and Romans, who normally recorded their *acta publica,* their public decisions and deeds, on stone). The letters of the text inscribed on a bronze model of a sheep's liver from Piacenza (see p. 347) were incised after casting, when the surface was already rigid; if they had been traced on the clay model, one would expect them to be rounded.

The largest number of Etruscan inscriptions on bronze occur on 1,000 or so figured mirrors (about 3,000 mirrors have survived in all). With a few notable exceptions whose decoration is in relief, the decoration on the reverse of these is engraved. A smaller but important category of bronze objects with inscriptions encompasses votive statues and statuettes. These include the beautiful large Chimaera of Arezzo. On the beast's paw is the inscription *tinścvil,* cut into the wax model before the bronze was cast, declaring it to be a 'gift to Tinia', that is Zeus or Jupiter. (The city of Arezzo was so famous for its bronzes in antiquity that the German word for metal, Erz, was derived from its name.) In Greece, in the early period, votive figures of gods and humans bore inscriptions scratched or engraved on their bodies, but the custom soon died out. In Etruria, and elsewhere in Italy under Etruscan influence, it survived, along with other Archaic forms and features. Some of the finest Etruscan statues and statuettes of the Classical period and later bear inscriptions carved into their mantles, on their bodies, or on their armour; for example the Arringatore in Florence and the Mars from Todi (Umbrian in language, Etruscan in style).

11–21
38–9

Other metals used include gold, silver and lead. On the three famous gold tablets from Pyrgi – in spite of their delicate appearance they are heavy plaques – the text is engraved in the soft gold surface and there are traces of words erased and written over. (A bronze tablet was also found with these.) The gold tablets were originally attached, perhaps to the wall of a temple; the nail holes, and some golden nails used for this purpose, are still extant. A gold *bulla* (pendant) has a relief design of a flying Daedalus and his son Icarus. Incised inscriptions identify the two: *taitle,* 'Daedalus' and *vikare,* 'Icarus'.

5

A cheap substitute for more expensive materials was lead, which had the added advantage of being soft and easy to write on. It was often used to make inexpensive religious or votive figures. Curses were written on lead tablets by Greeks, Etruscans, Romans and other peoples in ancient Italy. These so-called *tabulae defixionis* bore prayers, incantations and magic formulas designed to harm or incapacitate enemies and rivals. The tablets were rolled up and 'posted' in someone's tomb, for the Underworld. Lead was also used for inscriptions, such as a ribbon-like tablet from a sanctuary near Santa Marinella and a thin round plate from Magliano, with ritual, probably funerary, inscriptions (see p. 28). Epitaphs were incised on stone sarcophagi, cippi, urns, stelai and tombs, or painted in the rock-cut tombs of Tarquinia.

Inscriptions on coins and gems are short, but important. Etruscan coins, made of gold,

40

silver and bronze, were usually struck by dies (as coins are today); sometimes they were cast in moulds. Only a few issues carry 'legends' (inscriptions) or other symbols to identify their origin.

22-8   Gems, like mirrors, provide 'picture bilinguals': inscription and image explain each other. Some 3,000 gems have survived, but not all are inscribed. They are often extremely beautiful and provide important information about religion, mythology and language. Single figures, shown bending over to fit the rounded frame, or more rarely in groups, are labelled with names of Greek mythological characters: Achle (Achilles); the Trojan hero Paris; Taitle (Daidalos); Easun (Jason); Hercle or Herkle (Herakles). A gem

9   in the Bibliothèque Nationale with a youth reading the numbers written on a pair of tablets has the word *apcar,* which is Etruscan for *abacus,* the Latin word for a counting-board (*b* becomes *p* in Etruscan). Their great number is due to the fact that they were widely used as jewellery (rather than only to seal documents and containers by impressing the bezel of the ring into soft wax or clay). Like mirrors, they belonged to the luxurious world of wealthy Etruscans, who adorned themselves not only for pleasure but as a way of showing their status in society.

9   A gem showing a youth reading numbers from a tablet, *c.*450 BC (*TLE* 779). Paris, Bibliothèque Nationale.

4

Etruscan Inscriptions

Etruscan inscriptions – on stone, lead, clay, bronze, tomb walls, etc. – total about 13,000; a very large number if we consider how few we have for the other ancient non-Latin languages of Italy. Eleven inscriptions describing a religious ritual, the bronze Iguvine tablets from Gubbio – written partly in an Etruscan, partly in a Latin alphabet – are almost all that remains of the pre-Roman Umbrian language; a few hundred in Venetic and Oscan have come down to us; only three inscriptions in the Gauls' language, and none in the indigenous dialects of Sardinia and Corsica. The Faliscan language is attested by about 150 inscriptions; a large number, due to the close ties of Falerii with the literate Etruscan culture. In archaic Latin we have only nine inscriptions earlier than the third century BC, including one new one, and one, the Praenestine fibula, said to be a forgery.

Most of the 13,000 Etruscan inscriptions (more are continually being discovered) can be understood. Most are pitifully short. The majority are funerary inscriptions, consisting only of the name of the deceased, the patronymic, or father's name, sometimes the matronymic, or mother's name, and the surname or family name. What would be known of the English language if there were hardly anything but tombstones and other short inscriptions to read?

Longer inscriptions

The few long texts that have come down to us are described briefly below.

The Zagreb mummy

The longest and most exotic Etruscan inscription which survives is a religious text, a sacred linen book, parts of which were preserved by being used as linen wrappings on a mummy. The mummy, that of a 30-year old woman, was bought in Egypt by a Croatian traveller in the last century and given to the Zagreb National Museum in Yugoslavia, where it remains today. When the wrappings were removed from the body they were found to contain a neatly inked text of some 1,200 readable words, in at least twelve vertical columns. It was a liturgical calendar of sacrifices and prayers to be made to a number of gods, for instance Nethuns (Neptune), on specific dates. Though damaged and spotted by the unguents used for mummification, and largely unintelligible because of its technical vocabulary and the repetitions typical of religious texts, it is uniquely precious for our knowledge of the Etruscan language. A typical passage runs (column VIII, lines 3ff.): *celi* (the month of September) *huthis zathrumis* (the 26th [day]) *flerchva* (all the offerings) *nethunsl* (to the god Neptune) *sucri* (should be declared) *thezri-c* (and should be made).

The Capua tile

On a terracotta tile from Capua in Campania, dating from the fifth or fourth century BC, now in the State Museum in East Berlin, is incised a long funerary ritual, honouring the gods of the Underworld. Sixty-two lines are preserved, with almost 300 legible words. Among the gods mentioned are Calus, Laruns, Lethams, Tinia, Uni, and perhaps Bacchus.

The Santa Marinella lead sheet

On both sides of a lead sheet found in fragments during the 1964–5 excavations at a sanctuary near Santa Marinella, not far from Pyrgi, is a much damaged inscription, with very small letters. It is today in the Villa Giulia Museum, Rome. Several words are similar to those found on the Zagreb mummy cloth and the Capua tile; this too was evidently a religious document. It contains traces of 80 or more words, half of which can be read, and dates from the fifth century BC.

The Magliano plaque

The text of a lens-shaped lead plaque found at Magliano, in the Albegna river valley (now in the Archaeological Museum in Florence), contains some 70 words running in a spiral from the exterior inward to the centre. It was written during the fifth century BC, and mentions the gods Calus, Suri (Apollo Soranus?), Cautha, Maris, Thanr and Tins; the word for 'gods', *aiseras,* also occurs. The text seems to have been funerary in nature.

The Pyrgi tablets (Fig. 5)

Shorter, but very important because of their historical implications and because they provide us with the closest thing to a bilingual inscription, are the texts inscribed on the three gold tablets found at Pyrgi, the harbour of Caere (Cerveteri), in 1964. (Because of their great value they are kept in a bank vault in Rome. Reproductions are on view in the Villa Giulia Museum). Two are in Etruscan, one in Phoenician. A fourth tablet, in bronze and fragmentary, also had an Etruscan inscription, mentioning the goddess of dawn, Thesan. The tablets date from about 500 BC. The longest Etruscan text, which has 16 lines and 36 (or 37) words, parallels the Phoenician text but does not provide a word-for-word translation: it is no Rosetta Stone. It gives a free translation of the text of a dedication by the ruler of Cisra (Caere), Thefarie Velianas, as a thank-offering to the goddess Uni, identified as Astarte (*Štrt*) in the Phoenician text. *Turce* is translated in the Phoenician inscription as 'gave'; *zilac* is 'king' (*mlk*); *ci* is 'three'. The goddess 'held him in her hand three years' (*ci avil* = three years).

The Perugia cippus

A later (second or first century BC) inscription on a stone *cippus* or boundary-marker from Perugia (in the Perugia Museum) bears on two sides a finely carved text of 46 lines and 130 words. This was a property contract between members of the Velthina and Afuna families. The word *tular,* 'boundary' or 'boundaries', features prominently among the legal formulas and repetitions.

The epitaph of Laris Pulena

The epitaph of Laris Pulena of Tarquinia (Tarquinia Museum) is engraved on a representation of a long strip of cloth (the *volumen* of the Romans). Half-unrolled in the hands of its owner, it is proudly displayed by the deceased, who reclines on his stone sarcophagus as if on a couch. The 9 lines and 59 words can in large part be interpreted by comparing the text with the Latin *elogia* (honorary epitaphs) of the Scipios at Rome.

The Piacenza liver (Fig. 10)
An unusual document, providing invaluable evidence for Etruscan divination, is a bronze model of a sheep's liver which was discovered in 1877 near Piacenza in northern Italy (Museo Civico, Piacenza). Because of peculiarities of script and spelling, scholars think it was made near Chiusi about 150 BC. On the outer margin it is divided into sixteen regions, reflecting the sections of the sky; there are in addition twenty-four regions on the interior of the liver and two on the underside. It gives fifty-two names of divinities, mostly

10   Bronze model of a sheep's liver, from Piacenza, *c.* 150 BC (*TLE* 719).

abbreviated. Many are repeated. Some of these are known from other sources: *tin* = Jupiter, *uni* = Juno, *catha* = a sun god, *cel* – a mother goddess, *selvan* – Silvanus, *fufluns* = Bacchus, *hercle* = Hercules, *usil* = the sun, *tivr* = the moon. Many of the divinities are local Italic gods. Hercle, Fufluns, Usil, Uni and Tin are also represented and labelled on the backs of bronze mirrors, as is *celsclan*, 'son of Cel', who appears as a giant, son of Mother Earth.

Short inscriptions

Shorter inscriptions occur on mirrors and gems, vases, tableware, sarcophagi and urns, votive figures and coins.

Mirrors

The engraved decoration on Etruscan bronze mirrors contrasts with the three-dimensional decoration and supports of most Greek mirrors. The Etruscan examples provide us with a continuous series of line drawings, and often inscriptions, from the Archaic to the later Hellenistic period (*c.* 530–200 BC). They were produced in various Etruscan cities, but since such small luxury objects were given as gifts and widely exported, in ancient as well as in modern times, it is difficult to establish their provenance and to recognise the workshops where they were made.

Mirrors were probably given to women at their weddings or on other special occasions. Like most surviving luxury objects, they were found in the graves of their owners, who took their precious possessions with them. So far, mirrors have been found in women's tombs only. Inscriptions also make it clear that the mirrors were made for women, as on one which Tite Cale gave to his mother (*ati*):

> *tite cale:atial:turce:malstria:cver*
> 'Tite Cale to his mother gave this mirror as a gift'.

The sense of *cver* as a sacred object, like the Greek *agalma*, suggests that the mirror was dedicated to his dead mother, to take to the tomb.

Another mirror, from Sentinum in Umbria, says,

mi malena larthia puruhenas, 'I [am] the mirror of Larthia Puruhena'.

These two inscriptions give us the Etruscan words for 'mirror', *malstria* and *malena*, with
the characteristic ending in *-na*. Another, in the British Museum, says:

mi thancvilus fulnial, 'I [am the mirror] of Thancvil Fulni'.

11 Bronze mirror belonging to Thancvil Fulni, with
a man and a woman talking, *c.* 300 BC. Diam.
*c.*16 cm (BM Br 724, 1868.5–20.55; *TLE* 749).

12 Bronze mirror from Chiusi, 3rd
century BC, inscribed *śuthina*. Diam.
12.5 cm (BM Br 722, 1873.8–20.106).

Once dedicated to the grave, some were inscribed with the formula *śuthina* scratched on
the reflecting surface so as to preclude their re-use or theft.

Most inscriptions on mirrors, however, are of mythological names, often Etruscan
transcriptions and transformations of the names of Greek mythological figures, many of
which were known in Etruria from the plays of the Greek tragedians and their followers.
Other names of heroes and gods bring us close to Etruscan religion, literature and even
history. The broad range of subjects depicted includes remarkable examples of local
interpretations of Greek myths and legends, and local types. A popular figure in Etruria,
Hercle, or Herkle, the Etruscan Herakles, was introduced quite early to central Italy,

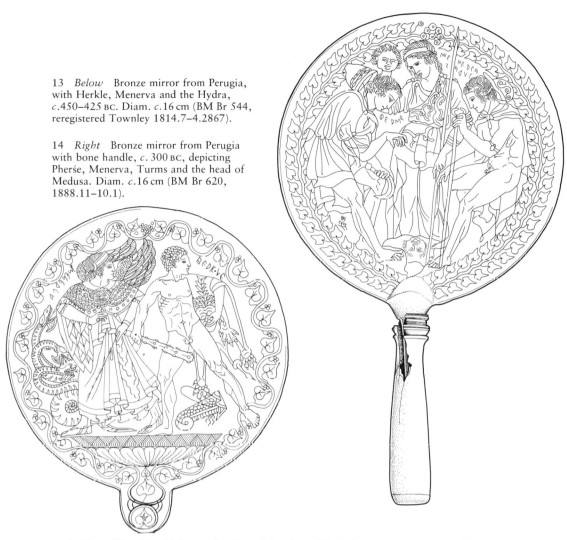

13 *Below* Bronze mirror from Perugia, with Herkle, Menerva and the Hydra, c.450–425 BC. Diam. c.16 cm (BM Br 544, reregistered Townley 1814.7–4.2867).

14 *Right* Bronze mirror from Perugia with bone handle, c.300 BC, depicting Pherśe, Menerva, Turms and the head of Medusa. Diam. c.16 cm (BM Br 620, 1888.11–10.1).

probably as Herakles Melqart, the Phoenician hero. He is shown on numerous mirrors, including an example in the British Museum's collection, dating from about 450–425 BC, accompanied by his divine patron and frequent companion, the goddess Menerva (this is the Archaic, unsyncopated form of her name; the Latin form of her name is Minerva). Menerva also appears on a mirror (about 300 BC) with another protégé, Pherśe (Perseus). Also shown is Turms, the god Hermes, who has lent Pherśe the cap of invisibility, here shown hanging down his back. All three gaze at the reflected image – appropriate for a mirror – of the decapitated Medusa, whose head Menerva holds up. Here, as elsewhere, the names are fitted into the spaces left blank by the design's composition. The direction of the writing follows the personages labelled: Pherse's and Menerva's names run left to right, starting from their images; Turms' starts near his head, on the right, and runs leftward.

On an ambitious mirror from Bolsena, the characters in the central scene are identified by inscriptions around the outer margins (a feature typical of a later series of mirrors). Menrva is shown in full regalia – crested, flowing-maned helmet, Gorgon-headed aegis, and spear: yet her role is that of a *kourotrophos,* the Greek word for a deity holding a

349

15 Bronze mirror from Bolsena,
c.300 BC, with Menrva and other
divinities, and three Mariś babies.
Diam. *c*.18 cm (BM Br 618,
1868.6–6.1; *CIE* 10840).

child. With her left hand she holds or pulls a child, Mariś Husrnana, out of a volute
krater. Next to her stands Turan, the goddess of love. She is not naked, as often, but
tightly wrapped in a handsomely bordered mantle which she holds up to her mouth so
that only her upper face is seen. (She is dressed in a similar manner on a mirror showing
Helen and Menelaos, and may represent a goddess of marriage.) Laran (the 'L' is ob-
literated), hand on spear, watches the scene. Two side figures, Turms (Hermes) on the
left and the female Amamtunia, hold two other children: Mariś Isminthians (on Turms'
knee) and Mariś Halna (on Amamtunia's left arm).

On another mirror, from Chiusi, with a similar scene, Menrva has bared her breast as
though to nurse a child and holds Mariś Husrnana with both hands. Turan helps her,
while Leinth (not Turms) holds another baby on his left knee. An unidentified fourth
figure has the pose, *chlamys* and spear of Laran on the Bolsena mirror. Both mirrors, and
a Praenestine cista or toilet box, showing Menrva helping an adult Mariś who is rising
out of a huge jar, represent indigenous scenes. Mariś is not Mars, but a local divinity
who, according to one interpretation, lived for the considerable period of 130 years, and
had three lives. The scene on the Bolsena mirror, in connection with the others on which
he appears, has been interpreted as showing Mariś' birth, life and death. There is no
general scholarly agreement, but a number of interesting possibilities are worth con-

16 Bronze mirror from Chiusi, late
4th century BC, with Fufluns, his
wife Areatha, his mother Semla and
a satyr. Diam. *c.*21 cm (BM Br 630,
1847.11–1.21).

sideration. Husrnana, perhaps connected with *husiur,* 'children' (with a double suffix,
-na-na) may refer to Mariś birth as the 'baby boy'. Various possible connections have
been suggested for *halna,* an epithet which would refer to the living, or mature Mariś.
Finally, Mariś Isminthians, whose epithet seems related to that of Apollo Smintheus,
would represent Mariś' encounter with death: the baby is held by Turms, as Hermes or
Mercury Psychopompus, guide of souls to the Underworld, on the Bolsena mirror.
Leinth, whose name is connected to *lein,* 'death', holds Mariś on the other mirror. The
three babies might be the children of Menrva and Hercle.

Fufluns (Dionysos, Bacchus, Liber) was an important Etruscan divinity, whose name
appears on the Piacenza liver. On a handsome mirror of the late fourth century BC, a 16
young Fufluns is shown with his partner Areatha (Ariadne). He holds a swan-headed
lyre. The divine couple, formed, as often in Etruscan art, of an older woman and a young
man, is flanked by Fufluns' mother Semla (Semele) and a Dionysiac reveler, a pug-nosed,
animal-eared satyr named Sime, 'snub-nosed'. The lush, stylised trumpet flowers of the
border betray an influence from the south, possibly from Apulian vases.

17 Bronze mirror with toilet scene,
late 4th century BC. Diam. 20 cm
(BM Br 626, 1865.1–3.39).

Helen, not surprisingly (given her legendary reputation for beauty), was a favourite subject for Etruscan mirror-makers and often appears in toilet and adornment scenes. One mirror, dating from the fourth century BC (all the figures are still dressed in heavy drapery rather than appearing in the graceful nudity preferred in the Hellenistic period), shows Malavisch dressing. Malavisch may be an Etruscan name or epithet for Helen, meaning something akin to 'the one adorned' and related to *malstria* and *malena,* both meaning 'mirror'. Assisting her are four female figures, depicted in the solemn, majestic style of the fourth century: Turan, Munthuch, Zipu and Hinthial. These names, too, have been connected with adornment scenes. *Hinthial,* 'ghost', 'shade', 'reflection', one of the most intriguing and important words in Etruscan, may, however, refer to the 'shade of Helen'. The fourth-century BC Tomb of Orcus in Tarquinia represents the shades, *hinthial*, of Teriasals (Teiresias) and [Ach]memrun (Agamemnon), and a contemporary Etruscan vase shows the *hinthial* of two Amazons, Turmuca (perhaps Aturmuca, Andromache) and Pentasila (Penthesilea).

Belief in the importance of divination and omens played an important role in Etruscan

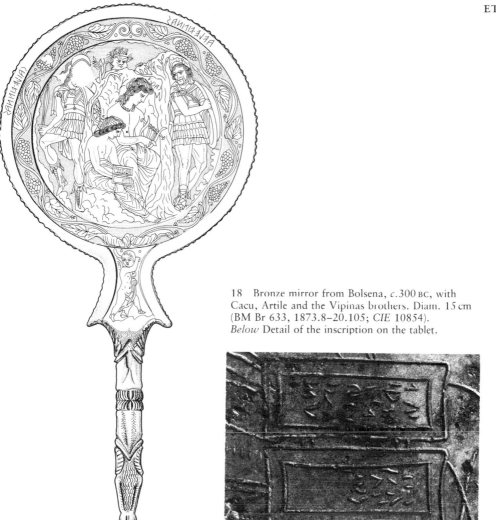

18 Bronze mirror from Bolsena, c.300 BC, with Cacu, Artile and the Vipinas brothers. Diam. 15 cm (BM Br 633, 1873.8–20.105; *CIE* 10854). *Below* Detail of the inscription on the tablet.

tradition and may lie behind another remarkable mirror in the British Museum. Like the Mariś mirror, it comes from the Bolsena region. This third-century mirror is justly *18* known as an example of Etruscan historical art, for it depicts a local myth or legend and records names known to us from Roman historical tradition. Two youths are seated in a sylvan landscape, indicated by the background as well as by the head of a satyr. Cacu plays a lyre; Artile reads from a hinged diptych, on which are inscribed some letters, impossible to decipher. Cacu, the Latin Cacus, is here a seer; thus his Apollo-like appearance. Artile, a boy, seems to be reading a prophecy. Two figures approach in a stealthy manner; their names, inscribed on the margin of the mirror, reveal that they are the brothers Caile Vipinas and Aule Vipinas, known to the Romans as Caeles and Aulus Vibenna. Roman historians place the story of Caeles Vibenna – whose name was remembered in the Caelian Hill in Rome – in the time of the Tarquins, the late sixth century BC.

A homogeneous group of later mirrors, dating from the Hellenistic period (third

19   *Left*   Bronze mirror showing the birth of Menrva from the head of Tinia, 3rd century BC. Diam. *c.*16 cm, H. 31.5 cm (BM Br 696, 1856.12–13.4; *CII* 2471 *bis*).

20   Bronze mirror from Cerveteri, 3rd century BC, with four figures from the story of the Trojan War: Menle (Menelaos), Uthste (Odysseus), Clutmsta (Clytemnestra), Palmithe, written Talmithe (Palamedes). Diam. *c.*14.5 cm, H.28 cm (BM Br 714, 1865.7–12.3).

century BC) are characterised by a number of features: (1) a border decoration in the form of a spiky garland, often fastened at the top, bottom and side, sometimes ending in two pine cones; (2) the frequent presence of the word *śuthina* scratched on the reflecting surface; (3) the use of the outer, plain border as a field for the inscriptions identifying the characters represented; (4) a cast handle terminating in a ram's head; (5) hair-styles shown as neatly arranged concentric circles; and (6) a standard size, usually 13–14 cm in diameter. They were evidently made in the same workshop, perhaps at Orvieto. Other features, such as the presence of the god Laran or 'conversation groups' of four gracefully lounging figures, characterise some, though not all, mirrors in this group.

The British Museum has several of these 'Spiky Garland' mirrors. One shows the birth of Menrva from the head of her father Tinia (Zeus, Jupiter), in the presence of four divinities: Laran, Thalna (a nymph), Uni (Tinia's wife) and Maris Tiusta, bearded like Tinia. The circumstances are unlike any we know of from Greek myth: Uni and Thalna assist Tinia; but the presence of a martial god, Laran, perhaps identified with Mars, and of the Italic god Maris, seem to refer to local stories unknown to us from literature.

Two other Spiky Garland mirrors show characters from the Trojan War. In one, a 'conversation group' of four figures, are included two seated male figures on the sides, labelled Talmithe, for Palmithe (Palamedes, here written with a *t* instead of a *p*), and Menle. In the centre stand Clutmsta, Clytemnestra (perhaps written *clupmsta,* with a *p* instead of a *t*) and Uthste, Odysseus (the *delta,* Δ, of the Greek is reproduced by O, *theta*). What story did the artist or craftsman have in mind when he showed Clytemnestra, Odysseus, Menelaos and Palamedes together? There were certainly Etruscan versions of Greek myths, and more versions of 'Trojan' stories than we perhaps know of. Menle and Talmithe wear Phrygian hats usually reserved for Easterners, Trojans, or the divine twins Castur and Pultuce (Castor and Pollux). On this inexpensive mirror, we may have stock figures from a standard repertoire of models, labelled with names picked at will. Books of such models may have been available in workshops of the Hellenistic period, when mirrors and relief-decorated funerary urns were practically mass-produced.

The second mirror represents an animated scene perhaps harking back to a theatrical performance. Troilos, the youngest of Priam's fifty sons, was killed and decapitated by a bloodthirsty Achilles, Achle, shown in the centre of the mirror with fellow-warrior Evas (Ajax). Achilles rests his knee on an altar after savagely murdering the boy. On the border of the altar is engraved Troilos' name, Truil(e), beside which, we realise with a shock, is the huge cadaver of the horse on which Troilos rode down from Priam's high place, into the ambush of Achilles. To the right stands Echtur, Achilles' mortal enemy, Hector (who would die later by Achilles' hand). The winged female demon on the left, Vanth, is a purely Etruscan divinity.

21   Bronze mirror with the death of Truile (Troilos), 3rd century BC. Diam. *c.*16 cm, H. 31 cm (BM Br 625, 1873.8–20.108; *CIE* 10862).

22 Hercle resting, *c.*400 BC. H.1.6 cm (BM Gem 769, 1814.7–4.1299).

23 Herkle and Kukne, 5th century BC. 15 × 11 mm (BM Gem 621, 1867.5–7.335).

24 Achle in retirement, 500–400 BC, 14 × 11 mm (BM Gem 632, 1867.5–7.414).

Engraved gems

One of the most characteristic and beautiful Etruscan gems in the British Museum, perhaps from Chiusi, bears a design with the stooped figure of Hercle (Hercules) sitting on a rock. Beside him is the lion skin. The letters of his name follow the curve of his arm, head and shoulder, filling in the blank space in a pleasing design. Hercules is by far the most popular figure on Etruscan gems. His name appears spelled either Hercle, as here, or Herkle, as on a remarkable late Archaic gem, showing him in action, lunging against his enemy Kukne or Cycnus. Here the name, written almost vertically, nicely fills the space behind the hero's back and muscular thighs, in the Archaic style.

Also very popular was Achilles, whose name appears variously as Achale, Achele, Achile, or in its syncopated form, Achle, as on a cornelian scarab from Tarquinia. The scene reminds us of his retirement from battle in the *Iliad*.

The Trojans occupied a special place in Etruscan myth (the later Romans, of course, thought of Aeneas as their founder). So it is not surprising to find a sardonyx gem in the Classical style representing the Trojan hero Paris as an archer, as he is described by Homer. Here again, the widely spaced letters of his name fill the empty spaces, following the course of the gem's border, with its characteristic dot pattern.

The craftsman Taitle, or Daedalus, appears three times on Etruscan jewellery of the fifth century BC: twice on gems and once on a golden *bulla*, where he is shown along with his son, Vikare (Icarus), and with his saw and adze. The British Museum gem illustrates their tragic voyage. Taitle's name is neatly written in a horizontal line above the hooked signs which represent the waves of the sea over which he soars.

Easun (Jason) is shown embarking on the ship *Argo,* whose furnishings or fittings fill the space all around the figure. The letters of his name are fitted in on either side of his legs and along the side of the cornelian bezel. The relatively free field of another gem, in contrast, is filled with the bold lettering of the Etruscan name given to a bearded, powerful, striding male figure: Tarchnas. He holds jumping weights, and so may be an athlete. Perhaps, however, this personal name, so common in Etruria, is the name of the owner.

25 Paris the archer, late 5th century BC. H.1.5 cm (BM Gem 631, 1772.3–15.475).

26 Taitle flying over the sea, 450–400 BC. H.*c.*1.6 cm (BM Gem 663, 1772.3–15.366).

27 Easun by his ship, late 5th century BC. 16 × 12 mm (BM Gem 669, 1872.6–4.1166).

28 Tarchnas as athlete, with jumping weights, 500–470 BC. 13 × 10 mm (BM Gem 643, 1849.6–23.5).

Vases

The Etruscans imported huge quantities of Greek vases and adopted the Greek names for them, as surviving inscriptions show. A *kylix* will bear an inscription saying, *mi chulichna (culichna, or culchna)*, 'I am the culichna', or *kylix*. Another cup says: *mi qutun karkanas*, 'I am the *kothon* of Karkana'. An oil jar is a *lechtumuza*, 'little *lekythos*', or *aska eleivana*, 'leather container (*aska*) for oil (*eleivana*)'. Etruscan *thina* derives from Greek *dinos*, a type of bowl; *ulpaia* from Greek *olpe*; *pruchum* from Greek *prochous*. Other names of vases are native Etruscan: *thafna, zavena*, the latter an indigenous Etruscan shape, the ancestor of the Greek *kantharos*.

29 Perfume vase of Velthur Hathiśna, in the form of a lion. From Veii, 7th century BC. H.6.5 cm (BM Terracotta 1683, 1852.1–12.8; CII 2561).

An early (seventh to sixth century BC) impasto (rough terracotta) perfume vase in the form of a reclining (couchant) lion, about 10 cm long, was found at Veii and is now in the British Museum. Below the left ear runs the vertical inscription:

velthur hathi {nas

The owner's name is given in the genitive case: '(I am the vase [or, 'I am the possession']) of Velthur Hathiśna'. Here the genitive ending *-s* is added only to the last name, Hathiśna. The form of the internal *s*, a five-bar ({) sigma, instead of the more usual three-bar sigma, testifies to its early date. The owner of the vase has a typically Etruscan name. Velthur is a common first name, while Hathiśna has the characteristically Etruscan ending in *-na*, as in Porsenna, Rasna, Karkana, Tarchna (Tarquin), etc. In small or more primitive societies an individual was easily identified by his or her first name, with the simple addition of the father's name, or patronymic. As society became more complex and cities developed, people needed a second name: a gentilicial, or family name (this name often developed from an original patronymic, like O'Connor or McDonald). So the appearance of the family (*gens*) name, recognisable by its adjectival form, with a *-na* ending, is a mark of the newly urbanised Etruscan society.

Another very early inscription is on a bucchero *kantharos*, or two-handled drinking cup. In the seventh and sixth centuries BC, such bucchero cups were exported from Etruria all over the Mediterranean, from Corinth to Carthage and beyond. The shape, typical of Etruria, was adopted by the Greeks, who represented it in the hand of the wine

30 Bucchero *kantharos* (drinking cup) of Avile Repesuna, *c*.600 BC. H. *c*.12 cm (BM 1953.4–26.1; *TLE* 765).

god Dionysos himself. The words, scratched on the smooth buffed black surface, again indicate ownership. The object speaks in the first person,

mi repesunas aviles 'I [am] of Repesuna Avile', that is, 'I belong to Avile Repesuna'.

The verb 'to be' (*am*) can be omitted, as in Greek and Latin and in Indo-European languages generally. The ending *-s* indicates the genitive case, which also functions as a dative. *Avile* is a common first name; it can sometimes, as here, follow the name of the *gens*, or family name. *Repesuna* again has the characteristic Etruscan ending *-na*.

Another drinking vessel, a *rhyton* in the shape of a mule's head, dating from the fifth century BC, also has connections with the drinking party or *symposium*, a Greek social function which the Etruscans adopted as a sign of civilisation. A *rhyton*, a kind of party cup or drinking horn, does not have a flat base, so it could not be put down until emptied. Scholars are divided as to whether the craftsman who made this example was Greek or Etruscan. There is no doubt about the inscription, however. It is Etruscan:

fuflunl pachies velclthi 'of [to] Fufluns Bacchus, at Vulci'.

The god to whom the cup was dedicated is the Etruscan Fufluns, known from numerous mirrors as well as two gold *bullae* and the Piacenza liver. Here, his name is written

31 *Rhyton* (drinking horn) in the shape of a mule's head, dedicated to Fufluns Bacchus. From Vulci, 5th century BC. H.19.25 cm (BM Vase F489, 1837.6–9.79; *TLE* 336). *Below* Detail of the inscription on the handle.

without the final -s, and with the genitive -l. *Pachies* is the Etruscan transcription of the Greek name Baccheios, a cultic epithet of the Greek Dionysos. This double name has been compared to the double name of Uni Astre in the Pyrgi tablet, where it is likewise found in the genitive, *unial astres* (both -al and -s are genitive forms). Two other fifth-century BC vase inscriptions may document the growing influence of the cult of Dionysos, or Bacchus (also known as Liber in Italy), and his identification with the local god Fufluns. Much later, in the second century, we find reference to the cult of a god Pacha (Fufluns on the Piacenza liver) on three sarcophagi. On that of Laris Pulena, they are mentioned together. On another epitaph, Lars Statlane is said to be *maru* (a magistrate) of Catha and Pacha (*cathas pachanac:* the ending -c, similar to the Latin enclitic -*que*, means 'and'). Most interesting is the locative *velclthi*, 'at Vulci' (-*thi* is the sign of the locative) appearing on all three inscriptions. It has been convincingly compared to other locatives of cities, *tarchnalthi* (*TLE* 131, 174), 'at Tarquinia', and *velsnalthi* (*TLE* 902), 'at Volsinii'.

A later vase has the letters scratched into its black glaze so that they show up by contrast in the light pink of the clay beneath. Carefully and boldly incised all around the widest part of the pot, they form an effective decoration of its plain black-glazed surface and highlight its shape. To be noted are the extremely long stroke used to render the *i* of *Fastis* at the centre of the inscription, and the two dots used to separate the words. The vase is quite tall (20 cm) and comes from Arezzo. This handsome inscription is easy to read:

> *larthia levei fastis aneinal sec*
> 'Larthia Levei, of Fasti Aneina, the daughter', that is, 'Larthia Levei, daughter of Fasti Aneina'.

32 'Black-glaze' vase of Larthia Levei, from Arezzo, 3rd century BC. H.20 cm (BM 1946.10–12.1; *CIE* 4639).

Larthia's names have the typical feminine endings in -*a* and -*i* in the nominative form. She is identified as the daughter of Fasti Aneina, as we see from the genitive endings -*s* and -*l*. This is an unusual inscription, even in Etruria where women had more independence than in Greece or Rome, but were normally identified by reference to their fathers (as daughter, *sec*) or husbands (as wife, *puia*).

Bronze tableware

Several groups of inscribed bronze tableware once buried with their wealthy owners can now be studied in the British Museum. They were all made around 300 BC, but may have been buried later as heirlooms. Such wine and banqueting services consisted of pitchers, bowls, buckets, strainers and ladles, for use at the feasts, banquets and *symposia* of Etruscan nobles. When the owners died, some of these objects were inscribed with their names, followed by the usual formula *śuthina,* signifying that they were dedicated to their graves, for their use in the Underworld. Often objects were simply marked *śuthina.*

A fragmentary bronze mirror and nine vases remain from a tomb group originally consisting of fourteen bronze serving pieces, found in 1865 at Castel Giorgio near Orvieto. The tomb belonged to a man, Larth Metie, and a woman, indicated by the presence of the mirror. Two wine jugs and three buckets with handles are inscribed (on one some of the letters are corroded). One of the buckets, or *situlae,* is particularly beautiful, decorated with relief heads of Menrva and of a satyr, whose large open mouth (with built-in strainer) was the spout, inscribed:

33

larth meties śuthina, 'Of Larth Metie, for the tomb'.

The genitive ending *-s* occurs only on the last name.

33 Bronze situla and wine jug from near Orvieto, part of the tomb group of Larth Metie, late 4th century BC. H.29.5 cm (BM Br 652–3, 1873.8–20.202 and 204; *TLE* 216, *CIE* 10876, 78).

A large bronze wine and banqueting service from nearby Bolsena is divided between the British Museum and the Museo Gregoriano in the Vatican. The two pieces in the British Museum are inscribed with the owner's name:

34

larisal havrenieś śuthina, 'Of Laris [Lars] Havrenie, for the tomb'.

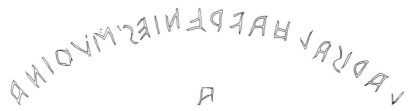

34 Inscription from a bronze wine crater, part of Laris Havrenie's tomb group from Bolsena, 350–300 BC (BM Br 651, cf. 655, 1868.6–6.5, cf.2; *TLE* 210, *CIE* 10830–31).

Of note are the two genitive endings *-al* and *-ś*. One piece has the letter *A* below the inscription: it is hard to tell what it stood for.

Part of another tomb group from Bolsena is also in the British Museum. The handsome bronze grave furnishings were dedicated to a woman: they included the important mirror showing the ambush of the Vipinas brothers. An incense burner (*thymiaterion*) is decorated with figures of a boy, a cat catching a bird, a rooster, and – on the basin – four birds. The inscription names the tomb's owner,

thania lucini śuthina, 'Of Thania Lucini, for the tomb'.

The name in the nominative with *śuthina* is unusual.

Sarcophagi and ash urns

Names of Etruscan men and women also occur on epitaphs, coffins and ash urns once in family tombs. An impressive terracotta sarcophagus from Chiusi (approx. 180 × 120 cm) dates from the Hellenistic period, about 150 BC. Reclining on the lid, as if on a comfortable banqueting couch, is an elegantly dressed, much bejewelled lady. Her epi- taph is carved in a large 'classical' script on the lower edge of the casket:

seianti hanunia tlesnasa

The first letter of the family name (Hanunia), because of its rounded form ⊖, looks like a *theta;* it is in fact a ⊟. The existence of six other inscriptions naming *velia seianti hanunia* or *senti hanunia* (without a first name), all from Chiusi and vicinity, make it clear that this was the lady's family name. The skeleton, still inside the sarcophagus, was analysed in 1989, revealing that the deceased woman was at least 80 years old.

Much more characteristic of Chiusi than such large, expensive sarcophagi are the cheaper stone or terracotta ash urns for cremation burials. One in the British Museum gives a good idea of the brightly coloured relief decoration which once ornamented them.

35 Terracotta sarcophagus of Seianti Hanunia Tlesnasa, from Chiusi, *c.*150 BC. H.122 cm, L.183 cm (Terracotta D786, 1887.4–2.1; *CIE* 1454).

The casket shows a battle between warriors. The figure of the deceased, reclining as usual on the lid, holds a patera with which to offer a libation to the gods. He wears a costume appropriate for a high rank in a Roman context: the vertical purple stripe of his *chiton* or tunic and deep red border of the toga, whose rounded edge is displayed just below the waist, and a gold ring, worn only by someone with the rank of knight or higher.

The casket bears an epitaph painted in brown along the upper border:

thana ancarui thelesa, 'Thana Ancarui Thelesa'.

The lower part of the ᛈ is erased; earlier scholars read the name as 'Ancapui,' ΑΗᏟΑᒋVΙ. But while the family name 'Ancapui' does not occur, the name 'Ancarui' recurs several times at Chiusi and Tarquinia. Although the figure on the lid is male, the name on the casket is that of a woman. Lids and caskets were often exchanged between the time of their discovery and their sale and final placement in museums. Perhaps, however, the heirs originally purchased an urn which was readily available, though it represented a man rather than a woman, and had it inscribed with the name of the deceased.

A sarcophagus of a member of the Vipinana family, from near Tuscania and now in the

36   British Museum, has the following inscription:

(1)   (2)   (3)   (4)   (5)   (6) (7)   (8)
vipinans śethre velthur[u]s meclasial thanchvilu avils cis cealchs

'Vipinans Sethre, [son of] Velthur [and of the daughter of] Meclas, Thanchvilu, [lived] years three-and-thirty.'

36   Stone sarcophagus of Sethre Vipinans from Tuscania, with the image of the deceased reclining on the lid. Hellanistic. H.60 cm, L.201 cm, W.64 cm (BM D31–2, 1838.6–8.4; *TLE* 180, *CIE* 5702). Below: Drawing of inscription.

We have here (1) the family name, Vipinans; (2) the first name, Sethre; (3) the patronymic, Velthur; the matronymic, including (4) the mother's family name, Meclasia, and (5) the mother's first name, Thanchvilu.

The word *avil* ('year') occurs more than a hundred times in funerary inscriptions. It is found with the single stem (*avil*) when used with the verbs *svalce* or *svalthas* ('to live'). When used with *lupu* ('dead'), we find *avils,* perhaps a dative of 'time when'. Evidently *avil* indicates a continuous action, 'he lived for X years ...', while *avils* expresses a precise action or occurrence, 'he died in such-and-such a year'. The following two inscriptions illustrate the difference:

> *velthur larisal clan cuclnial thanchvilus lupu avils XXV*
> 'Velthur, the son of Laris [and of] Thanchvil Cuclni, died at 25 years' (on a sarcophagus from Tarquinia).

> *atnas vel larthal clan svalce avil ↑XIII zi[la]th maruchva tarils cepta phechucu*
> 'Atnas Vel, son of Larth, lived years 63, [he was] *zilath maruchva* (a magistrate) ...' 37
> (the translation of *tarils cepta phechucu* is uncertain).

This inscription is on a sarcophagus from near Tuscania.

37 Stone (*nenfro*) sarcophagus of Vel Atna, with relief decoration showing a procession of magistrates. From Tuscania, *c.*250–200 BC. H.62 cm, L.213 cm, W.64 cm (BM D26, 1838.6–8.24; *TLE* 194, *CIE* 5755). Below: Drawing of inscription.

Another inscription in the British Museum, on an urn from Volterra, illustrates a different way of expressing age at death (for abbreviations of names, see Appendix 1):

> *ls. cala. ls. ril. ↑XX*
> 'Lars Cala, son of Lars, at the age of LXX', i.e. 'Lars Cala, son of Lars, [died] at the age of 70 years.'

Votive figures

Among the rare Etruscan objects found in non-funerary contexts are votive gifts. The inscriptions on these objects document the offerings people made to the gods, giving us a glimpse into their public and private religion, the divinities they worshipped and the gifts considered appropriate. Sometimes ambitious votive offerings, like the Chimaera of Arezzo, may have been made by a whole community. Inscribed on these gifts were the names of the individuals offering them and the names of the divinities to whom they were dedicated as a form of worship or cult. These were sometimes identified with Greek gods and therefore bear the names of Artemis (Aritimi), Minerva (Menrva), etc.; but in fact these gifts were deposited in the sanctuaries of local divinities. Many votive objects – where we know their actual provenance – come from the central Etruscan area around Lake Bolsena: Bolsena, Chiusi, Perugia, etc. This was a region of sanctuaries: as we have seen, the longest ritual inscriptions come from there.

From sanctuaries in Southern Etruria (Veii, Cerveteri, Pyrgi, Gravisca), Latium and Campania (Lavinium, Capua, Paestum), Magna Graecia and Sicily, come thousands of terracotta votive figures – models of eyes, uteri, breasts, genitals, feet and hands – as well as images of *kourotrophoi* (mothers and children) and other inexpensive votive figures asking favours or giving thanks for the health and protection of the faithful or for the birth and well-being of children. Such terracotta votive offerings came from a poorer class of people and were not identified with names. In contrast, more expensive gifts, bronze statuettes, incense burners, etc., proudly record the names of the rich donor and the divinity to whom the gift was offered. Two handsome bronze statuettes in the British Museum, in the late Classical style (about 400–350 BC) bear such inscriptions. Both are solid cast, both represent youths with short hair and both are dedicated to the god Selvans (Silvanus). One youth wears a mantle with rounded borders – the Etruscan *tebenna*, 38

38   Bronze statuette of a youth wearing a short mantle, dedicated to the god Selvans, 400–350 BC. H.16.2 cm (BM Br 678, 1824.4–97.3; *TLE 559, CIE 2403*).

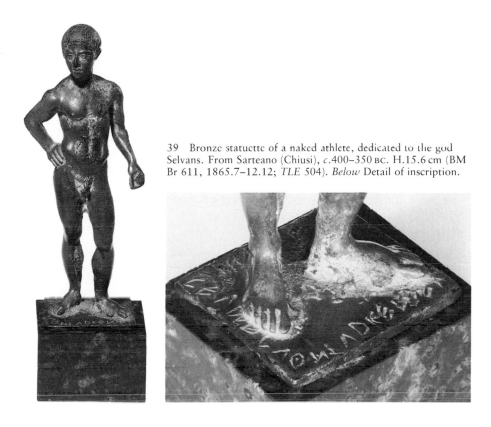

39 Bronze statuette of a naked athlete, dedicated to the god Selvans. From Sarteano (Chiusi), c.400–350 BC. H.15.6 cm (BM Br 611, 1865.7–12.12; *TLE* 504). *Below* Detail of inscription.

antecedent of the Roman toga. On the mantle, along the right leg, runs the inscription:

ecn turce larthi lethanei alpnu selvansl canzate
'This gave Larthi Lethanei as a gift to Selvans Canzate.'

Ecn, 'this', is the accusative of *eca, ika. Turce*, 'gave, dedicated', is the later (neo-Etruscan) form of the Archaic *turuce. Ecn turce* is the standard formula for the beginning of votive inscriptions in neo-Etruscan. *Alpnu* here seems to function as the direct object of *turce* (though scholars usually translate the word as 'gladly, willingly'). The donor was a woman: Larthi Lethanei. *Canzate,* an unknown word, seems to be a epithet of Selvans, perhaps referring to a particular region or cult-centre where he was worshipped.

The other bronze statuette, from Sarteano, near Chiusi, represents a naked youth in the Greek manner. The *kouros,* or handsome naked athlete, belongs to a Greek tradition beginning perhaps as early as 700 BC. Etruscans followed the artistic tradition, and at times the athletic custom as well. The dedication is incised into the flat rectangular base, cast in one piece with the statuette:

vel śapu th/n turke śel/van/ś[. . .]ran, or, more probably: *selvanś [. . .]ran)*
'Vel Sapu this gave to Selvans [. . .]ran.'

Thn is a variant of *ecn*, 'this'. This statuette was dedicated by a man, Vel Sapu; the epithet of Selvans ([. . .]*ran*) is unfortunately illegible. Both inscriptions seem to have Selvans in the genitive, but formed in different ways. One has the genitive suffix -*l*; in the other, nothing is added to the -*s* of the nominative to form the genitive -*ś* ending.

The importance of the god Selvans in Etruria is proved by the appearance of his name on the Piacenza liver (twice). It also appears on a significant group of ten dedications, eight of which are on bronze statuettes. One (from Tarquinia, now in the Vatican Museum) represents a baby wearing a good-luck charm, or *bulla*. The others, including two in the British Museum, show young men, either bare-chested with low-slung cloaks or nude. Three were dedicated by women (Larthi Lethanei, Velusa [. . .]ans, and Ramtha Uftatavi, the latter perhaps meant to be Uftavi: compare Latin Octavius).

One of these statuettes, in a private collection, is noteworthy for its unique inscription. Incised in vertical lines, it is scratched into the surface, starting from the right underarm. The words are divided by two dots:

> *ecn: turce: avle: havrnas: tuthina: apana: selvansl: tularis*
> 'This gave Aule Havrna, a votive gift (?), on behalf of his father, to Selvans of the Boundaries.'

Avle is the neo-Etruscan form of the Archaic Avile. In a parallel development, the form *Havrna* is related to the name Havrenie on the bronze wine service from Bolsena. The statuette also probably comes from Bolsena, where Havrenie (Havrna) was evidently an important name. *Apana*, 'paternal', agrees with a recently discovered inscription which refers to *apa atic*, 'father (*apa*) and mother (*ati*)'. The translation of *tuthina* here poses a problem; according to one scholar it means 'votive object'. But on the mantle of the famous life-size bronze Orator ('Arringatore') in Florence it has been translated as 'people'.

Coins

40 Etruscan coins, with their legends and symbols, give us a glimpse into another aspect of the life of these ancient and wealthy cities. The legends, like the designs, are in relief.

On the coin in Fig. 40b, *pupluna* identifies the city of origin as Populonia, whose coins have come down to us in great numbers. Also known as Fufluna, Pupluna is the city of Fufluns (just as Athens is the city of Athena). Many coins come from Volsinii (Velznani, abbreviated Velz): a unique gold piece is in the British Museum. Volsinii was so wealthy that when the Romans sacked it they carried off two thousand bronze statues.

The legend *thezl*, or *thezi*, on some beautiful silver coins, cannot be related to any city we know.

We also find the following marks of value on Etruscan coins.

)K = 100		)||X = 12½	
↑ = 50		X = 10	
XXX = 30		∧ = 5	
∧XX = 25		<|| = 2	
XX = 20		| = 1	

a. Silver stater of Thezle, uncertain mint, 4th century BC. Unique. 9.26 g. Obverse: three-quarter head of bull; around it, the inscription *thezle*. Reverse: swimming hippocamp (BM PCG III.C3.901315–4; *TLE* 786).

b. Bronze *sextans* of Populonia, 3rd century BC. 12.4 g. Obverse: head of Herakles. Reverse: bow, arrow and club with inscription below, *pupluna*; between the arrow and the club a mark of value: two pellets (BMC Populonia, Appendix 3; *TLE* 789).

c. Gold stater of Volsinii, *c*.300 BC. Unique. 4.67 g. Obverse: laureate young male head; below, on either side, a mark of value: X X. Reverse: a bull, with a dove flying above and a star; below, the inscription *Velznani* (BM PCG III.C2, 1848.8–19.1).

40 Silver, bronze and gold coins, inscribed Thezle, Pupluna, Velznani.

5

Etruscan Inscriptions as Historical Evidence

Inscriptions give evidence, direct and indirect, about Etruscan history, illuminating events and personages otherwise known to us only through the accounts of Greek and Roman authors. They testify to cultural, commercial and political contacts; and provide evidence about Etruscan society, religion, customs, magistracies and, through the mythological names, both local and those adapted from the Greeks, faint glimpses of the possible subjects of Etruscan literature and drama.

The gold tablets from Pyrgi record, around 500 BC, an historical event – the dedication of a cult place by Thefarie Velianas, king of Caere, to Phoenician Astarte (Ishtar, identified with Uni: Roman Juno) – and are consistent with the close alliance between Etruscans and Carthaginians mentioned by Aristotle in the fourth century. Just the names bring us closer to this historical past: Thefarie Velianas' first name would have been Tiberius in Latin. The ancient name of one of Caere's ports was Punicum, no doubt because of the intense traffic which at one time took place with Phoenician Carthage, whose citizens the Romans called Poeni. At the important sanctuary of Gravisca, the port city of Tarquinia, inhabited by Greeks from 600 to about 480 BC, gifts were offered and 'signed' by Eudemos (from Athens?); Paktyes, probably a Lydian; Ombrikos, perhaps a Hellenised Umbrian; and, most famous of all, Sostratos of Aegina, who dedicated a marble anchor to Apollo. This Sostratos was probably the same as the merchant mentioned by Herodotus (IV: 152) as trading with Tartessos in Spain.

Other names from inscriptions ring a bell that sounds across the centuries. The name of Hannibal, Rome's great enemy, appears on the epitaph of a certain Felsnas, son of Larth Lethe, who was buried at Tarquinia aged 106 years, and claimed to have fought at Capua during the war with Hannibal (*hanipaluscle*) at the end of the third century BC.

That the Vipinas brothers – pictured on an Etruscan mirror as well as in the wall-paintings of the François Tomb from Vulci, and mentioned in Roman traditions referring to the legendary period of their history in the sixth century BC – were real people is confirmed by a dedication scratched on bucchero vases of the same century from Veii: *avile vipiiennas*, Aulus Vipinas. The wall-paintings of the fourth-century François Tomb also record the names of other characters from Roman history: not only Aule and Caile Vipinas, but also Macstrna (Latin Mastarna, perhaps a title: *magister*?), elsewhere identified as Servius Tullius, Tarquin's heir and king of Rome, and Cneve Tarchunies Rumach, better known to us as Tarquin of Rome. In this 'historical' painting the killing of Tarquin accompanies a surprise attack on Etruscan allies of Rome by a group of heroes from Vulci. The victims came from Volsinii (*velznach*), Sovana (*sveamach*), Rome (*rumach*), and perhaps Falerii.

We have seen that most of the longest Etruscan texts which survive are religious or ritual in character: the Zagreb mummy wrappings, the Capua tile, the lead strip from Santa Marinella, the lead sheet from Magliano and the bronze model of a sheep's liver from Piacenza. This situation confirms the ancients' view of the Etruscans as a deeply religious people. They also wrote books on religion, recorded by Roman writers, which have not survived or been passed on through later copying.

We owe our knowledge of the Etruscans' religious reputation in antiquity to the fact that the Romans admired and adopted many Etruscan rites, rituals and traditions. They called in Etruscan *haruspices* (priests specialised in divination), and for a while young Roman aristocrats were sent to Etruria, as they were later sent to Athens, to complete their education (Livy IX. 36). These young aristocrats evidently learned in Etruria the art of reading signs and omens, essential for generals, who had to observe such signs and prudently interrogate the gods about their intentions before setting off on a campaign.

In the ancient Mediterranean, in Italy, in Rome and the Etruscan cities, where many gods held court, it was of the utmost importance to know precisely which god was involved in a particular affair. The divisions marked on the Piacenza liver reflected the regions of the sky and their boundaries, making it possible for the faithful to address their prayers, and their gifts, to the right god. Only thus could religious rites and prayers be effective. Ritual calendars like that on the Zagreb mummy wrappings specified which sacrifices and offerings were to be made to a particular god on a specific day. Votive offerings bore the name of the donor and that of the divinity as a reminder to the god.

Writing had a special significance then which it no longer has today: it was powerful magic. When you wrote down a name you acted on it, for good or bad. You gave it a force and a permanence far beyond that of the spoken word. A prayer, or a curse, was written down in order to make if efficacious, so that it would *work*. In the same way, centuries later, Scandinavian runes (themselves derived from Etruscan script) were incised on spears to ensure that they hit their mark.

Just as many inscriptions and public monuments in Athens, informing the people of even minor events and expenses, testify to the reality of fifth century democracy, so Etruscan epitaphs testify to the prestige of their noble families, while the religious inscriptions of the Etruscan cities testify to the importance of their religious rites and to their ideas of the importance of boundaries (*tular*) of space – regions of land and sky, places between the living and the dead – and of time, the *saecula*. These boundaries were marked in many ways. Epitaphs, or *elogia,* the praise of the dead, funeral ceremonies, memorial services: these all had a special importance because the Etruscans had a special regard for the family dead. This is borne out by the richly furnished tombs and the many representations of male and female figures which, once thought to be wholly divine or wholly human, are now better understood as representing images of ancestors – the 'heroised' dead. For an aristocratic family, the family tomb was a central symbol. So was the genealogy of the deceased, including the mother's family, and the visual reminder of their life, their marriage, their journey to the Underworld, the Greek mythology which bore witness to their culture. Later, when the 'middle class' family emerged, it adopted the symbols and insignia of the élite. The family tombs of Volterra, Perugia, Chiusi, Tarquinia and other cities were filled with ash chests and caskets bearing images of the deceased, epitaphs and representations of Greek myths. Even the cheapest burials – as, in Chiusi, terracotta *ollae* or vases containing the ashes of the dead – were painted or incised with the names of the deceased. When Pallottino called the Etruscans the 'People of the Book', he was calling attention to this ritual aspect of writing. 41

The number of surviving mirrors, their beauty and the interest of their scenes, often labelled with inscriptions, testify to the literacy, culture and wealth of the Etruscan women for whom they were made. The importance of women in religion is shown for example by the fact that three out of ten surviving dedications to the god Selvans (p. 366) were made by women (though it could be that Selvans was in fact more closely associated with women). From the very earliest periods women received burials as luxurious as those of men – we have seen several of these in the preceding pages – and in general were held in high esteem in aristocratic Etruscan society.

The importance of the woman's family is shown by the use of matronymics in many epitaphs. Yet Etruscan society was not matriarchal, as Bachofen believed (*Tanaquil,* 1870). Matronymics in fact occur less often than patronymics and are regularly placed after them. We do not even know the word for 'husband': we only know the name of the 'wife (*puia*) of so-and-so'; not 'so-and-so's husband'.

We know the names of many Etruscan magistracies and priesthoods which lasted as long as the Etruscan cities maintained their independence and their language. Prayers and magic spells in the Etruscan language survived beyond, into the Roman world, as exotic remnants. This was a world that spoke and wrote Latin and Greek, but on which the Etruscans had left their mark; and one which we cannot understand without taking into account what they have left behind, their monuments, their traditions and their inscriptions.

41   Red-figure crater from Vulci, *c*.350 BC, with Aivas (Ajax), despondent at his failure to win the arms of Achilles, committing suicide by impaling himself on his sword. His name is painted above, in white. H.39.75 cm (BM Vase F480, 1867.5–8.1328).

6
Oscan: The Agnone Tablet

The Italic branch of the Indo-European family of languages consists of Latin, Umbrian, the dialects of the central Italian mountain tribes – the Marsi, Marrucini, etc. – and Oscan. The Oscan language coincides with the territory inhabited by the Samnite tribes: inscriptions have been found in Samnium, Campania, Apulia, Lucania and Bruttium, but most come from Pompeii and Capua. The earliest are coin legends of about 400 BC; the latest, graffiti from the walls of Pompeii, probably dating from the early years of the first century BC. Over 200 inscriptions survive. Indeed, Oscan was not an unimportant dialect: after Etruscan, it was the chief language of central Italy, while Latin was limited to Rome and Latium.

Three alphabets were used: Oscan, Greek and Latin. The Oscan alphabet was usually written with finely traced letters. A reform of the writing system, in about 300 BC, added the letters ⊢ and ∨, transcribed as *í* and *ú*, to signify the long vowels. U was used – often but not always – for *o*. Characteristic is the A, ⊿ in its latest form. The *d* is written as R (the letter the Latins regularly used for the sound of *r*). There was thus an exchange of signs, since the sound of *r* was indicated by the letter ∩. Digamma (˥), pronounced like Latin *v* or English *w*), must have been semi-vocalic, since it often appears in diphthongs: for example, *thesavrum*, Latin *thesaurus*, Greek *thesaurós*. Z was pronounced (as in Etruscan) *t* + *s*. I was used to express an original *e*: *íst* = Latin *est*. The existence of the letter 8, pronounced *f*, was, in Oscan as in Umbrian, due to direct Etruscan influence. A Greek model, parallel to the Etruscan model, would account for the letters for *b*, *g* and *d* (B, G and R), which are absent or transformed in Etruscan: the reintroduction of the sounds *b*, *g*, *d* and the corresponding letters B, G and R resulted from contacts with the cities of Magna Graecia.

Apart from the Oscan alphabet, a Greek alphabet (Ionic-Tarentine) prevailed, not surprisingly, in the regions of Magna Graecia, in Lucania and Bruttium, as well as among the Mamertines in Sicily. Later the Latin alphabet was used in colonies: the Oscan Tavola Bantina, for example, is written in this alphabet. For a number of years the Greek alphabet, which was long-lived, overlapped with the use of the Latin.

Though we derive most of what we know about Oscan from inscriptions, certain observations on peculiarities of the language by ancient scholars, such as Varro (first century BC), have come down to us. These ancient scholars recognised Oscan, like Etruscan, as a distinct, separate language. We are told that Latin *quidquid,* 'whatever', was equivalent in pronunciation to Oscan *pitpit;* this means that the sound *kw* was rendered as a *p*. Varro also tells us (*Lingua Latina,* VII:29), '*senem* ...*Osci casnar appellant*', 'the Oscans call an old man *casnar*'.

Oscan, Umbrian, Latin, and the other Indo-European dialects of central Italy were spoken by neighbouring peoples for a considerable length of time, and influenced each other. But Oscan shows surprisingly close similarities with languages other than Latin, particularly with Greek and with the Germanic languages. For example, the word for

42

Etruscan	Oscan	Pronunciation (transcription)
		a
		b
		c, g
		d
		e
		v
		z
		h
		i
		k
		l
		m
		n
		p
		r
		s
		t
		u
		f
		i
		ú

'daughter' in Oscan is *futreí,* related to German *tochter,* English *daughter,* Greek *thugater;* in contrast, the Latin word *filia* is quite unrelated to Oscan.

The Romans did not pressure their neighbours to change over to Latin. The allies of Rome eventually felt it would be to their advantage to adopt the more prestigious Roman language: in 180 BC Cumae asked the Roman Senate for permission to adopt Latin as their official language instead of Oscan. For a long time, however, Oscan continued to be spoken and written in Pompeii and elsewhere as the unofficial but real language of the people.

The principal Oscan inscriptions are the Tavola Bantina, written in Latin characters; the *cippus* from Abella; the tablet from Agnone; and groups of ritual inscriptions known as the *iúvilas* and *eítuns,* from the appearance of these words in the texts. In addition to ritual, votive, commemorative and funerary texts, we have building inscriptions and magical inscriptions.

The famous bronze tablet from Agnone, in Samnite country (Molise), was discovered in 1848. Measuring 28 × 16.5 cm, the tablet has a handle, with an iron chain from which it could be hung. It is said to have been found in a sanctuary, some traces of which still survive. It has been variously dated: some consider it the oldest Oscan inscription (*c.* 250 BC), others date it somewhat later. Inscribed on both sides are the directions on the route to follow during the course of a ritual ceremony. The list of 'stations' inside and outside the *húrtín*

42 Etruscan and Oscan alphabets.

keríin, the 'garden, or enclosure, of Ceres', has been compared to the Christian ritual of the Stations of the Cross. Such a topographic route consists of separate 'stations' (*statíf*), each of which has a special significance, or is evocative of a particular event. In the case of the Oscan ritual, each refers to the altar of a particular divinity, which is mentioned at some length on side A, and listed again more summarily on side B. To be noted is the close relationship of the back and front of the tablet, with each divinity's 'station' lined up front and back.

Some scholars have interpreted *statíf* as 'statue' or 'construction', rather than 'station'. It seems clear, in any case, that it coincides with the placement of the altar (*aasa*) of each god. These are all divinities connected with agriculture. They belong to the circle of Ceres, or Demeter, and in some cases show the influence of Magna Graecia; we can compare, for example, the ritual on the Etruscan inscription from Capua, not too far from this area.

43   Bronze tablet from Agnone, *c.*250 BC, inscribed front and back (BM Br 888, 1873.8–20.119).

Side A

1. *statús. pús. set. húrtín.* | *kerríiin.* 2. *vezkei. statíf.* 3. *evklúi. statíf. kerrí. statíf.*
4. *futreí. kerríiai. státíf.* 5. *anter. statai. statíf.* 6. *ammaí. kerríiai. statíf.* 7. *diumpaís.*
kerríiaís. statíf. 8. *líganakdíkeí. entraí. statíf.* 9. *anafríss. kerríiúis. statíf.*
10. *maatúis. kerríiúis. statíf.* 11. *diúvei. verehasiúi. statíf.* 12. *diúvei. regaturei. statíf.*
13. *hereklúi. kerríiúi. statíf.* 14. *patanai. piistíai. statíf.* 15. *deivai. genetai. statíf.*
16. *aasai. purasiaí.* 17. *saahtúm. tefúrúm. alttrei.* 18. *pútereípíd. akeneí.*
19. *sakahíter.* 20. *fiuusasiaís. az. húrtúm.* 21. *sakarater.* 22. *pernaí. kerríiaí. statíf.*
23. *ammaí. kerríiaí. statíf.* 24. *fluusaí. kerríiaí. statíf.* 25. *evklúí. patereí. statíf.*

Latin translation

1. Ritus qui sunt in horto Cereali 2.*Vensici statio 3. Euclo statio. Cereri statio
4. Filiae Cereali statio 5.*Interstitae statio 6. Ammae Cereali statio 7. Lumpis
Cerealibus statio 8. Liganacdici *Interae statio 9. Imbribus Cerealibus statio
10. Matis Cerealibus statio 11. Iovi Iuvenali statio 12. Iovi Rectori statio 13. Herculi
Cereali statio 14. Patanae Pistiae statio 15. Divae Genitae statio 16–19. In ara
igniaria sanctum holocaustum altero quoque anno sanciatur 20. Floralibus ad hortum
sacratur 21. Pernae Cereali statio 22. Ammae Cereali statio 24. Florae Cereali statio
25. Euclo patri statio

English translation

1. The established ritual places which are in the enclosure of Ceres; 2. The stopping-
place for Vensicus; 3. The stopping-place for Euclus; the stopping-place for Ceres;
4. The stopping-place for Ceres' Daughter; 5. The stopping-place for Interstita; 6. The
stopping-place for Amma; 7. The stopping-place for the Nymphs of Ceres; 8. The
stopping-place for Liganacdix Interna 9. The stopping-place for the Rains of Ceres;
10. The stopping-place for the Matis of Ceres; 11. The stopping-place for Jupiter
Juvenal; 12. The stopping-place for Jupiter Rector, or Irrigator; 13. The stopping-
place for Hercules of Ceres; 14. The stopping-place for Patana Pistis; 15. The stopping-place for the Goddess Genita. 16–19. At the Altar of Fire let a holy burnt offering
(sacrifice) be sanctified every other year; 20–21. To the Florae by the enclosure let there
be a sacrifice; 22. The stopping-place for Perna of Ceres; 23. The stopping-place for
Amma of Ceres; 24. The stopping-place for Flora of Ceres; 25. The stopping-place for
Euclus the Father.

Side B

1. *aasas. ekask. eestínt.* 2. *húrtúi.* 3. *vezkei.* 4. *evklúi.* 5. *fuutrei.* 6. *anter. stataí.*
7. *kerrí.* 8. *ammaí.* 9. *diumpaís.* 10. *líganakdíkei. entraí.* 11. *kerríiaí.* 12. *anafríss.*
13. *maatúis.* 14. *diúvei. verehasiú.* 15. *diúvei. piihiúi. regaturei.* 16. *hereklúi.*
kerríiúi. 17. *patanaí. piistíaí.* 18. *deivaí. genetaí.* 19. *aasaí. purasiaí.* 20. *saahtúm.*
tefúrúm. 21. *alttrei. pútereípíd.* 22. *akeneí.* 23. *húrz. dekmanniúis. staít.*

Latin translation

1–2. Arae hae extant | horto 3.*Vensici 4. Euclo 5. Filiae 6. Interstitae 7. Cereri 8. Ammae 9. Lumpis 10. Liganacdici Interae 11. Cereali 12. Imbribus 13. Matis 14. Iovi Iuvenali 15. Iovi Pio Rectori 16. Herculi Cereali 17. Patanae Pistiae 18. Divae Genitae 19. In ara igniaria 20–21. sanctum holocaustum altero quoque anno 23. hortus pensionibus decimanis stat.

English translation

1–2. These altars stand in the enclosure: 3. for Vensicus; 4. for Euclus; 5. for the Daughter; 6. for Interstita; 7. for Ceres; 8. for Amma; 9. for the Nymphs; 10–11. for Liganacdica Interna of Ceres; 12. for the Rains; 13. for the Matis; 14. for Jupiter Juvenalis; 15. for Jupiter Pius Rector; 16. for Heracles of Ceres; 17. for Patina Pistia; 18. for Divine Genita; 19. At the Altar of Fire 20. a holy burnt offering 21–22. every other year. 23. The enclosure is at the disposal of the Decimani.

Notes

Side A

2.   *Vensicus:* uncertain. Related to Venus?
3.   Greek *Euklos*, a chthonic divinity, of the circle of Demeter.
4.   Ceres' Daughter = Persephone, Proserpina.
5.   'The Goddess Between' (the mother and the daughter?).
6, 23. *Amma:* 'mummy', mother
7.   Nymphs: divinities of the springs
8.   *Legifera* = Lawgiver? Latin *lex*, Oscan *ligud; Interna* = in between Nymphs, that is water of the earth, and rain, water from the sky = perhaps the dew.
10.   *Matis*, perhaps related to Mater Matuta, or an Italic divinity; related to *maturus* = 'ripe'?
13.   Hercules is not usually involved with Ceres, earth divinities or vegetation; but in the Roman world he is sometimes connected with Silvanus (Etruscan *Selvans*).
14.   *Patana* = *Panda* in Latin, goddess of opening, ripening plants. The epithet *Pistis* is related to either faith or threshing.
15.   *Genita:* birth of plants.
16.   *Aasai purasiaí;* compare Latin *ara,* 'altar'; Greek πῦρ, 'fire'.
17.   *Saahtúm tefúrún:* 'a sacrifice with fire'; *tefúrún* is probably connected with Greek τέφρα, 'cinders', 'ashes'. 20. *Fiuusasiasís:* compare Latin *Flora,* Italian *fiore.* 25. *Patereí:* 'father'.

Side B

1.   *aasas ekask:* the altars of the *hortus,* dedicated to the individual divinities. *eestínt:* elsewhere *stahínt.*
23.   *húrz dekmanniúís staít:* ceremonies in the *hortus,* where the offering of the tithe was carried out. The *Dekmannis* was apparently the priesthood in charge of performing these rites in the enclosure.

APPENDIX 1
Etruscan Names

PRAENOMINA (First Names)

Abbreviations

MASCULINE

A, Ar, Ath	Arnth, Aranth = Latin Arruns
Au, Av	Aule, Avle, Avile = Latin Aulus
C, Ca	Cae, Cai = Latin Caius, Gaius
V, Ve, Vl	Vel
Vth	Velthur
Lc	Larce
L, La, Lth	Larth
L, Li, Lr	Laris, Lars
M	Marce = Latin Marcus
S, Sth	Sethre
Ti	Tite = Latin Titus

FEMININE

H, Ha, F, Fa	Hasti(a), Fasti(a)
Th, Tha	Thana
Thch	Thanchvil = Latin Tanaquil
R, Ra	Ramtha
Rav, Rn	Ra(v)ntha, Raunthu

(*thana* + *cvil* = 'gift of Thana'?)

Other first names

MASCULINE	FEMININE
Cneve = Latin Cnaeus, Gnaeus	Sethra
Caile = Latin Caelus	Velia
Cuinte = Latin Quintus	Larthi(a)
Spurie = Latin Spurius	Arnthi
Mamarce	Tita
Thefarie = Latin Tiberius	

APPENDIX 2
Glossary of Etruscan Words

*Words preceded by an asterisk are reconstructed from forms given by Greek and Roman writers. For names of divinities, see Index. For further information see vocabulary lists in Pallottino, *Etruscans*; Pfiffig, *Etruskische Sprache*; and *Thesaurus*.

A ꙰

ac make, offer, act; *acazr* objects offered in the tomb
acale (*Aclus*) June
ais, eis (pl. *aisar, eisar*) god
aisiu divine, of the gods
aisna, eisna divine, of the gods
al give, offer
alpan, alpnu gift, offering; willingly
alphaze offering
alumnathe sacred society
am to be
an (*ana, ane, anc, ananc*) he, she
apa father
apana paternal
apcar abacus
ar-, er- to make, move, build
arac falcon
arim monkey
ars- push away?
aska type of vase (Gk *askós*)
athre building (Lat. *atrium*?)
ati, ativu mother, 'mummy'
ati nacna grandmother
avil year

C Ꙅ) Ꝁ

-c and
ca this
camthi name of a magistracy
cape, capi vase, container (cf Lat. *capiō*?)
capr- April
capra urn
capu falcon
car-, cer- make, build
cecha sacred things, ritual, ceremony, priestly; *zilch cechaneri* a title (see *zil* etc.)
cechase name of magistracy
cehen this one here
cela room (Lat. *cella*)

celi September
celu priestly title
cep-, cepen priestly title
ces- lie
cezp 8?
cezpalch 80?
ci 3
cialch-, cealch- 30
ciz three times
cisra Caere
clan (pl. *clenar*) son
cletram basin, basket, cart for offerings (Umbrian *kletra*)
cleva offering
clevsin Chiusi
creal magistrate
creice Greek (Lat. *Graecus*)
culichna vase, 'little kylix' (Gk *kylix*)
cupe cup (Gk *kúpē*, Lat. *cupa*)
cver, cvil gift, offering

Ch Ꙇ

chosfer (gloss) October

E Ꙓ

eca (see *ca*)
eleivana of oil; *aska eleivana* vessel for oil (Gk *élaion*)
-em minus
enac, enach then, afterwards
epl, pi, pul in, to, up to
eslz twice
etera, eteri foreigner; slave, client (serf?)
etnam and, also

F Ꝇ

falatu (gloss, *falado*) sky
fan- to consecrate?
fanu sacred place (Lat. *fānum*?)

favi grave, temple vault (Lat. *fauissa*?)
fler offering, sacrifice
flerchva all the statues, offerings
flere divinity, god
fleres statue
frontac interpreter of lightning; see *trutnuth* (Gk. *brontē*?)
fufluna see *pupluna*

H ꙞꙞ

hanthin in front of
hec-, hech- put, place in front of, add
herma, heramasva place, statue? (Gk Hermes)
herme, hermu sacred society of Hermes
hermi- (gloss, *Ermius*) August
hinthial soul, ghost, reflection
hintha, hinthu, hinththin below
hus- (pl. *husiur*) youth, children; *huzrnatre* group of youths
huth 6

I ꙇ

ic, ich, ichnac how
ica, ika this
ilu- verb of offering or prayer
in, inc it
ipa relative pronoun
ipe, ipa whoever, whatever
ister (gloss: Lat. *histrio*) actor
ita, itu this
itu- (gloss: *itus* or *ituare*) to divide? (Lat. *Idus*)

L Ꙇ

lauchum king (Lat. *lucumō*)
lauchumna 'belonging to a *lucumo*' (king or prince), palace

lautni 'of the family', freedman
lautnitha, lautnita freedwoman
lautun, lautn family, *gens*
lechtum vase for oil (Gk *lēkythos*)
lechtumuza little *lēkythos*
lein- to die?
les- offer sacrifice
leu lion
lucair to rule
luth sacred place
lup-, lupu to die

M ᛗ ᛙ

-m, -um and
mach 5
macstrev name of magistracy
mal- to give, dedicate?
malena, malstria mirror
man, mani the dead (Lat. *Manes*)
manin- to offer to the Manes?
maru, marunu name of magistracy (Lat. *marō*, Umbr. *maron-*)
masan, masn name of month?
matam, matan above, before
math honey, honeyed wine
maruchva type of *zilath*
mech people, league
men- offer
methlum district
mi, mini I, me
mul- to offer, dedicate as an *ex-voto*
mulach, malak, mlach votive offering, dedication
mun-, muni underground place, tomb
mur- stay, reside
murś urn, sarcophagus
mutana, mutna sarcophagus

N ᛈ ᛙ

nac how, as, because
nefts, nefś, nefis grandson (Lat. *nepos*)
nene nurse, wet-nurse
neri water
nesna belonging to the dead?
nethśra haruspicina
netśvis haruspex
nuna offering?
nurph- 9

P ᛖ

pachathur Bacchante, maenad
pachie- pachana Bacchic
pacusnaśie, pacuśnasie Bacchic, Dionysiac
papa, papacs grandfather
papals of the grandfather: grandson
parnich magistrate
patna name of vase (Gk *patane*, Lat. *patina*?)
penthuna, penthna cippus, stone?
pi, pul at, in, through
pruch, pruchum jug (Gk *próchous*)
prumathś, prumats great-grandson (Lat. *pronepos*)
puia wife
pul see *pi*
pulumchva stars?

pupluna, fufluna Populonia
purth, purthne name of magistrate or magistracy; dictator?
put-, puth- cup, vase, well? (Lat. *puteus, puteal*?)

Q ᛩ

qutun, qutum vase (Gk *kōthōn*)

R ᛉ

rach- prepare
*rasenna, rasna Etruscan, of Etruria
rath sacred thing
ratum according to law (Lat. *rite*)
ril aged, at the age of ... (years)
rumach Roman, from Rome
ruva brother

S, Ś ᛗ ᛊ

(*s* and *ś* are often interchangeable)
śa 4
sac- carring out a sacred act
sacni sanctuary
sacnisa consecrate?
sal- make, carry out
śar, zar 10
sath-, śat- put, establish, be put?
sealch 40
sec, sech daughter
semph 7?
semphalch 70?
slicaches sacred society?
snenath maid, companion (f)
spur- city
spurana, spureni having to do with the city
śran, sren ornament, figure
srencve decorated with figures?
suc- declare
suplu flutist (Lat. *subulo*)
śuth-, sut- to stay, place?
śuthi tomb, grave
śuthina for the tomb, sepulchral gift
sval alive, to live
sve similarly
sveamach from Sovana

T ᛏᛏ

ta this
tamera name of magistracy
tarchnalthi at Tarquinia
ten- to act as
tes-, tesam- to care for
tesinth caretaker
teta grandmother
tev- to show, set?
tevarath onlooker, judge at the games, umpire
tin- day
tiu, tiv-, tiur moon, month
tmia place, sacred building
-tnam see *etnam*
trin- to plead, supplicate
truth, trut libation
trutnuth, trutnvt priest (Lat. *fulguriator*)
tul stone

tular, tularu boundaries
tunur one at a time
tur- to give
tura incense
turza offering
tus funerary niche
tusurthir married couple? ('in the double urn'?)
tuthi, tuti- community, state (Umbrian *tota*?)
tuthin, tuthina- of the state, public
tuthina the people; votive object?

Th ⊙○

thafna cup
tham- to build, found
thapna vase (for offerings?)
thaurch funerary
thaure, thaura tomb
thez- to make an offering
thezl, thezi name of a city found on Etruscan coins
thi pronoun
thina vase, jar (Lat. *tina*, Gk *dinos*)
thu one
thucte name of month
thui here, now
thuni before
thunz once

U Y V

ulpaia jug (Gk *olpe*)
une then
usil the sun
uslane at noon
ut- carry out, perform

V ᛝ

vacal, vacil, vacl libation?
*velcitna (gloss, *Velcitanus*) March
velclthi at Vulci
velsnalthi at Volsinii (*velznani*); *velsnach* from Volsinii
vers- fire (or ladle?)
vinum, vinm wine (Lat. *uinum*)

Z ᛁ

zal, zel-, esal- 2
zanena cup
zar see *sar*
zathrum 20
zeri rite, legal action?
zich- to write, incise
zil- to rule?
zil, zilac, zilc, zilach, zilath a magistrate (Lat. *praetor*)
ziv having lived, dead at
ziva the dead, deceased

Further Reading

Etruscan

L. Banti, *The Etruscan Cities and their Culture*, Berkeley and Los Angeles, 1973.

G. Bonfante and L. Bonfante, *The Etruscan Language: An Introduction*, Manchester and New York, 1983; trans. as *Lingua e cultura degli Etruschi*, rev. trans. Rome 1985.

Corpus Inscriptionum Etruscarum (CIE), various places, 1873, 1970, 1980, ongoing.

M. Cristofani, 'Recent Advances in Etruscan Epigraphy and Language', in *Italy Before the Romans*, ed. D. and F.R.S. Ridgway, London, New York, San Francisco, 1979, 373–412.

N. de Grummond (ed.), *A Guide to Etruscan Mirrors*, Tallahassee (Florida) 1982.

C. de Simone, *Die griechischen Entlehnungen im Etruskischen*, 2 vols, Wiesbaden 1968–70.

E. Macnamara, *The Etruscans*, London 1990.

E. Macnamara, *Everyday Life of the Etruscans*, London 1973, 172–89.

M. Pallottino, *The Etruscans*, Bloomington (Indiana) and London 1975, 187–234.

M. Pallottino, *Testimonia Linguae Etruscae* (TLE), Florence 1968.

A. Pfiffig, *Die etruskische Sprache*, Graz 1969.

E.H. Richardson, 'An Archaeological Introduction to the Etruscan Language', in *Etruscan Life and Afterlife*, ed. L. Bonfante, Detroit, 1986, 215–31.

H. Rix, *Das etruskische Cognomen*, Wiesbaden 1963.

Thesaurus Linguae Etruscae, I, *Indice Lessicale*, Rome 1978.

L.B. van der Meer, *The Bronze Liver of Piacenza*, Amsterdam 1987.

P. Zazoff, *Etruskische Skarabäen*, Mainz 1968.

Oscan

A. Morandi, *Epigrafia Italica*, Rome, 1982, 66, 72, 115–17, 126–30.

V. Pisani, *Le lingue dell'Italia antica oltre il latino*, Turin 1953, 92–5.

A. L. Prosdocimi, 'L'Osco', in *Popoli e civiltà dell'Italia antica* 6, Rome, 1978, 830–38.

Inscriptions Cited but not Illustrated

Page

330–1	*TLE* 801–58 (glosses)
331	*TLE* ϼ
333	*TLE* 55
338	cf. *TLE* 504; *TLE* 282
339	*TLE* 399, 278, 282, 1
342–3	*TLE* 156
345	*TLE* 1
346	*TLE* 2, 878, 359 (*CIE* 5237), 570, 131 (*CIE* 5430)
347	*TLE* 719, 752
348	*TLE* 695
352	*TLE* 88, 335
356	de Simone 112–13
357	*TLE* 3, 63, 761, 762, 5, 62, 64; cf. 7–8
359	*TLE* 131 (*CIE* 5430), 190, 174, 902
360–1	BM Br 700, 73.8–20.109 (*CIE* 10875); BM Br 654, 73.8–20.203 (*TLE* 216, *CIE* 10877); BM Br 780, 73.8–20.211 (*TLE* 291–2, *CIE* 10855)
363	*TLE* 129
366	*TLE* 148, 559, 696, 719, 900; 651
368	*TLE* 890, 293–303, 35

Index